The Age of Charisma

An innovative examination of American society, culture, and politics, *The Age of Charisma* argues that the modern relationship between American leaders and followers grew out of a unique group of charismatic social movements prominent in the late nineteenth and early twentieth centuries. Drawing on hundreds of letters and testimonials, Jeremy C. Young illustrates how "personal magnetism" in public speaking shaped society by enabling a shift from emotionally inaccessible leadership to emotionally available leadership. This charismatic speaking style caused a rapid transformation in the leader–follower relationship, creating an emotional link between speakers and listeners, and the effects of this social transformation remain with us today. Young argues that, ultimately, charismatic movements enhanced American democracy by encouraging the personalization of leadership – creating a culture in which today's leaders appeal directly to Americans through mass media.

Jeremy C. Young is an assistant professor of history at Dixie State University.

The Age of Charisma

Leaders, Followers, and Emotions in American Society, 1870–1940

JEREMY C. YOUNG
Dixie State University

CAMBRIDGE
UNIVERSITY PRESS

CAMBRIDGE
UNIVERSITY PRESS

University Printing House, Cambridge CB2 8BS, United Kingdom

One Liberty Plaza, 20th Floor, New York, NY 10006, USA

477 Williamstown Road, Port Melbourne, VIC 3207, Australia

4843/24, 2nd Floor, Ansari Road, Daryaganj, Delhi – 110002, India

79 Anson Road, #06–04/06, Singapore 079906

Cambridge University Press is part of the University of Cambridge.

It furthers the University's mission by disseminating knowledge in the pursuit of education, learning, and research at the highest international levels of excellence.

www.cambridge.org
Information on this title: www.cambridge.org/9781107114623
10.1017/9781316335369

First published 2017

Printed in the United States of America by Sheridan Books, Inc.

A catalogue record for this publication is available from the British Library.

ISBN 978-1-107-11462-3 Hardback

To Chelsea McCracken

Contents

Illustrations

Acknowledgments

Just as a charismatic movement cannot succeed without the army of leaders, followers, and organizers that constitute it, this book about charismatic movements would have been impossible without the help and support of mentors, colleagues, and friends. At Indiana University, Michael McGerr mentored me as a writer, fought hard for me when professional challenges blocked my path, and responded with forbearance when I insisted I was going to write a biography of Woodrow Wilson. In the end, I did write about Wilson, but only after discovering what I really wanted to say about him. I remain grateful to Professor McGerr for his friendship, guidance, and steadfast support. John Bodnar's insightful questions about the Lincoln Republic and American national identity encouraged me to think about my dissertation in the broadest of terms. Judith Allen supervised my initial research on Aimee Semple McPherson and helped me craft a leaner, more concise writing style. Rebecca Spang rightly urged me to abandon an overly theoretical approach and to explain exactly why I wanted to use the term "charisma." Their encouragement, constructive criticism, and intellectual comradeship are much appreciated.

Throughout my career, I have invariably found my senior colleagues within and outside of the academy both welcoming and generous. During my undergraduate years at St. Mary's College of Maryland, Chuck Holden and Christine Adams nurtured my interest in the American Progressive Era and showed me that history could be weird, fascinating, and fun. At History Associates Incorporated, Mike Reis provided me with a crash course in archival research that has served me well in the ensuing years. Thanks as well to Ann Blair, Jane Calvert, Jason Crouthamel, Nick Cullather, Jonathan Dresner, Wendy Gamber, Russell Hanson, Carl

Ipsen, Robert D. Johnston, Michael Kazin, M. Alison Kibler, James Livingston, Kathryn Lofton, James H. Madison, Stephen P. Marrone, Khalil Gibran Muhammad, Paul Murphy, Mike Reis, William E. Scheuerman, Carolyn Shapiro-Shapin, Janet L. Six, and the anonymous reviewers at Cambridge University Press for their generous advice and help.

I am grateful to several individuals and institutions for their financial and professional support of my research. At Cambridge University Press, Debbie Gershenowitz has been an unfailing champion of this project; her steadfast belief in my work has meant a great deal. Kristina Deusch, Amanda George, Katherine Law, Sri Hari Kumar, and others at Cambridge have been friendly and helpful throughout the production process. The Indiana University History Department was extremely generous in providing me with financial support and time for research and writing. The Roosevelt Institute provided me with a timely grant for research at the Franklin D. Roosevelt Library. Thanks as well to the Grand Valley State University History Department and the Indiana University Graduate and Professional Student Association for their helpful financial assistance. The Dixie State University History Department has been a friendly and supportive environment in which to complete final revisions on the manuscript. Finally, please note that Chapter 3 contains material originally published in my article "Transformation in the Tabernacle: Billy Sunday's Converts and Emotional Experience in the Progressive Era," *Journal of the Gilded Age and Progressive Era*, Vol. 14, No. 3 (July 2015): 367–385. ©2015 Society for Historians of the Gilded Age and Progressive Era; reprinted with permission.

Those who have aided my research in libraries and archives also deserve special mention. I am particularly grateful to Rhonda Long, Isabel Planton, Ronald Luedemann, and the rest of the Herman B. Wells Library Document Delivery Services staff at Indiana University; without their help, I could not have completed this book in anything resembling a timely manner. William E. Darr at the Morgan Library, Grace College and Theological Seminary, offered research assistance and expertise on the various Billy Sunday collections. Grand Valley State University's Digital Studios generously provided digital scans for several images. Thanks also to the librarians and archivists at the Library of Congress, the Franklin D. Roosevelt Library, the Library Company of Philadelphia, and the Harry Ransom Center at the University of Texas-Austin, and to the staff at the Herman B. Wells Library at Indiana University; the Mary Idema Pew Library at Grand Valley State University; the Fondren Library at Rice

University; the Cline Library at Northern Arizona University; and the Flagstaff Public Library in Flagstaff, Arizona.

Throughout this project, a number of friends have provided helpful advice, offered thoughtful critiques, and listened patiently while I rambled on about Billy Sunday. Dustin Abnet, an outstanding friend and colleague, read and critiqued the full manuscript. Despite the many demands of his professional life, Brian David Jennings sharpened my thinking about political leadership and was consistently supportive of the book project. Thanks as well to Neal Coleman, Rachel Coleman, Kalani Craig, Karen Dunak, Christine Dunn, Keith Eberly, Susan Eckelmann, Justin Ellison, Silva Kahl, Nicole Kozdron, Hyon Ju Lee, Sean McKee, Elizabeth Nelson, Katherine Nelson, Bogdan Popa, Heather Roberts, Tara Saunders, Jim Seaver, Carl Suddler, Victoria Wheeler, and Drew Zaitsoff for their help, suggestions, and support. Natasha Hollenbach graciously took time from her own graduate work to help me with archival research at the University of Tennessee, Knoxville. I am also thankful to the students in my courses at Indiana University and Grand Valley State University for helping me workshop my ideas on charisma and for being as amused as I was by James Rush's horses and Jonathan Barber's bamboo cage.

Finally, I am grateful for the support and assistance of my family, particularly my father, Bill Young, who taught me to be a historian; my mother, Karen Raskin-Young, who taught me to be a storyteller; my sister, Meredith Young, who encouraged me to pursue my academic dreams; and my in-laws, Jack and Deborah McCracken, who generously opened their home to me during my research trips to the Library of Congress. This book is dedicated to my wife, Chelsea McCracken, who accompanied me to archives, helped me understand James Rush's linguistic theories, challenged my assumptions about the absence of women from positions of charismatic leadership, read and critiqued the entire manuscript, edited several of the images, assisted with compiling the index, and helped shape my thinking at every stage of the project. As observers of charisma would be the first to recognize, for some things, no words in any language are enough.

Introduction

On September 23 and 24, 1885, Patrick Sarsfield Gilmore began a series of concerts at the St. Louis Exposition's new music hall. Cutting a smart figure in his dress uniform, the most famous bandleader in America bowed to the hall packed with 4,300 wildly applauding audience members, plus an extra thousand crowding outside the doors. Raising his baton, Gilmore led his 22nd New York Regimental Band in virtuosic performances that amazed the assembled audiences. "Every note melted like moonlight," gushed the *St. Louis Globe-Democrat.* Bursting with pride, the paper congratulated Exposition organizers for bringing Gilmore to St. Louis. "Another triumph was scored for the management," the *Globe-Democrat* concluded, "and another proof given to the world that when St. Louis people undertake to do anything it is done with judgment, energy and liberality."[1]

As impressed as they were with the fine music and the large audience, the *St. Louis Republican* and *Globe-Democrat* reporters seemed especially taken with the relationship between Gilmore and the members of his band. "The master seems to, and actually does command music from the various instruments, as much as if he directly played upon them himself," marveled the *Republican* writer. "His men, all artists of high rank, have been asked to give expression to his wish, to become, severally,

[1] "Exposition," *St. Louis Republican*, September 25, 1885, 5; Rusty Hammer, *P. S. Gilmore: The Authorized Biography of America's First Superstar* (Gainesville, FL: Rusty Hammer, 2006), 242; "Magnetic Music," *St. Louis Globe-Democrat*, September 24, 1885, 8; *St. Louis Globe-Democrat*, September 24, 1885, 6; "Gilmore's Glory," *St. Louis Globe-Democrat*, September 22, 1885, 8.

the parts of one grand organ whose stops and frets he, and he alone, comprehends. It is in this way that his concentrated degree of skill and musical genius is focused and made to tell upon the popular emotions."[2] The *Globe-Democrat* reporter was similarly awed by the intimate connection between Gilmore's gestures and the music his band produced. "The music seems in him rather than around him," the paper wrote; "he is the instrument and the player." The editor of the *Globe-Democrat* summed up the effect in a headline: Gilmore and his band were creating "MAGNETIC MUSIC."[3]

It was not surprising that Gilmore's magnetic power over his band fascinated the St. Louis reporters. The relationship between Gilmore and his musicians represented in microcosm what was happening all across the United States – in revival tents and stump speeches, at lecture halls and whistle-stops. Beginning in the 1870s, American leaders deployed new techniques, particularly a unique brand of emotional public speaking, designed to attract large numbers of followers to their religious, political, and activist causes. Just as Gilmore conjured lyrical music from the restless tip of his baton, these leaders outlined visions of a better America and dramatized those visions through their onstage oratorical performances. The social and economic upheavals of the late nineteenth-century United States had left many Americans searching for meaning and purpose in their lives. Millions eagerly joined social movements led by dynamic orators. In the same way that the members of the 22nd Regimental Band willingly took their cues from Gilmore, these followers responded to leaders' visions and devoted themselves to a variety of religious, social, and political causes. Thanks to the development of transcontinental railway networks and the ability of leaders to spread their message in person to all corners of the United States, the resulting social movements were national in scope and ambition. Together, each group of followers formed a "grand organ," a powerful social instrument upon whose "stops and frets" its leader played. When such a movement was thoroughly motivated and effectively organized, the result was a harmonious ensemble whose members believed they could exert significant influence on society.

Americans who followed leaders in this way drew on a distinctly Protestant religious vocabulary to describe the phenomenon.

[2] "Exposition," *St. Louis Republican*, September 25, 1885, 5; Hammer, *P.S. Gilmore*, 242.

[3] "Magnetic Music," *St. Louis Globe-Democrat*, September 24, 1885, 8.

In letters, they referred to their chosen guides as Messiahs and compared them sometimes to George Washington or Abraham Lincoln, but more often to Moses or Jesus Christ. "I believe you the second Moses," Alphonse J. Bryan wrote to 1896 presidential nominee William Jennings Bryan (no relation) in a typical missive, "not of Egypt but of America, who will lead back the poor blind oppressed laborer ... to the road of Salvation."[4] Followers used similarly effusive language to describe their own connections with such figures. They were "united" with the leader, transfixed by "magic" and "electricity," or moved by words "echoing in their hearts." Followers themselves had undergone transformations at the leader's hands; they were "different" or "new men," "changed" and "shook up," with "new" or "awakened hearts" filled with "joy and love" – in short, new apostles ready to serve a noble cause. This religious language of followership appeared with remarkable consistency through the late nineteenth and early twentieth centuries and into the interwar years. Indeed, it was the defining feature of this type of leader–follower relationship – the necessary characteristic that separated these uniquely emotional connections from other more transactional movement relationships. As leadership and organizational practices shifted with cultural currents, the consistent rhetoric of follower experience made it clear that the underlying phenomenon remained the same.

Despite the persistence of this emotional type of leader–follower relationship, Americans had difficulty settling on a single name for leaders' ability to attract followers in this way. One leading contender was the term the *Globe-Democrat* had applied to Patrick Gilmore and his band: "personal magnetism." Leaders who exhibited this quality were called "magnetic men," and, less frequently, their followers were said to be "magnetized." But writers did not use "magnetism" to describe the relationship between leaders and followers or the social movements constructed out of that relationship. Furthermore, the term fell out of favor well before the qualities it described began to lose prominence in American culture – and some "magnetic" leaders specifically denied that they were magnetic at all. Accordingly, commentators soon developed other names for this type of leader. "Spellbinder" was one, used to describe the political stump orators who dominated national

[4] Alphonse J. Bryan to William Jennings Bryan, October 31, 1896, box 5, William Jennings Bryan Papers, Library of Congress.

campaigns beginning in the 1880s.[5] Others described such leaders as possessing a great deal of "personality," though that term, too, had other meanings. In the end, Americans were unable to find a name broad and comprehensive enough to reflect all the elements of this leader–follower relationship, just as they could not reach consensus on its effects or its value.

For this reason, it may be preferable to use the anachronistic term "charisma" to describe the phenomenon in its totality. The ancient Greeks first used "charisma" to denote a special ability given by the gods; St. Paul used the word in a similar way but cited Yahweh as the ultimate source of the ability.[6] The theologian Rudolf Sohm revived the term and introduced it into modern scholarship in an 1888 volume on church history.[7] It was the German sociologist Max Weber, though, in the late 1910s and especially in his posthumously published *Economy and Society* (1922), who decoupled charisma from religion and gave it its modern meaning.[8] Weber, born in 1864, was a contemporary of those Americans who experienced the phenomenon of personal magnetism firsthand. Like Americans of the period, Weber spent much of his life responding to the socioeconomic upheavals occasioned by industrial capitalism. In particular, Weber viewed with alarm the growing bureaucratic reorganization of society; memorably, he charged that this "rationalization" had stripped humanity of its individuality and locked it in an "iron cage."[9] Also like his American contemporaries, Weber lived in a society controlled by leaders who wielded immense power over popular ideas and culture – though many of these German figures, such as Kaiser Wilhelm II and Chancellor Otto von Bismarck, were monarchical or dictatorial rather than democratic.

5 J. Adam Bede, "Spellbinders: The Men Who are Talking from Maine to California," *Frank Leslie's Illustrated Newspaper*, August 1904, 388–390; William Bayard Hale, " 'Friends and Fellow-Citizens': Our Political Orators of All Parties, and the Ways They Use to Win Us," *The World's Work*, April 1912, 673–674; Curtis Guild, Jr., "The Spellbinder," *Scribner's*, November 1912, 561–562; William Dudley Foulke, "The Spellbinders," *The Forum*, February 1901, 658–659.

6 John Potts, *A History of Charisma* (Houndmills, UK: Palgrave Macmillan, 2009), 5; I Corinthians 7:7.

7 Potts, *A History of Charisma*, 118; Rudolf Sohm, *Outlines of Church History*, tr. May Sinclair (orig. pub. 1895; London: Macmillan, 1931), 66.

8 Joshua Derman, *Max Weber in Politics and Social Thought: From Charisma to Canonization* (Cambridge, UK: Cambridge University Press, 2012), 176.

9 Max Weber, *The Protestant Ethic and the Spirit of Capitalism*, tr. Talcott Parsons (orig. pub. New York: Charles Scribner's Sons, 1930; Los Angeles, CA: Roxbury Publishing Co., 1996), 181.

Writing in the 1910s, Weber argued that charisma was the only social force capable of challenging the inexorable advance of industrialized, bureaucratized society.[10] He defined the term as "a certain quality of an individualized personality by virtue of which he is considered extraordinary and treated as endowed with supernatural, superhuman, or at least specifically exceptional powers or qualities ... on the basis of [which] the individual concerned is treated as a 'leader.' "[11] Charisma could be either innate or acquired, Weber noted, and it could inhere in a person, an office, or an institution; the social movements it created were "charismatic communities."[12] Though Weber identified a "religious aura" surrounding charisma, charismatic techniques were present in politics, too. A "charisma of rhetoric" featured prominently in "modern democratic electioneering with its 'stump speeches' "; its effect was "purely emotional," designed "to convince [the masses] of the leader's charismatic qualification." At times, this charisma could overwhelm the political party structure it inhabited. Weber specifically identified American ex-president Theodore Roosevelt's 1912 presidential campaign as evidence that "the bureaucratization of the parties and of electioneering may at its very height suddenly be forced into the service of charismatic hero worship."[13]

For Weber, charisma was starkly opposed to bureaucracy. "In radical contrast to bureaucratic organization," Weber wrote, "charisma knows no formal and regulated appointment or dismissal ... Charisma is self-determined and sets its own limits. Its bearer seizes the task for which he is destined and demands that others obey and follow him by virtue of his mission." Charisma's transience and instability meant that followers could easily dethrone leaders they no longer deemed charismatic; the leader was only "master" of his followers "as long as he 'proves' himself."[14] Nevertheless, Weber felt, in the right circumstances charisma was a powerful agent of social upheaval that could "result in a radical alteration of the central attitudes and directions of action with a completely new orientation of all attitudes toward the different

[10] Charles Camic, Philip S. Gorski, and David M. Trubek, "Introduction," in Camic, Gorski, and Trubek, eds., *Max Weber's Economy and Society: A Critical Companion* (Stanford, CA: Stanford University Press, 2005), 2.

[11] Max Weber, *Economy and Society: An Outline of Interpretive Sociology*, Vol. 1, ed. Guenther Roth and Claus Wittich, tr. Ephraim Fischoff et al. (orig. pub. New York: Bedminster Press, 1968; Berkeley, CA: University of California Press, 1978), 241.

[12] *Ibid.*, Vol. 1, 243, 400; Vol. 2, 1140.

[13] *Ibid.*, Vol. 2, 1122, 1129–1130, 1132.

[14] *Ibid.*, Vol. 2, 1112–1113.

problems of the 'world.' "[15] Because charismatic followers obeyed the caprices of a leader rather than a predictable hierarchy of regulations, they could cut through the orderly process of rationalized governance and create immediate, transformative change in their societies. "Charisma," Weber declared, "is indeed the specifically creative revolutionary force of history."[16]

Weber failed to grasp that charisma was more a historically bounded phenomenon than a world-historical force, and it is debatable whether charisma truly possessed the "revolutionary" power he ascribed to it. Nevertheless, Weber was one of the few commentators to identify charisma's most significant social feature: its ability to empower followers. As the St. Louis reporters demonstrated, Americans tended to view the charismatic relationship as one between player and instrument or between an all-powerful conductor and a passive "grand organ." Weber knew better, though. Followers' emotional support for their leaders, he realized, constituted the crucial element in charismatic movements' success. When followers withdrew that support, their movements often faltered or even disbanded. "Pure charisma," Weber explained, "does not recognize any legitimacy other than one which flows from personal strength proven time and again. The charismatic hero derives his authority ... solely by proving his powers in practice." When a leader appeared to lose his charisma – or worse, when he failed in "*bringing well-being* to his faithful followers ... then his mission comes to an end, and hope expects and searches for a new bearer." Weber's insight about the balance of power between charismatic leaders and followers led him to a significant conclusion: "The genuinely charismatic ruler ... is responsible to the ruled."[17]

Weber's definition of charisma is useful, but not in itself sufficient to explain what Americans experienced between 1870 and 1940. Rather, charisma in the American context represents the aggregate of not one but three overlapping historical phenomena. First, charisma was a uniquely emotional style of public speaking – a set of oratorical and gestural techniques developed by American elocutionists and taught to several generations of American public speakers in the late nineteenth and early twentieth centuries. Many, though not all, of the public figures described as magnetic during this period displayed at least some elements of this speaking style, although most of them were unaware of the role their oratorical training played in their popular reception. Second, charisma

[15] *Ibid.*, Vol. 1, 245. [16] *Ibid.*, Vol. 2, 1117. [17] *Ibid.*, Vol. 2, 1114; italics in original.

was a specific type of relationship between a leader and his or her followers. Although this type of connection had some antecedents in American history, it was intense, emotional, spiritual, transformative, and enduring in ways that most earlier leader–follower relationships were not. Charismatic relationships often, but not always, began with magnetic oratory and made use of a related set of performance practices and organizational techniques developed by speakers and managers. The strength and emotional heft of these charismatic connections made them ideal components of broader social, religious, and political movements. Finally, charisma contributed to a turn-of-the-century discourse about American democracy. Advocates of charisma held a collection of related ideas concerning the role of emotion in the leader–follower relationship and the power of followers within social movements. Many defended the charismatic relationship as a valuable and socially redeeming method of social organization; some also saw a democratic and populist component in the leaders' reliance on emotional support from followers. Overall, they advanced an idea that became charisma's most lasting legacy: that leaders owed something of themselves to their followers and that emotional availability, rather than emotional remoteness, was a prerequisite for democratic leadership.

These three interrelated historical developments – charisma as speaking style, charisma as leader–follower relationship, and charisma as democratic discourse – challenge traditional assumptions about how Americans of the period participated in their society. Though contemporary critics charged charismatic followers with hysteria and charismatic leaders claimed the power to manipulate the public, followers were in fact volitional agents who helped to shape and control the movements they joined. As in Gilmore's band, there was no "magnetic music" without musicians to perform it; the players controlled the success or failure of the ensemble by their willingness to commit themselves to the charismatic enterprise and to take direction from its conductor. Followers' ability to influence charismatic movements by increasing or withdrawing their emotional investment afforded them a type of agency unavailable to Americans through other types of social organization. To dismiss charismatic followership as inchoate, reactive, or self-defeating behavior is to misunderstand the charismatic project. Followers believed they were participating in a type of social engagement every bit as effective as traditional partisan politics or voluntary associations. Ultimately, charismatic followership served democratic goals; it was a purposeful and constructive effort to reshape society in positive and dynamic ways.

Leaders and activists coveted the power inherent in a charismatic following; their activities, too, challenge popular narratives of political, social, and religious conflict in the late nineteenth and early twentieth centuries. Behavior often interpreted as showboating or demagoguery was actually a calculated effort by leaders to harness the power of charisma for the benefit of their personal or policy platforms. Figures as diverse as ministers Henry Ward Beecher, Billy Sunday, and Aimee Semple McPherson; politicians James G. Blaine, William Jennings Bryan, and Theodore Roosevelt; and activists "Big Bill" Haywood, Frances Willard, and Marcus Garvey made charismatic techniques a centerpiece of their self-presentation in an attempt to win followers and to promote their respective causes. They understood the stakes as Weber did: charisma, they felt, possessed transformative power and could unleash revolutionary change of a sort not possible through other types of social movements. Accordingly, many of the period's key battles had a charismatic subtext; numerous sacred and secular conflicts doubled as clashes over who would harness the power of charisma and to what end.

Although the historical record cannot show how effective charismatic techniques were in the tabernacle, the meeting room, or the polling place, charismatic movements often failed to achieve their stated goals. No president won election through a charismatic campaign between 1870 and 1940, though several candidates tried; several major charismatic social movements disintegrated spectacularly. In large part, this tendency toward failure was a matter of selection bias. Because it relied so much on the emotional responses of followers, the charismatic relationship was inherently unstable and destabilizing. Members of the political, corporate, or religious establishment, and those who could achieve success through traditional organizational techniques, had little incentive to try out the new methods or to place themselves so completely at the mercy of their followers. Accordingly, with some exceptions, charismatic leadership was the province of underdogs, outsiders, long shots, and others who could not reasonably have been expected to succeed in the first place. Their many failures do not necessarily prove that charismatic movements had little effect on society, but they do indicate that charismatic techniques were not the panacea some Americans hoped they could be – that the charismatic relationship could not by itself win an election or change society. Nevertheless, many leaders and followers were convinced that it could do these things; any analysis of charisma must take such views seriously, for the widespread belief in charisma's transformative power was itself the cause of historical change.

Finally, the role of the charismatic relationship in turn-of-the-century America underscores the importance of individual and collective emotion in shaping historical trends. The emotions evoked by charismatic leaders were not only an *effect* of cultural influences but also the *cause* of broad cultural shifts. While the themes and patterns present in American culture did inform emotional responses to charismatic figures, the relationship was a reciprocal one – Americans' emotional experience itself influenced society and culture in a variety of ways. Many followers' emotions translated directly into social activism, while many leaders subtly altered their self-presentation to attract emotional support. More important, simply by experiencing strong emotional attachments to charismatic figures and movements, Americans found they could reshape the connection between their leaders and themselves. By gravitating toward more emotionally available leaders, ordinary people altered the prevailing expectations about American leadership and forced politicians, activists, and evangelists to appeal to the new popular tastes. Charismatic movements, then, illustrate the power of emotions to do work in the world; simply by experiencing charisma, Americans transformed their culture.

* * *

Charisma emerged as an object of American fascination with the "magnetism craze" of the late nineteenth century. As Chapter 1 explains, the term "personal magnetism," borrowed from eighteenth-century hypnotist Franz Mesmer, became ubiquitous in American culture as a way of describing the power of one individual to influence another. Newspapers investigated the phenomenon, entrepreneurs advertised instruction manuals on it, and one enterprising huckster even founded a commune based on magnetic persuasion. After the Civil War, a variety of upheavals in American society – including the rise of industrial capitalism, a nationwide religious awakening, a cultural shift away from individualism, and the growth of a transcontinental railroad network – contributed to the growing national appetite for personal magnetism. The liberal minister Henry Ward Beecher, almost certainly the most accomplished charismatic orator of the nineteenth century, and the politician and "Magnetic Man" James G. Blaine were the first prominent charismatic leaders on the national scene. Their careers highlight both the promising and the troubling aspects of the charismatic relationship: both developed nationwide followings, yet both were accused, with some justification, of either sexual or fiscal improprieties stemming at least in part from their ability to influence others.

The term "personal magnetism" became increasingly anachronistic by the turn of the century, but the charismatic movements it described continued to grow in number and size. By 1896, when William Jennings Bryan's "Cross of Gold" speech landed him the Democratic presidential nomination and won him legions of followers, charismatic leadership had arrived as a major force in American culture. Chapter 2 investigates the origins of the charismatic speaking style and of charismatic organization more broadly. In the 1820s, eccentric researcher James Rush had invented a unique style of elocution based on both meticulous research and his own personal tastes. Coupled with an English gestural system and repackaged in textbook form, Rush's work became ubiquitous in higher education and formed the basis of the charismatic speaking style. Evangelist Charles Grandison Finney, an equally important forerunner of charismatic movements, made mainstream the idea that persuading audiences through emotional public speaking could be beneficial to American society. Influenced by a tradition of oratorical prowess and by Thomas Carlyle's writings extoling the virtues of heroism, a number of late nineteenth-century Americans adopted Finney's views and aspired to charismatic leadership. As charismatic movements began to proliferate, they developed their own set of performance practices and technologies: lecture circuits to facilitate speaking tours, new performance venues to maximize the reach of the speaker's voice, musical programs to prepare audiences, handshake events to enable direct interaction between followers and leaders, and lecture managers to oversee and implement the whole enterprise. Despite the ubiquity of charismatic movements by the early 1900s, women and African Americans often struggled to deploy charismatic techniques in an America that was hostile to female charismatic power and that marginalized or co-opted black charismatic oratory. Notwithstanding these obstacles, many female and African American leaders managed to circumvent opposition by challenging traditional views on the gendered and racial performance of oratory.

Charismatic movements depended for their success on the emotional investment of followers. Chapter 3 draws on hundreds of letters, oral histories, and archival and published testimonials to investigate the experience of charismatic followership. The decision to follow a charismatic leader such as Bryan, evangelist Billy Sunday, or Socialist politician Eugene Debs was not a self-defeating distraction from political commitments, as some scholars have argued; nor, as some contemporaries charged, were charismatic followers mere hysterical dupes. Rather, charismatic followership represented for many Americans a thoughtful response to their personal afflictions and to broader social concerns. Many charismatic followers experienced preexisting internal crises that they attributed to their own moral failings – even if their real problems arguably stemmed from broader social inequalities. Their own sense of unhappiness, coupled with familial and community pressures and the organizational efforts of charismatic movements, brought them into contact with charismatic orators who moved and inspired them. Joining a charismatic movement was a considered choice; it was also a powerful conversion experience that transformed their identities and invested their lives with new meaning and purpose. Followers described leaders using religious or sacralized language, fashioned new identities for themselves in keeping with the movement's ideals, convinced others to join the cause, and dedicated themselves to promoting the movement's political or religious platform. The charismatic relationship thus provided Americans with a way to translate their vague internal longings into external religious, social, and political action.

By the turn of the century, charisma had produced a variety of social, political, and religious movements that boasted millions of followers. As Chapter 4 notes, however, many Americans began to suspect the charismatic relationship could do more than that; they became convinced that charismatic movements possessed transformative political power that could change society in concrete ways. Gustave Le Bon's popular treatise *The Crowd*, translated into English in 1896, denigrated the intelligence of charismatic followers and urged leaders to manipulate audiences in order to bring about social change. Although most American thinkers adopted a less cynical approach to charisma, they, too, sought to utilize the charismatic relationship to promote various political platforms. In *The Promise of American Life* (1909), journalist Herbert Croly called for "some democratic Saint Francis" whose charismatic leadership would regenerate American society and bring about progressive policy goals. The irrepressible publicist Elbert Hubbard sought to create a charismatic relationship between readers and the subjects of serial biographies in service of a conservative, pro-business ideal. Even labor radicals, who savaged charismatic leaders as demagogues, viewed the work of "agitators" such as "Big Bill" Haywood and Eugene Debs as an acceptable use of the charismatic relationship. The diversity of voices who championed charisma as a force for political change underscored the widespread nature of such pro-charismatic views.

Following Croly's lead, a number of progressive leaders attempted to develop charismatic movements to promote their political programs; their efforts came to dominate discussions of charisma during the 1910s. Ex-president Theodore Roosevelt made the charismatic relationship the centerpiece of his 1912 presidential campaign. The winner of that election, fellow progressive Woodrow Wilson, viewed oratory as a key feature of political leadership; at the end of World War I, Wilson embarked on a charismatic speaking tour to promote congressional passage of the Treaty of Versailles. Chapter 5 demonstrates, however, that neither Roosevelt nor Wilson was able to maximize his charismatic appeal to American audiences. An idiosyncratic speaking style and, more important, a disastrous campaign strategy limited Roosevelt's access to the voters with whom he sought to forge charismatic connections. Meanwhile, Wilson's philosophy of oratory focused on improving followers' moral character rather than appealing to their emotions. Wilson's approach to public speaking largely precluded the use of charismatic practices; when he finally began to embrace charismatic techniques, he suffered a catastrophic physical collapse and had to abandon the project. Ultimately, Roosevelt, Wilson, and other progressives misunderstood the mutual nature of the charismatic relationship and failed to offer followers enough agency to win their allegiance – thus dooming the progressive charismatic enterprise.

The collapse of progressivism after World War I, Chapter 6 argues, soured many Americans on the charismatic connection that had become closely identified with progressive politics. The growth of the radio and other forms of electronic mass communication undermined the effectiveness of the charismatic speaking style and replaced it with a new conversational idiom that sounded better over the airwaves. At the same time, many commentators unhappy with the outcome of the war came to believe that unscrupulous charismatic leaders had manipulated Americans into supporting a disastrous militarism. These thinkers developed a new distrust of popular governance, leading them either to turn against charismatic movements or to advocate Le Bon's cynical form of charismatic manipulation. Despite a growing cultural hostility toward charisma which silenced William Jennings Bryan and other charismatic figures, women and minority leaders such as the pan-Africanist Marcus Garvey and the Pentecostal evangelist Aimee Semple McPherson continued to embrace the charismatic relationship and to develop new and innovative charismatic techniques. After his election as president in 1932, Franklin Roosevelt delivered a series of radio "fireside chats" that merged elements of charismatic leadership with mass communication strategies. Although Roosevelt adopted the conversational speaking style and avoided charismatic organizational techniques, his radio addresses created an intimate connection with voters and inspired letters that equaled or exceeded charismatic follower testimonials in their emotional fervor. Ultimately, Roosevelt absorbed the emotional content of charismatic connections into a new type of leader–follower relationship that would exert a lasting influence on American culture.

Today, the "grand organ" of charismatic leadership no longer operates in American society as it once did. The world inhabited by Patrick Gilmore and his band is gone, replaced by a seemingly less emotional style of leadership and more pervasive skepticism about the charismatic relationship's social merits. Nevertheless, as the conclusion shows, the intimate emotional bond between leaders and followers that formed the basic feature of charismatic movements has assumed a central place in modern American society. Every emotional sermon delivered by a televangelist, every effort by a politician to connect personally with voters, and every attempt by an activist to inspire new recruits is an echo and a reminder of America's charismatic past. Comprehending the leader–follower relationship in modern America requires understanding the period in American history when charisma was everywhere – in the actions of leaders, the aspirations of followers, and the magnetic music that thrilled audiences at the St. Louis Exposition. This is the story of that age of charisma.

1

Magnetic America

Personal Magnetism in American Culture, 1870–1900

"Have the Plants Souls?" The headline of an 1889 *Chicago Tribune* article posed the question with some urgency. After all, there seemed no other way to explain why some women could grow home gardens easily while others appeared doomed to failure. "Are flowers sentient beings?" the *Tribune* reporter asked. "Have they affections, likes and dislikes?" He interviewed "a demure little housewife," who "calm[l]y assured [the] reporter that flowers had souls, or hearts, or some other organ capable of receiving impressions from human beings." What sort of impressions, the reporter wondered, were good and bad gardeners imparting to their plants? "Personal magnetism in one case; the lack of it in the other."[1]

In 1884, watch repairer M. J. Valentine told a *Philadelphia Times* reporter the story of a particularly difficult timepiece: a watch that ran perfectly while in his possession but that often told incorrect time while out of the repair shop. Valentine suspected that the watch's inner workings were being magnetized – but by what? Finally, he read an article that "opened my eyes. It was simply a little item saying that sometimes delicately adjusted watches were affected by the temperament of their wearers." Valentine had already noticed that the watch's owner seemed nervous and high-strung. Now he had an epiphany: "The whole thing flashed upon me in a moment. The woman's watch was affected by herself." The *Times* reporter succinctly captured Valentine's point: "Affected by Personal Magnetism."[2]

1 "Have the Plants Souls?" *Chicago Tribune*, September 15, 1889, 26.

2 "Magnetized Watches," orig. pub. *Philadelphia Times; Chicago Tribune*, September 7, 1884, 3.

In 1905, the aging baseball player Jack O'Connor reminisced with a *Dallas Morning News* reporter about the games of O'Connor's youth. Unlike in the past, noted the St. Louis Browns catcher, today's fans were more interested in teams as a whole than in individual players. What had changed during the previous two decades? The obvious answer was the arrival of the "dead-ball era," in which a combination of rule and strategy changes led to uneventful games and an absence of star sluggers.[3] But O'Connor did not notice any difference in the game itself; instead, he felt the relationship between players and spectators had changed. "Both the players and the crowds are different," he explained. The *News* reporter elaborated: "There were men years back whose every appearance on the field was the signal for yell after yell of delight and admiration." But now, "The era of popular idols has passed, and the present epoch is that of team-work and the science of the game." In describing this disconnect between the "popular idols" and their supporters, O'Connor turned to a familiar phrase. "If there is one element of baseball which seems to be disappearing," he opined, "it is personal magnetism."[4]

Personal magnetism! What was this mysterious power that turn-of-the-century Americans thought capable of growing plants, stopping watches, and attracting fans to baseball games? "It cannot be defined in words," admitted singer Emma Abbott, though that did not stop Abbott's contemporaries from trying.[5] In essence, personal magnetism was the ability to appeal to others, and to affect their behavior, by means of nonrational, subverbal cues. "To me," wrote Dr. W. R. Latson, "personal magnetism means the power of one person to attract and influence other people."[6] "It is something in the voice or manner," wrote Senator and famed after-dinner speaker Chauncey M. Depew, who knew whereof he spoke, "which establishes a connection between the audience and the speaker."[7] "It is a sort of electrical force a man may put forth," agreed composer Frank L. Eyer, "which will draw other men to him, and secure, often command, their love, admiration, and co-operation in any undertaking he

[3] Harold Seymour and Dorothy Seymour Mills, *Baseball: The Golden Age* (New York: Oxford University Press, 1989), 122.

[4] "About Personal Magnetism," *Dallas Morning News*, November 12, 1905, 22.

[5] "What Is Personal Magnetism?" orig. pub. *Chicago Times; Bismarck Daily Tribune*, June 27, 1888, 1.

[6] W. R. Latson, "Personal Magnetism," *Grand Rapids Evening Press*, September 12, 1908, 4.

[7] Chauncey M. Depew, "Editorial Foreword," in Depew, ed., *The Library of Oratory: Ancient and Modern*, Vol. I (Akron, OH: The New Werner Co., 1902), i.

may be desirous of seeing accomplished."[8] Magnetic people "invite your confidence when first you meet them," the *Philadelphia Public Ledger* explained; "You feel at once the force of an irresistible attraction."[9] Such individuals "charm you towards them with an almost irresistable [*sic*] power," wrote the *Idaho Statesman*. "You like them at first sight, though you are not always able to give a reason why. Their very presence is an inspiration ... They 'grapple you to their souls with hooks of steel.' "[10] As such imagery suggested, magnetism meant control over others, for good or ill. It was "an invisible, mysterious force," maintained the *Langston City Herald*, "which we acknowledge and yield to, even against our convictions and reason."[11] The *Idaho Falls Times* defined the term more ominously: magnetism was the ability of "a man to make others believe he is right when they know he is wrong."[12]

At the end of the nineteenth century, what can only be described as a personal magnetism craze swept the United States. In an unstable and perilous world, many Americans wanted to learn about magnetism, to become magnetic, or to exert magnetic power over others. Writing in 1875 of his experiences as a Civil War nurse, Walt Whitman "found it was in the simple matter of Personal Presence, and emanating ordinary cheer and magnetism, that I succeeded" in helping wounded soldiers.[13] When dime novelist Joseph E. Badger, Jr., invented in 1889 a brave hero for whom "to will was to win," he named his protagonist "Major Magnet, the Man of Nerve."[14] A 1911 letter to newspaper columnist Dorothy Dix reflected such desires; if she could have three wishes, the young letter-writer stated, she would choose "a masterful mind, personal magnetism, and to marry a baseball player." Dix found the baseball player part funny, the rest understandable.[15] By the 1880s, popular interest in magnetism was so great that hucksters began to take out newspaper ads for correspondence courses on the subject. If the proliferation of their advertisements was any indication, these entrepreneurs did excellent business selling ordinary Americans the power to "Win ... the

[8] Frank L. Eyer, "Personal Magnetism," *The Etude*, Vol. 18, No. 10 (October 1, 1900), 360.

[9] "Personal Magnetism," orig. pub. *Philadelphia Public Ledger; Colorado Springs Gazette*, April 25, 1909, 12.

[10] "Personal Magnetism," *Idaho Daily Statesman*, June 23, 1888, 2.

[11] "Personal Magnetism," *Langston City Herald*, July 9, 1892, 1.

[12] *Idaho Falls Times*, May 19, 1898, 7.

[13] Walt Whitman, *Memoranda During the War* (Camden, NJ: Walt Whitman, 1875), 18.

[14] Joseph E. Badger, Jr., *Major Magnet, The Man of Nerve; or, the Muck-a-Mucks of Animas*, Beadle's New York Dime Library (New York: Beadle & Adams, 1889), 14.

[15] Dorothy Dix, "Three Wishes," *Tucson Daily Citizen*, October 28, 1911, 8.

Laurels in the Hardest-Fought Battles of Life." Magnetism, they promised, was "the Magic Wand that Rules the World Today."[16] It "turns life's failures into successes," wrote the Reverend Paul Weller in one such advertisement; "it makes you nobler, purer and better."[17] By 1909, these individuals had so commodified magnetism that actor David Belasco dismissed the term as "a cheap, tawdry word."[18] Nevertheless, the hordes of such "tawdry" salesmen reflected the broad appeal of their wares.

Though some Americans wanted to become magnetic themselves, most sought primarily to understand the phenomenon in others. Accordingly, newspaper discussions of magnetism focused on leaders who displayed magnetic abilities. As the response to Patrick Gilmore's band demonstrated, the emerging field of conducting was one of the key venues for audiences to observe the charismatic phenomenon. The influence of Richard Wagner in Europe created a tradition of charismatic orchestra conductors that eventually culminated with the career of Arturo Toscanini; two of these magnetic music directors – Anton Seidl and Arthur Nikisch – electrified listeners when they arrived in the United States in the 1880s.[19] Then there were the bandleaders such as Gilmore and John Philip Sousa, "[t]he magnetic man of marches and melodies," according to the *Maysville Daily Public Ledger*.[20] Concertgoers in the late nineteenth century were fascinated by the tableau of a baton-wielding leader molding his orchestral followers onstage into a mass movement whose "magnetic music," in turn, touched and moved listeners.

In general, however, Americans were more interested in the magnetic influence of public speakers in the religious, political, and activist realms – in other words, of leaders who sought to change society in concrete ways. "If you have ever sat under the eloquence of some great orator," wrote Frank Eyer, "and, in company with the hundreds about you, been moved to tears, to laughter, to enthusiasm, then you know the power of [personal magnetism]."[21] Political figures, in particular, seemingly could possess

[16] "Personal Magnetism is the Magic Wand that Rules the World Today," advertisement, *Charlotte Daily Observer*, October 2, 1910, 13.

[17] "Man's Influence over Man," advertisement, *Philadelphia Inquirer*, February 11, 1900, 11.

[18] "David Belasco Talks of the Theory of Magnetism," *New York Times*, May 23, 1909, SM9.

[19] Harold C. Schonberg, *The Great Conductors* (New York: Simon and Schuster, 1967), 176–177, 208, 212; Joseph Horowitz, *Wagner Nights: An American History* (Berkeley, CA: University of California Press, 1994), 90.

[20] *Maysville Daily Public Ledger*, January 25, 1897, 4.

[21] Eyer, "Personal Magnetism," 360.

or lack magnetism in sufficient quantities to influence their electoral fortunes. President Grover Cleveland's "Want of Personal Magnetism" ensured that "He Has No Friends," insisted the *Boston Daily Advertiser* in 1888.[22] California gubernatorial nominee George Stoneman "is not a man of great personal magneticism [*sic*]," lamented the sympathetic *San Francisco Examiner* in 1882 after Stoneman delivered a dull, rambling acceptance speech at the Democratic state convention.[23] Defeated Minnesota congressman Solomon G. Comstock wished he had lost instead to the third candidate in a three-way race in 1890, because the actual winner, "being a man of no particular personal magnetism or oratorical powers, it was out of the question to expect much of him as a congressman."[24] Historical leaders could be magnetic as well; writers often described Henry Clay and Abraham Lincoln in this way, and such figures as Napoleon and King David merited articles devoted to their attractive qualities.[25] Certain women, such as the social activists Anna Dickinson and Frances Willard, the Populist agitator Mary Lease, and the African American evangelists Amanda Berry Smith and "Aunt Susan," were also described as magnetic.[26]

Personal magnetism played a central role in charismatic movements; in fact, it was virtually synonymous with the modern popular definition of "charisma." In essence, magnetism served as the engine that drove the charismatic relationship. Charismatic leaders attracted followers and cemented their allegiance by demonstrating magnetic abilities and deploying magnetic techniques. Qualities such as organizational prowess, upright character, and popular issue positions could also help leaders

[22] "He Has No Friends," *Boston Daily Advertiser*, April 7, 1888, 8.

[23] *San Francisco Examiner*, June 24, 1882, 3, quoted in John F. Reynolds, "The Hustling Candidate and the Advent of the Direct Primary: A California Case Study," *Journal of the Gilded Age and Progressive Era*, Vol. 12, No. 1 (January 2013), 33.

[24] "Comstock on Halvorsen," *Duluth Daily Tribune*, November 21, 1890, 2; comment paraphrased by reporter.

[25] "Lincoln's Personal Magnetism," *New Hampshire Sentinel*, April 18, 1867; "How Lincoln Swayed Men," *Bismarck Daily Tribune*, May 3, 1899; "Personal Magnetism," *Portland Morning Oregonian*, March 29, 1891, 11; "Henry Clay's Personal Magnetism," orig. pub. *Louisville Courier-Journal; Trenton Evening Times*, February 20, 1887, 6; Ella W. Prattle, "David the Magnetic Man," *Omaha Sunday World-Herald*, March 27, 1892, 7.

[26] "Famous Female Orators," orig. pub. *Boston Herald; Boston Investigator*, October 14, 1891, 5; "Two Fair Chieftains," *Chicago Daily Inter Ocean*, October 18, 1888; "Just Like Her Ma," *Atchison Daily Globe*, June 7, 1897; "Colored Woman Evangelist," *New Orleans Daily Picayune*, October 14, 1897; Mary E. Leonard, "A Blind Evangelist," *Atchison Daily Globe*, October 21, 1898, 3.

attract large followings, but specifically charismatic leader–follower connections relied on magnetism for their power. To many Americans, magnetism explained the discrepancies between leaders' expected popularity, based on traditional measures of ability, and the support those leaders actually garnered. A writer for the *Springfield Republican*, for instance, confessed himself amazed by the outpouring of enthusiasm for Pennsylvania political boss Matthew Stanley Quay at the 1900 Republican National Convention. "Here is a man," fumed the journalist, "whom we have the very best possible reason to think of as unprincipled, who does violence to fundamental laws of morality, – and not only goes unpunished, but meets with salvos of applause." Only Quay's possession of "a great deal of [magnetism]" could explain the disconnect between his venality and his popularity.[27]

The American fascination with magnetism already had a long history by the late nineteenth century. The idea that people exerted a magnetic force on one another had originated with the Swabian hypnotist Franz Anton Mesmer as early as 1775; by the late 1830s, European lecturers were touring the United States transfixing American audiences with Mesmer's theories.[28] Mesmer's experiments in "animal magnetism," with their strange pseudoscientific discussions of electrical attractions and "magnetic fluids," occasionally left their mark on later American discussions of personal magnetism. Mesmer's influence could be seen in those who thought magnetic personalities could stop watches and grow plants, in Whitman's belief that "the magnetic touch of hands" could heal wounded veterans, and in the writer who suggested expert fishermen could "entice [fish] out of the water by a sort of personal magnetism or moral suasion."[29] And an 1896 *New York Journal* article certainly reflected the influence of magnetic fluid theory: "When you shake hands," the paper asserted, "something goes out of you and into the other person."[30] Most turn-of-the-century Americans, though, saw magnetism as a more practical matter than Mesmer had. "There is no such

[27] "Personal Magnetism," *Springfield Republican*, August 12, 1900, 13.

[28] Ann Taves, *Fits, Trances, & Visions: Experiencing Religion and Explaining Experience from Wesley to James* (Princeton: Princeton University Press, 1999), 125; Alan Gauld, *A History of Hypnotism* (Cambridge, UK: Cambridge University Press, 1992), 1, 3; Robert C. Fuller, *Mesmerism and the American Cure of Souls* (Philadelphia: University of Pennsylvania Press, 1982), 17, 20, 26.

[29] Whitman, *Memoranda During the War*, 40; "Fishing as an Art," *St. Louis Globe-Democrat*, September 5, 1885, 16.

[30] "Dangers in Handshaking," orig. pub. *New York Journal; Denver Evening Post*, November 23, 1896, 3.

thing as magnetism ... in the popularly accepted sense," insisted Belasco. "Magnetism is hard work; that's what it is."[31]

Magnetism had more mainstream antecedents, too. Thomas Carlyle's *On Heroes, Hero-Worship, and the Heroic in History*, for one, had been popular in the United States since its 1841 publication.[32] Carlyle urged his readers to venerate heroes and leaders for their magnetism and their superior nature: "No nobler feeling than this of admiration for one higher than himself dwells in the breast of man," he wrote.[33] At the same time, he promised that worshipping such leaders would benefit followers as well: "Does not every true man believe that he is himself made higher by doing reverence to what is really above him?"[34] Americans had also experienced magnetism of a spiritual nature beginning with the Second Great Awakening of the 1820s. Evangelical preachers such as Charles Grandison Finney and, later, Dwight Moody pioneered revival strategies designed to induce religious conversions; the ministers won souls by using magnetic speaking and organizational techniques to establish charismatic relationships with their audiences.[35] Finney and Moody themselves drew on a tradition of charismatic preaching and emotional response stretching back to George Whitefield and Jonathan Edwards in the eighteenth century.[36] Meanwhile, Phineas Quimby and his followers in the New Thought theological movement, inspired by the ideas of Swedish mystic Emanuel Swedenborg, adapted Mesmer's theories beginning in the mid-1800s to argue that magnetism offered physical health benefits for the magnetized.[37]

[31] "David Belasco Talks of the Theory of Magnetism."

[32] Barbara Sicherman, *Well-Read Lives: How Books Inspired a Generation of American Women* (Charlotte, NC: University of North Carolina Press, 2010), 291 n. 32.

[33] Thomas Carlyle, *On Heroes, Hero-Worship, and the Heroic in History* (London: James Fraser, 1841), 18.

[34] *Ibid.*, 23.

[35] William G. McLoughlin, Jr., *Revivals, Awakenings, and Reform: An Essay on Religion and Social Change in America, 1607–1977* (Chicago: University of Chicago Press, 1978), 123–130, 142–144.

[36] Taves, *Fits, Trances, & Visions*, 19, 122.

[37] *Ibid.*, 212–215; Catherine L. Albanese, *A Republic of Mind and Spirit: A Cultural History of American Metaphysical Religion* (New Haven, CT: Yale University Press, 2007), 140–141, 285–288; Richard Wightman Fox, *Jesus in America: Personal Savior, Cultural Hero, National Obsession* (New York: HarperCollins, 2004), 268–269; David G. Schuster, *Neurasthenic Nation: America's Search for Health, Happiness, and Comfort, 1869–1920* (New Brunswick, NJ: Rutgers University Press, 2011), 66–67.

Despite earlier interest in charisma, the post–Civil War magnetism craze was unprecedented in its popularity and scope. Several developments help to explain magnetism's meteoric rise to prominence. First and most important, the rise of industrial capitalism beginning in the 1850s caused dramatic shifts in American society. The growth of urban industry led to a torrent of migration to the cities, the rise of a substantial middle class and an ultra-rich upper class, and an influx of desperately poor immigrants from Europe. This transformation of the American socioeconomic structure made society seem unstable and frightening, particularly for members of the new middle class. Many Americans found themselves bewildered by a newly complicated world of shifting class status, in which some people seemed to get ahead effortlessly while others were left behind – and most worried they would end up in the latter category.[38]

Magnetism seemed to explain these easily observable societal discrepancies. Magnetic people won friends, arguments, and promotions more easily than their nonmagnetic counterparts. They were natural leaders who gained followers as predictably as a magnet attracting iron filings, and who got ahead in the world on the strength of their mysterious talent. Eligible young women could even win husbands through magnetism; Connecticut judge John Light argued that if female teachers "spent as much time cultivating personal magnetism as they did in dressing their hair ... three-fourths of them would be married."[39] Commentators disagreed as to the exact ways people became magnetic, but such attractive personalities clearly were doing something simple, natural, and maddeningly difficult to copy. "The great man carries in the calm dignity of his brow, the light in his eye, and the firm set of his lips the impress of his soul, of the work he has done, and the high thoughts he has lived with," explained Belasco. A man who tried to fake such things without talent or training would "have something self-conscious about him" and would fail.[40]

[38] T. J. Jackson Lears, *No Place of Grace: Antimodernism and the Transformation of American Culture, 1880–1920* (New York: Pantheon, 1981), 8–11; Theodore P. Greene, *America's Heroes: The Changing Models of Success in American Magazines* (New York: Oxford University Press, 1970), 114; Robert H. Wiebe, *The Search for Order, 1877–1920* (New York: Hill and Wang, 1967), 11–12; Richard Hofstadter, *The Age of Reform: From Bryan to F. D. R.* (New York: Knopf, 1955), 7–9.

[39] "Girls Can Win Husbands by Personal Magnetism," *Columbus Enquirer-Sun*, April 24, 1908, 3.

[40] "David Belasco Talks of the Theory of Magnetism."

The growth of industrial capitalism spawned three other developments that also contributed to the post–Civil War magnetism craze. Grasping for solid ground in an era of dramatic socioeconomic change, the new American middle class gravitated toward novel forms of engagement with Protestant religion. An upswing of religious revivalism not seen since the 1840s, coupled with a flowering of new Protestant sects in the emotive Pentecostal tradition, constituted the "Third Great Awakening" in American society.[41] At the same time, middle-class Americans' Protestant faith often engendered a moral response to industrialization; even those not involved in revivals or new denominations sought ways to strengthen the moral and religious fiber of American culture in order to restore balance to industrial society.[42] The language of Protestantism suffused encounters with both overtly religious and ostensibly secular magnetic leaders. Magnetic orators often used religious rhetoric to describe themselves and their causes, while their listeners described the experience of magnetic followership using the words of the Christian convert. Many Americans became receptive to magnetism for the same reason they embraced religious awakening: in a world filled with new and disturbing questions, they believed, powerful emotional experiences might lead to the answers they sought.

Industrial capitalism also created a transportation revolution that reshaped American society. The growth of a transcontinental railroad network, along with track standardizations and speed increases, enabled greater mobility by 1890 for those able to afford regular train tickets.[43] The result was greater exposure to magnetism for Americans across the country. Charismatic leaders who might previously have garnered only local followings were able to embark on nationwide speaking tours, gaining adherents wherever they went. In doing so, they unified the

[41] McLoughlin, *Revivals, Awakenings, and Reform*, 2, 145–146; Grant Wacker, *Heaven Below: Early Pentecostals and American Culture* (Cambridge, MA: Harvard University Press, 2001), 1–4.

[42] Paul Boyer, *Urban Masses and Moral Order in America, 1820–1920* (Cambridge, MA and London: Harvard University Press, 1978), 125, 132; Robert M. Crunden, *Ministers of Reform: The Progressives' Achievement in American Civilization, 1889–1920* (New York: Basic Books, 1982), 28.

[43] Alfred D. Chandler, Jr., *The Visible Hand: The Managerial Revolution in American Business* (Cambridge, MA: Belknap Press, 1977), 88; Barbara Young Welke, *Recasting American Liberty: Gender, Race, Law, and the Railroad Revolution, 1865–1920* (Cambridge, UK: Cambridge University Press, 2001), 5–16; Christian Wolmar, *The Great Railroad Revolution: The History of Trains in America* (New York: Public Affairs, 2012), 159, 215–219.

charismatic follower experiences of Americans in widely differing locales. Americans who had only read about antebellum political leaders, for example, could now experience the magnetism of postwar national politicians firsthand. As leaders increased their geographical reach, they in turn gained more power to influence society.

Finally, the development of an industrial economy changed how Americans viewed themselves in relation to their society. A deep strain of individualism ran through the American character during the early nineteenth century.[44] "Whoso would be a man, must be a nonconformist," Ralph Waldo Emerson declared in his 1841 essay "Self-Reliance"; "the great man is he who in the midst of the crowd keeps with perfect sweetness the independence of solitude."[45] Such a view of personhood was incompatible with personal magnetism, and indeed Emerson complained in 1840 about the "magnetic" President Andrew Jackson.[46] "Every decent and well-spoken individual," Emerson lamented the next year, "affects and sways me more than is right"; a person who could be changed by another, he felt, was not a full person at all.[47] This individualist relationship between self and society persisted into the late nineteenth century – as late as 1892, suffragist Elizabeth Cady Stanton was declaring that "Nothing adds such dignity to character as the recognition of one's self-sovereignty."[48]

By 1900, however, a new approach to social life had taken hold in the American consciousness. "A large body of people," reported social reformer Jane Addams in 1902, "feel keenly that the present industrial system is in a state of profound disorder, and that there is no guarantee that the

[44] Daniel Walker Howe, *Making the American Self: Jonathan Edwards to Abraham Lincoln* (Cambridge, MA: Harvard University Press, 1997), 4, 9; Wilfred M. McClay, *The Masterless: Self & Society in Modern America* (Chapel Hill, NC: University of North Carolina Press, 1994), 52.

[45] Ralph Waldo Emerson, "Self-Reliance," in Emerson, *Essays, First Series* (New York: Crowell, 1841), 36, 39.

[46] Ralph Waldo Emerson, journal entry for June 1840, in Emerson, *The Journals and Miscellaneous Notebooks of Ralph Waldo Emerson, 1838–1842*, ed. A. W. Plumstead and Harrison Hayward (Cambridge, MA: Harvard University Press, 1969), 376; Burton W. Peretti, *The Leading Man: Hollywood and the Presidential Image* (New Brunswick, NJ: Rutgers University Press, 2012), 18.

[47] Emerson, "Self-Reliance," 37.

[48] Elizabeth Cady Stanton, "The Solitude of Self," *Hearing of the Woman Suffrage Association*, Committee on the Judiciary, January 18, 1892 (Washington, DC: US House, 1892), 3.

pursuit of individual ethics will ever right it."[49] The tremendous social forces unleashed by both industrial capitalism and the Civil War led Americans to embrace solutions that sacrificed individual autonomy in favor of communal benefits. This shift in attitudes inspired a variety of government-based proposals to improve industrial society – from Henry George's Single Tax to Edward Bellamy's socialist utopia to the nascent progressive movement.[50] It also made personal magnetism a far more appealing social development. If mass movements could solve problems that individual effort could not, Americans reasoned, there was more to gain – and less to lose – by embracing the charismatic relationship as a means of motivating Americans to concerted action.

Despite magnetism's mass appeal, many Americans saw a disturbing side to the phenomenon. In the wrong hands, magnetism's coercive power could facilitate corruption, criminality, or even sexual misconduct. "Personal magnetism has no connection whatever with iron," quipped the *Galveston News* in 1880, "but … such metals as gold and silver are most likely to produce the desired effect."[51] The *Brooklyn Eagle* made a similar crack in 1879: "Candidate Charles Foster, of Ohio, is said to possess a great deal of personal magnetism. He can put his hand in his pocket, and bring it out charged with personal magnetism."[52] Actual criminals used such techniques as well. "Noted bunco man" Edward D. Snow, wrote the *Milwaukee Journal*, "has personal magnetism enough to paralyze the intended victim."[53] Fraudster W. J. St. Claire, according to the *Phoenix Republican-Herald*, "possesses a personal magnetism by which he draws dollars from the most suspicious."[54] Meanwhile, anxious jokes about men confusing their unwanted sexual advances with personal magnetism reflected a real fear that men and women who truly possessed such power might seduce others against their will.[55]

Ultimately, the magnetism craze revealed the degree to which charismatic leaders seemed both fascinating and frightening in the late nineteenth century. Personal magnetism appealed to Americans because

[49] Jane Addams, *Democracy and Social Ethics* (New York: Macmillan, 1902), 165–166.

[50] Jeffrey Sklansky, *The Soul's Economy: Market Society and Selfhood in American Thought, 1820–1920* (Chapel Hill, NC: University of North Carolina Press, 2002), 4–9; McClay, *The Masterless*, 74–75.

[51] "Personal Magnetism," *Galveston Daily News*, June 5, 1880.

[52] " 'Magnetism' in Ohio," orig. pub. *Brooklyn Eagle; Washington Post*, July 9, 1879, 2.

[53] "Crooks and Their Faces," *Milwaukee Journal*, December 19, 1891.

[54] "Picturesque Criminal," *Phoenix Republican-Herald*, December 28, 1899, 6.

[55] Orig. pub. *Burlington Hawkeye; New Haven Evening Register*, September 16, 1884, 3; "An Electric Spark," editorial cartoon, *Denver Rocky Mountain News*, May 3, 1896.

of its power to explain new developments in their culture, its potential to move and inspire them, and its ability to order society by spurring them to action in a meaningful and coordinated way. At the same time, they feared its misuse in the hands of criminals or seducers bent on exploiting their magnetic abilities to manipulate society to their own ends. The remarkable career of minister Henry Ward Beecher and the political campaigns of James G. Blaine illustrate both the promise and the pitfalls of charisma's newfound role in society. Few aspects of American culture carried such great rewards or such high risks as did charisma. It is surprising not that people discussed personal magnetism as much as they did, but that they did not discuss it even more.

* * *

In the summer of 1886, the Reverend W. J. Dawson attended a lecture at Exeter Hall, on the London Strand. The speaker that evening was the American clergyman Henry Ward Beecher, who had made a series of memorable pro-Union addresses in that city during the Civil War. Dawson knew of Beecher's considerable reputation, but at first he found the American's performance disappointing. Beecher's manner of speaking "was so quiet, so colloquial, so free from the usual artifice of the orator... He did not even try to make himself heard." Glancing around, Dawson noticed that other attendees looked as restless as he felt. He imagined their surprise: "Where were the brilliant paradox, the flash of epigram, the sonorous declamation which English audiences had learned to expect from their popular orators?" Meanwhile, "This quiet man" – Beecher – "went on talking with himself."

All at once, something changed. Beecher "suddenly ... emitted a spark of flame that ran kindling through the crowd." No one looked restless any more. Beecher changed his tone again, and "the audience quivered; a moment later frantic excitement seized upon the congregation. And still he was talking with the utmost quietness, complete master of himself as well as of his hearers." Dawson could not believe what had transpired in the hall. "It was a new kind of oratory," he remarked later; "it was the speech of the soul finding by unerring instinct its way to the deepest springs of life and thought in his hearers."[56]

Dawson had experienced the personal magnetism of one of nineteenth-century America's most extraordinary characters. Ask any ten educated

[56] W. L. Dawson, "An English Estimate of Beecher," in J. H. Tewksbury, ed., *Henry Ward Beecher as His Friends Saw Him* (New York: Pilgrim Press, 1904), 48–51.

Americans in 1870 who was the nation's most magnetic personality, and you would likely get a unanimous vote in favor of Henry Ward Beecher. "Probably no American of our century . . . has surpassed him in magnetic power, the faculty of drawing and holding men," wrote biographer John Henry Barrows in 1893.[57] Not only was Beecher the first national figure to be identified consistently with the phrase "personal magnetism," he was in many ways the archetype of the charismatic leader: ubiquitous, wildly popular, able to charm and inspire at will from the pulpit or the podium. "I have seen great audiences bow before his eloquence as a field of wheat goes down before the west wind," declared Amory H. Bradford.[58] Lyman Abbott, Beecher's biographer and friend, described Beecher's remarkable ability in terms that could typify charismatic leadership itself: "If the test of oratory is the power of the speaker to impart to his audience his life, to impress on them his conviction, animate them with his purpose, and direct their action to the accomplishment of his end, then Mr. Beecher was the greatest orator I have ever heard."[59]

It was not always this way with Beecher. In fact, one might have been forgiven for wondering, during his boyhood, whether Henry would amount to much of anything. He was born on June 24, 1813, the eighth of fiery Congregationalist minister Lyman Beecher's thirteen children. Lyman Beecher was a complex man, brilliant and intellectual, possessed of a bleak Calvinist worldview and the conviction that a moment not spent seeking salvation was a moment wasted. By temperament Henry's father was a loving parent, but after Henry's mother died in 1816, Lyman withdrew into morbidity and an ever-more-dogmatic theology. He encouraged his children's quick minds, drove them to academic excellence, and demanded that they achieve professional success – preferably as Calvinist preachers like himself. The Beecher children responded to this pressure in very different ways. Henry's older sister Harriet went on to write the wildly successful antislavery novel *Uncle Tom's Cabin*; two other sisters became noted women's rights activists. All of Henry's brothers became ministers at some point in their lives. Several achieved prominence; two, cracking under the burden of their father's expectations, committed suicide.[60]

[57] John Henry Barrows, *Henry Ward Beecher: The Shakespeare of the Pulpit* (New York: Funk & Wagnalls, 1893), 156.

[58] Quoted in Tewksbury, ed., *Henry Ward Beecher as His Friends Saw Him*, 126.

[59] Lyman Abbott, *Henry Ward Beecher* (Boston: Houghton, Mifflin, 1903), 403.

[60] Debby Applegate, *The Most Famous Man in America: The Biography of Henry Ward Beecher* (New York: Doubleday, 2006), 19–46; Clifford E. Clark, Jr., *Henry Ward*

Then there was Henry, the middle child who seemed to do nothing right. He chafed under his father's uncompromising expectations and unforgiving God; as a mediocre student and a sinner, he felt incapable of measuring up to the standards of either. He even tried to run away to sea, but lost his nerve.[61] What was worse, he had a speech impediment, "a thickness of speech arising from a large palate," he remembered, "so that when a boy I used to be laughed at for talking as if I had pudding in my mouth."[62] For a preacher's son expected to follow in his father's footsteps, such a defect was a terrible affliction. Between Henry's unfocused intellect and his slurred speech, "the last success that ever would have been predicted for him," wrote his sister Harriet, "would have been that of an orator."[63]

The story of Beecher's transformation from mumbling ne'er-do-well to meteoric success reveals two key components of charismatic performance: artifice and emotion. Artifice came first, along with hard work. As a teenage student at Amherst College, Henry encountered an instructor named John Lovell who agreed to train him in elocution. Lovell's system did more than simply remove Beecher's speech impediment; it was a comprehensive program consisting, Beecher recalled, of "the thorough practice of inflexions by the voice, of gesture, posture, and articulation."[64] Lovell drew his program of gestures and pronunciations from textbooks written in 1830–1831 by Harvard elocution professor Jonathan Barber. Barber's system was so precise that his own students, standing in a bamboo cage, placed their hands through different slats depending on the emotion they were trying to evoke.[65] For hours each day, Beecher rehearsed the precise techniques calculated to influence audiences. At times, he spent a whole hour repeating a single word over and over. "It was drill, drill, drill, until the motions almost became a second

Beecher: Spokesman for a Middle-Class America (Urbana, IL: University of Illinois Press, 1978), 6–12.

61 Applegate, *The Most Famous Man in America*, 49, 59.

62 William C. Beecher and Samuel Scoville, *A Biography of Rev. Henry Ward Beecher* (New York: Charles L. Webster, 1888), 95.

63 Harriet Beecher Stowe, *Men of Our Times; Or, Leading Patriots of the Day* (Hartford, CT: Hartford Publishing Co., 1868), 510.

64 "Inquiring Friends," *Christian Union*, July 14, 1880, quoted in Beecher and Scoville, *A Biography of Rev. Henry Ward Beecher*, 95.

65 David H. Grover, "Elocution at Harvard: The Saga of Jonathan Barber," *Quarterly Journal of Speech*, Vol. 51, No. 1 (February 1965), 65; Henry Ward Beecher, *Yale Lectures on Preaching*, Vol. 1 (New York: J. B. Ford, 1872), 135.

nature," Beecher wrote. "Now … my gestures are natural, because this drill made them natural to me."[66]

Minister Frank Gunsaulus, who heard Beecher speak many times, testified to the results of this training. Rhetorically speaking, Beecher had "simply the most multitudinous collection of forces" at his disposal, Gunsaulus reported. He wielded his voice like an artist's brush; "his painter-like sympathy for rightness of color, and his will to express himself in perfect draughtsmanship," gave him the skill and precision to fit perfectly any mood he chose. His body took part in the sermon, too. "It would not be adequate to say that Beecher's body … was 'the organ of his mind,' " Gunsaulus wrote. During a sermon, "The whole being called Beecher was organism; he was it and it was he."[67] Every gesture, every movement of his body, was carefully calibrated to influence his listeners. "His voice, his action, his look, his whole person *act* his meaning," noted *Scribner's Monthly* in 1872.[68] Indeed, Beecher found pulpits and podiums confining and refused to stand behind them when preaching or lecturing. "It is not the voice, or even the head alone, it is the whole man, informed with his subject, who preaches," he insisted.[69]

Even after he had gained the power of oratory and decided to become a minister after all, Beecher's theological doubts remained. At seminary, however, Beecher had a religious experience that clarified his approach to Christianity. "There rose up before me a view of Jesus as the Saviour of sinners," Beecher recalled, "because they were so bad and needed so much; and that view has never gone from me." Henry rejected his father's vision of a wrathful God eager to punish the slightest transgression. Instead, he "felt that God had a father's heart; that Christ loved me … and would help me out of sin."[70]

It was this emotional heart of Beecher's belief that distinguished him from other preachers of his time. Beecher was certainly not the only American of the mid-nineteenth century to receive training in elocution,

66 "Inquiring Friends," *Christian Union*, July 14, 1880, quoted in Beecher and Scoville, *A Biography of Rev. Henry Ward Beecher*, 95.

67 Frank W. Gunsaulus, "Henry Ward Beecher as an Orator," in Tewksbury, ed., *Henry Ward Beecher as His Friends Saw Him*, 38, 45.

68 "Mr. Beecher as a Social Force," *Scribner's Monthly*, Vol. 4, No. 6 (October 1872), 752–753; italics in original.

69 Beecher sermon delivered at City Temple, London, July 8, 1886, quoted in Halford R. Ryan, *Henry Ward Beecher: Peripatetic Preacher* (New York: Greenwood Press, 1990), 9.

70 Quoted in Barrows, *Henry Ward Beecher*, 66.

but he applied elocutionary techniques in a new and unique way. Unlike most ministers of his time, Beecher had little interest in articulating specific points or arguments to his congregation; instead, he played almost exclusively on the emotions of his listeners to win over their hearts to his faith.[71] Accordingly, he appeared to his audiences in a state of "mental *dishabille*" – he bared his whole soul onstage for their benefit. He wept, he laughed, he cracked jokes, he told stories; he took his listeners from the heights to the depths and back again with a wave of his hand and a quiver in his voice.[72] "He mounted up, as on wings, into the regions of Christian victory and hope taking us all with him," remembered Rev. Joseph H. Twichell, "and sang – I can liken it to nothing else – a song of the Resurrection, sweet, triumphant, uplifting, beyond description."[73]

This was the "new kind of oratory" Dawson heard that day on the Strand: an outpouring of emotion that was also carefully and professionally calibrated to move audiences to action. The combination of the two qualities made Beecher unique. Some orators used training and skill to reach heights of elocution; others spoke simply and touched the heart. But to do both at once was not only unprecedented but almost shocking. Nineteenth-century Americans believed in a "culture of character," the idea that the quality of one's inner self determined one's lot in life.[74] Sincerity and authenticity – two qualities with which Beecher had always struggled – were the keys to success.[75] So ingrained was this value that some commentators refused to believe that personal magnetism could be taught to someone who did not possess it from birth.[76] Now Beecher stood as living proof that magnetism could be acquired, even by one born with "a thickness of speech." He offered audiences a version of his innermost self that was constructed and artificial. His gestures were "natural" but only because he had practiced them so long they had become "a second nature." As an orator he was "the man of many moods" but only because he had perfected them all.[77]

71 Applegate, *The Most Famous Man in America*, 171.
72 Quoted in *Ibid.*, 212; italics in original.
73 Joseph H. Twichell, "A Hartford Admirer's Word of Appreciation," in Tewksbury, ed., *Henry Ward Beecher as His Friends Saw Him*, 156.
74 Warren I. Susman, *Culture as History* (New York: Pantheon, 1984), 273.
75 Applegate, *The Most Famous Man in America*, 212.
76 "Personal Magnetism," *Langston City Herald*, July 9, 1892, 1.
77 Moss Engraving Co., "The Man of Many Moods," engraving in Tewksbury, ed., *Henry Ward Beecher as His Friends Saw Him*, 25.

FIGURE 1.1 The 1904 engraving "The Man of Many Moods," based on various photographs of Henry Ward Beecher, captured the charismatic minister's ability to project a range of emotions from the podium.
Source: Moss Engraving Co., "The Man of Many Moods," engraving in J. H. Tewksbury, ed., *Henry Ward Beecher as His Friends Saw Him* (New York: Pilgrim Press, 1904), 25.

The more adept Beecher became at manipulating the emotions of his listeners, the better they loved him. His success struck at the heart of the culture of character, but Beecher also rejected the artificial quality that made some charismatic figures seem "tawdry." In Beecher's world, neither pure sincerity nor pure artifice was desirable; instead, the two should coexist in an emotionally charged balance that cemented people to one another and motivated them to a common purpose. Somewhere in between his elocution lessons and his religious awakening, Henry Ward Beecher had become the living embodiment of charismatic speech.

He served as chief evangelist, too, for the new outlook and method of communication he had helped to pioneer. In an 1876 address before the National School of Oratory in Philadelphia, Beecher defended himself eloquently against the culture of character. "Oratory," he remarked, "is looked upon ... as a thing artificial; as a mere science of ornamentation; as a method fit for actors who are not supposed to express their own sentiments, but unfit for a living man who has earnestness and sincerity and purpose."[78] Not so, Beecher countered; oratory merely aimed at "*influencing conduct with the truth set home by all the resources of the living man* ... It aims to get access to men by allaying their prejudices."[79] Because the goal of oratory was to convert sinners to Christ – a view Beecher borrowed from his father – all people should "study how skillfully ... to throw wide open the halls of emotion, and to kindle the light of inspiration in the souls of men."[80] Oratory was not artificial "because there has been so much of it, but because there has been so little of it"; if children were taught the techniques of oratory at a young age, they could integrate those skills into their identities just as they did walking and talking.[81] This was Beecher's ultimate vision: a world where everyone was magnetic, where magnetism came as naturally as breathing, where innate character and acquired techniques were one and the same. "Is there any reality in oratory?" he concluded. "It is all real."[82]

Through a series of cultural interventions, Beecher worked diligently to bring about the world he envisioned. First, he spread his own magnetic presence as far as possible. Taking advantage of the proliferation of railroads, he established himself as a regular on national

[78] Henry Ward Beecher, *Oratory* (Philadelphia: National School of Oratory, 1886), 20.
[79] *Ibid.*, 14; italics in original. [80] *Ibid.*, 21. [81] *Ibid.*, 35. [82] *Ibid.*, 21.

lecture circuits such as James Redpath's Lyceum Bureau.[83] In addition, Beecher used his speeches and writings to extol the virtues of cultivating a charismatic presence and to praise the personal magnetism of others. Orchestra conductor Theodore Thomas "must be a man of extraordinary magnetic power, he so completely imparts to the orchestra his own feelings," the minister wrote in 1871, foreshadowing the *St. Louis Republican*'s description of Patrick Gilmore. Thomas "carries them along with him in his interpretation of the music, as perfectly as if the orchestra were an organ, and he, with masterly ease and power, were manipulating the keys."[84] Meanwhile, Beecher lectured seminary students on the need for modern preachers to adopt magnetic techniques. "In speaking, a great deal depends on the personal, magnetic influence," Beecher told a Philadelphia seminary audience in 1870. Ministers should "dare to put their whole selves into their sermons ... [and] should draw on every faculty they possess; anything – only catch men."[85]

Finally, Beecher devised his own course of study in charismatic techniques. In his Yale Lectures on Preaching, delivered in 1871 and 1872, the minister offered a virtual textbook on how to gain and wield magnetic power over others. In part, Beecher recommended elocutionary methods similar to those Lovell had taught him in boyhood. He described specific vocal techniques that enhanced magnetism, such as speaking quietly when trying to "win [audiences] by persuasion" but in "sharp and ringing tones" when attacking something wicked.[86] He advised preachers to practice vocal exercises constantly, just as he had, through "a drill which will become so familiar that it ceases to be a matter of thought, and the voice takes care of itself." He recommended similar exercises for posture and hand gestures.[87]

Putting together the right speech, Beecher argued, mattered just as much as elocution in cultivating charismatic oratory. Here Beecher shared another of the hallmarks of his magnetic style: the use of anecdotes and word-painting to convey images to listeners. "Experience has taught that not only are persons pleased by being instructed through

[83] Mark Twain [Samuel Clemens], *Autobiography of Mark Twain: The Complete and Authoritative Edition*, Vol. 1, ed. Harriet Elinor Smith (Berkeley, CA: University of California Press, 2010), 151.

[84] Henry Ward Beecher, "One of Thomas' Concert [*sic*]," *Salem Register*, April 20, 1871, 1.

[85] Henry Ward Beecher, "Henry Ward Beecher on Preaching," *New York Evangelist*, May 5, 1870, 1.

[86] Beecher, *Yale Lectures on Preaching*, 132. [87] *Ibid.*, 134–137.

illustration," he advised, "but that they are more readily instructed thus, because, substantially, the mode in which we learn a new thing is by its being likened to something which we already know."[88] Visual descriptions and examples were particularly useful as memory devices, for stimulating listeners' imaginations, and for breaking up a sermon so as to hold the audience's interest.[89] Word choice mattered, too. "Use homely words, – those which people are used to, and which suggest many things to them," Beecher recommended. These "secret suggestions and echoes, multiply the meaning in the minds of men" and made them more receptive to the minister's message.[90] Finally, it was better to extemporize one's sermon than to write it down, so as to increase one's harmony with the congregation.[91]

Beecher did not merely want his readers to adopt his techniques, though; he wanted them to follow his lead in evangelizing for the charismatic leader–follower relationship itself. "Every man who means to be in affinity with his congregation must have feeling," he wrote. "Somewhere there must be that power by which the man speaking and the men hearing are unified; and that is the power of emotion."[92] The bias of many preachers toward rational argument slighted "a great many persons who want the truth presented in emotive forms ... They have as much right to be fed by their hearts as the others have to be fed by their reason."[93] Summing up, Beecher returned to the familiar organ metaphor that seemed so central to Americans' understanding of the charismatic relationship. "When you have before you a whole congregation or a whole community," Beecher declared, "what an instrument you have to play upon, and what a power it is when you have learned it, and have the touch by which you can play so as to control its entire range and compass! There is nothing more sublime in this world ... He is a great man who can play upon the human soul!"[94]

By that definition, Beecher was the greatest man in America by the 1870s. He constituted "a distinct social force acting upon an entire nation ... an element of power in the nineteenth century," wrote *Scribner's Monthly* in 1874.[95] "There is not a man in the land who has such a multitude that look upon him as if he were their brother," according to Oliver Wendell Holmes.[96] At the height of Beecher's powers,

[88] *Ibid.*, 154–155. [89] *Ibid.*, 159–161. [90] *Ibid.*, 230. [91] *Ibid.*, 235–236.
[92] *Ibid.*, 118. [93] *Ibid.*, 54. [94] *Ibid.*, 60. [95] "Mr. Beecher as a Social Force," 751.
[96] Oliver Wendell Holmes, "The Minister Plenipotentiary," *Atlantic Monthly*, Vol. 13, No. 75 (January 1864), 107.

he dominated the national discourse as few preachers had before him; he attracted unparalleled crowds and outpourings of feeling.[97] Then, his troubles began.

* * *

Sex was the Achilles' heel of the charismatic leader. Personal magnetism's popular association with sexual misconduct dated back to the 1780s, when a French royal commission had argued that mesmerism encouraged immoral sexual behavior.[98] As an anonymous American mesmerist wrote in 1845, it was very easy, and very tempting, for male hypnotists to molest their female patients. "Reader, let me tell you," explained the pamphleteer, "that to be placed opposite a young and lovely female [seeking to be cured by mesmerism], ... to look into her gentle eyes, soft and beaming with confidence and trust, is singular entrancing ... Then is her mind all your own. ... [She] will stop at no point beyond which [she] may afford you pleasure should you indicate it by thought or word."[99]

Though sorely tempted on a number of occasions, the author insisted he had never taken advantage of a woman in this way. However, he admitted to helping a client win back the affections of a former fiancée by mesmerizing the woman; afterward, he continued, he had hypnotized the same woman – now married – to fall in love with the mesmerist himself. Even his own wife was a former patient – "a young and beautiful female ... but just seventeen, and possessed of as perfect form and features, as one may have dreamed of, but never seen" – though he maintained that she "loved me through the natural channels of the heart's affection."[100] Other hypnotists were less scrupulous; one mesmerized women "for vile and sensual purposes," while another "openly avow[ed] that he could choose his wife from among his patients when he pleased." "Is not this a most dangerous agency," the mesmerist concluded, "that can so subject the most upright minds to the will of the unprincipled and oftentimes highly immoral practitioner?"[101]

Such sensational claims resonated with a public fearful of sexual deviance, and late nineteenth-century Americans, too, worried about the

97 William G. McLoughlin, Jr., *The Meaning of Henry Ward Beecher: An Essay on the Shifting Values of Mid-Victorian America, 1840–1870* (New York: Knopf, 1970), 254.

98 Robert Darnton, *Mesmerism and the End of the Enlightenment in France* (Cambridge, MA: Harvard University Press, 1968), 64.

99 "Confessions of a Magnetizer" (Boston: Gleason's Publishing Hall, 1845), 9–10; Fuller, *Mesmerism and the American Cure of Souls*, 33–34.

100 "Confessions of a Magnetizer," 15–16. 101 *Ibid.*, 10–11.

potential of the charismatic relationship for inspiring sexual immorality. They were willing to accept that a minister such as Beecher might manipulate their emotions to help them into heaven or that an orator might use magnetism to convince them of an argument. They could even understand more self-serving uses of magnetism by those who wanted a job, a contract, or a friendship. But the thought that a magnetic man might use his power to seduce an innocent woman – or even a helpless wife – horrified many middle-class Americans. Tirzah Miller, an attractive young resident of the utopian Oneida community in New York, found herself a frequent object of male lust. An Oneida leader explained to Miller that she was "one of those women ... who was liable to be magnetized by a certain class of men ... a fact which I had better calculate for."[102] Americans who disagreed with the commune's radical free-love doctrines would have been horrified by this situation; they would have seen the magnetism of Miller's lovers as fraudulent, designed to corrupt and ruin Miller. To steal a woman's heart and virtue by trickery was the ultimate betrayal of Victorian culture. Later, in the 1920s, charismatic women evangelists such as Aimee Semple McPherson and Rheba Crawford Splivalo inspired similar fears that they were seducing men through magnetism – but in Henry Ward Beecher's day, the public was primarily concerned with the sexuality of male, not female, charismatic figures.

Edward S. Van Zile's short story "A Magnetic Man," published in the August 4, 1889, issue of the *Pittsburg Dispatch*, captured the enormity of such fears. The title character, Marcus Rodney, is unpopular and standoffish until he invents a device that allows him to "manipulate ... electric current" at will – to use electricity to make himself personally magnetic to a nearly impossible degree. At first, he tells the narrator, "I had no scruples about taking advantage of my power." After all, he has used magnetism only to secure financial support for his inventions and to obtain membership in social clubs. But when he falls in love with the beautiful debutante Margaret Durand, he contemplates gaining sexual access to her using the same techniques. "I can win her consent to our marriage by the slightest effort," he laments. "You have no conception of the power I now wield ... Am I, then, to deny myself the only thing I crave because of a sentimental regard for that threadbare word 'honor?'" At first Rodney restrains

102 Robert S. Fogarty, *Desire & Duty at Oneida: Tirzah Miller's Intimate Memoir* (Bloomington, IN: Indiana University Press, 2000), 132.

himself, but soon Margaret's own magnetic attractiveness overwhelms Rodney's scruples. "Never was a man so tempted," he tells the narrator in anguished tones. "Her lips are so red! Her eyes are so bright! Her hair is so black!" Both the narrator and Margaret are terrified of what Rodney might do. "To sit there," remarks the narrator, "and see that electro-magnetic hawk poised to swoop down on his prey was agony." Finally Rodney advances on Margaret, device in hand. The sense of sexual menace is palpable: "I could see that she was strangely affected, though the expression on her face was one of repugnance. His will was stronger than hers."[103] Margaret is saved by Rodney's untimely death at the hands of his own magnetic device, but the story's message is clear: magnetic men could not resist the temptation to exploit women sexually.

It was a concern Beecher understood all too intimately. As early as his seminary years, the minister's infectious personality had inspired women to woo or seduce him. He had behaved responsibly then, but would he continue to do so at the height of his influence over his congregation?[104] In 1872, free-love advocate Victoria Woodhull charged that Beecher had in fact committed adultery with Elizabeth Tilton, the wife of his assistant Theodore Tilton. At the time, Beecher and both Tiltons denied the charge, but in 1874 Theodore sued Beecher for adultery. The entire incident became a national scandal; through two church inquests and a six-month civil trial, Beecher and the Tiltons hurled charges and countercharges at one another. Theodore stuck to his story once he had made the initial charge. Elizabeth first admitted to the adultery, then denied it under oath, and finally confessed again in 1878. Beecher maintained his innocence until the end of his life.[105]

Reluctant at first to outline the incidents in detail, Theodore eventually came right out and accused Beecher of seducing Elizabeth against her will. In doing so, he explicitly cited Beecher's "emotional and magnetic" qualities as a large part of what made the minister so dangerous.[106] Beecher had "sought out his trustful parishioner and

[103] Edward S. Van Zile, "A Magnetic Man," *Pittsburg Dispatch*, August 4, 1889, 9–10.

[104] Clark, *Henry Ward Beecher*, 32.

[105] Richard Wightman Fox, *Trials of Intimacy: Love and Loss in the Beecher-Tilton Scandal* (Chicago: University of Chicago Press, 1999), 39, 53–54, 57, 89, 156–157; Altina L. Waller, *Reverend Beecher and Mrs. Tilton: Sex and Class in Victorian America* (Amherst, MA: University of Massachusetts Press, 1982), 1, 7–11.

[106] Quoted in "The Social Scandal," orig. pub. *Chicago Tribune; Harrisburg Patriot*, August 18, 1874, 1.

craftily spread his toils about her, ensnaring her virtue and accomplishing her seduction," Theodore declared during the first church hearing. The seduction was "a strong man's triumph over her conscience and will."[107] Theodore made the same point more graphically during the adultery trial: Elizabeth "followed [Beecher's] beck and lead trustingly; she would go after him like one blinded; I think she sinned her sin as one in a trance; I don't think she was a free agent. I think she would have done his bidding if ... he had bade her fling her child into the Ganges or cast herself under the Juggernaut."[108] In Theodore's view, Elizabeth was so helpless before the force of Beecher's personality that the minister might as well have used Marcus Rodney's magnetic device on her.

Beecher denied everything, of course, and Elizabeth Tilton joined him in insisting nothing sexual had occurred between the two of them. Interestingly, however, both Beecher and Elizabeth agreed with Theodore that magnetism was to blame. According to them, Theodore's own magnetic power over his wife had forced her to write false confessions and to implicate Beecher in a made-up tryst for Theodore's ultimate gain. "There is a certain power that Theodore has over me, especially if I am sick," Elizabeth reported at the church hearing. "I have often thought whether I had any power, or whether his was a mesmeric condition brought to bear upon me; I certainly was indifferent to any act that I was doing, except to do as he willed me to do."[109] In the civil trial, Beecher corroborated this version of events. After Tilton confronted him, Beecher recalled, the minister had rushed to Elizabeth to ask her why she had falsely confessed to adultery. "My friend, I could not help it," she had told him; "I was wearied out ... with his [Tilton's] importunities."[110] Ultimately, the three of them agreed that Elizabeth had been manipulated into indiscretion by the magnetic personality of a man who desired her sexually; they disagreed only about the nature of the crime and the identity of the man.

National opinion concerning Beecher's guilt was decidedly mixed. Though some newspapers acquitted the pastor of all wrongdoing,

[107] Charles F. Marshall, *The True History of the Brooklyn Scandal* (Philadelphia: National Publishing Company, 1874), 525.

[108] Theodore Tilton vs. Henry Ward Beecher, *Action for Crim. Con. Tried in the City Court of Brooklyn*, vol. 1 (New York: McDivitt, Campbell, 1875), 619.

[109] Marshall, *True History of the Brooklyn Scandal*, 201–202.

[110] Tilton vs. Beecher, vol. 2, 763.

others thought he had indeed slept with Elizabeth Tilton – and they agreed with Theodore that Beecher's charismatic abilities had been a primary cause of his home-wrecking ways. "There is," said Dr. A. C. Stanton in a widely reprinted article, "a personal magnetism about [Beecher] which makes him irresistible with most women, and I do not doubt but that he could reveal some of the strangest stories regarding his feminine infatuations ever related by man." Stanton expressed skepticism that Beecher's resolve was any stronger than Marcus Rodney's in the face of such sexual opportunities: "Of course, the temptation surrounding such a man is almost too great to be resisted by flesh and blood, and if he should prove, after all, to have kept himself free from sin, it will be one of the most remarkable instances of self-control or the 'power of divine grace' ever witnessed."[111] The *Cleveland Daily Herald* concurred: "A large class of women act very foolishly toward a favorite preacher … A man like Mr. Beecher, with his emotional and fervent nature, his personal magnetism, his liberality and charity, would naturally be adored by those female parishioners whose pious zeal overcame their reasoning powers."[112] In these interpretations of the story, Beecher did not even need to try to seduce individual women – they came to him unbidden because of his charismatic power over them. "Don't go to church," warned the *Chicago Times* facetiously, "because clergymen may be magnetic, unawares."[113] Others viewed Beecher as the aggressor and Elizabeth as the helpless victim of his perverted magnetism. Condemning Beecher as "a clerical Don Juan," the *Rochester Express* defended Elizabeth as a "woman of gentle, susceptible nature, overpowered by her pastor's sophistry and magnetic influence."[114] Either way, magnetism contributed to Elizabeth's violation.

Magnetism was also responsible for protecting Beecher from the punishment he appeared to deserve. During the trial, Americans seemed to expect that the preacher's charismatic performances would sway the jury in his favor despite the evidence against him. Beecher "must convince twelve men that his letters have other meanings than those which their language seems to carry," opined the *New York Sun*. Given the minister's

111 "Beecher at Indianapolis," *Chicago Inter Ocean*, August 11, 1874.
112 "The Temptation of Ministers," *Cleveland Daily Herald*, August 7, 1874, 5.
113 Cameo, "Happy Thoughts," *Chicago Sunday Times*, August 23, 1874, 1.
114 "Is Mr. Beecher a Clerical Don Juan?" orig. pub. *Rochester Express; New York Herald*, July 24, 1874, 3.

"magnetic gift of speech and manner, ... can he do it? Yes, if any living man can."[115] The *Sun* was prescient. On the witness stand, Beecher acted out scenes from his interactions with Theodore, wept as he recalled confronting Elizabeth with her own false accusations, and used all the charismatic techniques at his disposal to win over the jurors.[116] His performance was just powerful enough to garner a hung jury. The result was not the resounding acquittal he had hoped for, but it was enough to conclude the scandal and allow him to go on preaching.

Still, Beecher had tarnished the very charismatic style of leadership he had helped to pioneer. Countless others would mimic his techniques, and millions of followers would flock to their speeches. But the questions Beecher had raised about charismatic leadership remained. Could a magnetic person be trusted in positions of high importance, or would he always use his power for social transgressions? Americans soon had the chance to judge for themselves, not in the pages of the sensational press but at the ballot box in a presidential election.

* * *

It was July 5, 1876, and the one they called the "Magnetic Man" was standing on the floor of the U.S. House of Representatives, clutching a sheaf of letters in his hand, his arm raised dramatically over his head as the gallery roared with applause. It was a spellbinding moment, made all the more theatrical by the identity of the man holding the letters. He was James Gillespie Blaine of Maine, Speaker of the House of Representatives and, at the moment, the likeliest candidate to win the Republican presidential nomination eleven days later. The House Judiciary Committee had been conducting an inquiry into a bribery allegation against the speaker; those letters, brought to Washington by one James Mulligan, allegedly proved the charge, but Blaine had gotten hold of the documents and refused the committee's repeated demands for them. The letters did not actually incriminate him, he insisted, but they were his personal correspondence and consequently were nobody's business but his.[117] Now, in a dramatic reversal, Blaine stood on the

[115] "Mr. Beecher's Great Task," orig. pub. *New York Sun; Little Rock Gazette*, March 6, 1875, 1.

[116] Fox, *Trials of Intimacy*, 106; Tilton vs. Beecher, Vol. 2, 762.

[117] *The Disposal of the Subsidies Granted Certain Railroad Companies*, Miscellaneous Documents, Report No. 176, House of Representatives, 44th Congress, First Session, 1876, 105–107 (June 1, 1876); David Saville Muzzey, *James G. Blaine: A Political Idol of Other Days* (New York: Dodd, Mead, 1935), 87–93.

House floor, letters in hand, and declared, "I am not afraid to show the letters. Thank God Almighty I am not ashamed to show them ... I invite the confidence of 44,000,000 of my countrymen while I read those letters from this desk." The applause this time was deafening.[118]

It was not the first sensational incident in the case, nor would it be the last. Earlier, Blaine had grandly assured the House, "I have never done anything in my public career for which I could be put to the faintest blush in any presence, or for which I cannot answer to my constituents, my conscience, and the great Searcher of hearts."[119] And six days after hoisting the Mulligan letters aloft, the Speaker fainted dead away in front of a Washington church – cementing, just five days before the nomination, his status as a martyr to the enviousness and underhanded tactics of his political opponents.[120]

The scene with the Mulligan letters, though, was Blaine at his most characteristic: unmatched in his ability to play to an audience, yet continually in trouble because of his rivals' jealousy and his own poor choices. As the controversy showed, the very actions that gained Blaine his magnetic reputation often earned him the sternest criticism from the press and public. Americans who believed the charges against Blaine saw him as a corrupt manipulator who used magnetism to cover up his crimes. Blaine's "personal magnetism" and "wonderful audacity" had "enabled him to violate all rules of the House without question," complained the *New York Tribune*, despite evidence which "prove[d] his unfitness to become a leader in a great reform campaign."[121] People questioned, too, the remarkable scene that unfolded at Mulligan's lodging one night during the hearing; face-to-face with his accuser, Blaine gained possession of the incriminating letters through what seemed to be magnetic techniques of persuasion. The speaker, Mulligan later testified, "rather prevailed upon me to give them up" by claiming that "they would ruin him for ever; he contemplated suicide ... He asked me if I would not like a consulship."[122] Blaine denied all this, of course, but his colleagues seemed inclined to believe Mulligan; if a magnetic man possessed the power to beguile incriminating documents out of the hands of his accuser, was it

[118] *Congressional Record*, 44th Congress, 1st Session, 3604 (June 5, 1876).

[119] *Mr. Blaine's Record: The Investigation of 1876 and the Mulligan Letters* (Boston: Committee of One Hundred, [1884]), 31; speech given before the House of Representatives, April 24, 1876.

[120] Muzzey, *James G. Blaine*, 100.

[121] "Mr. Blaine's Wonderful Audacity," *New York Tribune*, June 7, 1876, 1.

[122] *The Disposal of the Subsidies Granted Certain Railroad Companies*, 98, 102 (June 1, 1876).

plausible that he could refrain from using that power? The *New York Sun* went so far as to accuse Blaine of faking his attack of sunstroke to win the presidential nomination: "Was the sun that struck Mr. Blaine the orb that shone at Cincinnati," the location of the Republican convention, "rather than that which sent its rays to the church door at Washington? Any way, the Blaine opportune attack was an extraordinary one."[123]

Congress eventually acquitted Blaine of wrongdoing, but the allegations against him persisted. "No doubt it is [Blaine's] superabundance [of magnetism] that brings on those distressing attacks of sunstroke," quipped the *Galveston Daily News* in 1880; Blaine was "charged with electricity, and draws in everything in the neighborhood, including bonds, Mulligan letters and the like."[124] Blaine did not win the presidential nomination in 1876, nor did he earn it four years later. Yet it was Blaine's magnetism that made him attractive as a presidential candidate in the first place. Blaine was "the second Henry Clay," newspapers declared; the pre–Civil War Whig politician had been "a man of wonderful personal magnetism, of unrivaled power for attaching friends to his cause, of matchless sway over the masses of his party," and Blaine shared these characteristics.[125] Would the "unrivaled power" of personal magnetism propel Blaine to the presidency, or would it leave him, like Clay before him, a perennial also-ran?

Born in Pennsylvania on January 31, 1830, Blaine first came to prominence in Maine as a state legislator and the editor of several newspapers.[126] Like Beecher, Blaine began public life with a speech impediment and a bad case of nerves, but his discomfort about public speaking quickly passed.[127] He won election to Congress at the age of thirty-two; he had served less than a year before he began to clash with the powerful Republican floor leader Thaddeus Stevens. After one such confrontation in 1864, the exasperated Stevens complained that Blaine's "magnetic manner" had convinced the House to vote against Stevens' bill.[128] The nickname stuck, and soon commentators viewed

[123] "Blaine's Mysterious Attack," *New York Sun*, June 16, 1876, 2.

[124] "Personal Magnetism," *Galveston Daily News*, June 5, 1880.

[125] "Clay in 1844 – Blaine in 1884," orig. pub. *Brooklyn Union; Washington Post*, July 2, 1884, 2.

[126] Muzzey, *James G. Blaine*, 6, 22, 30, 33.

[127] Henry G. Roberts, "James G. Blaine," in William Norwood Brigance, ed., *A History and Criticism of American Public Address*, Vol. II (New York: McGraw-Hill, 1943), 878–879.

[128] *Ibid.*, 39, 47; Charles Edward Russell, *Blaine of Maine: His Life and Times* (New York: Cosmopolitan, 1931), 105.

Blaine's charismatic ability as his defining characteristic. "Mr. Blaine's personal magnetism is probably greater than that of any other man seen in publ[i]c life during the past quarter of a century," gushed the *Philadelphia Times*.[129] A Maine state senator recalled Blaine's "magnetism of such power that the greater the distance the greater was the intensity of the attraction."[130] Even the hostile *New York Sun* admitted that "Brother Blaine has a charm that binds men to him. His magnetism is something uncommon, and his tact in dealing with men is extraordinary."[131] "Like an armed warrior, like a plumed knight," declared orator Robert Ingersoll in his 1876 convention speech nominating Blaine for president, "James G. Blaine marched down the halls of the American Congress and threw his shining lance full and fair against the brazen forehead of every traitor to his country and every maligner of his fair reputation."[132] A "plumed knight" and a "magnetic man" – Americans agreed that Blaine epitomized charismatic leadership.

Blaine's magnetism was different from Beecher's. While Beecher oscillated between emotional extremes, Blaine's techniques were subtle and restrained; the Mulligan letters speech was probably the most dramatic of his life. And while Beecher exhorted his followers to become charismatic leaders in their own right, Blaine stayed silent on the subject. Blaine "does not act as though he was aware of … his wonderful magnetism," wrote a campaign biographer.[133] Nevertheless, Blaine understood the principles of charismatic performance. In an 1870 article on the oratory of former ambassador Anson Burlingame, Blaine demonstrated a perceptive grasp of Burlingame's charismatic techniques. Burlingame possessed "a peculiar power over those with whom he came in contact," Blaine wrote, "a power growing out of a mysterious gift, partly intellectual, partly spiritual, largely physical; a power … we designate as magnetism." This "subtile [*sic*], forceful, overwhelming

129 "Blaine's Great Magnetism," orig. pub. *Philadelphia Times; Milwaukee Daily Journal*, June 11, 1884.

130 Maine State Legislature, *Memorial Addresses on the Life and Character of James Gillespie Blaine of Augusta* (Augusta, ME: Burleigh & Flynt, 1893), 45 ("Address of Mr. Spillane of Lewiston").

131 "Blaine's Secret," *New York Sun*, June 19, 2.

132 Proceedings of the National Republican Convention, 1876, officially reported by M. A. Clancy and William Nelson (Concord, NH: Republican Press Association, 1876), 73–75, quoted in Muzzey, *James G. Blaine*, 110.

133 Thomas V. Cooper, *Biographies of James G. Blaine, The Republican Candidate for President, and John A. Logan, the Republican Candidate for Vice President* (Chicago: Baird & Dillon, 1884), 2.

power" made the ambassador "preeminently effective before an assemblage of the people." Burlingame's magnetism, Blaine continued, "was quite independent of his volition, not in any sense under his control"; neither was it "dependent on speech, though of course it was greatly deepened and strengthened by it." Instead, Blaine held, the ambassador's magnetism reflected the fervor of his beliefs and the freshness of his approach.[134] Clearly, Blaine comprehended how to use charismatic abilities to one's advantage.

Like Beecher, Blaine became magnetic through the development of his own unique style. As his many contemporary biographers and others who met him were quick to attest, Blaine gained followers primarily through direct interactions with them, not through his oratorical performance. Biographer Charles Russell, who had known Blaine personally, explained the Maine politician's technique: upon meeting someone for the first time, "Blaine would fix upon him a searching, comprehending but friendly gaze, absorbing every detail ... At the same time, he kept up a running fire of questions ... When next he met the man, an unusual memory recalled with the face some fact or incident of which conversation could be made, and the man went away magnetized."[135] Blaine's extraordinary memory made an impression on many Americans with whom he came into contact. Illinois attorney Robert E. Williams met Blaine briefly in 1848; thirty years later, he was astonished to discover that the Maine legislator still remembered him by name.[136] Similarly, a reporter for the *New York Herald* once wrote an article that briefly mentioned a white dove present at the Civil War battle of Chickamauga; eleven years later, Blaine buttonholed the journalist, whom he had never met before, to ask whether the dove story was true.[137]

Blaine owed his magnetism in small gatherings to more than mere mnemonic skill. His conversational abilities also served him well. "As a conversationalist Mr. Blaine has few equals," wrote campaign biographer William Ralston Balch. "He has a keen appreciation of fun, and can tell a story with wonderful simplicity ... yet ... he is quite willing

[134] James G. Blaine, "Mr. Burlingame as an Orator," orig. pub. *Atlantic Monthly*, November, 1870; reprinted in Blaine, *Political Discussions, Legislative, Diplomatic, and Popular, 1856–1886* (Norwich, CT: Henry Bill, 1887), 106, 108.

[135] Russell, *Blaine of Maine*, 349–350.

[136] Thomas W. Knox, *The Lives of James G. Blaine and John A. Logan, Republican Presidential Candidates of 1884* (Hartford, CT: Hartford Pub. Co., 1884), 125–126.

[137] *Ibid.*, 134–135.

to listen when any one has anything to say."[138] Blaine was particularly good at making his conversational partners feel important. "With the scholar he would talk of books and reading," noted a posthumous biography, but he was equally good at " 'talking horse' " with an equestrian; "in the presence of the fond parent he did not forget the promising son, and the son of a father who was in any way distinguished blushed with the reflected glory cast upon him."[139] The politician's regal bearing also contributed to his charismatic power. Encountering Blaine after the 1876 convention, newspaper editor James G. Holland recalled a line from an old Scottish tragedy: "Never before stood I in such a presence."[140] Even Blaine's handshake conveyed charismatic authority. "If you shake him by the hand once," commented Balch, "you will never forget the touch of his fingers."[141]

While Blaine's charisma was particularly notable in individual and small group settings, he could win over the masses as well. "He had above any man of his day that strange power of reading the mind of a people," remarked another contemporary biographer.[142] Blaine was in fact a talented public speaker. Though he lacked the formal training of Beecher, he shared the minister's belief that plain language was more persuasive than studied eloquence. One observer noted that Blaine "introduced [in Congress] a new style … deliberate, restrained, reasonable, persuasive."[143] "He had nothing of the affectation of the so-called orator," remarked another. "In his judgment the man who had the best literary style was the one who apparently had none."[144] Blaine also shared with Beecher a devotion to vocal technique. Commentators noted that his voice was "exceedingly pleasing, mellow, melodious, insinuating, sufficiently rangeful" and that it "had a metallic note … which vibrated upon the ear and in such a way as to produce a thrill of

[138] William Ralston Balch, *Life and Public Services of James G. Blaine, with the Facts in the Career of John A. Logan* (Philadelphia: Thayer, Merriam, 1884), 348.

[139] John Clark Ridpath and Selden Connor, *Life and Work of James G. Blaine* (Chicago: Dominion, 1893), 209.

[140] James G. Holland, "Blaine to Garfield," orig. pub. *Washington Post; Chicago Daily Inter Ocean*, January 6, 1894, 10. The play was *Douglas*, by John Home.

[141] Balch, *Life and Public Services of James G. Blaine*, 346.

[142] John Russell Young, "Introduction," in James P. Boyd, ed., *Life and Public Services of James G. Blaine, The Illustrious American Orator, Diplomat and Statesman* (Philadelphia: Publishers' Union, 1893), 30.

[143] Ridpath and Connor, *Life and Work of James G. Blaine*, 103.

[144] Theron Clark Crawford, *James G. Blaine: A Study of His Life and Career* (Cleveland, OH: Edgewood Pub. Co., 1893), 23–24.

emotion."[145] The ultimate result of this combination of traits was an individual of powerful magnetism and limitless political potential. "If one wishes to be Mr. Blaine's enemy," wrote Balch, "he must keep . . . beyond the reach of his voice."[146]

* * *

By the time Blaine, now a U.S. senator, finally secured the Republican presidential nomination in 1884, Americans viewed him as the national standard-bearer for charismatic leadership. Accordingly, commentators saw Blaine's triumph as a victory for personal magnetism as a political force. The massive outpouring of support for Blaine "is significant as a protest and at the same time as a demand," wrote the *Grand Forks Herald*. "It means that the people want a positive, absolute President of their own and not a mere do-nothing . . . 'The plumed knight' is no myth, this time."[147] The *Herald* painted the triumph of magnetism as a victory for the popular will; the charismatic relationship underlying Blaine's success made the leader dependent on the people rather than the political party establishment. Others saw Blaine's power in more practical terms. A candidate "whose qualities will call out the enthusiasm of the country will necessarily prove much the stronger at the polls," remarked the sympathetic *Minneapolis Tribune*.[148] T. McCants Stewart of the African American *New York Globe* agreed. Owing to the senator's magnetism, Stewart remarked, "I have yet to meet a poor or laboring man who has other than words of honest praise for 'Jim Blaine.' "[149] Even the *Buffalo Express*, which supported one of Blaine's opponents at the convention, acknowledged that "the mass of voters [in backing Blaine] excuse some things which the more thoughtful cannot excuse and lose their heads because their hearts are moved."[150] It seemed to even his most grudging supporters as if Blaine's charismatic abilities made him unbeatable in the November election.

[145] Ridpath and Connor, *Life and Work of James G. Blaine*, 104; Crawford, *James G. Blaine*, 23.

[146] Balch, *Life and Public Services of James G. Blaine*, 358.

[147] "Personal Magnetism," *Grand Forks Daily Herald*, May 2, 1884, 2.

[148] "Personal Magnetism," orig. pub. *Minneapolis Tribune*; *Chicago Tribune*, April 24, 1884, 12.

[149] T. McCants Stewart, "Blaine at Home," *New York Globe*, October 4, 1884.

[150] "The Greatest Political Leader of the Generation," orig. pub. *Buffalo Express*, reprinted in Cooper, *Biographies of James G. Blaine*, 47.

Recognizing his charismatic strengths, Blaine decided to leverage his abilities in a unique way during the campaign. At the time, most considered it beneath the presidential nominee to campaign actively during the election; his job was to remain at home while others waged the campaign in his name. In his eulogy for President James Garfield, however, Blaine had praised the slain president for violating this rule. Despite warnings that "anything of the kind seemed novel, rash, and even desperate," Garfield "spoke to large crowds" from his front porch throughout the 1880 race and consequently won the election.[151] Now Blaine would do the same thing, but to an even greater extent. He traveled through the East and the Midwest for six weeks, making over 400 brief speeches to audiences as large as 100,000 people.[152] Blaine justified his unprecedented public performances on the grounds that the significance of the tariff issue demanded it, but the tariff had figured in previous campaigns and would continue to do so in the future; everyone knew Blaine was trying to use his personal magnetism to win the presidency.[153]

For Blaine as for Beecher, magnetism proved a double-edged sword. The politician, like the preacher, inspired fears that charisma was a dangerous, unstable leadership quality. Though no one suspected the candidate of sexual misconduct, allegations of bribery and corruption followed him everywhere he went. If a magnetic man was not using his powers to seduce women, many Americans felt, he was probably busy relieving people of their money. The same anonymous mesmerist who had raised fears about magnetism and sexuality in 1845 had recounted the story of a "little scoundrel" who had used magnetism to steal another man's pocketbook over dinner.[154] Just as they had during the Mulligan letters controversy, many people simply took as a given that Blaine used his magnetic powers to mislead voters. "Mr. Blaine has one kind of personal magnetism on the stump in prohibition districts, and another in the cupboard of the cottage at Bar Harbor," insisted the *Kansas City Times*.[155] "Blaine, Blaine, James G. Blaine, continental liar from the State of Maine," chanted Democrats in New York City.[156] Even Henry

[151] James G. Blaine, "James A. Garfield Memorial Address," February 27, 1882 (Washington, DC: Government Printing Office, 1882), 41–42.

[152] Blaine, *Political Discussions*, 435; Crawford, *James G. Blaine*, 22; Michael E. McGerr, *The Decline of Popular Politics: The American North, 1865–1928* (New York: Oxford University Press, 1986), 36.

[153] Speech at Boston, November 3, 1884, in Blaine, *Political Discussions*, 465.

[154] "Confessions of a Magnetizer," 42–43.

[155] *Kansas City Times*, August 17, 1886, 6.

[156] Muzzey, *James G. Blaine*, 321.

Ward Beecher, the greatest American defender of magnetism, considered Blaine unscrupulous and opposed his election in 1884. "I do not wish to see a man as President whose opinions of the power of money are in the slightest degree doubtful," Beecher declared.[157]

In addition to fears that he might misuse his charisma in the nation's highest office, Blaine faced concerns about magnetism that had nothing to do with his personal failings. Some commentators felt that personal magnetism was bad for government, no matter who possessed it. "Magnetism is a very unsafe quality to tie to in politics," cautioned the *Springfield Republican* in opposing Blaine.[158] Journalist and author Mary Clemmer condemned Americans for even considering voting for a candidate whose strongest qualification was his charisma. "The man who would place its government on the surest basis, is not a 'magnetic' man," she sniffed; "therefore they will have naught of him."[159] Blaine also faced concerns that his magnetic personality was so divisive as to render him unelectable. "The very qualities" that made Blaine magnetic, argued the *Chicago Tribune*, "have also led him into hot-headed indiscretions which have raised up an unnecessary number of enemies in his path."[160] "The small minority which opposes him cannot be ignored," commented a Maine Republican. "Magnetic men are good to have ordinarily, but ... perhaps some less highly charged man may answer the purpose better."[161]

Harper's Weekly cartoonist Thomas Nast was perhaps Blaine's most implacable enemy.[162] In a series of images published during the early 1880s, Nast wickedly lampooned the presidential nominee – often as much for his charismatic reputation as for his policies or improprieties.[163] Many of the cartoons skewered the senator by playing on the nickname "Magnetic Man." In "The 'Magnetic' Blaine," Nast depicted the nominee

157 "Ovation for Cleveland," *New York Times*, October 16, 1884, 5; Neil Rolde, *Continental Liar from the State of Maine: James G. Blaine* (Gardiner, ME: Tilbury House, 2006), 275; Clark, *Henry Ward Beecher*, 253.

158 "Mr. Blaine as a Presidential Candidate," *Springfield Republican*, January 21, 1882, 4.

159 Mary Clemmer, quoted in the Chicago Daily Inter Ocean, January 8, 1880, 4.

160 "Personal Magnetism," orig. pub. *Minneapolis Tribune; Chicago Tribune*, April 24, 1884, 12.

161 New Haven Register, May 22, 1882, 2.

162 Fiona Deans Halloran, *Thomas Nast: The Father of Modern Political Cartoons* (Chapel Hill, NC: University of North Carolina Press, 2012), 257–259; Morton Keller, *The Art and Politics of Thomas Nast* (New York: Oxford University Press, 1968), 325–326.

163 Norman E. Tutorow, *James Gillespie Blaine and the Presidency: A Documentary Study and Source Book* (New York: Peter Lang, 1989), 86.

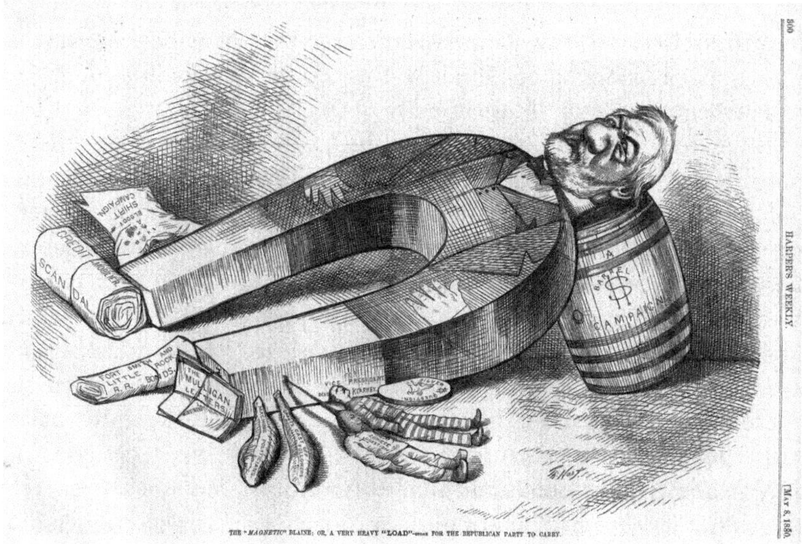

FIGURE 1.2 Thomas Nast's 1880 cartoon "The 'Magnetic' Blaine" skewered James G. Blaine by emphasizing the connection between personal magnetism and corruption.
Source: Thomas Nast, "The 'Magnetic' Blaine," editorial cartoon, *Harper's Weekly*, May 8, 1880, 300.

as a large horseshoe magnet attracting all manner of unscrupulous items, including the Mulligan letters and the allegedly illegal railroad bonds they referenced, the Crédit Mobilier scandal of 1872, "machine politicians," and a literal "barrel" of campaign dollars.[164] "Too Heavy to Carry" featured another horseshoe magnet, named "Magnetic Blaine," breaking the back of the Republican elephant.[165] "The Plumed Knight" showed Blaine donning a foppish hat covered in feathers; one of the plumes signified assistance from "the machine of bluster and brag."[166] "At His Old Tricks Again out West" represented the Maine politician as an unscrupulous magician who declared, in a parody of his Mulligan letters speech, "I will now, in confidence, take in 50,000,000 people."[167] Other

[164] Thomas Nast, "The 'Magnetic' Blaine," editorial cartoon, *Harper's Weekly*, May 8, 1880, 300.
[165] Thomas Nast, "Too Heavy to Carry," editorial cartoon, *Harper's Weekly*, June 14, 1884, 388.
[166] Thomas Nast, "The Plumed Knight," editorial cartoon, *Harper's Weekly*, June 5, 1884.
[167] Thomas Nast, "At His Old Tricks Again Out West," editorial cartoon, in Albert Bigelow Paine, *Th. Nast: His Period and His Pictures* (New York: Macmillan, 1904), 505.

Nast drawings parodied Blaine's writings, his manner, and his views, but the cartoonist clearly saw Blaine's charisma as the key to the problem: this was simply a man who could not be trusted, who covered up his crimes and inadequacies with "bluster and brag."

Ultimately, Blaine's career illustrates both personal magnetism's potential to influence American political life and the limits of that influence in the late nineteenth century. Aided by a Blaine supporter's intemperate anti-Catholic remarks just six days before the election, Democrat Grover Cleveland ultimately defeated Blaine by a narrow margin.[168] Whether Blaine's charismatic approach to politics helped or hurt his electoral chances is up for debate, but it probably did a little of both. Like Beecher before him, Blaine had discovered the paradoxical nature of late nineteenth-century attitudes toward charismatic leaders. The senator's magnetic abilities were designed to appeal directly to voters, and many Americans responded positively to what they deemed a populist approach to political leadership. The *Grand Forks Herald* had it right; Blaine's popularity reflected Americans' desire for more control over their political system, for a president who answered not to party leaders but directly to the people. At the same time, though, voters feared they themselves might become the ones answering to Blaine, rather than the other way around. An American president always held influence over the citizenry, but magnetic power was something else – more emotional, more intimate. All the fuss about Blaine's corruption and trickery came down to this: when it mattered, the American people were not completely sure who was in charge of the charismatic relationship between leader and follower. In the 1884 election, that uncertainty led them to reject the man they had a chance of controlling in favor of the man who had no chance of controlling them.

* * *

By the 1890s, personal magnetism had passed from genuine popular craze to relentlessly promoted product. Self-published authors dominated the discourse of magnetism; generally, they combined verbose paeans to magnetic power with fairly obvious self-help techniques. Orison Swett Marden, a New Thought acolyte, was characteristic of the trend. In *The Power of Personality* (1906), Marden presented magnetism as a commodity to be acquired for financial benefit: "The promoter knows

[168] Muzzey, *James G. Blaine*, 316–317.

the value of personal magnetism and persistently cultivates it. The business man understands it and tries to secure magnetic employees. The commercial traveler exploits it every day."[169] For Marden, magnetism was the great equalizer of wealth that could raise from poverty anyone who applied himself: "Poor boys and girls who are trying to get a start in the world often envy the rich youth who does not have to struggle for a living; yet many of them have a wealth in their own personalities, a power in possibility far exceeding that of money."[170] Marden suggested his readers achieve magnetism by spending time with other magnetic people, staying healthy, and practicing the Golden Rule.[171] Marden's depiction of personal magnetism may have appealed to his readers, but its sunny optimism about class mobility did little to explain the realities of actual experience; small wonder that interest in magnetism was waning.

That was not to say, however, that the self-help authors had nothing to contribute to the discussion of charisma. The irrepressible Webster Edgerly, who founded a commune dedicated to his particular brand of magnetism, probably went further than any other writer in defending even the most egregious contradictions and dangers of charismatic leadership.[172] In such books as *The Two Sexes* (1898) and *Sex Magnetism* (1924), for instance, Edgerly confronted directly the fear that magnetic men threatened women's virtue. It was not true, he insisted, that men such as the fictional Marcus Rodney who preyed upon women were practicing magnetism; instead, they were mesmerists or hypnotists. "The tendencies are opposite," Edgerly argued. "The hypnotist is usually an undesirable person ... The magnetizer is almost always a superior person."[173]

Instead, for Edgerly "sex magnetism" put two lovers on a superior footing from that of simple sexual attraction: "Allurement is not magnetism," he wrote, "and should never be taken as a basis for marriage."[174] The danger in sexuality, Edgerly explained, was that it encouraged emotionally impulsive acts; on that score, even orgasms should be avoided in order to strengthen "will power and capability of

[169] Orison Swett Marden, *The Power of Personality* (New York: T. Y. Crowell, 1906), 98.
[170] *Ibid.*, 95. [171] *Ibid.*, 106, 109–110.
[172] Janet L. Six, "Material Symbol: The Role of the Garden in the Transmission of Meaning," M.A. thesis (University of Pennsylvania, 2003), 65.
[173] Edmund Shaftesbury [(Albert) Webster Edgerly], *The Two Sexes* (Washington, DC: The Ralston Club, 1898), 160.
[174] *Ibid.*, 171.

restraint."[175] Magnetism, on the other hand, gave practitioners "eyes in their emotions" and allowed them to control themselves.[176] Sexual magnetism was a higher form of attraction that encouraged people to cultivate good behavior in front of magnetic members of the opposite sex. Over time, these improved behaviors gradually became part of one's character, just as Beecher believed oratory could become "second nature" to those who practiced it. Sex magnetism, then, was essential for the continuing development of civilization; it was also, for the white supremacist Edgerly, the key to maintaining racial purity.[177] Armed with this argument, Edgerly demonstrated his contempt for the dangers of magnetism by boldly proclaiming even its controlling aspects to be beneficial: "Every woman by magnetism ... can in time secure complete control over her husband. Every man by magnetism ... can in time secure complete control over his wife. This kind of control ... is willingly given even by magnetic persons; and the result, if both are magnetic, is that both will seek to yield subjection to the other."[178]

Notwithstanding the continued popularity of their works – Edgerly alone claimed to have sold at least 800,000 volumes – the popularizers represented the decline of personal magnetism in American culture.[179] While Marden's benign encomiums signaled the mainstream absorption of magnetism's less-controversial qualities, Edgerly's outlandish arguments demonstrated the increasing relegation of the term itself to the cultural fringes. With the dawn of a more scientific age, the sense of unexplainable mystery and wonder that had propelled the magnetism craze gradually dissipated; some cities even considered outlawing mesmeric stage acts as a public nuisance.[180] Accordingly, personal magnetism was no longer a vital phrase – it had become "tawdry," according to Belasco, or "barren," in the words of a posthumous Blaine biographer.[181] By 1920 it was archaic; newspapers remarked on how quaint "the genteel feminine phrase used to be, 'a very

[175] *Ibid.*, 157.

[176] Edmund Shaftesbury [(Albert) Webster Edgerly], *Sex Magnetism* (Meridien, CT: Ralston University Press, 1924), 339.

[177] *Ibid.*, 15. [178] *Ibid.*, 438.

[179] Janet L. Six, "Hidden History of Ralston Heights: The Story of New Jersey's Failed 'Garden of Eden,' " *Archaeology*, Vol. 57, No. 3 (May/June 2004), 32.

[180] Fred Nadis, *Wonder Shows: Performing Science, Magic, and Religion in America* (New Brunswick, NJ: Rutgers University Press, 2005), 91, 103.

[181] Young, "Introduction," in Boyd, *Life and Public Services of Hon. James G. Blaine*, 30.

magnetic man.' "[182] Yet personal magnetism remained very real for ordinary Americans, no matter how much scientists scoffed at the idea. A group of jewelers, for instance, complained to a *Baltimore Sun* reporter in 1927 that their customers continued to insist on the ability of personal magnetism to stop watches. The watchmakers dismissed the idea as nonsense, but they nevertheless added leather "insulation" to watches in order to "satisf[y] the owner of the watch that her personal magnetism is being recognized and offset."[183] Similarly, the phenomenon exemplified by Henry Ward Beecher and James G. Blaine proved more enduring than did the phrase their contemporaries used to describe it. Indeed, the personal magnetism craze was only a prelude to a deeper American engagement with charisma. The connection between charismatic leaders and followers remained a critical part of American culture in the decades that followed. As the twentieth century began, Americans continued to find that connection both seductive and troubling – and magnetism continued to play a key role in shaping American society.

[182] Sophie Treadwell, "Obregon's Men Bring New Life to Mexico City," *New York Tribune*, July 4, 1920, 8.

[183] "Jewelers Deny that Personal Magnetism Affects Watches," *Baltimore Sun*, January 15, 1927, 20.

2

Command Performances

Leaders and Their Technologies, 1890–1910

As he surveyed his audience from the platform of the 1896 Democratic National Convention in Chicago, William Jennings Bryan saw arrayed at his feet 900 delegates and 20,000 spectators, sweating in the July heat and regarding him with rapt attention.[1] Bryan, a young, relatively obscure former Congressman, had spoken to them on the question of free silver for twenty minutes; inspired by his magnetism and the weightiness of events, they had applauded enthusiastically at every break in his speech.[2] Now, at the close of his address, Bryan prepared to rouse his listeners to new heights of emotion. "We will answer their demand for a gold standard," he declared, "by saying to them: You shall not press down upon the brow of labor this crown of thorns" – here he brought his fingers to his temples, miming the actions of Jesus' tormentors – "you shall not crucify mankind upon a cross of gold."[3] As he uttered the final words, Bryan stretched out his arms and held the position of Christ upon the cross. Then he brought his hands to his sides.[4]

For a moment, the audience was silent. Then, something happened that newspaper reporters at the convention struggled to explain to their readers.

[1] Richard Franklin Bensel, *Passion and Preferences: William Jennings Bryan and the 1896 Democratic National Convention* (New York: Cambridge University Press, 2008), 69.

[2] Michael Kazin, *A Godly Hero: The Life of William Jennings Bryan* (New York: Knopf, 2006), 62.

[3] William Jennings Bryan, "In the Chicago Convention," July 8, 1896, in Bryan, *Speeches of William Jennings Bryan*, Vol. I (New York: Funk & Wagnalls, 1909), 249.

[4] Bensel, *Passion and Preferences*, 232; Donald K. Springen, *William Jennings Bryan: Orator of Small-Town America* (New York: Greenwood Press, 1991), 16; Paolo E. Coletta, *William Jennings Bryan, Vol. I: Political Evangelist* (Lincoln, NE: University of Nebraska Press, 1964), 141.

"The scene which followed beggars description," recorded the *Washington Post* correspondent. "Words may tell what actually happened, but words cannot impart the strange and curious magnetism which filled the atmosphere ... In the spoken word of the orator thousands of men had heard the unexpressed sentiments and hopes of their own inmost souls."[5] "Like the terrible premonitory rumbling that gives warning of the approach of ten thousand cattle stampeded," reported the *Columbia State*, "delegates and spectators began the ovation to the young Nebraskan. And then the volume of sound grew and grew until it could grow no more and everyone went mad."[6] Observers, wrote the *Lincoln News*, "saw 20,000 people, ... swayed like windswept fields; they heard the awful roar of 20,000 voices burst like a volcano against the reverberating dome overhead ... The applause was the spontaneous outburst of enthusiasm kindled by the torch of magnetic eloquence ... Old political generals were stupefied."[7]

Gold Democrats had expected resistance from the silver crowd, but the response to Bryan's speech showed that free silver was beyond "a mere ephemeral craze," as the *Washington Post* pointed out in another article. "They found themselves confronted by a living, palpitating, thrilling movement, into which men had flung their sentiments, their convictions, their very souls ... Five millions of living, breathing men in bitter, deadly earnest; five million men inflamed into an ecstasy ... overwhelmed them as a tidal wave obliterates an idle sentence scratched upon the sand."[8] Bryan alone seemed unsurprised by the popular reaction to his speech. "The audience," he wrote later, echoing the media descriptions of Patrick Gilmore's charismatically responsive musicians, had "acted like a trained choir."[9] Not only did Bryan carry the platform fight, but his speech in large part won him the presidential nomination – the first of three he would earn between 1896 and 1908. "A single sentence, it may be said, has made William J. Bryan the Presidential candidate of the silver-crazed Democratic National Convention," concluded the *Philadelphia Inquirer*.[10]

5 *Washington Post*, quoted in Bensel, *Passion and Preferences*, 233.

6 "Democracy's Big Day," *The State*, July 10, 1896, 1.

7 *Lincoln News*, July 10, 1896, 8, quoted in Myron G. Phillips, "William Jennings Bryan," in William Norwood Brigance, ed., *A History and Criticism of American Public Address*, Vol. II (New York: McGraw Hill, 1943), 903n.

8 "Side Lights on the Convention," *Washington Post*, July 14, 1896, 6.

9 William Jennings Bryan and Mary Baird Bryan, *The Memoirs of William Jennings Bryan* (Philadelphia: John C. Winston, 1925), 115.

10 "Bryan on the Fifth Ballot," *Philadelphia Inquirer*, July 11, 1896, 1. Michael Kazin points out that shrewd strategy as much as speechifying won Bryan the nomination; see Kazin, *A Godly Hero*, 62.

Bryan's 1896 convention triumph was the most significant moment in the history of American charisma up to that time. No longer was the charismatic relationship merely a preaching technique or a weapon in the arsenal of an already-successful politician, as it had been for Henry Ward Beecher and James G. Blaine, respectively, or the province of regional figures such as the Populists of the early 1890s.[11] Bryan's rise from also-ran to nominee largely through a single speech made charismatic oratory the centerpiece of a national political campaign in ways that surpassed even Blaine's efforts. Traveling nonstop by train, Bryan delivered hundreds of speeches heard by millions of Americans.[12] "We had during the last week of the campaign 18,000 speakers on the stump," wrote Republican Nannie Davis Lodge afterward; "He alone spoke for his party but speeches which spoke to the intelligence and to the hearts of the people, and with a capital P."[13] Financially and organizationally outgunned by his Republican opposition, Bryan sought to level the playing field through an unprecedented use of charismatic speaking techniques.

Nor was Bryan alone in his charismatic self-promotion. By the 1890s, the phenomenon of charisma had moved beyond the diffuse personal magnetism craze, with its bizarre fluid theories and inexplicable stopped watches. Instead, charisma had crystallized in a group of national movements headed by magnetic orators. These new movements emerged from a culture that valued heroism and powerful, even authoritarian, leadership more highly than in most other periods of American history. Politicians, religious leaders, and social activists used magnetic techniques to win large nationwide followings. In doing so, charismatic figures lent the force of numbers to their religious, political, or social platforms; honing their charismatic skills, they hoped, would win them enough supporters to carry the day for themselves and their ideas. Like Bryan, many of these leaders became highly skilled at their craft. "I might just as well put up a trapeze on my front lawn and compete with some professional athlete," 1896

[11] Lawrence Goodwyn, *Democratic Promise: The Populist Moment in America* (New York: Oxford University Press, 1976), 158, 174, 217; Charles Postel, *The Populist Vision* (New York: Oxford University Press, 2007), 157, 255; C. Vann Woodward, *Tom Watson: Agrarian Rebel* (New York: Oxford University Press, 1938), 308.

[12] Kazin, *A Godly Hero*, 68.

[13] Nannie Davis Lodge to Cecil Spring-Rice, quoted in Phillips, "William Jennings Bryan," 904.

Republican nominee William McKinley remarked, "as go out speaking against Bryan."[14]

The use of such theatrical metaphors for charisma was apt, for charisma was above all a performance. "What is the difference between Buffalo Bill and Bryan?" the former asked rhetorically. "Buffalo Bill has a show."[15] Bryan had a show too, but of a very specific type. Borrowing techniques from religious revivals, partisan politics, and popular lecture circuits, magnetic leaders put on pageants carefully designed to win the support of their audiences. Though a few leaders demanded control over all aspects of the performance, in most cases a company of professional organizers – managers, architects, musicians, and others – coordinated the new technologies of charisma and left leaders free to focus on their own self-presentation. The result was a group of movements varied in their message but unified in their style, structure, and effect. Despite a stagecraft that resembled such contemporary phenomena as advertised politics and Wild West shows, the charismatic movement was quite different from these performances. Charismatic leaders drew on many of the same materials as did other performing arts of the time, but they added an element all their own: a uniquely emotional speaking style rooted in the elocutionary techniques of early nineteenth-century American speech experts. Armed with these technologies of performance, charismatic figures sought and achieved an intense, durable, and directed bond between leader and follower.

Between 1890 and 1910 charismatic movements developed into a significant force in American national life. Whereas Beecher and Blaine had appeared unusual and even dangerous to many Americans in the 1870s and 1880s, by the turn of the century movements such as Bryan's began to seem almost normal. At the same time, charismatic movements developed a series of scheduling, marketing, and performing technologies, a unique structure, and their own unmistakable speaking style. By 1910, charisma had come of age as an organizing principle for social movements. With the decline of the term "personal magnetism," Americans lacked a way to describe this new and dramatic upswing in charismatic organization, but they surely sensed its progress. As charismatic leaders

[14] Quoted in William D. Harpine, *From the Front Porch to the Front Page: McKinley and Bryan in the 1896 Presidential Campaign* (College Station, TX: Texas A&M University Press, 2005), 41; Stanley Llewellyn Jones, *The Presidential Election of 1896* (Madison, WI: University of Wisconsin Press, 1964), 277.

[15] Quoted in Dixon Wecter, *The Hero in America: A Chronicle of Hero-Worship* (orig. pub. Scribner, 1941; Ann Arbor, MI: University of Michigan Press, 1963), 361.

proliferated and charismatic techniques improved, charisma seemed poised to reconfigure American society.

* * *

At first glance, James Rush seemed an unlikely candidate to have invented a unique American style of public speaking. Rush's father Benjamin was one of early America's most famous intellectuals; he had signed the Declaration of Independence, served as surgeon general of the Continental Army, and consulted on the Lewis and Clark expedition.[16] Benjamin was also a student of oratory, having received training under Samuel Davies and other First Great Awakening ministers.[17] James, a medical doctor like his father, seemed destined for a quieter existence. After training in medicine at the University of Pennsylvania and gaining further instruction in Europe, Rush returned to the United States and entered private practice. Brilliant, bookish, antisocial, and obsessed with the Enlightenment ideals of his father's generation of scientists, Rush became consumed with a desire to understand the workings of the mind – not in metaphysical terms, as his religious contemporaries did, but in scientific ones. As an Enlightenment thinker, Rush rejected the idea of mind–body dualism; he insisted that the mental functions were themselves physiological and could be explained by investigations of the body.[18] Mimicking Francis Bacon, Rush also possessed a fervent belief in the absolute truth of the repeatable experiment.[19]

In the early 1820s, Rush determined to undertake a study of the voice. By understanding how mental processes connected external stimuli with vocal responses, he believed, he could put his Enlightenment ideas into action. As he put it later, his goal was "to show the physicians of my time the practical meaning of the Baconian Philosophy … to bring the art of speech within the pale of science."[20] In addition, Rush hoped to

[16] Lester L. Hale, "Dr. James Rush," in Karl L. Wallace, ed., *History of Speech Education in America: Background Studies* (New York: Appleton-Century-Crofts, 1954), 220.

[17] Alyn Brodsky, *Benjamin Rush: Patriot and Physician* (New York: St. Martin's Press, 2004), 17–24; Wade Williams, "Religion, Science, and Rhetoric in Revolutionary America: The Case of Dr. Benjamin Rush," *Rhetoric Society Quarterly*, Vol. 30, No. 3 (Summer 2000), 56.

[18] Hale, "Dr. James Rush," 220–224.

[19] Melvin H. Bernstein, "Introduction: *The Philosophy of the Human Voice*," in James Rush, *The Collected Works of James Rush*, Vol. 1, ed. Melvin H. Bernstein (Weston, MA: M&S Press, 1974), 2, 11.

[20] James Rush, "Printer's Copy of the First Edition of *The Philosophy of the Human Voice*" (1833), Item 34, Rush Family Papers, Series 2, Library Company of Philadelphia.

FIGURE 2.1 Dr. James Rush, portrayed here in an 1829 painting by Anna Claypoole Peale, developed a style of elocution that figured prominently in later charismatic movements.
Source: Anna Claypoole Peale, *Jacob Ridgway (1768–1843); Phoebe Anne Ridgway Rush (1799–1857); James Rush (1786–1869)*, watercolor on ivory, 1829, courtesy of the Library Company of Philadelphia.

democratize and professionalize public speaking. While early American public speaking students memorized the flowery speeches of ancient Greek and Roman orators in hopes of emulating their brilliance, Rush wanted to break oratory down into its component parts – to allow anyone with a good education and rigorous study habits to speak well on any subject. "The high accomplishments in Elocution are supposed to be, universally, the unacquired gifts of genius," Rush scoffed. "So seem the plainest services of arithmetic to a savage."[21] His work, Rush explained, "will enable an Elocutionist of any nation, to reduce to established form, the best modes of speech in his language."[22]

[21] James Rush, *The Philosophy of the Human Voice* (Philadelphia: J. Maxwell, 1827), xxii.
[22] *Ibid.*, xv.

For three years beginning in March 1823, Rush conducted an exhaustive examination of speech. He read every elocution manual he could acquire in the United States and imported the more elusive ones from England. More important, he engaged in years of empirical testing of his ideas, using himself as a test subject. "Occasionally in the afternoon, but generally at night," he wrote later, "I would experiment with my voice sometimes for hours, whilst walking my room, and then note down the result of this progress; the ideas growing as I wrote." Documenting his progress, Rush filled thousands of manuscript pages with handwritten notes, drawings of intonation contours, vowel charts, and musical symbols. He wrote out the cadence of phrases – "In the fifteenth century of the Christian era" and selections from Milton's *Paradise Lost* were favorites – assigning each syllable to a musical note and then varying the notes to change the meaning of the passage. The sounds issuing from his study during these years were likely quite strange indeed. "Most of this inquiry," Rush noted while practicing a new vocal technique, "was conducted from ten at night till two in the morning, when … my family [was] most deaf to the queer noises, yowling and barking which the quoted authority of the ear, and an effective investigation of the subject required." "How many queer sounds," he concluded after completing his work, "were sent out of my mouth: and how many miles I paced my room, in thinking and experimenting with my voice, I myself, who did it, cannot even grasp." Though Rush sought to shield his family from the aural evidence of his research, others in his household were not so lucky; at one point, he determined the emotional connotations of what he termed "staccato speech" by testing it on his horses.[23]

The result of Rush's labors was *The Philosophy of the Human Voice* (1827), a nearly 600-page treatise on elocution. Most of the *Philosophy* consisted of what Rush termed "a methodical description of all the vocal phenomena" – essentially an astute, prescient description of what modern-day linguists would term suprasegmental phonetics.[24] The doctor painstakingly outlined the concepts of vocal quality, intonation, and syllable stress and structure; described the physical means of producing them; and created a comprehensive catalog of their uses.[25] Innovative as this research was, Rush had bolder goals in mind. Rush believed that individual vocal techniques were scientifically connected with specific emotional responses. "The fact is," he wrote in his notes, "that the various

[23] James Rush, "First Outline of *The Philosophy of the Human Voice*" (1827), Item 27, Rush Family Papers, Series 2.

[24] Rush, *The Philosophy of the Human Voice*, i. [25] *Ibid.*, 29.

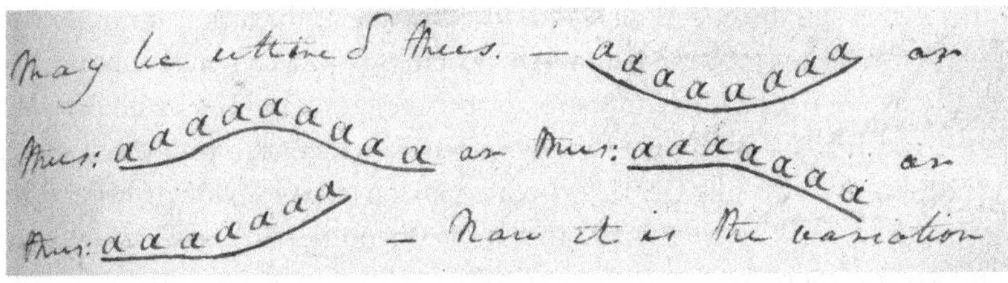

FIGURE 2.2 James Rush's notes reveal his development of specific intonation contours, an expanded pitch range, and other characteristics of the magnetic speaking style.
Source: James Rush, "First Outline of *The Philosophy of the Human Voice*" (1827), courtesy of the Library Company of Philadelphia, Rush Family Papers, Series 2, Item 27.

classes of ideas we call feelings, have a certain set of sounds offered by nature as their representatives."[26] By 1827, Rush felt he had conclusively identified "a system of principles ... which are accommodated to the temper and habits of the English ear; and which ... may be called the ideal beauty of speech."[27] Through his elocutionary system, in effect, Rush imposed his own aesthetic preferences on the structure of charismatic speech.

The speaking style Rush advocated contained several distinctive features. First, Rush instructed orators to embrace an expanded pitch range, to speak, as Rush put it, in musical intervals of the octave or fifth rather than the customary third.[28] The practical result was to pitch the highest point of a phrase much higher, and the lowest point much lower, than in ordinary conversational speech – an effect heard today only in some early sound recordings, but far more common among American charismatic orators of the late nineteenth century. Second, Rush pressed speakers to construct phrases in a way that privileged "the melody of speech"; he encouraged them to use poetic principles in compiling pleasing combinations of stressed and unstressed, long and short, rising

[26] Rush, "First Outline of *The Philosophy of the Human Voice*."
[27] Rush, *The Philosophy of the Human Voice*, xvi. [28] *Ibid.*, 207–212.

and falling syllables.[29] This focus on "melody" branded charismatic speech with what modern listeners would describe as a singsong quality. Finally, Rush urged his readers to adopt a vocal technique he christened "the orotund voice." This "fulness of voice, which at a low pitch has a certain hollowness like the reverberations of a cavity," was produced by lowering the larynx to enlarge the upper throat, creating a rich, round tone whose increased volume allowed it to be projected at great distances.[30] Commonly used today by opera singers, this sound quality, termed "advanced tongue root" by modern linguists, is quite difficult for native English speakers to produce consistently in speech; Rush's own attempts to master it resulted in the "yowling and barking" he described in his notes. Yet the orotund voice became perhaps the most distinctive feature of charismatic oratory.[31]

Rush's writings on elocution might have remained obscure if not for the intervention of Dr. Jonathan Barber – he of the bamboo cage, whose elocutionary system had so influenced Henry Ward Beecher. An English immigrant and, like Rush, a medical doctor, Barber was also a bit of a scoundrel whose debts and legal troubles had followed him across the Atlantic. Barber befriended Rush in 1827 and was soon borrowing liberally both from the American doctor's wealth and from his ideas.[32] By 1830, Barber had secured an appointment at Harvard and was teaching elocution courses based on Rush's principles.[33] Because Rush's *Philosophy* did not mention gesture, Barber combined Rush's teachings with the work of the British minister Gilbert Austin, whom Rush also admired.[34] Austin's *Chironomia* (1806) played the same role in prefiguring the physical movements of charismatic orators that Rush's

[29] *Ibid.*, 115–116, 172–179. [30] *Ibid.*, 101, 106.

[31] Greg Goodale, drawing on later elocution texts, provides a slightly different definition of the orotund style. Goodale, "The Presidential Sound: From Orotund to Instructional Speech, 1892–1912," *Quarterly Journal of Speech*, Vol. 96, No. 2 (May 2010), 171–173; Peter Ladefoged and Ian Maddieson, *The Sounds of the World's Languages* (Malden, MA: Blackwell Publishing, 1996), 300; Burton W. Peretti, *The Leading Man: Hollywood and the Presidential Image* (New Brunswick, NJ: Rutgers University Press, 2012), 40.

[32] Jonathan Barber to James Rush, March 17, 1827; Barber to Rush, September 24, 1827; Rush to Barber, April 13, 1828, Miscellaneous Correspondence of James Rush, Vol. 1, Rush Family Papers, Series 2.

[33] Marie Hochmuth and Richard Murphy, "Rhetorical and Elocutionary Training in Nineteenth-Century Colleges," in Wallace, ed., *History of Speech Education in America*, 162; Hale, "Dr. James Rush," 232; David H. Grover, "Elocution at Harvard: The Saga of Jonathan Barber," *Quarterly Journal of Speech*, Vol. 51, No. 1 (February 1965), 63.

[34] James Rush, "An Abstract of Authors Ancient and Modern Who Have Written On the Voice" (1837–1838), 244, Item 15, Rush Family Papers, Series 2.

work did in outlining their speech qualities. Rejecting previous gestural theories, Austin instead imagined public speakers inscribed in an invisible sphere and directed them to touch different points on the sphere's circumference to indicate distinct emotions. "The arm is projected forwards in authority," Austin wrote, prefiguring the forceful motion frequently used by Theodore Roosevelt. "They are both held forwards in imploring help," he continued, suggesting the supplicative motion favored by Eugene V. Debs.[35] The book's voluminous illustrations suggested extreme gestural precision, as even subtle changes could alter the movement's emotional meaning.[36] Barber himself diagrammed a speech, John Gay's "The Miser and Plautus," gesture by gesture; the resulting images demonstrated that speakers using the Barber–Austin system began a new gesture with each phrase, sometimes with each metrical foot.[37]

Barber's development of an actual bamboo cage to replicate Austin's spherical diagram of gestures angered students and led to the English doctor's departure from Harvard. His short textbooks on elocution and gesture, however, which were drawn directly from Rush and Austin's writings, achieved widespread popularity; along with other Rush-inspired texts, they became the most influential oratorical teaching volumes in nineteenth-century America.[38] Between 1821 and 1850, three of the four most widely used elocution texts by American authors were penned by devotees of Rush.[39] Filtered through these textbooks, Rush's recommendations became the most influential style of public speaking in nineteenth-century America.

The ideas of Rush and Austin left their mark on numerous charismatic speakers. Henry Ward Beecher's intensive training with Barber devotee John Lovell made him the most prominent, but by no means the only,

[35] Gilbert Austin, *Chironomia: Or a Treatise on Rhetorical Delivery* (London: T. Cadell and W. Davies, 1806), 483.

[36] *Ibid.*, plates between 308 and 309, 312 and 313.

[37] Jonathan Barber, *A Practical Treatise on Gesture* (Cambridge, MA: Hilliard and Brown, 1831), Plate XIII, unnumbered back matter.

[38] Grover, "Elocution at Harvard," 65–66; Jonathan Barber, *A Grammar of Elocution* (New Haven, CT: A. H. Maltby, 1830), 1–2, 177–181; Barber, *A Practical Treatise on Gesture*, unnumbered front matter; Nan Johnson, "The Popularization of Nineteenth-Century Rhetoric: Elocution and the Private Learner," in Gregory Clark and S. Michael Halloran, eds., *Oratorical Culture in Nineteenth-Century America: Transformations in the Theory and Practice of Rhetoric* (Carbondale, IL: Southern Illinois University Press, 1993), 143–144.

[39] The texts were by Barber, Merritt Caldwell, and William Russell. Mary Margaret Robb, "The Elocutionary Movement and Its Chief Figures," in Wallace, ed., *History of Speech Education in America*, 179, 187.

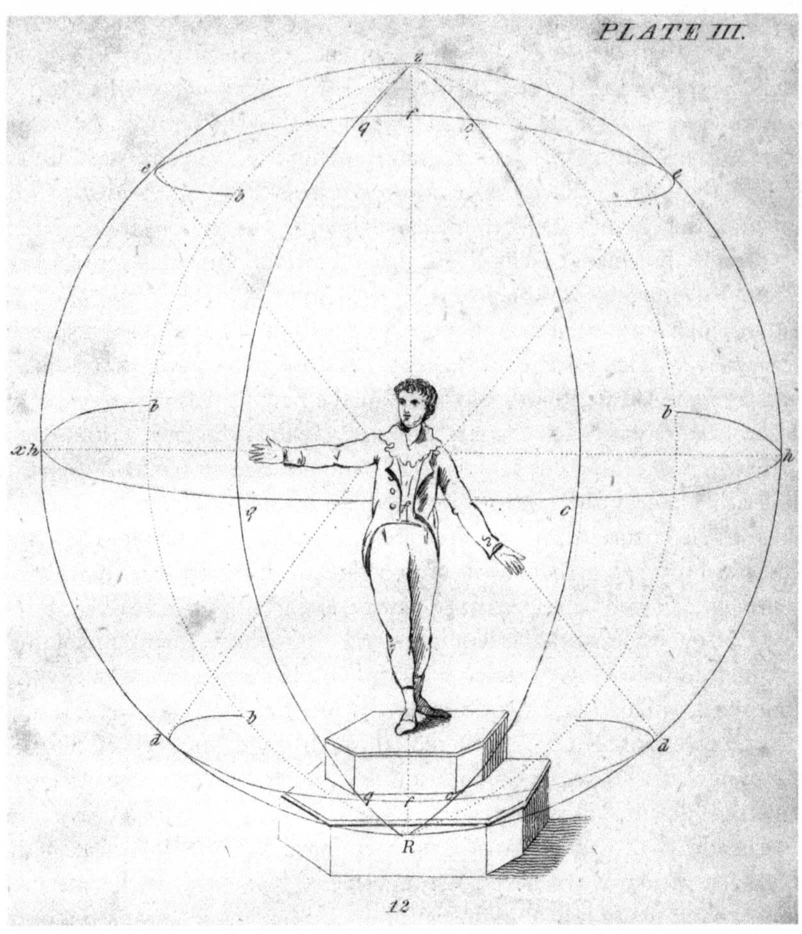

FIGURE 2.3 Jonathan Barber, like Gilbert Austin before him, imagined public speakers inscribed in an imaginary sphere; speakers would touch different points on the sphere to communicate different emotions.
Source: Jonathan Barber, *A Practical Treatise on Gesture* (Cambridge, MA: Hilliard and Brown, 1831), Figure 12, Plate III, unnumbered back matter.

practitioner of the Rush–Austin speech style. Wendell Phillips, the greatest orator of the abolitionist movement, developed his impressive speaking ability while studying with Barber at Harvard. "Whatever I have acquired in the art of improving and managing my voice," he wrote later, "I owe to Dr. Barber's system, suggestions, and lessons. No volume or treatise on the voice except those of Rush and Barber has ever been of any practical value to me."[40] Theodore Weld, another prominent abolitionist speaker, signed his name to a glowing testimonial after completing an elocution course with Barber's younger brother John in the late 1830s.[41] Edwin Forrest, the most popular American stage actor of the mid-nineteenth century, read Rush's *Philosophy* and recommended it to a fellow actor seeking to improve his vocal production.[42] And evangelist Billy Sunday, one of the most prominent charismatic speakers of the early twentieth century, briefly attended college at Northwestern University and benefited from Robert McLean Cumnock's course on oratory.[43] Cumnock's own elocution textbook reveals what Sunday learned in his college course: vocal slides and expanded pitch range, the orotund voice, and other speech characteristics unmistakably inspired by Rush.[44]

Bryan's career provided the most striking evidence of Rush's influence on the charismatic style. In 1877, Bryan "received the usual training in public speaking" at Illinois College under S. S. Hamill, yet another devotee of Rush; Hamill "trained us in modulation of the voice, gesticulation, etc.," the politician wrote in his memoirs, "and I presume that his instructions were beneficial to me."[45] "Beneficial" was an understatement. Bryan's rich, resonant voice, known for its ability to carry long distances, was a textbook example of the orotund voice.[46] The singsong quality and poetic rhythm of Bryan's rhetoric – "You shall not crucify mankind upon a cross of gold" was perfect iambic heptameter – followed Rush's recommendations, too.[47] The most dramatic evidence, however, was visual. At the 1908 Democratic National Convention, Bryan posed for a series of photographs displaying the gestures he typically made while speaking. Four of the surviving photographs reproduce almost exactly

[40] Quoted in James E. Murdoch, *A Plea for Spoken Language* (Cincinnati: Van Antwerp, Bragg, 1883), 101, quoted in Robb, "The Elocutionary Movement and Its Chief Figures," 185.

[41] Quoted in John Barber to James Rush, March 23, 1840, Miscellaneous Correspondence of James Rush, Vol. 1, Rush Family Papers, Series 2.

[42] Robb, "The Elocutionary Movement and Its Chief Figures," 189.

[43] "Northwestern Folks You Ought to Know," *Northwestern University Alumni News*, Vol. 4, No. 1 (November 1924), 25; William G. McLoughlin, Jr., *Billy Sunday Was His Real Name* (Chicago: University of Chicago Press, 1955), 7.

[44] Robert McLean Cumnock, *Choice Readings for Public and Private Entertainments*, rev. ed. (Chicago: McClurg, 1898), 103–104, 109, 297; Grace Mattern, "The Biography of Robert McLean Cumnock" (M.A. thesis, Northwestern University, 1929), 16.

[45] Bryan and Bryan, *The Memoirs of William Jennings Bryan*, 87; Hochmuth and Murphy, "Rhetorical and Elocutionary Training in Nineteenth-Century Colleges," 171; S. S. Hamill, *The Science of Elocution* (New York: Nelson & Phillips, 1872), 67, 103, 151.

[46] Kazin, *A Godly Hero*, 48. [47] Rush, *The Philosophy of the Human Voice*, 174–177.

FIGURE 2.4 William Jennings Bryan's public speaking style (photographed here in 1908) reveals the influence of Jonathan Barber's gestural theories (1831) on charismatic performance.
Source: Jonathan Barber, *A Practical Treatise on Gesture* (Cambridge, MA: Hilliard and Brown, 1831), Figure 10, 42, 48, and 55, Plates II, IX, and X, unnumbered back matter; photographs of William Jennings Bryan, c. July 3, 1908, orig. pub. June 25, 1920, courtesy of the Library of Congress, Prints and Photographs Division, LC-USZ62-16464, LC-USZ62-10291, LC-USZ62-34093, LC-USZ62-21973.

illustrations found in Barber's *Practical Treatise on Gesture*.[48] Bryan's characteristic speaking style – the source of his personal magnetism – was in large part the ideas of Rush and Austin performed effectively by a master of the form.

In the first edition of the *Philosophy*, Rush paused to ponder his own place in history. Imagining "the present age and posterity as rivals," so that "those who receive the favor of the one" were "outcasts from the

[48] Barber, *A Practical Treatise on Gesture*, Figure 10, 42, 48, and 55, Plates II, IX, and X, unnumbered back matter; photographs of William Jennings Bryan, c. July 3, 1908, orig. pub. June 25, 1920, LC-USZ62-16464, LC-USZ62-10291, LC-USZ62-34093, LC-USZ62-21973, Prints and Photographs Division, Library of Congress.

other," Rush noted hopefully that this formulation "does not exclude all prospect from those who are contented in the anticipation of deferred success."[49] It did not work out that way for Rush. Though he enjoyed modest renown among elocution experts during his lifetime, he was almost forgotten by 1900. Instead, it was Rush's elocution techniques themselves that grew famous after his death in 1869. The shift from an oratory of natural ability to a widespread course of training in a popularly accepted elocutionary aesthetic contributed greatly to the development of charismatic movements in the late nineteenth century. More important, by the end of the century, Rush's influence on public speaking was so great that even orators not trained in Rush's methods absorbed his techniques by learning from other speakers. More often than not, when Americans identified an orator as magnetic, they heard Rush's style issuing from the platform or the podium. Though turn-of-the-century commentators failed to make the connection between the magnetic speech they observed and the obscure elocution scholar who had first described it, Rush's elocutionary techniques formed the central and most unique element of personal magnetism. More than any other individual, James Rush had invented the charismatic speaking style. It would take a very different innovator, however, to convince Americans that the use of that style was morally justified.

* * *

On Wednesday evening, October 10, 1821, an important event in the history of the charismatic relationship transpired beside a fireplace in Adams, New York. As the young law clerk Charles Grandison Finney went to sit by the fire, he experienced a staggering religious conversion. "I received *a mighty baptism of the Holy Ghost*," he wrote later. "The Holy Spirit descended upon me in a manner that seemed *to go through me*, body and soul. I could feel the impression, *like a wave of electricity*, going through and through me." Overcome by "*waves of liquid love*," Finney could barely contain his emotions. "It seemed to me that I should burst," he remembered. "I wept aloud with joy and love; and I do not know but I should say I literally *bellowed out* the unutterable gushings of my heart."[50] Finney's conversion experience transformed him

49 Rush, *The Philosophy of the Human Voice*, xxvii.

50 Charles Grandison Finney, *The Memoirs of Charles G. Finney: The Complete Restored Text*, ed. Garth M. Rosell and Richard A. G. Dupuis (Grand Rapids, MI: Zondervan, 1989), 23–24; italics in original.

immediately from spiritual skeptic to true believer and made it impossible for him to continue his legal studies. "I had no longer any desire to practise law," he wrote. "Everything in that direction was all shut up . . . I had the impression, which has never left my mind, that God wanted me to preach the Gospel, and that I must begin immediately."[51]

Finney, it soon transpired, had some unorthodox ideas about just how God wanted him to "preach the Gospel." Combining the brash confidence of the budding American legal profession with the zeal of the religious convert, Finney was an unusual figure even in the 1820s. When three seminaries rejected his application for admission, Finney announced to the local ministers that he did not mind the rejection; he did not want to go to seminary anyway, for he "was confident that they [the ministers] had been wrongly educated" there![52] Finney's presbytery placed him under the tutelage of his minister, George Washington Gale – the same clergyman Finney had enjoyed tormenting with skeptical arguments before his conversion. Committed now to the divine doctrines he had gleaned from his conversion experience, Finney was no more receptive than he had been earlier to Gale's traditional Calvinist theology.[53] "The fact is that Brother Gale's education for the ministry had been entirely defective," Finney later asserted. "I finally said to Mr. Gale: 'If there is nothing better than I find in your library to sustain the great doctrines by our church, I must be an infidel.' "[54] Though Finney eventually reconciled with Gale and other traditionalists, he never achieved a thorough education in Calvinist theology; nor, despite his eventual ordination, did Finney ever feel comfortable ministering for years at a settled church as Gale had.[55]

Instead, Finney spent the next decade touring the country as the most successful revivalist in generations. Finney's preaching, like his theology, was dramatic and unorthodox. Like George Whitefield and Jonathan Edwards before him, Finney's pulpit personality was intense and charged with emotion. "He moved about like a caged lion on that great platform," recalled Oliver Willard after seeing Finney preach as an old man, "his light blue eyes blazing under those shaggy, white

[51] *Ibid.*, 28.

[52] *Ibid.*, 47; Keith J. Hardman, *Charles Grandison Finney, 1792–1875: Revivalist and Reformer* (Syracuse, NY: Syracuse University Press, 1987), 50–51.

[53] Hardman, *Charles Grandison Finney*, 49–50; Charles E. Hambrick-Stowe, *Charles G. Finney and the Spirit of American Evangelicalism* (Grand Rapids, MI: Eerdmans, 1996), 25.

[54] Finney, *The Memoirs of Charles G. Finney*, 55.

[55] Hardman, *Charles Grandison Finney*, 61–62.

eyebrows."[56] Unlike the staid local ministers whose towns he visited in the "burned-over district" – the revival hotspot of upstate New York – and eventually in major cities across America, Finney liked to shake things up. Where other preachers allowed their listeners to progress toward conversion at their own pace, Finney demanded immediate converts and chastised in open meeting those who resisted his call.[57] Where traditional Calvinists sought to maintain order in their meetings, Finney participated in the Methodist-inspired "shout tradition" of vocalized audience emotion.[58] In a typical revival, Finney recalled, "The congregation began to fall from their seats; and they fell in every direction, and cried for mercy. If I had had a sword in each hand I could not have cut them off their seats as fast as they fell."[59] Finney pioneered additional techniques, all wildly successful. He called upon members of the audience by name and castigated them for their sins; he installed an "anxious seat" at the front of the congregation and invited potential converts to come forward and occupy the bench if they planned to commit themselves to God.[60] Despite opposition from traditionalists and even such moderates as Lyman Beecher, Finney's record of success spoke for itself. Finney set down his "new measures" for revivals in an 1835 bestseller, *Lectures on Revivals of Religion*.[61] Partly because of his success at achieving conversions and partly because he mellowed in his dealings with traditionalists, Finney's methods eventually won acceptance from both orthodox Calvinist divines and mainstream American Protestantism as a whole.[62]

Finney was far from the first American revivalist, nor were most of his methods as "new" as he made them out to be.[63] Finney himself was not even a charismatic leader in the fully developed sense; while his tactics on

[56] Quoted in Frances E. Willard, *Glimpses of Fifty Years: The Autobiography of an American Woman* (Chicago: H. J. Smith, 1889), 60; Harry S. Stout, *The Divine Dramatist: George Whitefield and the Rise of Modern Evangelicalism* (Grand Rapids, MI: Eerdmans, 1991), 40–44, 79, 140–141, 151–154.

[57] Hambrick-Stowe, *Charles G. Finney and the Spirit of American Evangelicalism*, 36.

[58] Ann Taves, *Fits, Trances, & Visions: Experiencing Religion and Explaining Experience from Wesley to James* (Princeton, NJ: Princeton University Press, 1999), 132–133.

[59] Finney, *The Memoirs of Charles G. Finney*, 102.

[60] Hambrick-Stowe, *Charles G. Finney and the Spirit of American Evangelicalism*, 38–39.

[61] Charles G. Finney, *Lectures on Revivals of Religion* (New York: Leavitt, Lord, & Co., 1835).

[62] William G. McLoughlin, Jr., *Modern Revivalism: Charles Grandison Finney to Billy Graham* (New York: Ronald Press, 1959), 11.

[63] Hardman, *Charles Grandison Finney*, xii; R. Laurence Moore, *Selling God: American Religion in the Marketplace of Culture* (New York: Oxford University Press, 1994), 50.

the platform prefigured charismatic techniques, the structure of his revivals bore little resemblance to that of the later movements.[64] What made Finney unique was his insistence that the job of the public speaker was to transform the lives of his listeners. Finney's contemporaries included many skilled political orators, but these politicians sought to win votes or advance policy agendas, not to provoke conversion experiences. Among Protestant religious figures, only the marginalized Methodists believed that their preaching should produce an immediate and explosive emotional response. Finney's cheerleading for the art of transformational oratory, his belief that properly prepared audience members should undergo emotional "second conversions" right there in the revival meeting, made him a trailblazer for the charismatic figures who came after him. In essence, Finney opened a place in mainstream American culture for charismatic oratory – he made respectable the persuasive speaker who sought to change society by appealing to the emotions of his listeners.

In his preaching, Finney promoted two ideas that paved the way for a broad acceptance of charisma. First, he rejected predestination – the idea, central to the Puritan religious belief of mainstream American theologians, that God determined before birth whether a person was destined for heaven or hell. In his 1831 sermon "Sinners Bound to Change Their Own Hearts," Finney argued instead that people could choose whether or not to be saved by God; free will, not divine order, determined one's ultimate fate. "Holiness ... must consist in voluntary obedience to the principles of eternal righteousness," Finney declared. "Every human being possesses ... the power and liberty of choice ... It is evident that the requirement here, is to change our *moral character;* our *moral disposition;* in other words, to change that abiding preference of our minds, which prefers sin to holiness; self-gratification to the glory of God."[65]

Both Methodists and earlier Calvinist revivalists had agreed with Finney that salvation was a matter of individual choice. What Finney added was an understanding that rejecting predestination led inexorably to the use of persuasion in achieving conversions. If sinners really were bound to change their own hearts, then the job of the minister was to encourage them to do so; in fact, he should employ all possible means to

64 Hardman, *Charles Grandison Finney*, 192; Hambrick-Stowe, *Charles G. Finney and the Spirit of American Evangelicalism*, 158.

65 Charles G. Finney, *Sermons on Important Subjects* (New York: John S. Taylor, 1834), 7–8; italics in original.

ensure that conversions actually took place. "One grand design of God in leaving Christians in the world after their conversion," Finney declared in the *Lectures*, "is that they may call the attention of the thoughtless multitude to the subject [of salvation] ... What is wanted in the world is something that can be a sort of omnipresent miracle, able not only to arrest attention but to fix it, and keep the mind in warm contact with the truth, till it yields."[66] The "omnipresent miracle" was, of course, Finney and other Gospel preachers. Finney's acknowledgment of persuasion's beneficial role in American society prefigured the attitudes of later charismatic movements. Charismatic leaders agreed with Finney that Americans had the power to change their society for the better; accordingly, persuading them to use that power was a noble application of charismatic speech, not a nefarious one.

Finney's second innovation flowed from his first. Since ministers needed the most advanced persuasive techniques available, he reasoned, they should seek such tools among the slickest professional persuaders of all: political campaigners. "What do the politicians do?" Finney asked in the *Lectures*. "They get up meetings, circulate handbills and pamphlets, blaze away in the newspapers ... all to gain attention to their cause and elect their candidate. All these are their 'measures,' and for their *end* they are wisely calculated ... They know that unless there can be an excitement it is in vain to push their end."[67] In part through Finney's agency, the early part of the century witnessed a fertile interchange of persuasive techniques between revivalists and political actors. Just as Finney urged preachers to adapt political tactics to their ministries, antebellum politicians borrowed freely from revival techniques. They deployed armies of orators in service of national and local tickets, erected tents on the same meeting grounds evangelists frequented, held political camp meetings in direct imitation of religious revivals, and even collaborated with revivalist ministers in endorsing one another's causes.[68] At the same time, politicians became comfortable eliciting revival-style emotional responses from their audiences.[69] After the Civil War, this cross-fertilization of religious and political imagery became a hallmark of charismatic movements. Thanks in part to Finney's influence, Americans found nothing unusual

[66] Finney, *Lectures on Revivals of Religion*, 129. [67] *Ibid.*, 167; italics in original.
[68] Richard J. Carwardine, *Evangelicals and Politics in Antebellum America* (New Haven, CT: Yale University Press, 1993), 51–52.
[69] *Ibid.*, 52–54; Moore, *Selling God*, 75.

in Bryan using Christian imagery in his "Cross of Gold" speech or revivalist Billy Sunday advocating for alcohol prohibition laws from the tabernacle stage.

Finney added to these theoretical arguments two key innovations in practical technique. First were Finney's "new measures" – the anxious seat, calling out audience members by name, and so forth. Finney intended these techniques to create a personal connection between the leader and every member of the audience. "Preaching should be *direct*," he insisted in the *Lectures*. "The gospel should be preached *to* men, and not *about* them. The minister must address his hearers. He must preach *to* them *about themselves*, and not leave the impression that he is preaching to them about others."[70] Second, Finney developed a new style of preaching designed for effectiveness rather than propriety. He rejected prepared, written sermons as lacking "freshness"; he eschewed "ornate language" in favor of plainspokenness.[71] Instead, Finney drew on his legal background to create a rhetorical style all his own.[72] "I was bred a lawyer," he recalled in his memoirs. "I came right forth from a law office to the pulpit, and talked to the people as I would have talked to a jury."[73] His goal in the pulpit, he wrote, was "to express my thoughts with the greatest simplicity of language."[74] Finney used simple phrases and filled his sermons with examples designed to appeal to the everyday experience of his listeners. "The fact is," he concluded, prefiguring Henry Ward Beecher's views decades later, "if ministers have a single eye, and intend to reach and to save the people, ... they will come down to them, and will try to understand their language and accommodate their addresses to their capacities and positions."[75]

Although there is no evidence Finney and Rush ever communicated with one another, Finney was at least aware of Rush's techniques; the revivalist's onetime teacher and subsequent acolyte, George Washington Gale, attended an elocution course by John Barber in the late 1830s.[76] Finney's endorsement of simple language coincided with Rush's views on the subject. Later observers of charisma frequently noted that their subjects eschewed elocution and formal oratory in

[70] Finney, *Lectures on Revivals of Religion*, 185; italics in original.

[71] Finney, *The Memoirs of Charles G. Finney*, 81, 93.

[72] David B. Chesebrough, *Charles G. Finney: Revivalistic Rhetoric* (Westport, CT: *Greenwood Press*, 2002), xv.

[73] Finney, *The Memoirs of Charles G. Finney*, 89. [74] *Ibid.*, 81. [75] *Ibid.*, 88.

[76] John Barber to James Rush, March 23, 1840, Miscellaneous Correspondence of James Rush, Vol. 1, Rush Family Papers, Series 2.

favor of a more homespun idiom. James G. Blaine "was not eloquent in our American understanding of that word," confirmed Senator Chauncey Depew in a typical comment, "but he had a certain clearness of statement, directness of argument, plain and understandable way of putting things which carried his audience."[77] In 1890, the *Plattsmouth Journal* described William Jennings Bryan's speaking style, "so different from that of any other speaker ... There is no effort to produce an effect by high-sounding phrases, demagogic appeals to passion or prejudice ... His entire lack of artfulness makes him invincible."[78] Although Robert Ingersoll's political speeches were more florid than were typical charismatic utterances, his lectures on religion revealed him to be "a master of colloquial speech," according to the writer Hamlin Garland. "He bantered us, challenged us, electrified us. At times his eloquence held us silent as images and then some witty turn, some humorous phrase, brought roars of applause ... At other moments we rose in our seats and yelled."[79] In his support for extemporaneous speaking, on the other hand, Finney's recommendations clashed with Rush's mechanistic approach – and it was Finney's view, not Rush's, that influenced charismatic leaders. The night before suffrage orator Anna Howard Shaw was to speak at the 1893 Chicago World's Fair, her mentor Susan B. Anthony convinced her to scrap her prepared speech and talk extemporaneously instead. "You've polished and repolished that sermon until there's no life left in it," Anthony warned. "It's dead." Shaw heeded the advice and delivered a masterful performance.[80]

The use of verbal illustrations, also championed by Finney, became another trademark of charismatic oratory. A contemporary of Henry Ward Beecher noted that once, during a lecture, Beecher "managed to bring in trout fishing ... [and] dodged from one side of the rostrum to the other, up and down, giving line and reeling in, until the entire audience (nearly two thousand) leaned forward with expectant eyes and open

[77] Quoted in Willis Fletcher Johnson, *Life of James G. Blaine, "The Plumed Knight"* (Philadelphia: Atlantic Pub. Co., 1893), 554–555.

[78] Quoted in *Omaha World-Herald*, October 29, 1890, quoted in Keith Melder, "Bryan the Campaigner," Contributions from the Museum of History and Technology, Paper 46 (Washington, DC: Smithsonian Institution, 1965), 64.

[79] Hamlin Garland, *Roadside Meetings* (New York: Macmillan, 1930), 45; Susan Jacoby, *The Great Agnostic: Robert Ingersoll and American Freethought* (New Haven: Yale University Press, 2013), 89–90.

[80] Anna Howard Shaw and Elizabeth Jordan, *The Story of a Pioneer* (New York: Harper & Brothers, 1915), 176–178; Trisha Franzen, *Anna Howard Shaw: The Work of Woman Suffrage* (Urbana, IL: University of Illinois Press, 2014), 78.

mouths."[81] Billy Sunday, according to his music director Homer Rodeheaver, "was a past master" of such illustrations. "He had but to acquaint himself with the bare outlines of a good story, then he would amplify and embellish it in his own inimitable fashion and use it to clinch an argument or illuminate and emphasize some attribute of Christian living."[82] Often, Rodeheaver wrote, Sunday's storytelling impressed his audiences more than the rest of his performance did: "There was a magic in his word-painting which kept alive the spiritual truth of his stories so that those who heard them never forgot."[83] Bryan excelled at such illustrations, too. "We understand a thing more easily," he wrote in 1906, "when we know that it is like something which we have already seen."[84] And what image could be more powerful than Christ's ordeal on the cross, called forth by Bryan to dramatize public suffering under the gold standard?

Unlike Finney's oratorical recommendations, very few of his "new measures" survived intact into the era of personal magnetism. The mid-century evangelist Dwight L. Moody, for instance, moved the anxious seat into a separate "inquiry room" where an assistant could guide the spiritually affected through their conversions while the main revival proceeded uninterrupted. Still later, Billy Sunday did away with the concept altogether; instead, audience members were expected to "hit the sawdust trail" to the pulpit on their way to immediate conversions. Similarly, both religious and secular turn-of-the-century leaders avoided criticizing their audience members by name. These later figures sought a different response from their audiences than did Finney: less weeping and wailing, more positive energy and motivation to direct action. "No longer does one see the sinner go forward with tearstained eyes," noted a psychology graduate student observing a 1915 Sunday revival. "In fact, most of those who hit the [sawdust] trail seemed to be in a rather pleasant frame of mind."[85] Nevertheless, there was an important similarity between the "new measures" and the newer ones: both sought to bring the charismatic service home to the individual listener, to make every member of the audience feel personally touched by the leader.

[81] Leon Oliver, *The Great Sensation* (Chicago: Beverly, 1873), 17.

[82] Homer Rodeheaver, *Twenty Years with Billy Sunday* (Winona Lake, IN: Rodeheaver Hall-Mack, 1936), 47.

[83] *Ibid.*, 65. [84] Bryan, "Introduction," xiii–xiv.

[85] Henry Arthur Bentson, *A Psychological Study of a "Billy" Sunday Revival* (Ph.D. diss., Columbia University, 1916), 48; McLoughlin, *Billy Sunday Was His Real Name*, 127.

Appropriately, the new measures led indirectly to one of the most important features of later charismatic technique, a moment of direct physical touch between the leader and his followers: the postspeech handshake. Handshakes themselves predated the United States by millennia and had long been part of business deals, politics, and even diplomacy, but charismatic movements adapted them to a new purpose. Having spent their entire performance withholding their physical presence from listeners while inspiring them from the pulpit or the podium, charismatic figures dramatically relieved the tension by offering handshakes to audience members after the speech. Sunday astutely built the handshake into the climax of his revivals; those who chose to "hit the sawdust trail" at the end of the service found a Sunday handshake waiting for them at the front of the tabernacle. Often, Sunday would make his listeners wait through weeks of revival sermons before issuing the first call to conversion – building up the audience's longing for contact with him and then offering them release only if they converted.[86] For their part, politicians and activist lecturers rarely made handshakes an official part of the program, but they regularly made themselves available after their speeches for as many handshakes as possible. Blaine, Bryan, and Debs, among others, won wide acclaim for the quality of their postspeech handshakes.[87]

Some charismatic politicians even organized receptions at which the parade of handshakes itself served as the main event. Theodore Roosevelt was the acknowledged champion of these events; the president engaged in many such activities every year, shaking thousands of hands at each. At a White House reception on New Year's Day, 1907, Roosevelt shook hands with over 8,500 people, setting a record that stood for seven decades.[88] African Americans, too, were welcome to partake of the president's generosity, though the *Trenton Evening Times* noted ominously that their numbers seemed to have dropped off from the previous year. "Although he was shaking hands at the rate of nearly 40 a minute from first to last," reported the *Times*, "the President had a smile for every one of the thousands, and at least a word for every one of two or

[86] McLoughlin, *Billy Sunday Was His Real Name*, 98–99.

[87] William Ralston Balch, *Life and Public Services of James G. Blaine, with the Facts in the Career of John A. Logan* (Philadelphia: Thayer, Merriam, 1884), 346; Sara N. Cleghorn, quoted in Ruth Le Prade, ed., *Debs and the Poets* (Pasadena, CA: Upton Sinclair, 1920), 75; Alexander MacDonald to Theodore Debs, December 18, 1935, microfilm: reel 5, Debs Collection, Indiana State University, Terre Haute, Indiana.

[88] "President Shakes Hands with 8,500," *Aberdeen Daily American*, January 2, 1907, 1.

three ... A continuous gattling [*sic*] gun fire of similar exclamations fell from his lips as the throng moved along at almost a quick step." It took Roosevelt over three and a half hours to work his way through the crowd.[89] The prevalence of such handshake receptions testified to Finney's insight about the importance of the personal connection between leader and follower; even with all other elements of the charismatic performance removed, that connection alone could provide a fulfilling experience for followers.

Everything William Jennings Bryan did during his night of triumph on the convention platform bore the imprint of James Rush, Jonathan Barber, and Charles Grandison Finney. When Bryan addressed the audience in his resonant voice; when he used gestures to play on the emotions of his listeners; when he spoke in a popular idiom; when he used verbal illustrations and drew those illustrations from the Bible; and when he allowed his followers, half-crazed with emotion, to carry him from the stage on their shoulders, Bryan drew on the tradition of charismatic stagecraft Rush, Barber, and Finney had pioneered. Other influences, too, shaped the leadership attitudes of Bryan and other charismatic figures – even if the leaders themselves did not recognize their importance.

* * *

As the sun rose one morning in 1887, Mary Baird Bryan found herself awakened by her husband. William Jennings Bryan had just returned from a speaking engagement, and the news could not wait. "Sitting on the edge of the bed," Mary remembered, "he began: 'Mary, I have had a strange experience. Last night I found that I had power over the audience. I could move them as I chose. I have more than usual power as a speaker. I know it. God grant I may use it wisely.' " Having reached this conclusion, Bryan raised his voice in prayer.[90]

It is telling that this account appeared in Mary Bryan's half of their joint memoirs, not in her husband's portion of the text, and that William Jennings Bryan offered no opinions on the source of his charismatic abilities or the wisdom of using it to persuade others. Many charismatic leaders after 1890 seemed incurious about their charismatic strengths and unafraid of their consequences, despite the controversies that had

[89] "President Shakes Hands with 10,000 at His Reception," *Trenton Evening Times*, January 1, 1907, 1–2.

[90] Bryan and Bryan, *The Memoirs of William Jennings Bryan*, 248–249.

surrounded personal magnetism only a decade earlier. To many in this new generation of charismatic practitioners, magnetism was simply a helpful tool that increased their persuasiveness on the stump; its possession led naturally to its use. Municipal reformer Brand Whitlock launched his charismatic oratorical career when his fellow reformer, Toledo mayor Samuel "Golden Rule" Jones, appeared in Whitlock's office with a request: "I want you to come out and speak." "On what subject?" Whitlock asked incredulously. "There's only one subject," responded Jones, "life ... Just speak what's in your heart." Without any further introspection, Whitlock agreed to help the mayor; soon Whitlock was speaking every week in favor of Jones' platform.[91] It was the same for religious leaders. Billy Sunday's autobiography contains a detailed description of his childhood, baseball career, and conversion, but only a sentence about his decision to become an evangelist: "I felt I was called definitely to enter Christian work."[92]

Sunday, of course, was participating in a long tradition of Christian prophets and preachers "called" to religious leadership by God, so he was unlikely to question such a revelation once he experienced it. Late-1800s American culture contained a tradition of secular oratory that boasted similar features. Despite the indifference of figures such as Bryan and Whitlock, other magnetic leaders evinced a deep interest in the rhetorical culture of previous generations. Noted political speakers such as Woodrow Wilson, Tom Watson, Jonathan P. Dolliver, Albert Jeremiah Beveridge, Robert Marion La Follette, and William E. Borah grew up reading the speeches of Abraham Lincoln, Daniel Webster, and Henry Clay, plus a cast of international orators that included Edmund Burke, William Gladstone, Demosthenes, and Cicero.[93] These young Americans imbibed the notion that an early American ideal of oratorical statesmanship had fallen into decline since the Civil War – but could, they hoped, be revived by their own generation.[94] Seventeen-year-old Watson filled his

[91] Brand Whitlock, *Forty Years of It* (New York: D. Appleton, 1914), 115–116.

[92] Billy Sunday, *The Sawdust Trail: Billy Sunday in His Own Words* (orig. pub. *Ladies' Home Journal*, September, October, November, December 1932, February, April 1933; Iowa City: University of Iowa Press, 2005), 69.

[93] Robert Alexander Kraig, "The Second Oratorical Renaissance," in J. Michael Hogan, *Rhetoric and Reform in the Progressive Era* (East Lansing, MI: Michigan State University Press, 2003), 15.

[94] *Ibid.*, 1,13; Robert Alexander Kraig, *Woodrow Wilson and the Lost World of the Oratorical Statesman* (College Station, TX: Texas A&M University Press, 2004), 4, 7–9, 27; Kenneth Cmiel, *Democratic Eloquence: The Fight over Popular Speech in Nineteenth-Century America* (New York: William Morrow, 1990), 248; Harry

journal with "Hints on Oratory" and similar comments during the 1873–1874 college term. "The power of the orator," he noted in one entry, "lies in the sympathy between him and the people. This is the chord which binds heart to heart; and when it is struck, thousands burst into tears or rouse into passion, like a single individual."[95] The twenty-year-old Dolliver wrote in 1878 that he wished to become "a fluent and attractive orator. It is the best hold a man can get in the world. It is the sure forerunner of influence among men."[96] Bryan summed up the ideal of the oratorical statesman in a 1906 essay. "The age of oratory has not passed," he wrote, "nor will it pass ... As long as there are human rights to be defended; as long as there are great interests to be guarded; as long as the welfare of nations is a matter for discussion, so long will public speaking have its place."[97]

This society-wide interest in oratory dovetailed closely with a corresponding tradition of heroism stemming from the writings of Thomas Carlyle. Middle-class Americans who had grown up with Carlyle's *On Heroes, Hero-Worship, and the Heroic in History* imbibed a version of the Carlylean ideal of heroism, with its uncompromising individualism and hard-nosed drive for success. M. Carey Thomas, later a social activist and president of Bryn Mawr College, was "carried away by Carlyle" as a teenager. "The fact is," she wrote at the age of fourteen, "I don't care much for any thing except dreaming about being grand & noble & famous."[98] "For a time I was a thrall of Carlyle," remembered sociologist Edward A. Ross; looking back at his twenty-year-old self, Ross recalled that "In my Carlyle *furore* ... I reached the apex and at the same time the end of

Thurston Peck, "Some Notes on Political Oratory," *The Bookman*, Vol. 4 (November 1896), 208–209.

95 Tom Watson, Journal, Watson Papers, University of North Carolina-Chapel Hill, quoted in C. Vann Woodward, *Tom Watson: Agrarian Rebel* (orig. pub. New York: Macmillan, 1938; New York: Oxford University Press, 1963), 28.

96 Quoted in Thomas Richard Ross, *Jonathan Prentiss Dolliver: A Study in Political Integrity and Independence* (Iowa City, IA: State Historical Society of Iowa, 1958), 31; Kraig, *Woodrow Wilson and the Lost World of the Oratorical Statesman*, 15.

97 William Jennings Bryan, "Introduction," in Bryan, ed., *The World's Famous Orations*, Vol. 1 (New York: Funk and Wagnalls, 1906), x.

98 M. Carey Thomas journal, November 10 and February 26, 1871, microfilm: reel 1, *The Papers of M. Carey Thomas in the Bryn Mawr College Archives*, ed. Lucy Fisher West (Woodbridge, CT: Research Publications, 1982), quoted in Barbara Sicherman, *Well-Read Lives: How Books Inspired a Generation of American Women* (Chapel Hill: University of North Carolina Press, 2010), 109.

my hero worship."[99] Reformer and social worker Jane Addams had a similar experience with Carlyle. She remembered reading *On Heroes* "with great enthusiasm" at the age of fifteen. "Carlyle," she wrote a few years later, "has a way of saying things that strikes me as it were my keynote."[100]

For many Americans, the historical figure of Napoleon Bonaparte seemed to embody this Carlylean model of heroic individualism. "The year 1894 was a Napoleon year," magazine publisher S. S. McClure noted in his autobiography.[101] In that year and the two after it, twenty-eight biographies of the French emperor reached publication in the United States; many achieved wide popularity.[102] Ida M. Tarbell's *A Short Life of Napoleon Bonaparte*, which McClure credited with doubling his magazine's circulation when it appeared in serial form, was a representative example.[103] Tarbell's narrative closed with a full-throated endorsement of Napoleon as a charismatic leader. "One may feel that he frequently sacrificed personal dignity to a theatrical desire to impose on the crowd as a hero of classic proportions, a god from Olympus," Tarbell wrote, "[b]ut he was greater as a man than as a warrior or statesman; greater in that rare and subtile [*sic*] personal quality which made men love him." Napoleon's power over others, Tarbell explained, stemmed from a "native, untrained" personality that awed followers with its vibrancy and unbridled force. Upon the announcement of Napoleon's death in the French parliament, "Sincere and deep emotion prevailed ... The whole House was under the sway of that strange and powerful emotion which Napoleon, as no other leader

[99] Edward Alsworth Ross, *Seventy Years of It: An Autobiography* (New York: D. Appleton-Century, 1936), 21, 30; Sicherman, *Well-Read Lives*, 291 n. 32.

[100] Jane Addams, *Twenty Years at Hull-House, with Autobiographical Notes* (New York: Macmillan, 1910), 36; Jane Addams to Eva Campbell, July 25, 1879, Eugene Goodrich Papers, York, Nebraska, quoted in Victoria Bissell Brown, *The Education of Jane Addams* (Philadelphia: University of Pennsylvania Press, 2004), 83; Louise W. Knight, *Citizen: Jane Addams and the Struggle for Democracy* (Chicago: University of Chicago Press, 2005), 68–69, 95.

[101] Samuel Sidney McClure, *My Autobiography* (New York: Frederick A. Stokes, 1914), 220; Theodore P. Greene, *America's Heroes: The Changing Models of Success in American Magazines* (New York: Oxford University Press, 1970), 110.

[102] T. J. Jackson Lears, *No Place of Grace: Antimodernism and the Transformation of American Culture, 1880–1920* (New York: Pantheon Books, 1981), 113.

[103] McClure, *My Autobiography*, 220.

who ever lived, was able to inspire."[104] The 40,000 new subscribers to *McClure's Magazine* testified to the broad interest in both experiencing and acquiring such a leadership style.

Despite their fascination with Carlyle and Napoleon, Americans recognized the authoritarian underpinnings of these figures and sought to channel their insights into a more socially conscious model of leadership. African American writer and activist W. E. B. Du Bois, another college-aged Carlyle devotee, delivered an 1888 commencement speech on Carlyle's favorite living leader, German chancellor Otto von Bismarck.[105] "The life of this powerful Chancellor illustrates the power of purpose, the force of an idea," Du Bois told his classmates. "It shows what a man can do if he will." Nevertheless, Bismarck's life "carries with it a warning lest we sacrifice a lasting good to a temporary advantage; lest we raise a nation and forget the people, become a Bismarck and not a Moses."[106] Americans hungry for moral heroism would have to find a gentler model of leadership than the one promoted by Carlyle.

Seekers of heroism found such a model in the figure of Abraham Lincoln, perhaps the most eulogized – and contested – figure in American history by the late 1800s.[107] Notwithstanding competing interpretations of the sixteenth president's heroism, Ida Tarbell's 1895 *Life of Abraham Lincoln* was a representative example of popular Lincoln literature. Tarbell's serialized biography increased subscriptions to *McClure's* by over three times as much as had her work on Napoleon.[108] Lincoln's leadership style involved not the promotion of his own power, Tarbell wrote, but a "lofty moral courage ... [that] was the logical result of life-long fidelity to his own conscience." Lincoln had achieved secular sainthood through "dogged struggle [and] constant repetitions of the few truths which he believed to be

104 Ida M. Tarbell, *A Short Life of Napoleon Bonaparte* (orig. pub. *McClure's Magazine*, 1894; New York: S. S. McClure, 1895), 223, 225, 228.

105 David Levering Lewis, *W. E. B. Du Bois, 1868–1919: Biography of a Race* (New York: Henry Holt, 1993), 74–75, 77.

106 W. E. B. Du Bois, "Bismarck ... My Hero," speech at Fisk University, 1888, microfilm: reel 80, W. E. B. Du Bois Papers, University of Massachusetts Amherst.

107 Roy P. Basler, *The Lincoln Legend: A Study in Changing Conceptions* (Boston: Houghton Mifflin, 1935), 3; David Donald, "Getting Right with Lincoln," in Donald, *Lincoln Reconsidered: Essays on the Civil War Era* (New York: Knopf, 1956), 12–13; Jason R. Jividen, *Claiming Lincoln: Progressivism, Equality, and the Battle for Lincoln's Legacy in Presidential Rhetoric* (DeKalb, IL: Northern Illinois University Press, 2011), 4–5.

108 McClure, *My Autobiography*, 221.

essential."[109] Tarbell's message was clear: in a democracy, good leadership took hard work, a steadfast moral compass, and a degree of unselfishness lacking in the careers of Bismarck and Napoleon.[110]

In such a cultural context, it is unsurprising that some charismatic leaders were not more introspective about their magnetism. Unlike their mid-nineteenth-century predecessors, turn-of-the-century Americans saw no contradiction between charisma and morality. Like many Americans of the period, charismatic leaders were openly ambitious, but they wanted to become both a Bismarck *and* a Moses, a Napoleon *and* a Lincoln – to use their persuasive powers to better their society. Most likely shared Bryan's prayer concerning charismatic ability: "God grant I may use it wisely." At the same time, charismatic leadership was about more than simply the choices and training of leaders themselves. When Bryan embarked on his national speaking tour in 1896, for instance, the organization of his travels had little to do with his views on leadership or his training in oratory. Instead, Bryan embedded his performance in a structure that was as important a part of charismatic movements as were the attitudes of leaders or the techniques of Rush, Barber, and Finney.

* * *

"Major James B. Pond," declared the writer and sometime vaudeville personage Elbert Hubbard, "was big, brusk, quibbling, insulting, dictatorial, painstaking, considerate and kind. He was the most exasperating and lovable man I ever knew." When Pond served as Hubbard's lecture manager on the vaudeville circuit, the cantankerous major proved remarkably effective at planning and executing a tour. "As a manager he was perfection," Hubbard recalled – "he knew the trains to a minute, and always knew, too, what to do if we missed the first train, or if the train was late. At the hall he saw that every detail was provided for. If the place was too hot, or too cold, somebody got thoroughly damned ... He regulated my hours of sleep, my meals, my exercise." Unfortunately, Pond matched this perfection as an impresario with a perfectly impossible temper. "When I lectured at Washington a policeman appeared at the box-office and demanded the amusement-license fee of five dollars ... Pond kicked him down the stairway, and kept his club as a souvenir.

[109] Ida M. Tarbell, *The Life of Abraham Lincoln*, Part Two (orig. pub. *McClure's Magazine*, 1895; New York: S. S. McClure, 1895), 262.

[110] See also Basler, *The Lincoln Legend*, esp. 103–163.

We got out on the midnight train before warrants could be served." As Hubbard soon learned, his manager considered such behavior normal. "Pond had so many notches cut on the butt of his pistol that he had ceased to count them," Hubbard concluded. "He left a trail of enemies wherever he traveled ... I cut my relationship with him because I did not care to be pained by seeing his form dangling from the crossbeam of a telegraph-pole."[111]

James Burton Pond was the antithesis of a charismatic leader; professional persuaders were rarely strung up by their audiences or arrested for assault. Nevertheless, Pond represented a type of personality, the lecture manager or organizer, that was indispensable to the business of charismatic movements. Given the daunting array of tasks required to keep such movements in working order – preparing and executing travel plans, renting halls, selling tickets, distributing literature, coordinating with local establishments, interacting with audiences – no speaker was prepared to handle the business alone. Every charismatic campaign had one or more Major Ponds lurking somewhere, whether coming along for the ride (as the real Major Pond was wont to do) or coordinating activities from home. Charismatic leaders might look to a friend or family member to serve as organizer for the movement; five-time Socialist presidential candidate Eugene V. Debs used his brother Theodore in this role.[112] Or leaders might rely on a volunteer campaign chairman; Debs did this too, in 1908, when Socialist leader J. Mahlon Barnes orchestrated the "Red Special" railroad campaign.[113] Finally, speakers might hire a professional manager–organizer, such as Major Pond. In any case, the choice was among the most important of any charismatic figure's career.

Leaders and managers had a close relationship, but a complex one. Next to the leader, the manager stood to gain more than anyone if a charismatic movement succeeded and to lose more than anyone if it failed. Depending on the type of manager used, that gain or loss might be financial as well as emotional. Managers were so important to the

[111] Elbert Hubbard, *In the Spotlight: Personal Experiences of Elbert Hubbard on the American Stage*, comp. John T. Hoyle (East Aurora, NY: The Roycrofters, 1917), 120–121.

[112] Nick Salvatore, *Eugene V. Debs: Citizen and Socialist* (orig. pub. 1982; 2nd ed., Urbana, IL: University of Illinois Press, 2007), 71–72.

[113] Ralph Tillotson, "Memory of the Red Special," in J. Robert Constantine, ed., *Debs Remembered: A Collection of Reminiscences* (Terre Haute, IN: Indiana State University (unpublished), 1981), reel 5, Papers of Eugene V. Debs microfilm edition.

charismatic enterprise that in some cases formal contracts listed the leader as the manager's employee. Bandleader John Philip Sousa inadvertently demonstrated the power of charismatic managers during a contract dispute in 1897. The incident concerned a managerial contract Sousa had signed five years earlier; after the manager's death, his widow, Ada P. Blakely, insisted on enforcing the document against Sousa in an unusually restrictive manner. Citing a clause that allowed her late husband to control the name of Sousa's band, Blakely charged in court that Sousa had violated his contract by using his own name in other enterprises. Blakely then astonished the court by claiming to own the rights to the name "Sousa" and demanding that the conductor be banned forever from using it to promote his own performances![114]

Charismatic organizers may not actually have owned their clients, body and soul – the court rejected Ada Blakely's interpretation of her contract – but organizers exercised a great deal of control over charismatic movements. As with charisma's platform techniques, its organizing networks and methods had a long history. Religious revivals, for instance, had been tightly organized and expertly promoted affairs since George Whitefield's time; Dwight Moody's campaigns in the mid-1800s were particularly renowned for their professionalized structure, which included weeks of local press appeals before Moody ever delivered a sermon.[115] It was the secular world, however, that provided the most far-reaching networks for charismatic speakers. In 1826, what was originally called the "lyceum movement" began under the auspices of geologist and teacher Josiah Holbrook.[116] As Holbrook conceived it, the lyceum was a local association offering a series of lectures on scientific and mechanical subjects for the purpose of educating rural Americans in technical skills. Though he did not say so explicitly, the lyceum also had a secondary purpose: to spread a budding middle-class ideology of edification and uplift to rural lower-class Americans.[117]

114 Paul E. Bierley, *John Philip Sousa, American Phenomenon* (Westerville, OH: Integrity Press, 1973), 62–64.

115 Thomas S. Kidd, *George Whitefield: America's Spiritual Founding Father* (New Haven: Yale University Press, 2014), 49; Bruce J. Evensen, *God's Man for the Gilded Age: D. L. Moody and the Rise of Modern Mass Evangelism* (New York: Oxford University Press, 2003), 40–41.

116 Carl Bode, *The American Lyceum: Town Meeting of the Mind* (Carbondale, IL: Southern Illinois University Press, 1956), 9–10.

117 *Ibid.*, 11–13; Angela G. Ray, *The Lyceum and Public Culture in the Nineteenth-Century United States* (East Lansing, MI: Michigan State University Press, 2005), 18, 30, 34; John E. Tapia, *Circuit Chautauqua: From Rural Education to Popular Entertainment*

Unsurprisingly, the resulting movement appealed more to the middle class themselves than to those they sought to influence; the mechanical element quickly lost prominence, too. What remained by the Civil War was a loose network of lyceums hosting a wide variety of speakers: educators, ministers, theater and entertainment acts, and early charismatic leaders, all uncomfortably sharing the same podiums.[118] Despite the popularity of its lectures, the lyceum system was completely disorganized. Individual lyceums had to coordinate their own schedules by soliciting speakers directly; the speakers themselves determined which offers to accept and coordinated their own travels to numerous unfamiliar locations. Once they arrived, they had little control over their accommodations. They might speak in a hall, a temporary structure, a tent, or the open air; their presentation might follow another act, an introduction, or nothing at all.[119] Simply put, the system was a mess; that it functioned as well as it did was surprising.

It was at this juncture that Major Pond entered the lyceum business. "I drifted into it," he wrote later, "the same as most people do who have to find some place for which they are fitted, or try to."[120] Pond, a Union army veteran and young newspaperman, volunteered in 1873 to serve as manager for a woman – an estranged wife of Mormon leader Brigham Young – who wanted to go on the lecture circuit. Pond procured a contract for his client from the prestigious Redpath Lecture Bureau.[121] Six years earlier, Bureau founder James Redpath had come up with an ingenious solution to the problem of lyceum organization. The growth of the American railroad network, Redpath recognized, made it possible for the first time for lecture booking and travel to be coordinated from a central location. "Mr. Redpath satisfied these lecturers that he could save them the trouble and annoyance of voluminous correspondence," Pond wrote, "and at the same time could obtain such fees as the lectures were worth ... By paying Redpath ten per cent. on all their business transactions they could be relieved of the care of bookings, and their income

(Jefferson, NC: McFarland & Co., 1997), 12; Charlotte M. Canning, *The Most American Thing in America: Circuit Chautauqua as Performance* (Iowa City: University of Iowa Press, 2005), 8; James R. Schultz, *The Romance of Small-Town Chautauquas* (Columbia, MO: University of Missouri Press, 2002), 1; Andrew C. Rieser, *The Chautauqua Moment: Protestants, Progressives, and the Culture of Modern Liberalism* (New York: Columbia University Press, 2003), 100–101.

118 Bode, *The American Lyceum*, 251. 119 *Ibid.*, 187.

120 James Burton Pond, *Eccentricities of Genius: Memories of Famous Men and Women of the Platform and Stage* (New York: G. W. Dillingham, 1900), xvii.

121 *Ibid.*, xx–xxi.

would not be diminished to say the least."[122] Redpath transformed the lecture circuit into an effective moneymaking enterprise. "His bureau revolutionized the lyceum and lecture field," Pond concluded. "It created a profession, and made the management of the work a business requiring skill and systematic care."[123] The lecture manager had arrived.

Pond himself ultimately became one of the greatest of the managers, first by buying out the Redpath Bureau itself and then by leaving to create his own successful organization.[124] Pond represented dozens of the most prominent American charismatic leaders and skilled public speakers, including Elbert Hubbard, Patrick Gilmore, Mark Twain, prohibitionist John Bartholomew Gough, abolitionists Wendell Phillips and Anna Elizabeth Dickinson, suffragists Elizabeth Cady Stanton and Susan B. Anthony, noted orator and Senator Chauncey M. Depew, African American advocates Frederick Douglass and Booker T. Washington, and even ministers Lyman Abbott and Newell Dwight Hillis.[125] He considered Henry Ward Beecher "my nearest and dearest friend" and served as his lecture promoter for eleven years; Pond was responsible for the minister's 1886 trip to England during which the Reverend Dawson reveled in Beecher's "new kind of oratory."[126] Beecher, Phillips, and Gough were, Pond wrote, "the triumvirate of lecture kings" whose enduring popularity made possible the survival of the lecture circuit. It is worth noting that two of the three were students, directly or indirectly, of Jonathan Barber.[127]

To read *Eccentricities of Genius* (1900), Pond's narrative of his managerial experiences, is to glimpse the crass commercial underbelly of the charismatic enterprise. Though Pond was surely skilled at managing railroad timetables, coordinating bookings, and preparing orators for their performances, his own interest remained with the financial part of the operation. "I had booked the balance of the tour of ninety more lectures at a very handsome profit," Pond boasted in a typical passage, "the lowest fee being £80 a lecture, and in some instances £250 ... Eleven weeks booked for five lectures a week, twenty-five per cent. of the guarantees paid in advance and in my bank in London. Good prospects indeed."[128] Pond crowed about his ability to wheedle clients and lecture venues into arrangements that profited him. He bragged about persuading novelist F. Marion Crawford to surrender a third of the profits from his lecture tour – far more than the 10 percent fee Redpath had charged.[129]

[122] *Ibid.*, 541. [123] *Ibid.*, 540. [124] *Ibid.*, xxv. [125] *Ibid.*, vii–ix. [126] *Ibid.*, 37, 64.
[127] *Ibid.*, 3. [128] *Ibid.*, 107. [129] *Ibid.*, 106, 456–457.

Once, Pond recalled, he had convinced Wendell Phillips to speak to a smaller audience in order to obtain a higher per capita speaking fee.[130] He even admitted to tricking the Danish violinist Ole Bull out of half the proceeds of a performance.[131] When Pond insisted "that the object of my work has never been simply to make money," he was likely the only person who believed the statement.[132]

Given Pond's attitude, it was not surprising that the most successful charismatic leaders – particularly those associated with religious revivalism and political campaigning – struck out on their own. Some charismatic figures continued to travel the lecture circuit – now rebranded "circuit Chautauqua" after the middle-class educational retreat in upstate New York – well into the twentieth century; Bryan and Billy Sunday became two of the main touring attractions.[133] "Men with soaring political ambitions have been heard this year with special interest," wrote circuit Chautauqua lecturer Robert Stuart MacArthur in 1905. "They have profoundly moved great audiences ... It is not too much to say that they can largely change the political complexion of the Central West."[134] Many other figures, however, developed their own separate touring apparatus, complete with in-house managers who were volunteers or employees of the leaders. There were many benefits to becoming independent in this way. For one thing, the more altruistic leaders could free themselves from the money-grubbing ways of Major Pond and his competitors. For another, they could gain power over two elements of the charismatic performance that even Major Pond could not control: the architecture of the performance space and the preparation of the audience before the speaker appeared. These two components represented the final elements of the charismatic operation; taken together with the speaking techniques inspired by Rush and Finney and the touring structure pioneered by the lecture managers, they comprised the technologies of charisma.

Charismatic leaders on speaking tours had four primary options when choosing a performance space: they could rent an existing lecture hall, erect a temporary structure of their own, set up a large canvas tent such as those used by camp meetings and circuses, or speak to their audiences in the open air. Each architectural type had its advantages. Renting a hall

[130] *Ibid.*, 541. [131] *Ibid.*, 546. [132] *Ibid.*, 554.

[133] Canning, *The Most American Thing in America*, 14; Tapia, *Circuit Chautauqua*, 56, 58.

[134] Robert Stuart MacArthur, "Chautauqua Assemblies and Political Ambitions," *The World To-Day*, Vol. 9, No. 4 (October 1905), 1074–1075.

allowed local representatives to schedule meetings without much feedback from the charismatic campaign and was thus the favored method of Pond and other managers. Some larger and newer halls were scientifically designed by sound engineers to maximize the acoustic quality and reach of onstage performances.[135] Tents, on the other hand, were popular among local office-seekers and partisan political organizations, as well as some Chautauqua circuits.[136] "Both sides, I should say all sides, will go to tent meetings," noted charismatic Cleveland mayor Tom L. Johnson, "while as [a] rule only partisans go to halls ... In a tent there is a freedom from restraint that is seldom present in halls."[137]

Nevertheless, the temporary structure and the open-air meeting became most popular speaking locations among charismatic figures. Temporary structures could be specially designed to control the flow of audience members and to maximize the acoustic properties of the space. For this reason, traveling evangelists found them particularly suited to the revival. Billy Sunday, for instance, refused to preach in a city unless its inhabitants agreed to erect a wooden tabernacle according to his exact specifications. In-house architect Joseph Spiece "was responsible for the 'turtle-back' roof which made it possible for the speaker's voice to be heard in remote corners of the big structure," according to Homer Rodeheaver. Spiece "also constructed the first device to hang directly above the speaker's head, which acted as a sort of sounding board. He named this the 'augiphone.' " Meanwhile, the tabernacle's two aisles channeled "trail-hitters" toward the pulpit in orderly rows so Sunday could shake hands on both sides of the podium at once.[138]

Unlike temporary structures, open-air meetings were cheap and required little preparation or travel time. The downside was that the audience was often distracted by outside events. Political "spellbinder" Curtis Guild, Jr., recalled having to compete with all manner of fire engines, streetcars, children shouting, food merchants hawking their wares, and even a drunk "bronco-buster" performing equestrian

[135] Emily Thompson, *The Soundscape of Modernity: Architectural Acoustics and the Culture of Listening in America, 1900–1933* (Cambridge, MA: MIT Press, 2002), 17–18.

[136] William Lawrence Slout, *Theatre in a Tent: The Development of a Provincial Entertainment* (Bowling Green, OH: Bowling Green University Popular Press, 1972), 40.

[137] Tom L. Johnson, *My Story*, ed. Elizabeth J. Hauser (New York: B. W. Huebsch, 1911), 82.

[138] Some sources spell the name "Speice." Rodeheaver, *Twenty Years with Billy Sunday*, 122; tabernacle blueprints, microfilm: reel 26, Papers of William and Helen Sunday, Grace College and Theological Seminary, Winona Lake, Indiana.

tricks.[139] Given the lack of structured space or police protection, audiences often became unruly. "An unpopular orator," New York governor Al Smith recalled, "might expect to meet almost anything from an egg to a tomato can."[140] Nevertheless, the style was particularly useful for national political candidates who wanted to speak to as many people as possible during a limited election cycle. Bryan, for example, chose this method for his 1896 whistle-stop campaign. The Democratic nominee traveled to some 250 scheduled lectures and made hundreds of unscheduled stops wherever he met a group of people crowded around the tracks.[141] Some of the scheduled speeches took place in rented halls, but Bryan delivered all of the unscheduled addresses from the rear platform of his train car.[142] The candidate averaged over six speeches a day during the campaign season and in some cases was barely introduced to spectators before the train began moving again; this pace was only possible because Bryan could reach his audiences without leaving his train.[143] Both major parties had adopted Bryan's rear-platform strategy by 1900, when Cleveland Frederick Bacon noted "a unique phase of political oratory" in which "Formal addresses in the large towns yielded chief place to the new spellbinding from the special car."[144] Meanwhile, J. Mahlon Barnes updated this train-platform oratory for Eugene Debs' 1908 "Red Special" campaign. Not only did the "Special" allow Debs to speak from the platform, it contained a mobile headquarters for his campaign, a vast store of socialist literature and campaign memorabilia, and even a sixteen-piece brass band to warm up the audience at each stop before Debs spoke.[145]

As the "Red Special" demonstrated, preparation of a lecture audience with music had a long history in American politics; similarly, Christian churches had long placed hymn-singing immediately before the sermon. Surprisingly, however, neither Finney nor Pond recognized the importance of the musical element in charismatic performance. Pond viewed music primarily as a competitor to oratory; he lamented the rise of light

[139] Curtis Guild, Jr., "The Spellbinder," *Scribner's*, November 1912, 565.

[140] Alfred E. Smith, "Spellbinding," *Saturday Evening Post*, Vol. 202, No. 47 (May 24, 1930), 3.

[141] Kazin, *A Godly Hero*, 68. [142] Harpine, *From the Front Porch to the Front Page*, 17.

[143] William Jennings Bryan, *The First Battle: A Story of the Campaign of 1896* (Chicago: W. B. Conkey, 1896), 301–302.

[144] Cleveland Frederick Bacon, "Itinerant Speechmaking in the Last Campaign," *Arena*, Vol. 85 (1901), 410.

[145] H. Wayne Morgan, *Eugene V. Debs: Socialist for President* (Syracuse, NY: Syracuse University Press, 1962), 100–101.

opera as the primary reason for a decline in lyceum ticket sales.[146] Finney, for his part, dismissed music as an inherently cheerful activity that detracted from the seriousness of the revival. "I never knew a singing revival [to] amount to much," he scoffed.[147] Both men misunderstood the curious power of music to move people and the connection, observed by Patrick Gilmore's audiences, between that power and the equally strange emotional potency of charismatic performance.

In fact, music and charisma were closely linked phenomena. John Philip Sousa saw his ensemble as "a one-man band," he told the *London Daily Express* in 1905. "Only, instead of having actual metallic wires to work the instruments, I strike after magnetic ones. I feel every one of my fifty-eight musicians is linked up with me by a cable of magnetism … Every single member of my band is doing exactly what I make him do."[148] His own leadership of his musicians, Sousa felt, mirrored charismatic leaders' hold over their audiences. Accordingly, a musical prelude to a charismatic speech helped mold the audience into a unified body and made them more receptive to the speaker's persuasive techniques.

Only certain types of music would do, however. Just as with the Finney speaking style, audiences responded best to music they considered simple, informal, and memorable. It was Finney's revivalist successor Dwight Moody who first recognized that preparatory music must mimic a popular idiom in order to have the desired effect on the audience. When Moody met Gospel singer Ira D. Sankey at an 1870 convention in Indianapolis, he knew at once that the two of them could create such music together. "You will have to … come to Chicago and help me in my work," Moody informed the astonished Sankey, "I have been looking for you for the last eight years."[149] Moody and Sankey coauthored a series of gospel hymnals during the 1870s, with Moody writing the words and Sankey the music. The Moody and Sankey hymnals made gospel music the standard style for American camp meetings.[150] Later, Homer

146 Pond, *Eccentricities of Genius*, 543.

147 Finney, *Lectures on Revivals of Religion*, 127.

148 *London Daily Express* interview reprinted in *Musical Courier*, February 8, 1905, 23, quoted in Neil Harris, *Cultural Excursions: Marketing Appetites and Cultural Tastes in Modern America* (Chicago: University of Chicago Press, 1990), 210.

149 Ira D. Sankey, *My Life and the Story of the Gospel Hymns* (Philadelphia: The Sunday School Times Co., 1906), 21.

150 Lyle W. Dorsett, *A Passion for Souls: The Life of D. L. Moody* (Chicago: Moody Press, 1997), 226; Sandra S. Sizer, *Gospel Hymns and Social Religion: The Rhetoric of Nineteenth-Century Revivalism* (Philadelphia: Temple University Press, 1978), 5.

Rodeheaver updated the gospel song repertoire at Sunday's revivals; he added more popular tunes and even secular songs that fit Sunday's message.[151] The goal, Rodeheaver explained, "was to bridge that gap between the popular song of the day and the great hymns and gospel songs, and to give to men a simple, easy lilting melody which they could learn the first time they heard it, and which they could whistle and sing wherever they might be."[152] Secular political campaigns, with their brass bands and standard march tunes, followed the same principle: audience members linked to one another by appealing music were thoroughly prepared to become charismatic followers and, hopefully, political volunteers.

This, then, was the charismatic structure in which Bryan participated during his 1896 campaign tour. It was largely the structure he found waiting for him, for Bryan himself possessed little formal campaign organization, and the Democratic Party apparatus, alienated by his brash free-silver campaign, was not eager to help him. When Bryan embarked on his trip, only his wife and a cadre of reporters traveled with him.[153] Seemingly overnight, the elements of the charismatic movement took shape around him. Speaking invitations poured in from across the country; parties met Bryan's train at rural depots to listen to impromptu open-air speeches; brass bands materialized in small towns to prepare audiences for his remarks.[154] Bryan brought the speaking techniques and handshakes of personal magnetism; his audiences supplied the rest. It was an almost miraculous convergence of charismatic speaker and receptive audience. But Bryan was lucky; not all Americans possessed of charismatic qualities could command such audiences successfully. Bryan found Americans predisposed to see him as a savior, but many less fortunate leaders found themselves portrayed as comical, threatening, or worse.

* * *

"My intuitions told me," Frances E. Willard recalled thinking as an eighteen-year-old in 1857, "that a woman ought to be at least as good a speaker as a man, and quite as popular."[155] Nine years later, Willard experienced similar feelings after listening to charismatic orator Anna

[151] McLoughlin, *Billy Sunday Was His Real Name*, 82.
[152] Rodeheaver, *Twenty Years with Billy Sunday*, 78. [153] Bryan, *The First Battle*, 300.
[154] Melder, "Bryan the Campaigner," 73.
[155] Willard, *Glimpses of Fifty Years*, 569–570.

Dickinson.[156] "What she said," Willard wrote later, "set vibrating within my spirit the sacred chord of patriotism . . . Going home that night I could not sleep, for I heard as clearly as I had done in the audience the cadence of that wondrous voice, its courage, its martial ring, and its unmeasured pathos."[157] Soon, it was Willard's turn to speak in the charismatic style when Chicago temperance leaders asked her to address an 1874 meeting. "I was frightened by the crowd and overwhelmed by a sense of my own emptiness and inadequacy," Willard wrote. "What I said I do not know except that I was with the [temperance] women heart, hand and soul, in this wonderful new 'Everybody's War.' "[158] Willard had found a calling, she realized: she would become a charismatic leader.

At first, Willard's oratorical career was a success. She spoke on the temperance question and religious subjects in numerous pulpits, lecture halls, and conferences.[159] She soon mastered extemporaneous speaking and other charismatic techniques; Willard and her friends noted marked improvement in her performances.[160] Finally, Willard got her big chance: Dwight Moody invited her to join his tour as chief minister for his women's meetings, and she agreed.[161] Once Willard began touring with the revivalist, however, things began to unravel. First, Moody neglected to pay Willard for her services; she was forced to give additional temperance lectures in order to earn enough to stay with the revival. When Moody found out Willard was giving outside lectures, he paid her belatedly but ordered her to end her lecturing career: "I want all there is of you for the Boston [revival] meetings."[162] Ultimately, Willard was unable to continue working with Moody. "It was my dream to do this," Willard lamented later, "to rally under Mr. Moody's indirect influence, all the leaders, men and women, of our growing [temperance] host." But Moody's domineering behavior and Willard's independence made such a partnership impossible. "The jacket was too straight," Willard concluded, "I could not wear it."[163]

A straitjacket was a fitting metaphor for the experience of many women who aspired to charismatic leadership. Certainly there was no shortage of women speakers who used magnetic techniques. Anna Dickinson, whose oratory against slavery and gender inequality had kept Willard awake at

[156] Ruth Bordin, *Frances Willard: A Biography* (Chapel Hill, NC: University of North Carolina Press, 1986), 84.
[157] Willard, *Glimpses of Fifty Years*, 570. [158] *Ibid.*, 336. [159] *Ibid.*, 344–347.
[160] *Ibid.*, 336–337, 347. [161] *Ibid.*, 356. [162] *Ibid.*, 358–359. [163] *Ibid.*, 361.

night, remained the "Queen of the Lyceum," in Major Pond's words, until her 1874 retirement.[164] Willard's friend Mary A. Livermore, a women's rights advocate, ruled the platform during the last few decades of the nineteenth century.[165] Suffragist pioneers Susan B. Anthony and Elizabeth Cady Stanton lectured widely, while suffrage leader Anna Howard Shaw, a full-time orator trained as a Methodist preacher, dazzled audiences with her rhetorical talents.[166] Jane Addams promoted social welfare policies from the platform in Chicago and elsewhere.[167] Feminist author Charlotte Perkins Gilman, whose great-uncle was Henry Ward Beecher, took part in the family profession by lecturing to large crowds around the nation; the *Oakland Enquirer* described her as "a most brilliant and effective platform speaker … [who]never fails to rivet the attention of her hearers."[168] Hatchet-wielding prohibitionist Carry A. Nation toured the nation inciting her listeners to violence against saloon-keepers.[169] Radical suffragist and free-love advocate Victoria Woodhull, who had exposed the Beecher–Tilton scandal, was frequently described as magnetic during her 1870s lecture tours.[170] Mary Harris "Mother" Jones won adoring followers as a labor lecturer.[171] And fiery Populist Party orator Mary Elizabeth Lease stumped the country in the

[164] Pond, *Eccentricities of Genius*, 152; J. Matthew Gallman, *America's Joan of Arc: The Life of Anna Elizabeth Dickinson* (New York: Oxford University Press, 2006), 136–137.

[165] Willard, *Glimpses of Fifty Years*, 572; Pond, *Eccentricities of Genius*, 155; Wendy Hamand Venet, *A Strong-Minded Woman: The Life of Mary A. Livermore* (Amherst, MA: University of Massachusetts Press, 2005), 120–121.

[166] Pond, *Eccentricities of Genius*, 144; Wil A. Linkugel and Martha Solomon, *Anna Howard Shaw: Suffrage Orator and Reformer* (New York: Greenwood Press, 1991), 13–15; Franzen, *Anna Howard Shaw*, 12–13, 46–47; Susan Schultz Huxman, "Passing the Torch of Women's Rights: Elizabeth Cady Stanton, Anna Howard Shaw, and Carrie Chapman Catt," in Martha S. Watson and Thomas R. Burkholder, eds., *The Rhetoric of Nineteenth-Century Reform* (East Lansing, MI: Michigan State University Press, 2008), 357.

[167] Brown, *The Education of Jane Addams*, 1, 253; Knight, *Citizen*, 265–266.

[168] *Oakland Enquirer*, 1900, quoted in Judith A. Allen, "Charlotte Perkins Gilman, Progressivism, and Feminism, 1890–1935," in Hogan, ed., *Rhetoric and Reform in the Progressive Era*, 432; Judith A. Allen, *The Feminism of Charlotte Perkins Gilman: Sexualities, Histories, Progressivism* (Chicago: University of Chicago Press, 2009), 270, 274.

[169] Fran Grace, *Carry A. Nation: Retelling the Life* (Bloomington, IN: Indiana University Press, 2001), 2.

[170] Amanda Frisken, *Victoria Woodhull's Sexual Revolution: Political Theater and the Popular Press in Nineteenth-Century America* (Philadelphia: University of Pennsylvania Press, 2004), 124.

[171] Elliott J. Gorn, *Mother Jones: The Most Dangerous Woman in America* (New York: Hill and Wang, 2001), 3–4.

1890s, urging farmers to "raise less corn and more hell"; her "golden voice" had such "hypnotic qualities," wrote journalist William Allen White, that "she could recite the multiplication table and set a crowd hooting or hurrahing at her will."[172] These and many other women speakers played highly visible roles in American society.

Magnetic though many of these women were, contemporaries were more likely to view them as motherly or matronly. With exceptions such as Dickinson and Woodhull, most of the leading women orators of the period began their lecturing careers after the age of forty; some were much older. Many women leaders actively embraced elements of the domestic, maternal mythology prevalent in American culture. "Mother" Jones probably went the furthest in remaking her public image to fit common maternal ideals.[173] Jones was "the new type of mother," explained labor journalist Mary Field, "the mother whose brooding, yearning motherhood extends beyond the nursery where its own child is fed ... anywhere, the world over, that a child cries for bread and love."[174] When Jones traveled, Field reported, "At every stop of the train, brakemen, roadmen, laborers came aboard just to shake their Mother's hand, to bless her, to bring her baskets of fruit and boxes of candy."[175] Listening to one of Jones' speeches "is one of the mileposts in my life that I can easily locate," recalled activist Kate Richards O'Hare. "Like a mother talking to her errant boys she taught and admonished that night in words that went home to every heart." The oration convinced O'Hare to become a Socialist.[176] Despite Jones' charismatic reception, she and others, including Shaw, Livermore, and Addams, tended to downplay their own personal magnetism.[177] To some degree, these women eschewed charismatic techniques in favor of a clear, logical, and less-controversial speaking style. To some degree, too, male

[172] The quote was not Lease's, but she approved of its substance. Rebecca Edwards, "Mary E. Lease and the Populists: A Reconsideration," *Kansas History: A Journal of the Central Plains*, Vol. 35 (Spring 2012), 27; William Allen White, *The Autobiography of William Allen White* (New York: Macmillan, 1946), 218.

[173] Gorn, *Mother Jones*, 118, 228–229; Mari Boor Tonn, "Radical Labor in a Feminine Voice: The Rhetoric of Mary Harris 'Mother' Jones and Elizabeth Gurley Flynn," in Watson and Burkholder, eds., *The Rhetoric of Nineteenth-Century Reform*, 241–243.

[174] Mary Field, "She Stirreth Up the People," *Everyman*, April–May 1914, 8.

[175] *Ibid.*, 10.

[176] Kate Richards O'Hare, "How I Became a Socialist Agitator," *The Socialist Woman*, Vol. 2 (October 1908): 4.

[177] Venet, *A Strong-Minded Woman*, 182–183; Linkugel and Solomon, *Anna Howard Shaw*, 15–17.

commentators and audiences misinterpreted or ignored female charismatic speech – as when Socialist writer Floyd Dell accused the often-charismatic Addams of failing "to imbue the movement in which she is a leader with her own spirit."[178]

The landscape of female public speaking in late-nineteenth-century America was a complex one. In the early 1800s, young women had regular access to elocution textbooks, along with certain, mostly academic, opportunities to speak in public; Barber's *Practical Treatise on Gesture* included numerous illustrations of female oratory.[179] These opportunities evaporated as quickly as they had appeared, however.[180] By midcentury, American society was fully immersed in what historians have termed "sentimental culture" – a focus on the emotion, or "sensibility," of private experience. Sentimental culture ordained women the high priests of sensibility and decreed that they should exercise their influence, and their speech, exclusively within the home or parlor.[181] Accordingly, public speech came to be gendered masculine, private speech feminine. James Rush himself condemned women's use of "offensive" falsetto and "careless pronunciation" in public.[182]

As sentimentalism declined in the second half of the century, however, women began to argue once again that their voices belonged in the public square. Relying on a combination of domestic and egalitarian arguments, women preachers and elocution teachers penned treatises demanding an increase in female public speaking.[183] "The mother-heart of God will never be known to the world," argued Willard in one such volume, "until translated into terms of speech by mother-hearted

[178] Floyd Dell, *Women as World Builders: Studies in Modern Feminism* (Chicago: Forbes, 1913), 36; Allen, *The Feminism of Charlotte Perkins Gilman*, 276; Nan Johnson, *Gender and Rhetorical Space in American Life, 1866–1910* (Carbondale, IL: Southern Illinois University Press, 2002), 121–122.

[179] Barber, *A Practical Treatise on Gesture*, unnumbered back matter; Carolyn Eastman, *A Nation of Speechifiers: Making an American Public after the Revolution* (Chicago: University of Chicago Press, 2009), 62–64; Lindal Buchanan, *Regendering Delivery: The Fifth Canon and Antebellum Women Rhetors* (Carbondale, IL: Southern Illinois University Press, 2005), 12–13, 44–47.

[180] Buchanan, *Regendering Delivery*, 44.

[181] Karen Halttunen, *Confidence Men and Painted Women: A Study of Middle-Class Culture in America, 1830–1870* (New Haven: Yale University Press, 1982), 56–59; Johnson, *Gender and Rhetorical Space in American Life*, 49–50.

[182] Rush, *The Philosophy of the Human Voice*, 147.

[183] Jane Donawerth, *Conversational Rhetoric: The Rise and Fall of a Women's Tradition, 1600–1900* (Carbondale, IL: Southern Illinois University Press, 2012), 73–75, 108–109, 116–117.

women."[184] Suffragists, temperance organizers, and other women leaders also advocated for an increased female presence on the lecture platform; Stanton and Anthony ran an informal school of oratory in New York for the purpose of training suffragist speakers.[185] Women's colleges, long a center of female rhetorical training, even sparked an oratorical craze in the 1880s and 1890s by promoting an elocution system devised by musician François Delsarte. The Delsarte system, later satirized in the musical *The Music Man*, coupled a distinctive speaking style with neoclassical togas for women practitioners.[186] Yet popular male opposition to women's public speaking continued.[187] Echoing Rush's complaints, the novelist Henry Adams spoke for many American men when he wrote in 1907 of his dismay at hearing female seminary students who "shrieked and bawled to each other." Women's careless colloquialism of speech, Adams warned, risked turning the English language into "an inexpensive generalized mumble or jumble, a tongueless slobber or snarl or whine," as debased as "the moo of the cow, the bray of the ass, and the bark of the dog."[188]

Though they were concerned about women's public speech in general, American men felt particularly threatened by female charismatic oratory. While they acknowledged that some modes of speaking might be better suited to women, men tended to identify charismatic performance

[184] Frances E. Willard, *Woman in the Pulpit* (Boston: D. Lothrop, 1888), 46–47.

[185] Elizabeth Cady Stanton, Susan B. Anthony, and Matilda Joslyn Gage, *History of Woman Suffrage*, Vol. II: 1861–1876 (Rochester, NY: Susan B. Anthony, 1881), 400; Barbara A. White, *The Beecher Sisters* (New Haven: Yale University Press, 2003), 158.

[186] Lisa Suter, "The Arguments They Wore: The Role of the Neoclassical Toga in American Delsartism," in David Gold and Catherine L. Hobbs, ed., *Rhetoric, History, and Women's Oratorical Education: American Women Learn to Speak* (New York: Routledge, 2013), 134–139; Joanne Wagner, "'Intelligent Members or Restless Disturbers': Women's Rhetorical Styles, 1880–1920," in Andrea A. Lunsford, ed., *Reclaiming Rhetorica: Women in the Rhetorical Tradition* (Pittsburgh, PA: University of Pittsburgh Press, 1995), 186–188; Kathryn M. Conway, "Woman Suffrage and the History of Rhetoric at the Seven Sisters Colleges, 1865–1919," in Lunsford, ed., *Reclaiming Rhetorica*, 221–222; Meredith Willson, *The Music Man*, dir. by Morton DaCosta (Burbank, CA: Warner Bros., 1962).

[187] Caroline Field Levander, *Voices of the Nation: Women and Public Speech in Nineteenth-Century American Literature and Culture* (Cambridge, UK: Cambridge University Press, 1998), 12–21.

[188] Henry James, "The Speech of American Women," in James, *Henry James on Culture: Collected Essays on Politics and the American Social Scene*, ed. Pierre A. Walker (Lincoln, NE: University of Nebraska Press, 1999), 69, 76, 77; Mary Beard, "The Public Voice of Women," *London Review of Books*, Vol. 36, No. 6 (March 20, 2014), 12–13.

specifically with masculinity – with the muscular Christianity of a Billy Sunday or the "strenuous life" of a Theodore Roosevelt.[189] Accordingly, male commentators often lampooned women charismatic speakers as masculine, unwomanly, or worse. "When I see and hear women speak in public," future president Woodrow Wilson wrote to his fiancée while a young graduate student, he experienced two emotions: a "chilled, scandalized feeling" and "a good deal of whimsical delight." A woman orator, he concluded, could not possibly be "more manly in her bearing."[190] William Allen White mirrored such revulsion toward charismatic women when he wrote that Mary Lease "often looked like a kangaroo ... was at least as sexless as a cyclone ... either her homemaking qualities had been frustrated or they had come to some calamitous close."[191]

As Willard's experience made clear, men who opposed female charismatic leadership could do much more than ridicule women speakers of whom they disapproved. Once, in the Michigan wilderness, a wagon driver got Anna Howard Shaw alone and threatened to rape her; she pulled a gun on him and forced him to drive her the rest of the way to her destination. In another Michigan city, temperance opponents actually set fire to the lecture hall while Shaw was delivering a speech inside; Shaw bravely marched the audience members out of the hall, waiting until she could see the flames and smell the smoke before making her own exit.[192] Carry Nation experienced the demoralizing effects of anti-charismatic men when she befriended the young journalist E. A. Braniff in 1901. At first, Braniff praised Nation in his articles, but soon his letters to her turned critical and patronizing.[193] "I don't care a rap about your anti-saloon work," he wrote her on March 21. "I wish you were out of it ... I'd like to know you were safe, that you were going to live quietly the rest of your life, just be nice and respectable and

[189] Clifford Putney, *Muscular Christianity: Manhood and Sports in Protestant America, 1880–1920* (Cambridge, MA: Harvard University Press, 2001), 59; David Morgan, "Protestant Visual Culture and the Challenges of Urban America during the Progressive Era," in John M. Giggie and Diane Winston, eds., *Faith in the Market: Religion and the Rise of Urban Commercial Culture* (New Brunswick, NJ: Rutgers University Press, 2002), 48–49.

[190] Woodrow Wilson to Ellen Axson, October 31, 1884, *The Papers of Woodrow Wilson*, Vol. 3, ed. Arthur S. Link (Princeton: Princeton University Press, 1967), 389.

[191] White, *The Autobiography of William Allen White*, 218–219.

[192] Shaw and Jordan, *The Story of a Pioneer*, 75–78, 169–171; Franzen, *Anna Howard Shaw*, 1.

[193] E. A. Braniff, "How I Ran Out on Carrie Nation," *The Commonweal*, March 19, 1948, 558.

contented and happy."[194] When Nation failed to stop her "unrespectable" charismatic activities, Braniff refused to be seen with her at a speech she delivered in his hometown.[195] Similarly, Alma White, who in 1878 had a conversion experience very similar to Finney's, ran into trouble when she sought to become a revivalist preacher in her own right.[196] Male leaders in both the Methodist and Holiness church organizations – including White's own husband – systematically discriminated against White by criticizing her choices, opposing her ordination, and passing her over for opportunities to preach. Frustrated and angry, White had to found her own denomination in order to pursue her evangelism unfettered.[197]

The case of Maria Woodworth-Etter stood as a stark warning to women who defied American men's distrust of female charismatic leadership. One of the most dramatic evangelists of the period, Woodworth-Etter's meetings combined two of the most controversial and emotional revival techniques – faith healing and sending audience members into a trance during which they often spoke in tongues.[198] Her approach provided a model for the emerging Pentecostal movement.[199] Yet when Woodworth-Etter set up her revival tent in St. Louis in August 1890, two local male doctors charged her with clinical insanity.[200] To exert such influence over her followers, Dr. Theodore Diller insisted, Woodworth-Etter must be crazy. "The woman is densely ignorant," Diller announced to the press. "I view with alarm the idea of such a woman exerting hypnotic powers promiscuously." Diller believed Woodworth-Etter was insane because he simply could not accept that her charismatic abilities could have caused her audiences' reactions: "I do not regard the woman as being endowed with any special degree of personal magnetism, and think the effects she produces are due to her peculiar method of preaching and to the

194 E. A. Braniff to Carry A. Nation, March 21, 1901, Carry Amelia Nation Papers, Kansas Historical Society, Topeka, Kansas.

195 Braniff, "How I Ran Out on Carry Nation," 560.

196 Alma White, *The Story of My Life* (Zarephath, NJ: Pillar of Fire, 1919), 224; Susie Cunningham Stanley, *Feminist Pillar of Fire: The Life of Alma White* (Cleveland, OH: Pilgrim Press, 1993), 10–12.

197 *Ibid.*, 43–44.

198 Wayne E. Warner, *The Woman Evangelist: The Life and Times of Charismatic Evangelist Maria B. Woodworth-Etter* (Metuchen, NJ: Scarecrow Press, 1986), xi, 75; Priscilla Pope-Levison, *Building the Old Time Religion: Women Evangelists in the Progressive Era* (New York: New York University Press, 2013), 37–38.

199 Warner, *The Woman Evangelist*, 159. 200 Taves, *Fits, Trances, & Visions*, 241.

surroundings."[201] Woodworth-Etter eventually won a reprieve from a local judge and continued her tour, but the message was clear: female charismatic performance led to punishment from powerful men.[202]

Yet women leaders did not simply give up on the charismatic leadership style that had proved so powerful in the hands of their male compatriots. Some, such as White and Woodworth-Etter, went right on using charismatic techniques as if nothing had happened. Others chose to downplay the charismatic elements of their speech in order to preserve their effectiveness on the stump.[203] Willard herself partially adopted this approach; after the unsavory experience with Moody, she adopted a new rhetorical style – featuring more "practical common-sense" with none of "the sentimental stuff," according to the *Leavenworth Daily Press*.[204] Still other women found ways to mask their charisma while preserving its effectiveness. The leaders of the 1873–1874 "Women's Crusade" for temperance, many of whom were charismatic speakers in their own right, followed this model. Early on, the crusaders learned that asking a charismatic male temperance lecturer to speak at the beginning of a local campaign could legitimize charismatic speech within the movement and pave the way for female speakers to use the same techniques.[205] A temperance meeting in Stryker, Ohio, began with "some very able and appropriate remarks by Col. E. D. Bradley," which warmed up the audience and made them receptive to charismatic stagecraft. Next, the female president of the Stryker temperance league dramatically held aloft her drunken husband's wine bottle. "Look at it, rumseller," she announced, "here is the poison dealt out by you to the once loved husband of my youth ... Can you wonder that I raise my voice against this terrible evil? Sisters, will you help me?"[206] Bradley's speech set the tone for the meeting, but

201 "Mrs. Woodworth's Mind," *St. Louis Globe-Democrat*, September 2, 1890, 4.

202 Taves, *Fits, Trances, & Visions*, 242.

203 Karlyn Kohrs Campbell, *Man Cannot Speak For Her*, Vol. I (New York: Praeger, 1989), 12–13.

204 *Leavenworth Daily Press*, May 16, 1880, microfilm: reel 32, Women's Christian Temperance National Headquarters Historical Files, quoted in Amy R. Slagell, " 'Making the World More Homelike': The Reform Rhetoric of Frances E. Willard," in Watson and Burkholder, eds., *The Rhetoric of Nineteenth-Century Reform*, 159, 161; Bordin, *Frances Willard*, 179. See also the description of Willard's speaking style by C. J. Little in Anna A. Gordon, *The Beautiful Life of Frances E. Willard: A Memorial Volume* (Chicago: Woman's Temperance Publishing Association, 1898), 321.

205 Jack S. Blocker, Jr., *"Give to the Winds Thy Fears": The Women's Temperance Crusade, 1873–1874* (Westport, CT: Greenwood Press, 1985), 31–32.

206 *Christian Advocate*, May 7, 1874, quoted in *ibid.*, 94.

it was ultimately the charismatic woman, not the man, with whom the audience connected.

The "straitjacket" of American culture certainly hampered women's efforts to exercise charismatic authority. Many women, however, accepted the challenge and forged successful charismatic speaking careers despite the strong headwinds they faced. In doing so, women such as Willard challenged the connection between charisma and masculinity. "It was my dream to do this," Willard wrote of her charismatic career; she and other American women were unwilling to give up easily on that dream.

* * *

The Atlanta Exposition's opening-night program on September 18, 1895, began with a performance by "Gilmore's Band," though Patrick Gilmore himself had died three years earlier. New bandleader Victor Herbert began with the national anthem and then switched to "Dixie" – eliciting cheers from his mostly white listeners.[207] With the audience thus prepared, the speakers mounted the podium. Some white audience members shouted angrily when they saw that one of the speakers was African American, but their tone changed to delight as Tuskegee Institute president Booker T. Washington began to speak.[208] "Within ten minutes," wrote *New York World* reporter James Creelman, "the multitude was in an uproar of enthusiasm ... It was as if the orator had bewitched them ... The whole audience was on its feet in a delirium of applause." Both white listeners and the few African Americans present were moved by Washington's speech. "Most of the Negroes in the audience were crying, perhaps without knowing just why." Creelman, like many listeners, found Washington's performance electrifying. "A Negro Moses," he concluded, "stood before a great audience of white people and delivered an oration that marks a new epoch in the history of the South."[209]

The Atlanta Exposition speech – later known as the "Atlanta Compromise" – propelled Washington overnight to national stardom of a sort no black leader since the great Frederick Douglass had enjoyed. In the aftermath of Washington's speech, Creelman was far from the only

[207] "Hail to the New South," *Philadelphia Inquirer*, September 19, 1895, 1, 3.

[208] David W. Blight, *Race and Reunion: The Civil War in American Memory* (Cambridge, MA: Belknap Press of Harvard University Press, 2001), 329.

[209] *New York World*, September 18, 1895, quoted in Booker T. Washington, *Up from Slavery: An Autobiography* (New York: A. L. Burt, 1900), 238, 240, 241.

American, white or black, to compare the college president with Moses.[210] "You are our Moses," wrote W. J. Cansler, an African American affiliated with Knoxville College, to Washington; he added that the orator was "destined to lead our race out of the difficulties and dangers which beset our pathway and surround us on all sides."[211] "God undoubtedly has exalted you to be our Moses," concurred Washington's former classmate Henry B. Rice.[212] Meanwhile, white U.S. Steel magnate Andrew Carnegie seemed determined to outdo all others in praising Washington's leadership: "Booker Washington," he declared, "is the combined Moses and Joshua of his people."[213]

As this religious imagery suggested, Washington was every inch a charismatic leader. "He has fire and magnetism and gifts of oratory which few of our Northern orators possess, whether they be black or white," confirmed the ubiquitous Major Pond.[214] Like many charismatic speakers, Washington trained as a debater in college and through church organizations.[215] He developed a conversational and extemporaneous style of address, filled with narrative examples and punctuated by well-timed "stops" designed to convey emotional significance to his audiences.[216] Washington himself reveled in his charismatic abilities: "It seems to me," he wrote in his autobiography, "that there is rarely such a combination of mental and physical delight in any effort as that which comes to a public speaker when he feels that he has a great

210 See examples in Wilson Jeremiah Moses, *Black Messiahs and Uncle Toms: Social and Literary Manipulations of a Religious Myth* (University Park, PA: Pennsylvania State University Press, 1982), 246 n. 2; David H. Jackson, Jr., *Booker T. Washington and the Struggle against White Supremacy: The Southern Educational Tours, 1908–1912* (New York: Palgrave Macmillan, 2008), 63.

211 W. J. Cansler to Booker T. Washington, September 26, 1895, in Louis R. Harlan, ed., *The Booker T. Washington Papers, Volume 4: 1895–98* (Urbana, IL: University of Illinois Press, 1975), 30.

212 Henry B. Rice to Booker T. Washington, December 28, 1898, in Harlan, ed., *The Booker T. Washington Papers, Volume 4*, 551.

213 Andrew Carnegie, "The Negro in America," speech delivered October 16, 1907 (Inverness: Committee of Twelve, 1907), 28; Emma L. Thornbrough, "Booker T. Washington as Seen by his White Contemporaries," *Journal of Negro History*, Vol. 53, No. 2 (April 1968), 162.

214 Pond, *Eccentricities of Genius*, 31.

215 Louis R. Harlan, *Booker T. Washington: The Making of a Black Leader, 1856–1901* (New York: Oxford University Press, 1972), 68, 85.

216 Jane Gottschalk, "The Rhetorical Strategy of Booker T. Washington," *Phylon*, Vol. 27, No. 4 (4th Quarter 1966), 390–391; Carla Willard, "Timing Impossible Subjects: The Marketing Style of Booker T. Washington," *American Quarterly*, Vol. 53, No. 4 (December 2001), 631–632.

audience completely within his control."[217] In the years after his Atlanta speech, Washington made several lecture swings through Southern states; his charismatic speaking style during these tours cemented his leadership and won him an army of supporters.[218] Like other charismatic figures, Washington elicited an intensely emotional response from his followers. "There is a thread of sympathy and oneness," he wrote of his own experiences as a speaker, "that connects a public speaker with his audience, that is just as strong as though it were something tangible and visible."[219] Hundreds of African Americans named their children after Washington, just as charismatic followers did with other leaders.[220] A college freshman at Tuskegee heard Washington speak there in 1912 and found that the speech "well-nigh revolutionized his life."[221]

As an African American charismatic leader, Washington was both typical and unique. On one hand, Washington participated in a tradition of African American messianism and charismatic speaking techniques going back to the antebellum period.[222] "Cultivate the oratorical," African American college professor William G. Allen urged listeners in 1852, "do it diligently, and with purpose; remembering that it is by the exercise of this weapon, perhaps more than any other, that America is to be made a free land, not in name only, but in deed and in truth."[223] Much of this tradition centered on charismatic ministers who became some of the nation's most visible black leaders. "The Preacher is the most unique personality developed by the Negro on American soil," wrote W. E. B. Du Bois in 1903. "A leader, a politician, an orator, a 'boss,' an intriguer, an idealist, – all these he is, and ever, too, the centre of a group of men, now twenty, now a thousand in number."[224] Black ministers embraced the Methodist "shout tradition"; Du Bois noted "the stamping, shrieking, and shouting, the rushing to and fro

[217] Washington, *Up from Slavery*, 243.

[218] Jackson, *Booker T. Washington and the Struggle against White Supremacy*, 3, 58.

[219] Washington, *Up from Slavery*, 243.

[220] Robert J. Norrell, *Up from History: The Life of Booker T. Washington* (Cambridge, MA: Belknap Press of Harvard University Press, 2009), 333.

[221] Quoted in Samuel R. Spencer, Jr., *Booker T. Washington and the Negro's Place in American Life* (New York: Little, Brown, 1955), 81.

[222] Moses, *Black Messiahs and Uncle Toms*, 9.

[223] William G. Allen, "Orators and Oratory," speech delivered June 22, 1852, in Philip S. Foner and Robert James Branham, eds., *Lift Every Voice: African American Oratory, 1787–1900* (Tuscaloosa, AL: University of Alabama Press, 1998), 246.

[224] W. E. Burghardt Du Bois, *The Souls of Black Folk: Essays and Sketches* (Chicago: A. C. McClurg, 1903), 190.

and wild waving of arms, the weeping and laughing, the vision and the trance" that were omnipresent in black churches.[225] African American preachers were able to translate this enthusiasm into an advocacy program to promote political, economic, and even social equality. By the 1890s, ministers such as Alexander Crummell, Henry McNeal Turner, and Reverdy C. Ransom, along with secular leaders such as Frederick Douglass and Virginia congressman John Mercer Langston, were putting Allen's exhortation into practice.[226]

These charismatic ministers and orators were unquestionably successful leaders within the African American community. Unlike in Washington's case, however, their success was confined to black audiences, and their ability to bring about concrete social change was therefore limited. The white audience cheering for "Dixie" at the Atlanta Exposition always stood between them and the societal changes they sought. Though African Americans such as Douglass and anti-lynching campaigner Ida B. Wells–Barnett achieved some success before white audiences, they did not have the ear of presidents and politicians as Washington did.[227] They could not move freely through the South as Washington could. They could not mobilize their followers to activism without risking a beating or a lynching. Instead, they found themselves facing one of the most vicious and restrictive of all racial systems: full-throated Jim Crow segregation at its nadir, enforced by systematic violence, state power, and cultural dehumanization.[228] In the North and especially in

[225] *Ibid.*, 191.

[226] Benjamin Brawley, *The Negro in Literature and Art in the United States* (New York: Duffield, 1921), 86; Kirt H. Wilson, "The Politics of Place and Presidential Rhetoric in the United States, 1875–1901," in James Arnt Aune and Enrique D. Rigsby, eds., *Civil Rights Rhetoric and the American Presidency* (College Station, TX: Texas A&M University Press, 2005), 35; Jackson, *Booker T. Washington and the Struggle against White Supremacy*, 8, 78–79; Philip S. Foner and Robert James Branham, "Introduction," in Foner and Branham, eds., *Lift Every Voice*, 14–15; Richard W. Leeman, "Fighting for Freedom Again: African American Reform Rhetoric in the Late Nineteenth Century," in Watson and Burkholder, eds., *The Rhetoric of Nineteenth-Century Reform*, 23, 45; H. Viscount "Berky" Nelson, *The Rise and Fall of Modern Black Leadership: Chronicle of a Twentieth Century Tragedy* (Lanham, MD: University Press of America, 2003), 11, 13–14.

[227] Louis R. Harlan, *Booker T. Washington: The Wizard of Tuskegee, 1901–1915* (New York: Oxford University Press, 1983), 331, 406; Shirley Wilson Logan and Martha S. Watson, " 'The Clear, Plain Facts': The Antilynching Agitation of Ida B. Wells," in Watson and Burkholder, eds., *The Rhetoric of Nineteenth-Century Reform*, 45.

[228] Leon F. Litwack, *Trouble in Mind: Black Southerners in the Age of Jim Crow* (New York: Knopf, 1998), xiii–xiv; Rayford W. Logan, *The Negro in American Life and Thought: The Nadir, 1877–1901* (New York: Dial Press, 1954), 52.

the South, African Americans experienced a sociocultural straitjacket far tighter than that inhabited by white women. Whites limited black educational opportunities, undermined black culture, and terrorized blacks who stepped out of line. African Americans found ways to resist these depredations, but in the face of such an existential threat, most leaders could do little more than counsel their followers to wait, educate themselves, and prepare for better days.[229]

That Washington escaped the fate of his fellow charismatic leaders – that he gained the ear rather than the ire of the whites who cheered for "Dixie" – was due largely to his ideology. The key descriptor for Washington's "Atlanta Compromise" speech was "compromise"; in fact, "accommodation" was a more apt term. In an attempt to win white sympathy for African Americans, Washington argued that blacks were willing to give up social, political, and economic equality for the opportunity to become skilled laborers. "Ignorant and inexperienced," he said apologetically, "it is not strange that in the first years of our life we began at the top instead of at the bottom."[230] Now, however, newly chastened African Americans were prepared "to dignify and glorify common labour and put brains and skill into the common occupations of life."[231] "The wisest among my race," he concluded, "understand that the agitation of questions of social equality is the extremest folly."[232] To win the cooperation of whites, Washington was willing to abandon virtually the entire program of equality African Americans had sought for generations. The strategy worked about as well as could be expected: Washington won whites' approval in a way no other black leader could match, but his presence on the national stage served largely to bolster the Jim Crow system and undermine the cause of black equality.[233]

African Americans, then, faced a difficult choice between political relevance and meaningful activism. Unlike the men who opposed female charismatic leaders, few whites challenged black charisma directly because African Americans' style of leadership had little effect on their

[229] Robin D. G. Kelley, *Race Rebels: Culture, Politics, and the Black Working Class* (New York: The Free Press, 1994), 32–33; Edward L. Wheeler, *Uplifting the Race: The Black Minister in the New South, 1865–1902* (Lanham, MD: University Press of America, 1986), 97; Timothy E. Fulop, " 'The Future Golden Day of the Race': Millennialism and Black Americans in the Nadir, 1877–1901," *Harvard Theological Review*, Vol. 84, No. 1 (January 1991), 78.

[230] Booker T. Washington, speech at Atlanta Exposition, September 18, 1895, in Washington, *Up from Slavery*, 218.

[231] *Ibid.*, 220. [232] *Ibid.*, 223.

[233] See, among others, Du Bois, *The Souls of Black Folk*, 50.

ability to be heard by white audiences; their only reliable means of influencing white centers of power was to abandon their calls for equality and better treatment. Faced with a choice between internal community uplift and external self-abnegation, most black leaders opted for the former.[234] Washington chose the latter, but the end result was the same: neither the "negro Moses" nor anyone else was able to lead African Americans to meaningful societal change during the nadir of Jim Crow. It was not until the late 1910s that the emergent ideology of pan-Africanism and the experiences of black soldiers rekindled the question of African American charismatic leadership as an agent of social change.

* * *

For turn-of-the-century women and African Americans, among others, charisma presented some difficulties as an organizational strategy for building movements and achieving social change. But for those fortunate enough to be born white, male, and middle class, educated in elocution, and capable of commanding the various elements of charismatic technique, charisma was a potent weapon. In the hands of skilled practitioners such as Bryan, true believers such as Finney, and canny organizers such as Major Pond, the technologies of charisma promoted religious, political, and social causes, raised leaders to prominence, and amassed legions of devoted followers. A leader who possessed charismatic ability and knew how to use it no longer seemed rare, odd, or dangerous; instead, he appeared as an asset to any cause.

Despite its success, charismatic speech was far from the only persuasive technique being performed on the national stage by 1896. Indeed, across the political aisle from Bryan, the Republican presidential campaign of William McKinley was building a new campaign style of its own. McKinley's campaign manager Marcus Alonzo Hanna fused the techniques of professional advertising with more traditional political tactics to create a new "advertised politics." Wary of the charismatic trapeze, McKinley did not travel the country as Bryan did, but he spoke daily from his front porch to handpicked audiences brought in for the occasion. Hanna printed copies of McKinley's speeches and sent them to campaign headquarters throughout the country for further distribution to voters. Along with the speeches, Hanna sent posters of McKinley's likeness, campaign memorabilia, catchy slogans designed to stick in voters'

[234] Kevin K. Gaines, *Uplifting the Race: Black Leadership, Politics, and Culture in the Twentieth Century* (Chapel Hill, NC: University of North Carolina Press, 1996), 1–5.

minds, and even a silent film clip of the candidate.[235] Hanna "has advertised McKinley," Theodore Roosevelt allegedly complained, "as if he were a patent medicine!"[236]

Advertising was part of the charismatic organization, too. Major Pond could fill halls for his clients only because local organizers advertised their speeches in advance.[237] Revivalists sold copies of their biographies, both to raise money and to enhance their stature as charismatic figures, and often convinced newspapers to print their sermons.[238] Dwight Moody was a master at obtaining free advertising through the press; he diligently "worked" local newspaper reporters and encouraged competition between papers so they would increase their coverage of his revivals.[239] "There was never a better advertised affair," noted the *Christian Register* during an 1877 Moody revival in Boston.[240] Meanwhile, Bryan and other charismatic politicians published numerous books and periodicals by mail order; Bryan's self-published weekly magazine *The Commoner* garnered him a captive audience in the hundreds of thousands and was the candidate's primary means of keeping his followers engaged between election cycles.[241]

For charismatic movements, though, advertising was merely a means of filling seats, fanning followers' enthusiasm, or making money on the side; it was never the main event. Charismatic leaders could not be sold like patent medicines in the way McKinley was, because charisma was not a product but a performance, conducted live in front of an audience. Because Hanna's advertised politics could cover the country while McKinley stayed on his front porch, the style was more flexible than was charisma. But Hanna could win only votes for McKinley; Bryan and his fellow charismatic leaders were after something more. When Bryan stretched out his arms on that Chicago stage, he won the lifelong

[235] Michael E. McGerr, *The Decline of Popular Politics: The American North, 1865–1928* (New York: Oxford University Press, 1986), 144–145; Harpine, *From the Front Porch to the Front Page*, 41–42; David Greenberg, *Republic of Spin: An Inside History of the American Presidency* (New York: W. W. Norton, 2016), 27.

[236] Thomas Beer, *Hanna* (New York: Knopf, 1929), 165.

[237] Pond, *Eccentricities of Genius*, 444.

[238] Kathryn E. Lofton, "The Preacher Paradigm: Promotional Biographies and the Modern-Made Evangelist," *Religion and American Culture: A Journal of Interpretation*, Vol. 16, No. 1 (Winter 2006), 96–97.

[239] Evensen, *God's Man for the Gilded Age*, 63, 156, 165.

[240] *Christian Register*, April 28, 1877, 2, quoted in *ibid.*, 173.

[241] William Jennings Bryan, *The Commoner Condensed*, Vol. 1 (New York: Abbey Press, 1902).

devotion of followers eager to participate in a national movement that lasted beyond a single speech or election cycle. Ultimately, the charismatic relationship's most original feature was not the techniques of its leaders but the emotions of its adherents. It was followers' experience of followership as a transformative, life-affirming activity that afforded charismatic movements their curious power and bridged the gap between charismatic performances and broader social trends.

3

Transformations

The Follower Experience, 1890–1920

On the night of February 17, 1910, Thomas Jenkins did something remarkable: he stood up. Thomas and his wife Mary had traveled through a storm to attend a Billy Sunday revival meeting in Youngstown, Ohio.[1] Since Thomas, a forty-six-year-old street peddler, had never been particularly religious, his interest in the revival took his devout wife by surprise.[2] In a letter she later wrote to Billy and Nell Sunday, Mary recounted having prayed for weeks, without any sign of success, for her husband's conversion; she was "very near being discouraged." Thomas "is a man that dont say much," Mary explained, "but he is a deep thinker." That night, while the congregation sang and Sunday delivered his energetic sermon, a momentous change took place within Thomas Jenkins' mind. When Sunday invited audience members to "hit the sawdust trail" – to come up to the pulpit and pledge themselves to Christ – Thomas answered Sunday's call. "He leaped from his seat without saying a word to me," Mary wrote. Down the tabernacle aisle Thomas strode until he reached Sunday and shook the evangelist's hand. Back at home, the conversion continued. Thomas told Mary, "I made the final step, & by the Grace of God I mean to stand by my Saviour, untill [*sic*] he calls me home." Mary opened her Bible and read aloud: "Blessed is the man that walketh not in the counsel of the ungodly, nor standeth in the way of sinners, nor sitteth in the seat of the scornful."[3] Then she uttered a

[1] Dates for Youngstown and all other campaigns can be found in William G. McLoughlin, Jr., "Professional Evangelism: The Social Significance of Religious Revivals since 1865" (2 vols., Ph.D. diss., Harvard University, 1953), II, 771–784.

[2] U.S. Bureau of the Census, *United States Census of Population*, 1910.

[3] Psalm 1:1.

prayer. Thomas prayed, too, for the first time in his life. "And I tell you he made a beautiful Prayer," Mary wrote, "with tears streaming down his face, and asked God to forgive his many sins, 46 yrs. old & wasted so much time serving the Devil but Lord I am going to serve Thee from now on." Overcome with emotion, Mary went to Thomas "and sat on his lap, and we embraced one and other, weeping with joy."[4]

On November 7, 1904, Guy Bogart did something scarcely less remarkable: he changed his mind.[5] Bogart, a cub reporter for the Democratic *Terre Haute Toiler*, was covering the election eve address of Socialist presidential candidate Eugene Victor Debs.[6] Bogart's editor had procured him a seat on the stage at the Terre Haute Grand Theatre, right next to the podium. From that vantage point, Bogart witnessed Debs' spellbinding speech. The Socialist nominee was "so worn and exhausted from weeks of campaigning that he could hardly stand," Bogart remembered later. Nevertheless, when Debs came over after the speech to shake Bogart's hand, the young journalist had a life-changing experience. "When Gene grasped my hand that night," he recalled, "there was a spiritual touch that was as convincing as the terrible earnestness of his loving pleading."[7] In a poem about the experience, Bogart wrote, "You clasped my hand and I thrilled as at touch of a sweetheart; / The love of all humanity surges through your handclasp."[8] That night, Bogart turned the incident over in his mind. By the next morning, he had reached a decision: "As I entered the Building Trades Hall on my rounds for news, I said to one of the leading business agents, 'Tom, let's vote the straight Socialist ticket today!' He shook hands on the pact – and Gene got two more votes." Bogart's conversion to Socialism was complete and long-lasting; he remained a party member sixteen years later.[9]

Despite the obvious differences between coming to Christ and casting a vote, these two conversion narratives share several remarkable parallels. Both Thomas Jenkins and Guy Bogart began their conversions by

[4] Mrs. Thomas Jenkins to Billy and Helen Sunday, n.d., folder 1, box 31 (microfilm: reel 27), Papers of William and Helen Sunday, Grace College and Theological Seminary, Winona Lake, Indiana.

[5] Bogart's age suggests this anecdote took place during the 1904 election, but it may have been 1908.

[6] Mike McCormick, *Terre Haute: Queen City of the Wabash* (Charleston, SC: Arcadia Publishing, 2005), 56.

[7] Quoted in Ruth Le Prade, ed., *Debs and the Poets* (Pasadena, CA: Upton Sinclair, 1920), 72.

[8] Guy Bogart, "My Big Brother 'Gene'," in Le Prade, ed., *Debs and the Poets*, 35.

[9] Le Prade, ed., *Debs and the Poets*, 72–73.

attending the speeches of charismatic leaders whose views they did not share. After hearing the speeches and shaking hands with the leaders, each experienced a dramatic and unexpected emotional response. Each took time to reflect on his experience before making a conscious decision to proceed with conversion. Eventually, each underwent a comprehensive personal transformation, consecrating himself permanently to the leader's cause. Finally, each found meaning and purpose in the results. When Bogart felt "the love of all humanity" surge through him, when Jenkins held his wife "weeping with joy," they were experiencing not a transient emotion but a deep and enduring sense of happiness and fulfillment.

In the historical record, just as in charismatic movements themselves, the voices of leaders boom the loudest. Stories such as those of Jenkins and Bogart, however, offer a window into the quieter, but equally important, half of the charismatic equation: the follower experience. Remarkably, the historical record includes thousands of such windows. The papers of Sunday and Debs contain large collections of follower testimonials. During the 1896 election, William Jennings Bryan and his campaign kept 5,000 of the letters Bryan received from followers. In 1920, the young Socialist poet Ruth Le Prade collected forty-nine prose and poetic responses to Debs' magnetism in *Debs and the Poets*. In 1981, historian J. Robert Constantine published thirty-two remembrances collected in the 1960s from Socialist followers and colleagues of Debs.[10] In 1982, at the behest of sociologist Ivan J. Fahs, twenty-seven elderly North Carolinians filled out questionnaires detailing their experiences at a Sunday revival nearly six decades earlier.[11] And in 1989, scholar Jeannette Smith-Irvin published interviews with six aging followers of the New York–based pan-Africanist leader Marcus Garvey in *Footsoldiers of the Universal Negro Improvement Association*.[12] Dozens of other charismatic followers wrote published and unpublished testimonials in book, article, and poetry form, or shared their stories in interviews. Far from being silent, charismatic followers were eager to share their experiences with anyone who cared to listen.

[10] J. Robert Constantine, ed., *Debs Remembered: A Collection of Reminiscences* (Terre Haute, IN: Indiana State University (unpublished), 1981), reel 5, Papers of Eugene V. Debs microfilm edition.

[11] Introductory material for Collection 295, Charlotte Evangelistic Campaigns Research Project, Archives of the Billy Graham Center, Wheaton College, Wheaton, IL, www.wheaton.edu/bgc/archives/GUIDES/295.htm.

[12] Jeannette Smith-Irvin, *Footsoldiers of the Universal Negro Improvement Association: Their Own Words* (Trenton, NJ: Africa World Press, 1989).

Taken together, the available testimonials represent a somewhat idiosyncratic cross-section of charismatic movements. Sunday's evangelical successor Billy Graham received up to 15,000 letters per day from eager admirers; if Sunday's epistolary haul was in any way comparable, the few hundred letters in his personal correspondence file constitute only a tiny fraction of the total receipts.[13] The letters that do survive appear to have been chosen, either by Nell Sunday or by a secretary for the revival campaign, to emphasize eloquently written narratives of conversion. This selection process effectively obscured the demographic diversity of Sunday's followers.[14] Similarly, the 5,000 letters retained by Bryan's 1896 campaign constitute a small portion of the nearly 200,000 letters the campaign received – and evidence suggests that the surviving letters feature a higher percentage of middle-class writers than did the original collection as a whole.[15] In addition, the surviving collections skew heavily toward the followers of white, and especially male, leaders.

Nevertheless, the testimonials constitute a detailed and valuable record of the emotional experience of charismatic followership. As historians have recognized, late nineteenth- and early twentieth-century Americans experienced a set of emotions unique to their time and place. The economic, social, and cultural upheavals occasioned by industrial capitalism led many middle-class Americans to seek a potent emotional fulfillment that would provide them with the purpose and direction they felt they lacked.[16] In part, this desire manifested itself in the "Third Great Awakening," the broad revival movement in which Billy Sunday's evangelism played a key role.[17] It also contributed to a newly emotional form of politics based on charismatic oratory – a politics of which William Jennings Bryan was the outstanding representative by 1900. "By your personal magnetism you won all hearts," wrote Thomas Colfer to Bryan

13 Grant Wacker, *America's Pastor: Billy Graham and the Shaping of a Nation* (Cambridge, MA: Belknap Press of Harvard University Press, 2014), 266.

14 William G. McLoughlin, Jr., *Billy Sunday Was His Real Name* (Chicago: University of Chicago Press, 1955), 16, 76–78, 311.

15 Michael Kazin, *A Godly Hero: The Life of William Jennings Bryan* (New York: Knopf, 2006), 73.

16 T. J. Jackson Lears, *No Place of Grace: Antimodernism and the Transformation of American Culture, 1880–1920* (New York: Pantheon, 1981), xiii; Peter N. Stearns, *American Cool: Constructing a Twentieth-Century Emotional Style* (New York: New York University Press, 1994), 42, 52.

17 William G. McLoughlin, Jr., *Revivals, Awakenings, and Reform: An Essay on Religion and Social Change in America, 1607–1977* (Chicago: University of Chicago Press, 1978), 2, 145–146; Josh McMullen, *Under the Big Top: Big Tent Revivalism and American Culture, 1885–1925* (New York: Oxford University Press, 2015), 33, 54–55.

after an 1888 debate performance, "and you gave us the day."[18] In response to troubling socioeconomic realities, middle-class American hearts longed to be "won" by both sacred and secular means, to "give the day" to someone who could fulfill their emotional and spiritual needs.

Scholarly interpretations of this type of charismatic followership experience have tended to deemphasize the agency of both followers and their emotions. Recent scholarship in religious history and "emotionology" has pointed out that emotions are experienced and recorded only after being filtered through a fog of social expectations, ritualized narrative forms, and social and linguistic traditions.[19] Narratives such as those of Jenkins and Bogart, then, were reflections of the culture in which they appeared; accordingly, such conversions were not entirely self-determined. Meanwhile, other interpretations have suggested that the impulse to follow was misguided or its consequences counterproductive. After all, though the charismatic relationship fulfilled followers' emotional needs, it could not in itself solve the underlying economic and social problems that inspired their dissatisfaction.[20]

Some contemporaries, drawing on the Emersonian individualism still present in American culture, developed a shriller interpretation of charismatic followership. "This movement led by Bryan is a wholly hysterical movement," New York City police commissioner Theodore Roosevelt was reported to have said in 1896, "and hysteria is not to be cured by one dose of medicine ... I really believe the sentiment now animating a large proportion of our people can only be suppressed, as the Commune in Paris was suppressed, by taking ten or a dozen of their leaders out ... and shooting them dead!"[21] "Billy Sunday is a shocking example of the license

[18] Thomas Colfer to William Jennings Bryan, September 21, 1888, quoted in Keith Melder, "Bryan the Campaigner," *Contributions from the Museum of History and Technology*, Paper 46 (Washington, DC: Smithsonian, 1965), 58.

[19] Baird Tipson, "How Can the Religious Experience of the Past Be Recovered? The Examples of Puritanism and Pietism," *Journal of the American Academy of Religion*, Vol. 43, No. 4 (December 1975), 696; Peter N. Stearns and Carol Z. Stearns, "Emotionology: Clarifying the History of Emotions and Emotional Standards," *American Historical Review*, Vol. 90, No. 4 (October 1985), 813, 816, 825; Stearns, *American Cool*, 2–3; Robert H. Sharf, "Experience," in Mark C. Taylor, ed., *Critical Terms for Religious Studies* (Chicago: University of Chicago Press, 1998), 97–98, 110–111. For a more nuanced discussion, see David D. Hall, "Review Essay: What Is the Place of 'Experience' in Religious History?" *Religion and American Culture: A Journal of Interpretation*, Vol. 13, No. 2 (Summer 2003), 242–245, 250.

[20] McLoughlin, *Billy Sunday Was His Real Name*, 35, 252; Lears, *No Place of Grace*, 58.

[21] *New York Journal*, quoted in "Who Are the Anarchists?" unidentified newspaper clipping, box 5, William Jennings Bryan Papers, Library of Congress. For Roosevelt's

which the modern purveyor of religion and virtue, so called, allows himself and is allowed by the public," wrote *Louisville Courier-Journal* editor Henry Watterson in a similar passage. "Hysteria in religion is … the most dangerous form of emotion … It leads to fanaticism and fanaticism is the devil's chosen instrument for the misleading of man."[22] In this view, charismatic followership was merely a mental disease whipped up purposefully, and shamefully, by unscrupulous leaders. At the same time, Watterson's and Roosevelt's uses of the term "hysteria" to describe followers' behavior reflected a fear common among critics of the charismatic relationship: that participation in mass movements had an emasculating effect on followers.[23]

The testimonials show that the reality of charismatic followership was more complicated – and more interesting – than these portrayals suggest. Notwithstanding the claims of Roosevelt and Watterson, followership was a considered and volitional activity that often involved long periods of reflection prior to any emotional commitment.[24] And while the emotions of converts certainly reflected themes already present in American culture, the testimonials help explain how followers translated those themes into their everyday lives. Some followers, particularly those in secular movements, specifically referenced their unhappiness about the widespread poverty, corporate control of government, and financial tyranny they perceived in American society. In many cases, letter-writers advocated for reformist legislation and outlined their desired political platforms in striking detail. Yet other letters, similar in tone and import, contained only vague or inaccurate mentions of political goals. These converts navigated the boundary between self and society by recasting external forces as internal ones; rather than connecting economic and social struggles directly with their unhappiness, they felt motivated by feelings of inadequacy and failure and by family and community pressures.

denial of these statements, see Richard Hofstadter, *The American Political Tradition and the Men Who Made It* (orig. pub. New York: Knopf, 1948; New York: Vintage Books, 1989), 284.

22 Henry Watterson, "The Preacher in Politics" and "Temperance in Religion," undated editorials, *Louisville Courier-Journal*, Henry Watterson Papers, University of Louisville, microfilm edition, Reel 3.

23 T. J. Jackson Lears, "Sherwood Anderson: Looking for the White Spot," in Richard Wightman Fox and T. J. Jackson Lears, eds., *The Power of Culture: Critical Essays in American History* (Chicago: University of Chicago Press, 1993), 14.

24 See Wacker, *America's Pastor*, 258, for a similar conclusion about Graham's followers.

While followers' motivations differed, the consequences of their followership were remarkably uniform. They declared themselves radically transformed, changed forever by their conversions and by the new principles to which they had dedicated their lives. "Lord I am going to serve Thee from now on," Thomas Jenkins insisted. Furthermore, conversion shaped followers' actions as well as their identities. Having transformed themselves, many followers sought to remake their society in the image of their new movement. They pursued this goal by helping to convert others to their cause and by serving as activists for the leader's political or religious platform. Often, groups of followers formed quasi–spiritual armies that sought to promote and amplify the programs of charismatic leaders on a national level. Magnetic leaders provided the blueprints for societal change; their converts hoped to put those plans into action.

To many turn-of-the-century Americans, then, charisma seemed far from unproductive; rather, it appeared to be a viable method of changing society. Those interested in creating social or political change had other choices, of course. Partisan politics, a key change agent since before the Civil War, remained at the center of American society and was one of the primary ways citizens participated in their government. Though the traditional torchlight parades and campaign festivals faced challenges from newer political styles by the 1890s, many Americans continued to participate in these time-honored democratic methods.[25] Voluntarism – the interest group–based politics pioneered by Frances Willard's Women's Christian Temperance Union and other women's associations – was another possibility, particularly for middle-class women whose inability to vote lessened their interest in partisanship.[26] Charismatic followership, however, appeared to combine some of the most meaningful qualities of each of these activities. Membership in a charismatic movement offered followers an emotional rush at least as powerful as that provided by partisanship. At the same time, the wide array of available charismatic leaders allowed followers to target relevant issues and platforms with as

[25] Michael E. McGerr, *The Decline of Popular Politics: The American North, 1865–1928* (New York: Oxford University Press, 1986), 5, 106.

[26] Paula Baker, "The Domestication of Politics: Women and American Political Society, 1780–1920," *American Historical Review*, Vol. 89, No. 3 (June 1984), 640, 642; Nancy F. Cott, *The Grounding of Modern Feminism* (New Haven, CT: Yale University Press, 1989), 85; Michael McGerr, "Political Style and Women's Power, 1830–1930," *Journal of American History*, Vol. 77, No. 3 (December 1990), 864; Theda Skocpol, "The Tocqueville Problem: Civic Engagement in American Democracy," *Social Science History*, Vol. 21, No. 4 (Winter 1997), 469.

much specificity as did voluntarist lobbying organizations. This combination of passionate experience and programmatic precision made charismatic followership seem a uniquely powerful activity.

The available evidence can neither verify nor disprove charisma's power to change society. Nevertheless, the testimonials show that charismatic followership was more than a momentary expedient, a misguided attempt at emotional fulfillment, an ineffective response to socioeconomic change, or – notwithstanding the denunciations of Roosevelt and Watterson – a national wave of hysteria. Ultimately, the charismatic follower narratives reveal how emotional experience mediated the transformation of cultural trends into movements of collective social action. Reacting to deep and unsettling changes in American society, Thomas Jenkins and Guy Bogart engaged in acts of conversion that in turn contributed to broad shifts in American culture. To understand what inspired such people, and to identify the forces they unleashed, is to grasp the significance of the charismatic relationship in American society.

* * *

It was February 6, 1901, and Frederic C. Howe was miserable.[27] Nine years earlier, he had graduated from Johns Hopkins University fired with "a pressing need in me to help the world along."[28] Yet here he was, a struggling thirty-three-year-old lawyer in Cleveland, with little to show for his efforts. "I worked listlessly at the law during the day and played cards in the evenings," he wrote later. "My university training gave me little comfort, it made me no friends ... So far as I could see, my life was a failure."[29] Howe lived for some years in a progressive settlement house, but he recalled this social work experience as "anything but fruitful."[30] He became involved with a political campaign for city council, but when the councilman died of appendicitis, Howe wrote, "My interest in life seemed pretty much ended."[31] Despite an outwardly promising career in law and politics, Howe's emotional well-being was at an all-time low. Everything, however, was about to change.

One evening, Howe attended the announcement speech of Democratic mayoral candidate Tom L. Johnson. Johnson, a businessman turned

[27] Howe indicated that the event in question was Johnson's announcement speech, which was on February 6; however, newspaper coverage indicates that Johnson announced at his Euclid Ave. home, not at the Hollenden House as Howe stated. Frederic C. Howe, *Confessions of a Reformer* (Kent, OH: Kent State University Press, 1925), 88; "The Johnson 'Surprise' Party," *Cleveland Plain Dealer*, February 17, 1901, 1.

[28] Howe, *Confessions of a Reformer*, 50. [29] *Ibid.*, 75. [30] *Ibid.*, 76. [31] *Ibid.*, 84.

progressive reformer and Single Taxer in the model of popular economist Henry George, earned Howe's ire at first by his self-presentation. "I could see why my friends distrusted him," Howe recalled. "He was not going at it the way I felt he should." Nevertheless, Howe could not stop thinking about Johnson: "I walked slowly homeward that night pondering on the enigma of Tom Johnson's personality, as I was to ponder on it for weeks to come."[32] Despite the fact that he himself was running for city council on the opposing ticket, Howe became more and more intrigued by Johnson's campaign. "The riddle of Tom Johnson remained ... He was an enemy of my opinions, my education, of my superior position. It hurt my ego, my self-respect, to be told that I was not much better than the politician ... But I continued to go to his meetings."[33] Howe was not quite sure what he saw in Johnson. "Perhaps his personality was winning me," he speculated; "perhaps somewhere in the back of my mind there was approval of his ideas. I fluttered about him mentally, accepting, withdrawing, irresistibly attracted."[34] Eventually, Howe confronted Johnson in the latter's office. Their conversation reassured Howe that Johnson was in earnest, but "I still had a moment of hesitation. I did not see clearly enough what he wanted to do." In the end, emotion prevailed, and Howe's conversion fell unbidden from his lips: "Suddenly I found myself saying: 'I think I will withdraw from the Republican ticket and come out and support you.' "[35] Howe had embarked on "the greatest adventure of my life";[36] he became Johnson's political follower and lieutenant, serving the mayor faithfully for the next eight years.

One of the most striking aspects of Howe's unusually detailed conversion narrative is the author's description of his morose emotional state before his conversion began: "My interest in life seemed pretty much ended ... So far as I could see, my life was a failure." Howe's sense of unhappiness was above all a personal one; despite his profile as a reformer, he was more dissatisfied with himself and his own life than with external social realities. Howe's experience was common. Conversion, the psychologist William James wrote in 1902, began when individuals felt "consciously wrong inferior and unhappy."[37] Converts in all periods generally experience a preexisting mental state of "crisis" or

[32] *Ibid.*, 90. [33] *Ibid.*, 93, 94. [34] *Ibid.*, 94–95. [35] *Ibid.*, 98.

[36] *Ibid.*, 115; Kevin Mattson, *Creating a Democratic Public: The Struggle for Urban Participatory Democracy During the Progressive Era* (University Park, PA: Pennsylvania State University Press, 1998), 30.

[37] William James, *The Varieties of Religious Experience: A Study in Human Nature* (New York: Longmans, Green, 1902), 189.

"destabilization" that sparks their interest in conversion.[38] Accordingly, turn-of-the-century conversion narratives often began with admissions of unhappiness or unworthiness. Billy Sunday convert Edgar G. Gordon's experience was a good example. Prior to his conversion, the schoolteacher had been consumed by self-criticism for his "pool-playing, card-playing, dancing, 'suds'-sipping" ways. Though Gordon knew his behavior was wrong, his lack of emotional fortitude had frustrated his previous attempts at self-correction. "I had long had a vision of service and of my duty," he wrote to Sunday in frustration in 1913, "but until you challenged, until you dared me to be a man, I had not the decision [to act upon it]."[39] Similarly, Charles H. Thurston detailed his struggles with alcoholism prior to his encounter with Sunday. "In spite of all I could do the appetite [for alcohol] held me fast," he lamented. "This continued for seven or eight years" until a tabernacle conversion finally sobered him up.[40] For Gordon and Thurston, Sunday's revivals were a godsend, a ready-made solution to the flaws they perceived in their own character.

Other charismatic followers located their crises not in themselves but in their society. While the majority of followers were middle class, many others were members of economically disadvantaged groups such as farmers, African Americans, or the urban poor.[41] Both Harry Sherman, "a heater in a roll mill" who had "stopt going to school when I was nine years old," and Olcott R. Derby, a retired lumber salesman who noted ruefully that he "live[d] in a shanty by the road," wrote letters to Sunday.[42] Many Bryan followers were farmers whose livelihoods had been ruined in the financial Panic of 1893. But even middle-class followers took societal problems personally; Howe himself expressed this idea when he described his frustrating inability to "help the world along."

[38] Lewis R. Rambo, *Understanding Religious Conversion* (New Haven, CT: Yale University Press, 1993), 9, 13, 44–46; Massimo Leone, *Religious Conversion and Identity: The Semiotic Analysis of Texts* (London: Routledge, 2004), 1.

[39] Edgar G. Gordon to Billy Sunday, November 16, 1913, folder 42, box 1 (reel 2), Papers of William and Helen Sunday.

[40] Charles H. Thurston, "From One of the Converts," in "Personal Gains from the Sunday Campaign: A Sheaf of Testimonies," *The Congregationalist*, February 22, 1917, 257.

[41] Kazin, *A Godly Hero*, 195.

[42] Harry Sherman to Billy Sunday, February 13, 1914, folder 23, box 1 (reel 1), Papers of William and Helen Sunday; O. R. Derby to Billy Sunday, June 1, 1930, folder 39, box 1 (reel 1), Papers of William and Helen Sunday; U.S. Bureau of the Census, United States Census of Population, 1920; U.S. Bureau of the Census, United States Census of Population, 1930.

Like those who suffered from internal crises, followers who located their problems in society saw charismatic leadership as a panacea for what ailed them. Hugh Mulzac, an African American sailor trained as an officer, spent years working as a ship's cook because racial prejudices prevented him from commanding white men at sea.[43] When Mulzac met Marcus Garvey in 1920, he "sat transfixed with awe" as the leader "outlined the greatest 'Back to Africa' movement the world has ever seen." Mulzac saw in Garvey's plan a miraculous solution to the harsh realities of American racism: " 'Yes, yes,' I assented, entranced by the enthusiasm of this man who was obsessed with what he considered the great idea."[44] Mulzac knew the cause of his own suffering without having to be told by Garvey, but other followers were only able to identify a specific social problem responsible for their unhappiness after learning the term from a leader. "My life has been a tragedy," Zachary Arms wrote Bryan in 1896, "in great part owing to the damnable and dastardly legislation against Silver and the money of the people."[45] Arms certainly had reason to lament the effects of the 1873 and 1893 financial panics on his economic well-being, but he may not have connected these panics with the gold standard until becoming acquainted with the free silver movement and its leader, Bryan.

A third group of followers appeared not to have any preexisting unhappiness at all; they experienced a crisis only at the moment of conversion, often at the hands of the magnetic leader him- or herself. Laura Danzeisen was both religious and outwardly happy in 1915 when she sang in a choir for Sunday's Philadelphia revival campaign. But "after hearing several of the messages," her daughter reported, Danzeisen "realized that she had to walk the sawdust trail for herself."[46] While some followers undoubtedly shared Danzeisen's lack of internal crisis, others likely left their feelings of dissatisfaction unstated when writing to leaders; why dwell on the past when charismatic followership promised a brighter future? Moreover, some of the more "sudden" conversions seemed rushed or even amusing. Laura Weeks opened her door on October 26, 1896, to

[43] Hugh Mulzac, *A Star to Steer By*, as told to Louis Burnham and Norval Welch (New York: International Publishers, 1963), 70.

[44] *Ibid.*, 77.

[45] Zachary T. Arms to William Jennings Bryan, October 29, 1896, box 4, William Jennings Bryan Papers, Library of Congress.

[46] The exact spelling of "Danzeisen" is not known, as the relevant oral history exists only in audiotape format. Kathryn Marie Hess Feldi interview by Robert Shuster, May 7, 1993, audiotape, side 1, tape 1, Collection 487, Archives of the Billy Graham Center.

find a Republican neighbor proclaiming that "Bryan is going to be elected. As sure as I am living Bryan is going [to be elected] I know it." Weeks inquired as to the cause of her neighbor's change of heart. "I'll tell you," replied the woman; "I had a dream last night." In the dream, the neighbor's husband "came home and tossed down such a heap of silver enough for every body ... I know there is going to be free Silver Bryan is going to be elected I know it."[47]

Every movement had such members, but most followers agreed that the cause of their crisis was personal, not societal – even if they sought social change or legislation to fix it. Even those such as Zachary Arms who saw problems in their society experienced those problems through direct consequences in their own lives. While some testimonial authors identified the exact cause of their discontent, converts more commonly experienced a vague dissatisfaction with themselves, a frustration with the unfairness of society, a lack of willpower, or an abiding sense of weakness. As Thomas Jenkins told his wife, the problem from his perspective was not with his job, his marriage, or even his behavior – it was that he had "wasted so much time serving the Devil."

Charismatic leaders connected with their followers at the point of personal crisis. Indeed, the charismatic relationship was an attempt to address followers' perceived problems, not to alter societal realities independently of followers' goals. Accordingly, magnetic leaders did their best to validate followers' self-criticism and dissatisfaction. William Ward Ayer, later a prominent New York minister, recounted that prior to his conversion by Billy Sunday most preachers had little to offer him, because they were always "saying, 'Be good! Be good!' and there were two things wrong with that. One was that I knew I couldn't be good if I wanted to, and the other was I didn't want to be good in the first place." Sunday's tactics were different. "Billy Sunday said I was a sinner," recalled Ayer, "and that I needed Christ."[48] Ayer and others in crisis found Sunday's criticisms of them reassuring; after all, the evangelist was only acknowledging what they already suspected about themselves. After his conversion, Edgar Gordon urged Sunday to continue using this approach: "Go on telling men how much they are worth. When this fails convince

47 Laura A. Weeks to William Jennings Bryan, October 27, 1896, box 4, William Jennings Bryan Papers; underscore in original.

48 Interview with William Ward Ayer in *The Billy Sunday Story*, dir. Irvin S. Yeaworth, Jr. (orig. pub. Chester Springs, PA: Sacred Cinema/Westchester Films, ca. 1960; Garland, TX: Beacon Video Ministries, 1989).

them of their worthlessness and insignificance so long as they are out of Christ."[49]

For their part, secular leaders worked to assure followers that the flaws and fissures they perceived in society were real and required immediate action. "We are fighting in the defense of our homes, our families, and posterity," Bryan insisted in his "Cross of Gold" speech. "We have begged, and they have mocked when our calamity came. We beg no longer; we entreat no more; we petition no more. We defy them!"[50] Followers responded to such language. Joseph Crider's 1896 letter to Bryan quoted a phrase from the "Cross of Gold" address: "We of this sparsely settled farming and stock-raising country recognize you to be the great leader of our cause," Crider wrote, " 'the cause of humanity.' "[51] Meanwhile, college student Elizabeth Stebbins reported "feeling quite ill, – from perplexity and loneliness mainly," until she read social reformer Jane Addams' book *Democracy and Social Ethics*. The pages "seemed actually to make me quite well," she wrote to Addams in 1909, because the reformer's "sympathy for college girls" resonated with her own vague but "desperate attempt to solve the problems of college life."[52] The problems faced by Ayer, Crider, and Stebbins differed greatly from one another, but each follower appreciated his or her leader's efforts to understand those problems and to offer meaningful solutions.

Pressure from friends and family members played a large role in translating private crises into charismatic conversions. After a group of local ministers came upon Charles Thurston drunk at the Cambridge city hall, they urged him to attend Sunday's tabernacle service. Meanwhile, Thurston recalled, his wife had "induced me to promise months in advance that I would go to the Sunday meetings."[53] The combined pressure of family and community led directly to Thurston's conversion. "My father has four sons," James Austin wrote to Bryan after learning of the politician's 1896 defeat, "and if by God's grace we shall all be living in

[49] Gordon to Sunday, November 16, 1913, folder 42, box 1 (reel 2), Papers of William and Helen Sunday.

[50] William Jennings Bryan, "In the Chicago Convention," July 8, 1896, in Bryan, Speeches of William Jennings Bryan, Vol. I (New York: Funk & Wagnalls, 1909), 241.

[51] Joseph W. Crider to William Jennings Bryan, October 24, 1896, box 4, William Jennings Bryan Papers.

[52] Elizabeth D. Stebbins to Jane Addams, July 18, 1909, microfilm: reel 2, Jane Addams Papers, Swarthmore College Peace Collection, Swarthmore College, Swarthmore, Pennsylvania; Jill Conway, "Women Reformers and American Culture, 1870–1930," *Social History*, Vol. 5, No. 2 (Winter 1971–1972), 173.

[53] Thurston, "From One of the Converts," 257.

1900, the unbroken ballot of our family will be cast for you for president."[54] For the Austin brothers, voting was a family affair; family ties reinforced charismatic followership.

Particularly in religious movements, class and especially gender considerations played key roles in the social pressure to convert. Wealthy Sunday backers such as industrialist John D. Rockefeller, Jr., and department store magnate John Wanamaker doubtless hoped converted workingmen would be more docile and less likely to challenge the authority of foremen and owners.[55] Nonetheless, women were by far the most important source of community pressure within the Sunday movement. Though Sunday's gender politics were often parochial at best – he called his wife "Ma" and encouraged female audience members to become motherly housewives – women such as Mary Jenkins saw him as a valued ally against their alcoholic, dissolute, or distant male family members.[56] Sunday's energetic, masculine delivery and his previous career as a baseball player made him the embodiment of "muscular Christianity," a movement that equated religious fervor with masculinity and physical prowess.[57] This approach to religion held particular appeal for men; accordingly, the preacher boasted a higher proportion of male converts than did any other evangelist of the time.[58] Converted husbands, their wives assumed, would refrain from drinking, participate in church activities, and be more attentive to their families. Alcoholic ex-mayor Charles Thurston recalled that his wife had "induced me to promise months in advance that I would go to the Sunday meetings."[59] Sunday's mail was filled with letters from similar women thanking him for his benevolent influence on their husbands, brothers, or sons.[60]

54 James W. Austin to William Jennings Bryan, November 5, 1896, box 7, William Jennings Bryan Papers.

55 McLoughlin, *Billy Sunday Was His Real Name*, 252–253.

56 Robert F. Martin, *Hero of the Heartland: Billy Sunday and the Transformation of American Society, 1862–1935* (Bloomington, IN: Indiana University Press, 2002), 85.

57 Clifford Putney, *Muscular Christianity: Manhood and Sports in Protestant America, 1880–1920* (Cambridge, MA: Harvard University Press, 2001), 59.

58 Thekla Ellen Joiner, *Sin in the City: Chicago and Revivalism, 1880–1920* (Columbia, MO: University of Missouri Press, 2007), 176; William G. McLoughlin, Jr. "Billy Sunday and the Working Girl of 1915," *Journal of Presbyterian History*, Vol. 54 (Fall 1976), 377; Henry Arthur Bentson, "A Psychological Study of a 'Billy' Sunday Revival" (Ph.D. diss., Columbia University, 1916), 58.

59 Thurston, "From One of the Converts," 257.

60 Mrs. W. T. Skates to Billy Sunday, January 3, 1931, folder 40, box 1 (reel 2), Margaret Bowman Morningstar to Billy Sunday, September 28, 1915, folder 24, box 1 (reel 1),

FIGURE 3.1 Though artist George Bellows considered Billy Sunday "the worst thing that ever happened to America," his lithograph of the evangelist captured Sunday's hypermasculine pulpit performance.
Source: George Bellows, *Billy Sunday*, lithograph, 1923, courtesy of the Columbus Museum of Art and the Bellows Trust.

Americans became charismatic followers through a process that began with their own internal crises. Their dissatisfaction with self and society led them to seek help from charismatic leaders, often at the behest of their families or friends. Once they made contact with a leader, however, the structure of the charismatic movement propelled them the rest of the way.

* * *

Andrew Wyzenbeek realized something was afoot when the six Swedes showed up to work in clean white shirts. Wyzenbeek, a shop superintendent in Ottumwa, Iowa, knew that these particular workers had earned their nickname "the six dirty Swedes" by their filthy appearance. "Ole, what happened to you fellows?" Wyzenbeek asked one of the men. "You're different." Ole responded, "Yeah, Mr. Wyzenbeek. We ... we are different. We are new men. We are born again." The men, it transpired, had hit the sawdust trail the night before. Wyzenbeek dismissed the Swedes as "fanatical," but he could not stop thinking

Mary Ellen Reiff to Billy Sunday, 1916, folder 25, box 1 (reel 1), and Mrs. E. H. Cole to Billy Sunday, December 18, 1911, folder 20, box 1 (reel 1), Sunday Papers.

about their experience. "I couldn't sleep well that night. It worried me. But I says, 'Is there anything to this?' . . . I was so curious. I had no idea what they did there [at the Sunday revival]. So I went in."[61]

When Wyzenbeek entered the tabernacle, he found himself caught up in a system designed to translate his vague longings into purposive action. Not for nothing had the *Chicago Tribune* declared the Sunday campaign a model of organizational efficiency.[62] Wyzenbeek himself was unimpressed with Sunday's sermon: "He spoke rapidly. He used big words. In biblical terms. I couldn't understand him at all." When Sunday called for converts, however, Wyzenbeek found himself heading toward the front of the tabernacle anyway, thanks to one of the many "personal workers" assigned by Sunday to manage the crowds during the service.[63] "She grabbed me by the arm and yanked me off the seat because I was outside and shoved," Wyzenbeek recalled. Though he found the revival experience underwhelming, Wyzenbeek transformed into an enthusiastic convert after community members, acting on information gathered at the Sunday meeting, took him to hear an inspiring speaker at a local church. Wyzenbeek related these events seven decades later; then ninety years old, he had remained in the same church ever since.[64]

Wyzenbeek's experience was unusual in that his conversion occurred despite the revival service, not because of it. His story was typical, however, in that his journey to followership involved significant interaction with Sunday's organizational system. Wyzenbeek sought out Sunday through the influence of some of the many new converts who formed a key part of the revivalist's advertising and recruiting force. He sat in a wooden tabernacle carefully designed to maximize the reach of Sunday's voice and to channel trail-hitters toward the pulpit in orderly rows.[65] He listened to a musical service designed to elicit an emotional response

[61] The name "Ole" has been changed from "Ollie" in the transcript to better accord with Wyzenbeek's pronunciation on the audiotape. Andrew Wyzenbeek interview by Robert Shuster, May 16, 1978, audiotape, side 1, tape 1, Collection 43, Archives of the Billy Graham Center, transcript accessed March 9, 2014, available at www.wheaton.edu/bgc/archives/trans/040t01.htm.

[62] Chicago Tribune, March 6, 1918, 13, quoted in Joiner, *Sin in the City*, 179.

[63] Wendy A. Danforth Wilson, "The Theatricality of Revivalism as Exemplified in the Artistry of Billy Sunday and Aimee Semple McPherson" (M.A. thesis, University of Oregon, 1974), 19.

[64] Wyzenbeek interview.

[65] Homer Rodeheaver, *Twenty Years with Billy Sunday* (Winona Lake, IN: Rodeheaver Hall-Mack, 1936), 122; tabernacle blueprints, reel 26, Papers of William and Helen Sunday.

before Sunday even appeared at the pulpit.[66] Finally, he flew headlong toward his eventual conversion thanks to the overzealous personal worker. Other charismatic leaders, especially political candidates and union activists, used similar techniques to bring followers into the fold.

Followers responded enthusiastically to such efforts, often remembering them long after they had forgotten the charismatic speeches themselves. The elderly trail-hitters who responded to Ivan Fahs' survey evinced a particular fondness for Sunday's musical program. "The singing touched and impressed me most," wrote R. G. Lineberger. "The huge crowd singing 'The Old Rugged Cross,' I'll never forget."[67] Florence Walker agreed: "The singing was so beautiful ... When a crowd sings you have to feel happy, and more receptive to the message."[68]

Music was also present at political events, as the brass band that accompanied Debs' 1908 campaign demonstrated. However, followers of political leaders often valued the politicians' orations more highly. Debs' correspondents were a good example. Clement Wood recalled the magic of a Debs speech: "His words spoke to our hearts, and woke them again."[69] Victor L. Greenwood wrote Debs that his "sermons are love incarnate. I cannot wait until I hear you & when I do I must find a corner where the tears will not be seen."[70] In many cases, Debs' followers were as impressed with the leader's self-presentation as with his oratory. "It was the spirit," Louis Untermeyer recalled of his Socialist conversion, "even more than the speech of Debs that remained with me; ... and it was the force of Debs that ... battered down my Ivory Tower."[71] "It didn't matter what Gene said or how he said it," author and editor Harry Golden agreed. "He won men by the force of his magnificent personality and the power of faith within him."[72] Edward A. Ross made a similar remark about Bryan: the Nebraska Democrat's "organ like voice was so pleasing," he wrote, "that often while listening to him I lost the thread

[66] Rodeheaver, *Twenty Years with Billy Sunday*, 72.
[67] R. G. Lineberger questionnaire, folder 17, box 1 (microfilm: reel 1), Charlotte Evangelistic Campaigns Research Project.
[68] Mrs. John E. Walker questionnaire, folder 17, box 1 (reel 1), Charlotte Evangelistic Campaigns Research Project.
[69] Quoted in Le Prade, ed., *Debs and the Poets*, 64.
[70] Victor L. Greenwood to Eugene V. Debs, February 16, 1921, microfilm: reel 3, Debs Collection, Indiana State University, Terre Haute, Indiana.
[71] Quoted in Le Prade, ed., *Debs and the Poets*, 62.
[72] Harry Golden, "Debs as 'Riler Up of the People'," in Constantine, ed., *Debs Remembered*.

of his discourse in my enjoyment of his rich, musical tones."[73] At a speech by Marcus Garvey, William Lander Sherrill had a similar experience to that of the Debs and Bryan followers: "I stood there like one in a trance, every sentence ringing in my ears, and finding an echo in my heart. When I walked out of that Church, I was a different man."[74]

Turn-of-the-century audiences responded to charismatic oratory much as had Henry Ward Beecher's listeners decades earlier. Debs, for instance, "held complete sway over the crowd," remembered Roy J. Owens; "one minute he would have us almost crying, and the next minute we would be laughing."[75] "There were moments when he would bring them up cheering, moments when he would have them laughing with him, ... moments when he would have them in tears," agreed Shubert Sebree.[76] Ralph Tillotson, sitting behind the podium one night during Debs' "Red Special" campaign, noticed listeners' "eyes and heads ... turning unconsciously from side to side, moving with [Debs'] pointing finger!"[77] "I'll never forget," sculptor Louis Mayer told an interviewer, "the old gentlemen who stood just drinking in whatever Debs said with tears running down their cheeks, and ... an Italian newsboy ... leaning on the table with his eyes riveted on Debs like some of the little murals of cherubs in the Madonna pictures."[78] Judge Jacob Panken, recalling a Debs speech, confirmed these reports: "I can still see the thousands in the audience. I can still feel their response as Gene spoke. They united themselves with him. They became part of him as he became part of them."[79]

Sunday was a peculiar case. The evangelist did not create many trail-hitters through oratorical eloquence; in fact, recordings of his hoarse, raspy voice and rapid-fire delivery suggest that audiences may have had

73 Edward Alsworth Ross, *Seventy Years of It: An Autobiography* (New York: D. Appleton-Century, 1936), 87–88; Malcolm O. Sillars, "William Jennings Bryan: The Jeffersonian Liberal as Progressive," in J. Michael Hogan, ed., *Rhetoric and Reform in the Progressive Era* (East Lansing, MI: Michigan State University Press, 2003), 219.

74 Quoted in Amy Jacques Garvey, *Garvey and Garveyism* (Kingston, Jamaica: United Printers, 1963), 251.

75 Roy J. Owens, "Recollections of a 16-Year-Old Boy," in Constantine, ed., *Debs Remembered.*

76 Shubert Sebree, "Gene Debs, My Beloved Comrade," in Constantine, ed., *Debs Remembered.*

77 Tillotson, "Memory of the 'Red Special'," in Constantine, ed., *Debs Remembered.*

78 Louis Mayer, "A Real Bruderschaft Drink with Debs," oral history interview by Edward K. Spann, in Constantine, ed., *Debs Remembered.*

79 Jacob Panken, "... A Pilgrimage to Jesus Reborn in Gene Debs," in Constantine, ed., *Debs Remembered.*

difficulty even making out his words.[80] Instead, Sunday perfected two techniques for persuading his audience: an enthusiastic, fist-pounding physical delivery, and the effective use of storytelling as a rhetorical device.[81] Sunday's athletic pulpit performances, which often drew on theatrical and vaudeville techniques or mimicked movements from his ball-playing days, transfixed the evangelist's audiences.[82] Survey respondent Howard Arbuckle, Jr., clearly remembered Sunday's "execution of a perfect baseball slide which was so different from the stiff demeanor of most preachers."[83] When Sunday "came up to bat or slid in home or stole a base," reported J. W. Booth, "we were on the edge of the seats."[84] Once he had his audience's attention, Sunday made the case for conversion through Biblical parables and stories of his own baseball career.[85] For survey respondent James Pickard, one particular story from Sunday's athletic past stood out: "He said he was chasing a fly or ground ball, and he prayed if God would let him catch it it would mean that he would know he was called to preach."[86] And no fewer than six testimonials mention a sermon in which Sunday broke ten painted vases in succession to symbolize sinners' breaking of the Ten Commandments.[87] Leslie A. Outterson, an eleven-year-old child during Sunday's 1915 Philadelphia

[80] *The Billy Sunday Story*; McLoughlin, *Billy Sunday Was His Real Name*, 158; Frederick W. Betts, *Billy Sunday: The Man and Method* (Boston: Murray, 1916), 18.

[81] William T. Ellis, *"Billy" Sunday: The Man and His Message* (Philadelphia: John C. Winston, 1914), 139; Wilson, "The Theatricality of Revivalism as Exemplified in the Artistry of Billy Sunday and Aimee Semple McPherson," 41–42.

[82] Matthew Bowman, *The Urban Pulpit: New York City and the Fate of Liberal Evangelicalism* (New York: Oxford University Press, 2014), 183–185.

[83] Howard B. Arbuckle, Jr., questionnaire, folder 17, box 1 (reel 1), Charlotte Evangelistic Campaigns Research Project.

[84] J. W. Booth questionnaire, folder 17, box 1 (reel 1), Charlotte Evangelistic Campaigns Research Project.

[85] Rodeheaver, *Twenty Years with Billy Sunday*, 24.

[86] James B. Pickard questionnaire, folder 17, box 1 (reel 1), Charlotte Evangelistic Campaigns Research Project.

[87] Myron James, who was interviewed by Wendy Wilson, attributed the performance to Homer Rodeheaver rather than to Sunday. John Franklin Boyd., Jr., questionnaire, folder 17, box 1 (reel 1), Charlotte Evangelistic Campaigns Research Project; Eugene F. Davis questionnaire, folder 17, box 1 (reel 1), Charlotte Evangelistic Campaigns Research Project; Alice B. Whitener questionnaire, folder 17, box 1 (reel 1), Charlotte Evangelistic Campaigns Research Project; questionnaire from unidentified respondent, folder 17, box 1 (reel 1), Charlotte Evangelistic Campaigns Research Project; Leslie A. Outterson, *This I Believe – Thank You, Billy Sunday, for the Goodness and Mercy Which I Know* (Hicksville, NY: Exposition Press, 1977), 18; Wilson, "The Theatricality of Revivalism as Exemplified in the Artistry of Billy Sunday and Aimee Semple McPherson," 30.

revival, was riveted by the scene: "I somehow connected the broken vases with the tragedy of my own broken home."[88] Later in life, he mused, "I am wondering about Billy Sunday and his ten symbolic vases. How many vases would he smash in describing my record today?"[89]

Bryan's grueling 1896 campaign schedule left him largely unable to make detailed political arguments in his brief whistle-stop speeches. Accordingly, his followers devoured published versions of his few longer addresses, as well as the daily coverage he received in Democratic newspapers. "I have read all of your speaches [*sic*]," bragged Leroy Lyon, "& I truly believe your heart is in them all for the poor & crushed."[90] "Ever since you made your speech at the convention," wrote Frederick De Graw, "I have kept track of you and read all your speeches ... and convinced many to your support."[91] "Day after day I have read your speeches," another writer agreed, "and I have thrilled with hope for this land, at the reading."[92] Nevertheless, Bryan's written words alone could not bind his followers to him; followers needed the in-person interaction of a public speech to become charismatically attached to their leader of choice. "I have daily followed you through the columns of the Journal," wrote David Weisiger to Bryan, but only after "I sat near you and heard your grand speech."[93] Similarly, Alphonse J. Bryan (presumably no relation) had "read all the work done ... since the Convenstions [*sic*]," but remembered more clearly having "had the pleasure to see you on Boston Common."[94]

Music and oratory drew in charismatic followers, but the most meaningful part of the performance was the moment of direct personal contact at the end of the speech: the opportunity to shake the leader's hand. In an 1896 editorial on Bryan, the *New Orleans Times Democrat* commented that "men and women are crazy to get a touch of his hand – as though it

[88] Outterson, *This I Believe*, 18; U.S. Bureau of the Census, United States Census of Population, 1910.

[89] *Ibid.*, 141.

[90] Leroy Lyon to William Jennings Bryan, October 29, 1896, box 4, William Jennings Bryan Papers; underscore in original.

[91] Frederick L. De Graw to William Jennings Bryan, October 30, 1896, box 4, William Jennings Bryan Papers.

[92] Unidentified correspondent to William Jennings Bryan, November 3, 1896, box 5, William Jennings Bryan Papers.

[93] I have been unable to determine to which newspaper Weisiger was referring. David J. Weisiger to William Jennings Bryan, October 29, 1896, box 4, William Jennings Bryan Papers.

[94] Alphonse J. Bryan to William Jennings Bryan, October 31, 1896, box 5, William Jennings Bryan Papers.

possessed supernal virtue."[95] "Last night thousands fought like tigers to shake my hand," Debs wrote to his parents after delivering a speech in the same year.[96] The Sunday movement, of course, institutionalized this form of physical contact, since a Sunday handshake awaited each convert at the end of the sawdust trail. Paradoxically, however, the handshake played an even more central role in cases where it was not an official part of the charismatic program. Sunday listeners such as Thomas Jenkins had to commit to conversion before they could receive the benediction of a handshake. Guy Bogart and other followers of secular leaders, on the other hand, reversed the process: the handshake itself often triggered a conversion experience. Charles Lionel James spoke for many charismatic followers when he recalled the importance of his first contact with Marcus Garvey: "When I shook his hand, I was shook up because right then and there I felt the electricity. I saw a man with flashing eyes ... His presence was irresistible and the first meeting was almost indescribable, and it drew me to him."[97]

Bryan's correspondents also wrote frequently about the importance of obtaining a handshake from the politician. Despite a limited grasp of standard spelling, James Jones' letter was otherwise a typical one. "[I] am the man," he wrote, "that com to you in the city of Charleston on Oct 2 when you waire on your way to speake when i shouck hans with you ... i could not call your name at that time for my sole waire fill with Jorey [joy] & love i have for you."[98] As the somewhat excessive level of detail in such descriptions suggested, the main purpose of these letters was to lend the permanence of the printed page to their all-too-fleeting moments of physical contact. Other writers, regretting their decision not to seek a handshake when they had the chance, memorialized in their letters the moment when they *should* have grasped Bryan's hand – as if to experience in memory what they had missed in reality. "I [saw] you at Albany N.Y. but had not yet rec'd your letter," Jacob Engle noted ruefully, "or I should have insisted on shaking you by the hand. I was only about two feet distant

[95] "A Tribune of the People," New Orleans Times Democrat, undated clipping (likely October 1896), in Alvan R. Purson to William Jennings Bryan, October 31, 1896, box 5, William Jennings Bryan Papers.

[96] Eugene V. Debs to Jean Daniel and Marguerite Debs, October 12, 1896, reel 1, Debs Collection.

[97] Quoted in Smith-Irvin, *Footsoldiers of the Universal Negro Improvement Association*, 65.

[98] James A. Jones to William Jennings Bryan, November 2, 1896, box 5, William Jennings Bryan Papers; spelling errors in original.

at one time being kept back by police, and others more fortunate than myself."[99] William Willoughby recalled making the noblest of sacrifices: he refrained from interfering with a Bryan speech to gratify his desire for a handshake. "I was on the iron fence, and platform, right in front, and could have taken hold of your hand," he wrote. "But . . . I did not want to draw your attention from the mass of people, who had been standing more than three hours to see and hear you."[100]

Debs' followers found the handshake particularly important, mostly because Debs was so good at it. Many reported that the Socialist politician was able to inspire them simply through the touch of what Sara Cleghorn called "those magnetic hands of which everybody speaks."[101] Debs' "handclasp was different to all others – I can feel it still," recalled Alexander McDonald. "It bound my adoring soul to his."[102] When T. T. Ritter "climbed over the footlights" to shake Debs' hand in 1904, the carpenter experienced a bona fide conversion: "As you grasped my hand you settled for all time the principle of the socialist movement for me."[103] Union activist Kate Steichmann remembered attending a Debs speech at the age of sixteen: "Over many heads of the crowd in Indianapolis I won the benediction, the clasp of your hand."[104]

Followers responded in a deeply personal fashion to the elements of charismatic organization. The musical programs prepared their emotions; the oratory inspired them; the physical contact of handshakes committed them to the cause. Nevertheless, the charismatic presentation itself was rarely enough to inspire immediate conversions. The final element of the process had to come from the followers themselves.

* * *

The letter to Bryan contained a variety of odd features. Written just days before the 1896 election, it provided only the barest of details about its author: "J. Johnson" of Aurora, Nebraska. Rather than discussing the author's background or the state of the campaign, Johnson's letter launched into a long narrative concerning an event that had happened a

99 Jacob Engle to William Jennings Bryan, October 31, 1896, box 5, William Jennings Bryan Papers.
100 William M. Willoughby to William Jennings Bryan, November 2, 1896, box 5, William Jennings Bryan Papers.
101 Sara N. Cleghorn, quoted in Le Prade, ed., *Debs and the Poets*, 75.
102 Alexander MacDonald to Theodore Debs, December 18, 1935, reel 5, Debs Collection.
103 T. T. Ritter to Eugene V. Debs, November 7, 1921, reel 4, Debs Collection.
104 Kate Steichmann, "I See the Light," in Constantine, ed., *Debs Remembered*.

few weeks earlier. "About 30 of the leading gold men" in Aurora, Johnson reported, had confronted a free-silver advocate named Sharp in the Sharp Bros. hardware store. Ignoring the implied threat the men posed, Sharp had "talked against all for over two hours, and done them all up." Only after describing the incident in detail did Johnson admit that he himself was one of the "leading gold men" who had menaced Sharp! "Only a few of us went up to [Republican Party] Headquarters" after that, he continued; "the rest went home. They had been convinced – I had been ... I was so provoked at myself for being such a party partisan, that I took my McKinley button and pounded it out of recognition." Even after deciding to support Bryan, however, Johnson was not brave enough to make his allegiance public in his hometown: "No one will know it around here, but I will give you all I dare, my sincere vote ... Please destroy this when you read it, as I do not wish any mention made of this letter privately or publicly."[105]

As Johnson's letter reveals, even after a follower was convinced of a leader's value, the final decision to convert publicly was often fraught with peril. The cause of Johnson's fears was no secret. In the 1890s, partisanship was a key aspect of most Americans' identities, and party organizations formed the nucleus of many people's social and professional networks; switching one's allegiance could mean estrangement from coworkers, friends, and even family members.[106] Accordingly, converts to the Bryan campaign often required weeks or months of soul-searching before they could bring themselves to support the Democratic ticket openly. In fact, follower testimonials of all types reflected this need for time to process charismatic experiences in solitude. William Sherrill, who entered a church to hear Marcus Garvey speak and "was a different man" when he left, was an unusual case. More often, a period of reflection either before or after meeting a leader was a key part of the decision to dedicate oneself to a charismatic movement. In some cases – Frederic Howe's was a typical example – followers required weeks of deliberation and multiple encounters with the leader before they were ready to convert.

Some Bryan converts showed less concern for political or social pressures than did Johnson; they simply needed time to evaluate the candidate outside of his momentary public appearances. "Why do I vote for you?" Fred Clerihew asked rhetorically in an 1896 letter to Bryan.

[105] J. Johnson to William Jennings Bryan, October 31, 1896, box 5, William Jennings Bryan Papers.

[106] McGerr, *The Decline of Popular Politics*, 13–14.

"Inasmuch as I have always been a Republican I had no use for you … [I] considered you no better than the average office seeker." A random encounter with Bryan on a riverboat changed Clerihew's view, however: "I carefully studied your face and then decided for myself that you were sincere in your declarations and meant every word you said." After months of reading Bryan's printed words and listening to the orator speak, Clerihew was finally a true convert: "As 'Men' trusted Christ in his utterances so I trust you with my ballot."[107] Meanwhile, traveling salesman and lifelong Republican S. B. Morris became a Bryan supporter only after experiencing a religious vision. "On the night of August 2d," Morris wrote to Bryan, "while in my room in the city of Schenectady N.Y. A convicting Power fell on and I was Brought to believe that you were advocating a Righteous Cause." After his experience with the "convicting Power," Morris switched his vote.[108]

Conversion was just as complicated for the followers of Billy Sunday. The evangelist recognized that conversion was often a lengthy and challenging process, prone to uncertainties and reversals. Sunday's most trenchant critics charged that his revivals had little lasting effect on the people or cities he visited; every short-term convert or insincere backslider the preacher produced threatened to prove these criticisms correct.[109] Accordingly, Sunday encouraged audience members to hit the sawdust trail only when they were certain of their choice. To ensure that trail-hitters had time to consider their actions, he did not begin asking for converts until at least a week after his revival campaigns had begun.[110] Even so, some who converted too hastily failed to receive the full spiritual benefit of the experience. Charles Thurston first hit the sawdust trail, "moved by an irresistible impulse," while drunk – though he returned three days later to "reaffirm … in my sober senses what I had already expressed."[111] In different ways, Andrew Wyzenbeek and Thomas Jenkins needed time to ponder the possibility of conversion before, as Thomas put it, they "made the final step."

As they decided whether to hit the sawdust trail, potential Sunday converts wrestled with a variety of fears. Felicite Clarke, a self-published

107 Fred C. Clerihew to William Jennings Bryan, October 30, 1896, box 4, William Jennings Bryan Papers.

108 S. B. Morris to William Jennings Bryan, October 31, 1896, box 5, William Jennings Bryan Papers.

109 Francis Hackett, *The Invisible Censor* (New York: B. W. Huebsch, 1921), 30–31; "Billy Sunday Dies; Evangelist Was 71," *New York Times*, November 7, 1935, 23.

110 McLoughlin, *Billy Sunday Was His Real Name*, 97–98.

111 Thurston, "From One of the Converts," 257.

poet and the estranged wife of a prominent attorney, found that her experience at the revival meetings challenged her sense of rationality.[112] In a poem entitled "Heart versus Brain," Clarke described her emotional response to the tabernacle: "A chord did resound, mid the music profound, / To the soulful vibration of light and of sound, / And darkness of night gave way to the light / That shines on the heart of the man who is right." Reason, wrote Clarke, was of little use to her in understanding "the problem of life"; Sunday offered her a more fulfilling "music and light" in its place. "Is religion naught but emotion?" she wondered, concluding in frustration, "Why reason should faint when I would be a saint, / Is a problem to stagger the sages."[113] Storekeeper T. J. Hutchison experienced the uncertainty of conversion in a different way. Despite weeks of listening to Sunday's sermons, Hutchison found himself "resisting the call of the Holy Spirit. I had not yet made up my mind." Hutchison finally decided to follow Sunday only after experiencing a full-blown vision not unlike Morris' "convicting Power." "The room lit up most glorious," Hutchison wrote, "and my what a scene. The most beautiful picture any one ever seen or ever will see until they get inside the portals of glory." Within the vision, Hutchison sensed the presence of God: "Its impossible for me to describe him to you. But he was there. And when he left I was ready Sunday afternoon to walk down the saw dust trail for time and eternity."[114]

As indicated by Hutchison's frequent Biblical references, narratives such as these were not entirely self-determined. Followers participated in a long history of American conversion and "enthusiasm" experiences dating back to the early 1700s; in a sense, even Hutchison's emotional response to the "beautiful picture," or Thomas Jenkins' vulnerability while "weeping with joy" in his wife's arms, reflected merely the "feminine" emotion prominent within the revival context.[115]

[112] "R. F. Clarke, Lawyer, Cuts off Wife in Will," *New York Times*, September 30, 1921, 11.

[113] Nomad [Felicite Clarke], *Varied Verse on Billy Sunday* (Tarrytown, NY: Roe Printing Co., 1924), 9–10.

[114] T. J. Hutchison to Billy Sunday, 1933, folder 42, box 1 (reel 2), Papers of William and Helen Sunday.

[115] John Corrigan, *Business of the Heart: Religion and Emotion in the Nineteenth Century* (Berkeley, CA: University of California Press, 2002), 261, 266–267; R. Marie Griffith, "'Joy Unspeakable and Full of Glory': The Vocabulary of Pious Emotion in the Narratives of American Pentecostal Women, 1910–1945" in Peter N. Stearns and Jan Lewis, eds., *An Emotional History of the United States* (New York: New York University Press, 1998), 219–220.

FIGURE 3.2 In "The Sawdust Trail," George Bellows imagined Billy Sunday's followers shouting, weeping, and fainting in the aisles.
Source: George Bellows, *The Sawdust Trail*, lithograph, 1917, courtesy of the Metropolitan Museum of Art, Purchase, Charles Z. Offin Art Fund, Inc. Gift, 1978, www.metmuseum.org.

Nevertheless, the length and difficulty of such transformations suggests that the decision to convert was considered and volitional. When Howe, Clerihew, and others finally decided to follow charismatic leaders, they meant it. And when converts actually declared themselves converted "for time and eternity," they felt their internal crises melt away in the joy of self-transformation. Mary Jenkins crowed to the Sundays about the "wonderful change" that had come over her husband; his relief at no longer "serving the Devil" was overwhelming.[116] During the religious vision that unfolded in T. J. Hutchison's bedroom, "the heart of stone was removed and he [God] gave me a new one. Lifted me up out of the miery clay plased my feet on the solid rock Christ Jesus, and put a new song in my mouth praise his holy name."[117] Perhaps the most eloquent statement of the conversion experience was Ole the Swede's testimony to his employer after he and his friends had walked the sawdust trail: "We . . . we are different. We are new men. We are born again . . . We have come to accept the Lord Jesus Christ as our Savior. And He put a new spirit and a new heart in us."[118] As Ole recognized, conversion marked the end of one phase of charismatic followership and the beginning of another. Freed from their internal shackles, followers would soon undergo a series of dramatic changes – transformations that would not only alter their identities and goals, but that would have consequences for American culture as a whole.

* * *

"I'm just one of those 'modern' girls," wrote Frances Elder to Sunday in 1929, "but please God, I'm going to change. No one [c]ould help it after listening to you!" The seventeen-year-old Elder, who worked in a beauty parlor, had listened to Sunday numerous times during his Buffalo, New York, revival in that year; "I would have walked all the way" into town, she declared, "if I couldn't have heard you any other way." Having converted to Sunday's brand of Christianity, Elder recognized that she would need to alter aspects of her life, even of her identity. "You've hit me a lot of times, Bill," she wrote, referring to the aptness of Sunday's criticisms, "but I hope to god the next time you come – you won't be able to hit once!" She vowed to "forget this dancing-drinking craze that has struck us – I'll live as God wants me to live – thanks to you!" Elder seemed firm in her desire to transform herself into Sunday's model of a good person, but at the end of her letter her resolution wavered. Solemnly considering the task that lay ahead of her, she asked Sunday to "drop me a

116 Jenkins to Billy and Helen Sunday, n.d., folder 1, box 31 (reel 27), Papers of William and Helen Sunday.

117 Hutchison to Billy Sunday, 1933, folder 42, box 1 (reel 2), Papers of William and Helen Sunday.

118 Wyzenbeek interview.

line wishing me 'good luck' in my new found happiness." She added ruefully, "I'll need it."[119]

As followers began to conceive of themselves in the context of their new movements, they quickly discovered that charismatic followership was hard work. Committing to a charismatic leader may have resolved followers' internal crises, but – as Elder's letter makes clear – it also presented them with a set of daunting new tasks. Although the specifics differed from movement to movement, followers generally embarked on a double mission: remaking themselves and reshaping society according to the principles of the movement they had joined. Each goal grew out of the requirements of the charismatic relationship, yet each had important effects on society at large.

For Billy Sunday's converts, hitting the sawdust trail was the inaugural action of a dramatic self-refashioning – a process that could be both liberating and confusing. Some followers, uncertain of their identities after conversion, sought to model their own personalities after Sunday's. Jamie Biggerstaff Goldsmith boasted to the evangelist that "I am called 'Billy Sunday' here where I work because I go every night and always talking of the Sunday party." A bit uncomfortably, he added, "Didn't know you had a namesake did you ha ha."[120] More commonly, followers sought more metaphorical guidance from their leader by cultivating an affinity with him. Often, they addressed Sunday with familiarity or irreverence or even imagined him as a personal friend. "When you and Mrs. Sunday want a 'flapjack,' " declared railroad dispatcher John P. Fox and his wife Eleanor in 1918, "don't come to the back door – walk in the front way and give your orders."[121] Many of Sunday's correspondents, including Frances Elder, addressed the evangelist by his first name. A correspondent named "Mit" achieved a similar sense of camaraderie with Sunday by aggressively defending the preacher's reputation. Mit wrote to a local storekeeper that "I always thought you were a good old scout untill [*sic*] you started to knock my best friend 'Billy' but if you think you are making any thing by it you are crazy. I myself know of dozens of

119 Frances Elder to Billy Sunday, 1917, folder 26, box 1 (reel 1), Papers of William and Helen Sunday; underscore in original; U.S. Bureau of the Census, United States Census of Population, 1930.

120 Jamie Biggerstaff to Billy Sunday, 1924, folder 33, box 1 (reel 2), Papers of William and Helen Sunday.

121 Eleanor and John P. Fox to Billy Sunday, n.d., folder 1, box 1 (reel 1), Papers of William and Helen Sunday; underscore in original; U.S. Bureau of the Census, United States Census of Population, 1920.

people who never will buy a thing in your store again." To ensure Sunday was aware of his status as Mit's "best friend," the letter-writer cheekily sent the evangelist a copy of this missive.[122]

For most converts, though, following Sunday ultimately meant living according to his teachings, not copying his mannerisms or becoming his friend. In a leaflet that his staff distributed to every new convert, Sunday made clear what he expected from his followers. According to the handout, walking the sawdust trail constituted a commitment to give up vices such as drinking, smoking, dancing, and card-playing; communicate with God through prayer and Bible study; support a local church both financially and through membership; and convert others to Sunday's brand of Christianity.[123] Trail-hitters could not have been surprised by these precepts; after all, Sunday's sermons repeatedly emphasized the same points.

Sunday's followers took their leader's commandments seriously, and their commitment to his program was often long-lasting. When journalist Bruce Barton surveyed the churches of Decatur, Illinois, a year after Sunday's 1908 revival there, he determined that 80 percent of converts who had signed up for local churches remained on the membership rolls, with 60 percent "in active membership, contributing, attending services and expressing their interest in various ways."[124] Followers found Sunday's list of proscribed activities a particularly impressive part of his movement. Elder was not the only Sunday convert who vowed to "live as God wants me to live." Thanks to Sunday's influence, wrote Evangeline George in 1930, "I have yet to enter my first theatre, my first dance hall and appear at my first card table."[125] In the same way, Edgar Gordon's sense of shame at his earlier "pool-playing, card-playing, dancing, 'suds'-sipping ways" suggested that he had internalized Sunday's own condemnations of such behavior. Even the elderly survey respondents clearly recalled Sunday's rules. Fifty-eight years after she had attended the revival meetings, Margaret Booth explained that she had avoided "cards and alcohol" and "never learned to dance" because of Sunday's memorable exhortations against these amusements.[126]

[122] "Mit" to "Mr. Jeffray," n.d., folder 1, box 1 (reel 1), Papers of William and Helen Sunday; original full-capitalization removed.
[123] Reproduced in Ellis, *"Billy" Sunday*, insert between 310–311.
[124] Bruce Barton, "In the Wake of Billy Sunday," *Home Herald*, Vol. 20, No. 22 (June 2, 1909), 4.
[125] Evangeline M. George to Billy Sunday, May 29, 1930, folder 39, box 1 (reel 2), Papers of William and Helen Sunday.
[126] Margaret H. Booth questionnaire, folder 17, box 1 (reel 1), Charlotte Evangelistic Campaigns Research Project.

For Elder and other trail-hitters, changing their lives to accord with Sunday's value system was among the more challenging aspects of followership. Simply by altering their behavior in these ways, though, the trail-hitters shaped society outside the confines of the tabernacle community. Just as Ole the Swede's white shirt and changed demeanor helped motivate his employer's conversion, Sunday's nationwide following served as a constant advertisement to nonconverts across the country. Over time, Sunday's movement created a natural ripple effect. Syracuse bank president Lucius A. Eddy – after hitting the sawdust trail himself – singlehandedly procured over 4,000 converts over a twelve-year period.[127] By 1960, William Ward Ayer's decades of evangelism had plausibly "seen thousands of people come to a saving knowledge of Jesus Christ." Ayer concluded that "what happened to them, happened to them because of what happened to me through Billy Sunday."[128] Whether they were ministers or laypeople, other trail-hitters likely had similar impacts on their own communities simply through the public display of their transformed selves.

Evidently, such dramatic personality modifications were limited to followers of charismatic religious movements. While Sunday's converts boasted of their improved moral character, Americans who followed political and activist leaders had little to say on the subject. Conversion for members of secular charismatic movements was a shift in allegiance, but not in personality. Politicians and activists, after all, were looking for votes and volunteers; the success of their platforms did not require that followers assume new identities. Only rarely did secular testimonials discuss the effects of followership on their authors' spiritual or personal lives. As J. Johnson's letter showed, some secular converts would not even declare their support in public; this option of secrecy was not available to trail-hitters, since publicly walking the sawdust trail formed a key part of their conversions.

Apart from their lack of lifestyle changes, however, secular followers shared a common view of followership with their religious brethren. Like the trail-hitters, Bryan's supporters came to see the candidate as their friend or even as a second identity for themselves. "My dear friend," began Joseph Crider's letter to Bryan, "I address you as my friend, for I believe you are the friend of every poor man not only of the United States but of the world."[129] "You are surely ... becoming to seem like one of our

[127] Rodeheaver, *Twenty Years with Billy Sunday*, 125.

[128] Ayer interview in *The Billy Sunday Story*; Ann Weldon, "William Ward Ayer: 50 Years of Ministry and Still Going Strong," *Evening Independent*, October 11, 1975, 4.

[129] Crider to Bryan, October 24, 1896, box 4, William Jennings Bryan Papers.

own near relatives," Jacob Engle agreed.[130] Other letters addressed Bryan as "My Dear Brother" or "Dear Bro" or "Billy Bryan," or identified Mary Baird Bryan as "My Dear Sister."[131] Just as Eleanor and John Fox promised Sunday a "flapjack," Bryan's correspondents offered him all manner of gifts signifying their friendship; alligators, handcrafted walking canes, and oddly symbolic potatoes constituted some of the more outlandish offerings.[132] And just as Jamie Goldsmith had boasted that community members had nicknamed him "Billy Sunday," the affinity between Bryan and his followers sometimes threatened to collapse into a unified identity – as when William J. Shaw bragged to Bryan that "They call me William Jennings around here."[133]

Similarly, just as "Mit" had stuck up for "my best friend 'Billy,' " Bryan's correspondents gleefully recounted their often physical defenses of their candidate's honor and good name. "Yesterday I was discussing your wonderful success as a campaigner," patent-medicine salesman W. J. Thurmond boasted to Bryan, when "a Republican called you a Lunatic and a Liar, before I [k]new what had happened, I had smashed his nose and blacked both Eyes."[134] S. B. Morris "attended a Gold meeting . . . and after the meeting, I yelled for Bryan and I got struck several times on the head, but I am still shouting for Bryan just the same."[135] Such antics were particularly common for political followers, in part because of contemporary conceptions of masculinity; in the absence of female suffrage, few women wrote letters to Bryan. Meanwhile, followers who lacked the opportunity to advocate for Bryan with their fists expressed their emotional commitment in other ways. "Our hearts are throbbing for you here in Maryland," wrote H. L. Powell.[136] "My heart and mind is

[130] Engle to Bryan, October 31, 1896, box 5, William Jennings Bryan Papers.

[131] Tyrus L. Burger to William Jennings Bryan, November 5, 1896, box 7, William Jennings Bryan Papers; John F. Teeling to William Jennings Bryan, October 30, 1896, box 4, William Jennings Bryan Papers; D. Young to William Jennings Bryan, October 30, 1896, box 4, William Jennings Bryan Papers; unidentified correspondent to Mary Baird Bryan, October 30, 1896, box 4, William Jennings Bryan Papers.

[132] Gregory P. Downs, *Declarations of Dependence: The Long Reconstruction of Popular Politics in the South, 1861–1908* (Chapel Hill, NC: University of North Carolina Press, 2011), 178.

[133] William J. Shaw to William Jennings Bryan, November 2, 1896, box 5, William Jennings Bryan Papers.

[134] W. J. Thurmond to William Jennings Bryan, October 28, 1896, box 4, William Jennings Bryan Papers.

[135] Morris to Bryan, October 31, 1896, box 5, William Jennings Bryan Papers.

[136] H. L. Powell to William Jennings Bryan, October 31, 1896, box 5, William Jennings Bryan Papers.

overflowing with joy to you for leading us out of bondage," Eugene O'Brien concurred.[137] George Boorman put the matter more simply: "I am one of your worshipers."[138] As such letters indicated, the distance between sacred and secular followership was not so great after all.

* * *

"What personality could be more insignificant than that of [Benjamin] Harrison?"[139] *Louisville Courier-Journal* editor Henry Watterson was not alone in thinking the question rhetorical. The twenty-third president of the United States was renowned for his cold, forbidding persona and his inability to connect with voters.[140] Still, Harrison was an effective orator, though not an especially magnetic one, and during the 1888 election he conducted one of the earliest front-porch campaigns – speaking extemporaneously from his home to crowds who had traveled across the country to see and hear him. Voters listened to the Republican candidate's speeches in person or, more frequently, read them after they were published in the press.[141] After encountering Harrison's public speaking in this way, followers often wrote letters to him; their missives were affable, encouraging, and relatively unemotional in tone. "I have read from day to day your addresses to visiting delegations," wrote attorney E. B. Johnson, "and Democrat though I am, as I have always been, yet your views and politics satisfy me and fill the measure of my ideas of what should be."[142] "I have read with a good deal of interest," agreed William F. Ryan, "every speech that you have made, and am free to say they are full of good American common sense."[143] Even those voters who had direct contact with Harrison betrayed only a calm sense of satisfaction in their letters. "I shook hands with your honorable self at Indianapolis on September, 27th 1888," Ohio State University student and campaign volunteer

137 Eugene O'Brien to William Jennings Bryan, November 3, 1896, box 5, William Jennings Bryan Papers.

138 George E. Boorman to William Jennings Bryan, November 3, 1896, box 5, William Jennings Bryan Papers.

139 "Hon. Henry Watterson," *Dallas Morning News*, May 1, 1891, 8.

140 Charles W. Calhoun, *Benjamin Harrison* (New York: Henry Holt, 2005), 70.

141 Charles W. Calhoun, *Minority Victory: Gilded Age Politics and the Front Porch Campaign of 1888* (Lawrence, KS: University Press of Kansas, 2008), 88, 133; Harry J. Sievers, *Benjamin Harrison, Hoosier Statesman: From the Civil War to the White House, 1865–1888* (New York: University Publishers, 1959), 372.

142 E. B. Johnson to Benjamin Harrison, October 20, 1888, microfilm: reel 12, Benjamin Harrison Papers, Series 1, Library of Congress.

143 William F. Ryan to Benjamin Harrison, October 26, 1888, reel 57, Benjamin Harrison Papers, Series 2.

Albert C. Buss wrote the candidate; "at that time did not know that you were a Phi [Delta Theta fraternity member], or I should have given you the grip."[144]

The letters to Harrison do not suggest that voters were apathetic or indifferent toward the Indiana senator; on the contrary, many Republicans were happy to have Harrison as their nominee and looked forward to his becoming president. Emotionally and rhetorically, however, Harrison's letters were entirely different from the missives charismatic leaders received. Unlike Harrison's correspondents, charismatic followers used the language of Protestant religious experience to describe their participation in charismatic movements. Indeed, they were the only group of followers in this period to do so other than actual Christian converts (and, as in the case of Billy Sunday's movement, the two groups often overlapped). A follower testimonial containing religious allusions, describing a conversion experience or comparing a leader to Moses or Jesus, was an unmistakable sign that the relationship between follower and leader was charismatic in nature. Leaders of traditional partisan campaigns and those who helmed voluntary associations did not regularly attract such sentiments.[145] Although both types of organization welcomed emotional investment from followers, this type of sacralization was not part of their recruitment approach. Frances Willard, for instance, indulged in charismatic oratory during the Women's Crusade but switched to a less emotional speaking style when she became president of the Women's Christian Temperance Union. For movements that relied on charisma as a significant part of their appeal, however, sacralization was an essential component of the follower experience.

Accordingly, eight years after voters had written cordially to Harrison, William Jennings Bryan received letters of an altogether different sort. "If you win this battle," J. E. Tibbins wrote to Bryan, "you will not only be President, but you will be King of Kings, and Lord of Lords."[146] While Tibbins connected Bryan with Jesus, furniture store owner W. B. McCormick drew a parallel between Bryan and Moses. "I further believe," McCormick wrote, "that God has brought you forth, and ordain[e]d you, to lead the people out of this state of oppression, and

144 Albert C. Buss to Benjamin Harrison, undated letter [c. October 1888], Reel 12, Benjamin Harrison Papers, Series 1.

145 McGerr, *The Decline of Popular Politics*, 3–5.

146 J. E. Tibbins to William Jennings Bryan, October 31, 1896, box 5, William Jennings Bryan Papers.

FIGURE 3.3 Listening to William Jennings Bryan speak in Georgetown, Kentucky, in 1906, this predominantly male group of charismatic followers was outwardly reserved; according to their letters, however, Bryan's followers were inwardly very emotional.
Source: Courtesy of the Nebraska State Historical Society, image RG3198-44-02.

despondency, into the Canaan of peace and prosperity."[147] Garvey's followers saw their leader in similarly religious terms. "Marcus Garvey was sort of a god, an idol," John Rousseau recalled. "I was fully aware that he was our savior."[148] Debs' supporters, too, saw their leader as a quasi-religious figure. "He was a messiah to his believers," George Caylor remembered. "They all wanted to hear him, and the precious message from his lips."[149] Ethel Truman praised Debs' "Christ mind" and assured him, "You are spiritual you are eternal"; after one of his speeches, she insisted, "I saw the Angel of Life hold your hand!"[150] "Comrade Jesus walks beside [you]; / and we – we throng behind," wrote Miriam Allen De

[147] W. B. McCormick to William Jennings Bryan, October 29, 1896, box 4, William Jennings Bryan Papers.

[148] Interview with John Rousseau by Stanley Nelson, "Marcus Garvey: The Film and More," accessed November 21, 2015, <www.pbs.org/wgbh/amex/garvey/sfeature/sf_interviews_jr.html>.

[149] Caylor, "That Was Debs," in Constantine, ed., *Debs Remembered.*

[150] Ethel Truman to Eugene V. Debs, October 6, 1923, reel 4, Debs Collection; Ethel Truman to Eugene V. Debs, November 2, 1920, reel 3, Debs Collection; underscore in original.

Ford in a 1920 poem about Debs.[151] Jacob Panken saw "Jesus reborn in Gene Debs."[152] Meanwhile, Sara Cleghorn treated Debs' apparel as a veritable saintly relic: "I wish," she wrote, "when the coat wears out that Eugene Debs wore at his trial, I could have a little piece of it to keep in my Bible."[153]

This widespread sacralization of leaders, this use of religious imagery in follower testimonials, was common to all charismatic movements; it was one of the most significant aspects even of secular followership. Figures such as Bryan, Debs, and Garvey used religious imagery to promote their respective causes and often lectured on religious subjects, but usually they were careful to erect clear boundaries between themselves and truly religious figures. Notwithstanding this caution on leaders' parts, secular followers giddily broke down such barriers by comparing leaders to all manner of prophets, saints, and the Son of God himself. This equivalence suggested that, for many followers, the line between theology and politics was a blurry one; religion and charisma formed a continuum in which one style of worship might blend seamlessly into another. Indeed, some followers openly declared that secular charismatic leaders were divine agents. "I feel (I Know) God sent Christ to save sinners, Abraham Lincoln to free the 4,000,000 black slaves and God has sent you to save 50,000,000 white slaves," O. C. Coulter proclaimed without a hint of irony in an 1896 letter to Bryan.[154]

When they were not "worshiping" charismatic leaders, secular followers venerated their heroes in a different way: by naming their children after Debs and Bryan. "On Oct. 2 1920," C. W. Van Horn wrote to Debs, "there was born to us our fourth child a girl and which we named ... Mable 'Gene ... after ...' our own dear 'Gene.' "[155] After Bryan's defeat in 1896, the campaign operation turned this tendency to its advantage. When Bryan's daughter Ruth promised in 1897 to respond directly to correspondents who named their children after Bryan, thousands of letters poured in.[156] "Dear sir," Laura Penny wrote in a typical

151 Miriam Allen De Ford, "Debs in Prison," in Le Prade, ed., *Debs and the Poets*, 24.

152 Panken, "... A Pilgrimage to Jesus Reborn in Gene Debs."

153 Quoted in Le Prade, ed., *Debs and the Poets*, 40.

154 O. C. Coulter to William Jennings Bryan, November 2, 1896, box 5, William Jennings Bryan Papers; underscore in original.

155 C. W. Van Horn to Eugene V. Debs, November 13, 1920, reel 3, Debs Collection.

156 William Jennings Bryan and Mary Baird Bryan, *The Memoirs of William Jennings Bryan* (Chicago: John C. Winston, 1925), 269; Dixon Wecter, *The Hero in America: A Chronicle of Hero-Worship* (orig. pub. New York: Scribner, 1941; Ann Arbor, MI: University of Michigan Press, 1963), 369–370.

missive, "i seat myself to drop you a few lines to let you know that you have a grand name sake was borned November 8, 1896 his name is Bryan every one far and near sent me word to name him Bryan because he was born on lection day and will be a strong old Bryan man."[157] J. B. Whitney explained the reasoning behind such choices: "I was told by Republicans not to name him for you would be defeated I told them I was naming him for you because I thought you was right."[158] Other proud parents named twins or even triplets (William, Jennings, and Bryan) after the candidate or his wife and daughters; one couple named their daughter Bryanette.[159] Followers often enclosed photographs or locks of hair from the infants, or bragged to Bryan about their babies.[160] "Was born unto us the Twenty Third of Oct 1896," Sadie Young wrote of one Bryan namesake, "and has never been sick a minute in his life . . . and if I do say it my self he is as smart a baby as any body has got. He never cries unless he is hungry."[161]

Naming their children after charismatic leaders was a way for followers to demonstrate the depth and permanence of their own attachments to charismatic movements. Such children served as living advertisements for their namesakes and effectively precluded their parents from changing allegiances; a man whose child was named after William Jennings Bryan would likely find it difficult to switch his vote to McKinley in 1900. Similarly, the sacralization of leaders in follower testimonials reflected the powerful emotional connection between secular leaders and followers. Motivated by this connection, both religious and secular converts were not content simply to write letters to their idols. They hungered for more direct ways of helping their movements – and their leaders were happy to oblige.

* * *

157 Laura B. Penny to William Jennings Bryan, August 9, 1897, box 44, William Jennings Bryan Papers; spelling errors in original.

158 J. B. Whitney to William Jennings Bryan, June 27, 1897, box 43, William Jennings Bryan Papers; A. F. Wiggerly to William Jennings Bryan, June 27, 1897, box 43, William Jennings Bryan Papers.

159 Mrs. G. H. Waterman to William Jennings Bryan, May 29, 1897, box 43, William Jennings Bryan Papers; Mrs. Isaac Wolfe to William Jennings Bryan, [illegible] 28, 1897, box 43, William Jennings Bryan Papers; Bryan and Bryan, *The Memoirs of William Jennings Bryan*, 269; Wecter, *The Hero in America*, 369–370.

160 Sylvester S. Gathers to William Jennings Bryan, May 27, 1897, box 43, William Jennings Bryan Papers; Mrs. and Mr. Lafayette Davis to William Jennings and Mary Baird Bryan, April 13, 1897, box 43, William Jennings Bryan Papers.

161 Sadie Young to William Jennings Bryan, February 1, 1897, box 43, William Jennings Bryan Papers.

In 1914, twenty-one-year-old Carl William Aschan, who lived at home with his widowed mother and four siblings, watched Sunday's train depart from Des Moines, Iowa, with a sense of spiritual emptiness – "as though the very soul of the city went away."[162] Dejectedly, Aschan and his friend H. E. Benson wondered aloud, "What are we going to do now we can't go to the meetings any more[?]" "Let's write to Mr. Sunday," Benson suggested, "and perhaps he could give us some work to do, so we could be trying to do some good for humanity." Aschan put the question to Sunday in a letter. "Mr Sunday if you have any thing for a couple of clean cut fellows to do would be more than glad to hear from you and do any thing for you we can."[163]

On election night in 1896, druggist E. D. Holmes sent a similar missive to Bryan. "We are evidently defeated now," he admitted, but "it may be that I can be of use to you in the fight ahead . . . In the next four years please consider me as absolutely at your service." Holmes, who admitted to having been a lifelong Republican before his conversion to Bryanism, stressed that he was not looking for prestige or an official position: "If you have at any time any work to be done in which there is neither honor nor pay please call on me and I will do what I can." To punctuate his lack of interest in notoriety, Holmes asked Bryan not to publish the letter.[164]

Aschan, Holmes, and other followers longed to take part in a great collective work that would invest their conversions with an enduring sense of purpose. Many trail-hitters found such a mission in Sunday's exhortation to convert others; some went on to become ministers, while followers who were already ministers roused themselves to greater exertions after hearing Sunday preach.[165] "The second Sunday after my return from [Sunday's 1916 revival in] Boston," exulted Maine pastor John Graham, "twenty-eight out of thirty-eight in my congregation came forward, some accepting Christ and others for reconsecration."[166] Laura Danzeisen began her missionary work by converting

162 U.S. Bureau of the Census, United States Census of Population, 1910; U.S. Bureau of the Census, United States Census of Population, 1920.

163 Carl William Aschan to Billy Sunday, December 22, 1914, folder 23, box 1 (reel 1), Papers of William and Helen Sunday.

164 E. D. Holmes to William Jennings Bryan, November 3, 1896, box 5, William Jennings Bryan Papers.

165 Martin, *Hero of the Heartland*, 138; George Christian to Billy Sunday, September 29, 1932, folder 41, box 1 (reel 2), Papers of William and Helen Sunday.

166 John Graham, "From a Maine Pastor," in "Personal Gains from the Sunday Campaign," 257.

her future husband; after attending religious school, the two of them traveled to Tanzania to continue spreading their faith.[167] Lucius Eddy and others who remained laypeople also participated in the work of conversion. Meanwhile, followers who were less successful vowed to redouble their efforts. Jamie Goldsmith confessed to Sunday that he had not "done very much in trying to save souls" before he went to the revival meetings; now, however, Sunday had "shown me where I stand."[168]

Followers' determination to share Sunday's message with others also manifested itself in more formal structures. Male trail-hitters formed numerous "Billy Sunday Clubs," which were designed to produce new converts, promote Bible study, and perform good works in the community. Women joined "Virginia Asher Clubs" – named after a prominent organizer in Sunday's campaigns – which fulfilled the same functions as the men's organizations.[169] Testimonials published in a Chattanooga Billy Sunday Club booklet reveal that members viewed the organizations as sites of spiritual renewal and reminders of the work they were undertaking. The Club "means more to me than any human organization I have ever been in," wrote school headmaster James P. McCallie. Salesman Albert S. Lyons agreed: "The Club has meant more to me, in Spiritual fellowship," he wrote, "than my church." School commissioner Hugh D. Huffaker added that the organization was "a constant reminder ... of my obligation to be a loyal and true soldier of the Cross."[170] These clubs often persisted for decades after the revivals that spawned them; in Charlotte, North Carolina, for instance, the Virginia Asher Society was still in existence fifty-eight years after its founding.[171]

Club membership of this type played an important part in political followership, too, particularly during the fallow periods between elections. In the days surrounding his 1896 defeat, Bryan received many letters offering to set up voluntary associations dedicated to his platform. "In the event of your defeat," Saul H. Drew wrote the candidate, "I shall with

[167] Feldi interview.

[168] Biggerstaff to Billy Sunday, 1924, folder 33, box 1 (reel 2), Papers of William and Helen Sunday.

[169] Lyle W. Dorsett, *Billy Sunday and the Redemption of Urban America* (Grand Rapids, MI: Eerdmans, 1991), 151.

[170] "Historical Sketch of Billy Sunday Club, Chattanooga, TN" (1926), 10, 13, folder 35, box 1 (reel 2), Papers of William and Helen Sunday; U.S. Bureau of the Census, United States Census of Population, 1930.

[171] Wade R. Todd questionnaire, folder 17, box 1 (reel 1), Charlotte Evangelistic Campaigns Research Project.

others, organize a Bimetallic League in N. Y. & Blyn [Brooklyn] to further instruct the people on this question in this state, so that they will know how to vote two and four years hence."[172] "I have this evening," John Burke wrote to Bryan, "drawn up hurriedly the form for a free silver club which it is my purpose to organize for future work ... I forward you the form and will be more than pleased with any sugestions [*sic*] you may be pleased to present."[173] Just as with the Sunday and Asher Clubs, political organizations of this type were particularly important when the charismatic candidate was not available in person to promote his cause; Drew and Burke hoped their free-silver clubs would help preserve Bryan's movement for a future presidential campaign.

More commonly, political followers externalized their commitment to the cause by participating in the work of the campaign itself. "Ever since you made your speech at the convention," Frederick De Graw assured Bryan, "I have been talking and working for you and the cause you are striving for."[174] The storekeeper Sharp "was the best Silver man in the County," admitted one of J. Johnson's pro-McKinley friends – "and was doing more damage by his arguments than all the rest combined ... I don't doubt but that he has made 100 Silver Republicans alone, besides keeping others in line."[175] Such tireless campaigning often represented a significant sacrifice. "So anxious am I that you shall be successful in the election to the president," W. H. Hildebrand wrote to Bryan, "that I have given up my business and doing all that lay in my power to help you in this grand caus that you advocate."[176] "If you desire it," wrote medical doctor J. M. Hays, "I would throw up my practice here, and serve you as private secretary or in any other way you desire – incidentally keeping you in good health."[177] Such commitments were long-lasting and spanned more than one campaign season. "I shall commence work for you Wednesday, Nov. 7, 1900," F. D. Byington wrote Bryan two days earlier on the eve of the candidate's

172 Saul H. Drew to William Jennings Bryan, November 2, 1896, box 5, William Jennings Bryan Papers.

173 John Burke to William Jennings Bryan, November 5, 1896, box 7, William Jennings Bryan Papers.

174 Frederick L. De Graw to William Jennings Bryan, October 30, 1896, box 4, William Jennings Bryan Papers.

175 Johnson to Bryan, October 31, 1896, box 5, William Jennings Bryan Papers.

176 W. H. Hildebrand to William Jennings Bryan, October 29, 1896, box 4, William Jennings Bryan Papers.

177 J. M. Hays to William Jennings Bryan, July 17, 1896, box 4, William Jennings Bryan Papers.

second election, " – that is if you are defeated."[178] Even without knowing whether Bryan would run for president a third time, Byington was preparing eagerly for the next battle.

The campaign work of political followers often overlapped with the more traditional style of partisan politics. Nellie Habig recounted her encounter with an old-fashioned torchlight parade in Bryan's honor: "They soluted our house and when they would go by they all would yell as loud as they could hurra for Bryan I got up on the gate post and waved my flag and blew my horn and howled hurra for Bryan, and they would say you are all right."[179] Nevertheless, there were key differences between partisan followers and charismatic ones. Partisanship stressed the party itself as an identity; it privileged the party platform and the entire slate of candidates while deemphasizing the role of the individual presidential nominee. Shouting for Bryan at a parade was one thing, but followers such as Byington and Hildebrand, who put the candidate himself before their economic well-being and supported him personally election after election, were participating in politics in a new and intensely personal way.

Political campaigning was surprisingly important for the Sunday movement, too. Sunday's message contained a public policy platform that reflected his focus on sinful individual behavior, particularly by men, as the source of social turmoil. Among other causes, the evangelist supported woman suffrage, child labor laws, anti-vice legislation, and American involvement in World War I; once, during a wartime revival meeting, Sunday engaged in a tabernacle fistfight with an audience member who sympathized with the Central Powers.[180] Most of all, he was an indefatigable champion of alcohol prohibition. The evangelist's fiery sermons attacking the liquor industry were legendary, and revivals often doubled as political campaigns for local or state prohibition legislation.[181] Sunday's nationwide army of followers promoted his prohibition policies

178 F. D. Byington to William Jennings Bryan, November 5, 1900, box 25, William Jennings Bryan Papers.

179 Nellie Habig to William Jennings Bryan, November 1, 1896, box 5, William Jennings Bryan Papers; spelling errors in original.

180 McLoughlin, *Billy Sunday Was His Real Name*, 143–145, 257–260; South Bend Tribune, "Sunday Favors Woman's Suffrage," n.d., quoted in Theodore Thomas Frankenberg, *Billy Sunday, His Tabernacles and Sawdust Trails: A Biographical Sketch of the Famous Baseball Evangelist* (Columbus, OH: F. J. Heer, 1917), 190; Matthew Avery Sutton, *American Apocalypse: A History of Modern Evangelicalism* (Cambridge, MA: Belknap Press of Harvard University Press, 2014), 61.

181 Rodeheaver, *Twenty Years with Billy Sunday*, 32.

enthusiastically – and converts' sheer number and depth of commitment made their movement a force to be reckoned with.

Indeed, many of Sunday's contemporaries believed the evangelist and his followers wielded considerable political power. Some local mayors feared that Sunday could seriously damage their political careers simply by speaking against them in the tabernacle. Omaha mayor James C. Dahlman was a typical case. The evangelist had made no secret of his antipathy toward the mayor; the *Omaha Bee* reported that Sunday would like nothing better than to "inundate Jim and sweep him out of the city hall."[182] When Sunday arrived in Omaha in September 1915, Dahlman protected himself by treating the preacher with perfect solicitude. The mayor sang hymns in the front row of the tabernacle, praised Sunday in the press, provided city facilities for the revivals free of charge, and gave every sign that he was about to walk the sawdust trail himself – until Sunday left Omaha, whereupon Dahlman abruptly withdrew his support for all Sunday-affiliated organizations. Dahlman earned the nickname "Foxy Jim" from the press for his skillful manipulation of Sunday, but not all mayors were so confident in their ability to outfox the evangelist.[183] Sunday's comment to a Columbus, Ohio, reporter that mayor George Karb might have been "elected by the whiskey ring" was enough to send Karb skittering to address the tabernacle crowd in that city.[184]

Dahlman and Karb, who supported the "wet" cause, feared Sunday in part because prohibition legislation seemed to blossom in the evangelist's wake.[185] In November 1916, for instance, Michigan voters passed a statewide ban on alcohol after Sunday preached in support of the bill in three of the state's largest cities. Even where Sunday lost prohibition battles, his supporters usually ran up larger-than-expected vote totals for the "dry" cause.[186] Meanwhile, mayors who supported prohibition essentially adopted Sunday's team as their campaign field organization

[182] Omaha Bee, October 27, 1915, quoted in Leslie R. Valentine, "Evangelist Billy Sunday's Clean-Up Campaign in Omaha: Local Reaction to His 50-Day Revival, 1915," *Nebraska History*, Vol. 64 (1983), 222–223.

[183] Valentine, "Evangelist Billy Sunday's Clean-Up Campaign in Omaha," 222–224.

[184] "Sunday Comes Late Today," *Columbus Citizen*, December 28, 1912, 1, quoted in Donald Elden Pitzer, "The Ohio Campaigns of Billy Sunday with Special Emphasis upon the 1913 Columbus Revival" (M.A. thesis, Ohio State University, 1962), 95, 124.

[185] Joiner, *Sin in the City*, 199–201.

[186] McLoughlin, *Billy Sunday Was His Real Name*, 233. On the Michigan vote, see Maynard Donavon Hilgendorf, "Billy Sunday: 'I Am Glad I Came to Detroit,' A Study of Rhetorical Strategies in the 1916 Campaign" (Ph.D. diss., University of Michigan, 1985), 319.

on the liquor issue. "Over a year ago," wrote Burlington, Iowa, mayor J. S. Caster to Sunday in 1905, "I said to the preachers and the public, that whenever public sentiment would sustain me I would close the saloons on Sunday." Caster had been able to keep this promise, he reported, because Sunday's Burlington revival campaign had swayed voters in favor of the measure. "This result," Caster concluded gratefully, "was brought about by your work in Burlington."[187] Similarly, voters in Decatur, Illinois, enacted prohibition just months after Sunday had conducted a revival there; Bruce Barton noted that Sunday's presence had galvanized local churches and converted the city's most important newspaper to the dry cause.[188]

Whether or how much the charismatic relationship actually altered electoral outcomes is unclear, but many charismatic followers saw no need for empirical evidence. Their collective power at the ballot box, they believed, could frighten mayors, pass laws over the objections of local governments, and fuel great national political campaigns. This sort of broad political influence may seem a surprising goal for followers to have adopted, given the vague and personal internal crises that triggered conversions in the first place. After all, most converts wanted to find emotional fulfillment, not to drive national policy debates – at least at first. Yet by attaching themselves to leaders and movements with definite political platforms, many followers decisively entered the public sphere. Charismatic engagement did not divert followers' political commitments into fruitless quests for self-improvement; rather, the charismatic relationship encouraged them to redirect their internal conflicts toward external political goals. Charismatic followers began by trying to change themselves and ended by trying to transform society.

* * *

"This movement led by Bryan is a wholly hysterical movement." Theodore Roosevelt later denied having said these words, but many Americans certainly shared the sentiment. Yet the notion that charismatic followers were mindless and hysterical could not have been further from the truth. Followership was a volitional process that melded intense emotion with purposive action in the hope of achieving concrete

[187] J. S. Caster to Billy Sunday, December 20, 1905, folder 14, box 1 (reel 1), Papers of William and Helen Sunday.
[188] Barton, "In the Wake of Billy Sunday," 4.

results. Followers viewed charismatic movements not as a therapeutic release but as a pragmatic solution to problems they perceived in their own lives. Nor was followership an exercise in futility. Through dedicated work on behalf of their movements' values, converts were able to translate their emotional fulfillments into stable organizations with social and political aspirations. As such, charismatic followership was a meaningful activity that connected the inner lives of millions of Americans with external forms of social engagement.

How effective were charismatic movements at achieving social change? Charismatic movements may have worried anti-prohibition mayors such as Dahlman and Karb, but they failed to elect William Jennings Bryan to the presidency in 1896, 1900, or 1908. To be sure, some Bryan supporters argued that McKinley owed his 1896 victory to the massive cash advantage his campaign enjoyed, while Bryan's magnetism succeeded in keeping the race closer than it otherwise would have been. "You have convicted and converted more men in one month than St. Paul ever saw," Saul Drew wrote to Bryan on the eve of the 1896 election. "You have made more friends in four months than Blaine made in a whole lifetime."[189] "You have had to combat the money power of the whole world," Levi Myers agreed. "Will it be any wonder if you do not win to-morrow? No, the wonder is that you have accomplished so much."[190]

Even some McKinley supporters recognized the significance of Bryan's accomplishment. "Alone, penniless, without backing, without money, with scarce a paper, without speakers," Nannie Davis Lodge wrote after the 1896 campaign, "that man fought such a fight that even those in the East can call him a Crusader, an inspired fanatic – a prophet!" Notwithstanding the opposition of "trained and experienced forces, with both hands full of money, with the full power of the press and prestige – … he almost won."[191] "A man that could sway 900 delegates to the extent of being chosen their standard-bearer," agreed the pro-Republican *Chicago Journal* in October 1896, "and who has moved to intense enthusiasm some of the greatest audiences ever gathered together, can accomplish much in the way of influencing voters … If the republican

[189] Drew to Bryan, November 2, 1896, box 5, William Jennings Bryan Papers.

[190] Levi W. Myers to William Jennings Bryan, November 2, 1896, box 5, William Jennings Bryan Papers.

[191] Nannie Davis Lodge to Cecil Spring-Rice, quoted in Myron G. Phillips, "William Jennings Bryan," in William Norwood Brigance, ed., *A History and Criticism of American Public Address*, Vol. 2 (New York: McGraw-Hill, 1943), 904.

managers do not appreciate the importance of what impends they display evidence of such total blindness that it is hard to believe they are shrewd politicians."[192]

The *Journal* was right about charisma's importance, but the paper missed the mark somewhat on charisma's practical effects, at least in 1896. In the absence of controlled experiments, claims that charismatic movements raised or lowered candidates' vote totals cannot be verified. Primarily, what distinguished charismatic movements from other contemporary reform efforts was not their ability to win elections or pass laws, but their role in empowering ordinary Americans. Whether or not followers promoted the most effective solutions to America's problems or succeeded in achieving those solutions, the agency they wielded in advocating for their political goals was real and significant. While scholars have long analyzed how emotional experience grows out of cultural influences – in essence, how emotions are an *effect* of historical trends – the follower testimonials highlight the ways emotions can also be a *cause* of social and cultural change. The emotional experience of followership itself played a central role in providing converts with the power to influence their society. By responding so strongly and in such numbers to charismatic movements, followers increased leaders' visibility and afforded them a national platform from which to promote their views. By committing themselves emotionally to a cause, too, followers refashioned themselves into activists capable of advancing a social policy platform. The fact that they came to this external mission in a quest to solve perceived internal problems reveals how emotional experience mediates the relationship between cultural influences and personal ones, between individual choices and broader social change.

Consider once more the case of Thomas Jenkins. When Jenkins stood and prayed and wept with joy on that rainy February night, he was reacting to his own sense of moral inadequacy. Jenkins' conversion was personal in origin, yet its consequences were social and political in nature. Just as thousands of voices joined into a single hymn that echoed through the Youngstown tabernacle, the conversions of Jenkins and thousands of his fellow charismatic followers formed movements whose activities influenced American society in profound ways. By the

192 "This Man Bryan," Chicago Journal, October 27, 1896, clipping in R. S. Haynie to William Jennings Bryan, October 30, 1896, box 4, William Jennings Bryan Papers.

dawn of the twentieth century, Jenkins and millions of other followers had transformed charisma into a phenomenon capable of spawning a multitude of national social, political, and religious movements. The stage was set for a new generation of leaders to capitalize on the new-found strength of the charismatic relationship – and it was Theodore Roosevelt, not charismatic followers, who would have to change to meet the new social realities.

4

Competing Visions

Imagining Charisma and Social Change, 1890–1910

Simply put, Henry Watterson loathed charismatic leaders. For one thing, the Democratic politician and *Louisville Courier-Journal* editor was unconvinced that the magnetic power wielded by James Blaine and others actually translated to votes at the ballot box. "The question of the personality of the [presidential] nominee cuts no figure in the race," Watterson insisted in 1891. "Henry Clay was beaten by a man without magnetism. The next most popular American, James G. Blaine, was beaten by a man without magnetism." Meanwhile, the "insignificant" personality of Benjamin Harrison "beat [Grover] Cleveland at a time when Cleveland's personality was very attractive."[1] Watterson's skepticism formed only part of his opposition to personal magnetism; in fact, the editor disliked everything about the charismatic style. After the Democratic Party nominated William Jennings Bryan in 1896, Watterson briefly bolted the party in protest. Faced in 1904 with the arduous task of championing the colorless Democratic presidential nominee Alton B. Parker against the charismatic Theodore Roosevelt, Watterson boldly asserted that Parker's dullness was his best quality. Watterson found in Parker "not a cast iron magnetic man showing three rows of front teeth … but a gentleman." The best thing about Parker was that "there is no stuff and nonsense about him. He is as plain and unpretending as an old shoe; and he fits like one and wears like one." In that plainness lay safety, for "he may be relied upon to do no trivial or foolish thing for the sake of the suppose[d] effect." Unlike Roosevelt, Parker "will not make civic righteousness speeches from the front portico of the White House, with the spoilsmen laughing and joking

[1] "Hon. Henry Watterson," *Dallas Morning News*, May 1, 1891, 8.

the while ... He will not require old women and old men to stand uncovered in the presence of his family and himself." President Parker would be neither a hypocrite nor a dictator, Watterson insisted; upon Parker's election, "The one-man power will be scotched ... and the would-be man [Roosevelt] will have taken himself off ... to find his consolation in the genial society of the Kaiser and the Czar."[2]

The most interesting aspect of Watterson's anti-charismatic argument was that by 1900 he stood almost alone in making it. Turn-of-the-century Americans held a variety of views on the charismatic relationship, but few agreed with Watterson that personal magnetism was insignificant "stuff and nonsense" that "cut no figure" in society. Over the previous twenty years, they had seen James Blaine stir up crowds with his magnetism and William Jennings Bryan dominate two presidential election cycles with his charismatic performances. The fact that Blaine and Bryan had lost did not suggest that charismatic abilities were unimportant, only that they were not invincible. In fact, charismatic speakers were ubiquitous in turn-of-the-century America – at lyceums and Chautauquas, revivals and churches, mayoral races and club meetings. Driven by political "spellbinders," popular lecturers, and religious evangelists, charismatic speech had fueled what historians have termed the "second oratorical renaissance" – a flowering of popular oratory that recalled the early days of the republic.[3] Watterson's increasingly shrill attacks on magnetism proved only that the charismatic style had become impossible to ignore.

Despite the political failures of Blaine and Bryan and the lack of evidence of charisma's political potency, by 1900 a variety of American commentators had become convinced that the charismatic relationship was a powerful organizing tool that could be harnessed to power national political movements. While these intellectuals and activists hailed the charismatic relationship as an emergent force in American society, they disagreed about the nature and value of its influence. Two questions in particular animated intellectual debates about charisma. First, did charismatic leaders benefit society, or were they a threat that needed to be managed and controlled? Second, how exactly would charismatic movements change society at a national level – would they reinforce the

[2] Henry Watterson, "Alton B. Parker the People's President," *Bisbee Daily Review*, October 18, 1904, 2.

[3] Robert Alexander Kraig, "The Second Oratorical Renaissance," in J. Michael Hogan, ed., *Rhetoric and Reform in the Progressive Era* (East Lansing, MI: Michigan State University Press, 2003), 1, 19–22.

established order, create political change, or spark a revolution? American thinkers wrestled with these questions at the turn of the century in a more systematic way than they had in the past. By 1910, at least three distinct intellectual camps had emerged, each with its own vision of how charismatic techniques could be harnessed to improve society. The utopian nature of these visions, and their fundamental incompatibility with one another, ensured that battles over charisma would become a fixture in American culture over the next decade.

* * *

"The era we are about to enter," proclaimed Gustave Le Bon in 1896, "will in truth be the ERA OF CROWDS."[4] It was not a prospect the French sociologist relished. In *La psychologie des foules* (translated into English as *The Crowd: A Study of the Popular Mind*), Le Bon condemned crowds as "always intellectually inferior to the isolated individual," possessed of "impulsiveness, irritability, [and] incapacity to reason." Such qualities "are almost always observed in beings belonging to inferior forms of evolution – in women, savages, and children, for instance."[5] Crowds were heedless of the consequences of their actions; they could commit murder one moment, weep for the slain the next. "By the mere fact that he forms part of an organized crowd," continued Le Bon, "a man descends several rungs in the ladder of civilisation. Isolated, he may be a cultivated individual; in a crowd, he is a barbarian."[6]

Above all, crowds were the playthings of leaders. "A crowd is a servile flock that is incapable of ever doing without a master," Le Bon insisted; the leader's "will is the nucleus around which the opinions of the crowd are grouped and attain to identity." In a criticism echoing Watterson's charges of crowd hysteria, Le Bon described the leader–follower relationship as a gendered one; while leaders might be masculine and virile, crowds feminized and emasculated their members.[7] Leaders themselves were scarcely more reputable than the crowds that followed them: such figures "are more frequently men of action than thinkers, ... especially recruited from the ranks of those morbidly nervous, excitable, half-deranged persons who are bordering on madness." Nevertheless, "The intensity of their faith gives great power of suggestion to their words. The multitude is always ready to listen to the strong-willed man, who knows how to impose himself upon it."[8]

4 Gustave Le Bon, *The Crowd: A Study of the Popular Mind*, tr. of *La psychologie des foules* (New York: Macmillan, 1896), xv.

5 *Ibid.*, 14, 17. 6 *Ibid.*, 13. 7 *Ibid.*, 118. 8 *Ibid.*, 118–119.

According to Le Bon, leaders used three simple techniques to control crowds. A leader must first affirm a belief or political program, then repeat the affirmation multiple times, and finally enable the operation of "a contagious power as intense as that of microbes" to spread the program through the crowd.[9] "The arousing of faith ... has always been the function of the great leaders of crowds," continued Le Bon. "To endow a man with faith is to multiply his strength tenfold."[10] Most important, leaders could only arouse faith in their followers, could only achieve the power of contagion, if they themselves possessed the power of prestige. Prestige "is a sort of domination exercised on our mind ... [that] entirely paralyses our critical faculty, and fills our soul with astonishment and respect," Le Bon explained.[11] "Prestige constitutes the fundamental element of persuasion. Consciously or not, the being, the idea, or the thing possessing prestige ... forces an entire generation to adopt certain modes of feeling and of giving expression to its thought."[12]

Though Le Bon deployed his own unique vocabulary, he was clearly describing a familiar phenomenon: "prestige" was the same thing as personal magnetism, "leaders" meant charismatic leaders, and "the crowd" represented charismatic followers. The feeling of prestige "would appear to be of the same kind as the fascination to which a magnetised person is subjected," he noted.[13] "Personal prestige ... [is] possessed by a small number of persons whom it enables to exercise a veritably magnetic fascination on those around them ... They force the acceptance of their ideas and sentiments on those about them, and they are obeyed as is the tamer of wild beasts by the animal that could easily devour him."[14] Similarly, "an individual immerged for some length of time in a crowd in action soon finds himself ... in a special state, which much resembles the state of fascination in which the hypnotized individual finds himself in the hands of the hypnotiser."[15]

Le Bon recognized the ascendancy of the charismatic relationship as a method of social organization, but he was cynical about charismatic leaders. As a conservative Frenchman, he had in mind men such as Maximilien Robespierre, so consumed with his political beliefs that he became a mass murderer; Louis-Napoleon, whose popularity led to dictatorship and served feckless and ineffectual government policies; and most recently General Georges Boulanger, a dissolute and corrupt cabinet minister who nevertheless nearly led a successful coup in

[9] *Ibid.*, 126–128. [10] *Ibid.*, 120. [11] *Ibid.*, 133. [12] *Ibid.*, 144. [13] *Ibid.*, 133. [14] *Ibid.*, 136. [15] *Ibid.*, 11.

1887.[16] Le Bon was even more contemptuous of the charismatic followers who rallied around such men as Boulanger and Louis-Napoleon. But he found hope in the ability of leaders to manipulate followers; using Le Bon's methods, reasonable men could assume charismatic leadership and manipulate the masses toward socially desirable ends. "To know the art of impressing the imagination of crowds," declared Le Bon, "is to know at the same time the art of governing them."[17]

Le Bon's translated volume achieved popularity when it arrived in the United States in 1896. Le Bon spoke for Americans who agreed with Watterson that the charismatic relationship was a dangerous and negative political force – although Le Bon, unlike Watterson, believed it could be channeled in productive directions through the cynical manipulation of charismatic followers. Nevertheless, the political landscape in 1890s America was very different from the one Le Bon occupied in France. The United States was in the throes of a personal magnetism craze; adoring crowds met Bryan's train at every whistle stop. Furthermore, America did not share France's history of dangerous charismatic leaders. For many Americans, the charismatic relationship was fascinating, its potential limitless and exciting.

The philosopher and psychologist William James articulated this position in a review of *The Crowd* published in the May 1897 issue of *Psychological Review*. James rejected Le Bon's cynicism about the charismatic relationship. In *The Varieties of Religious Experience* and other works, James argued that a well-ordered society required "regeneration" or "new birth" from its citizens – "a firmness, stability, and equilibrium succeeding a period of storm and stress and inconsistency."[18] Religious conversion was one way "by which a self hitherto divided, and consciously wrong inferior and unhappy, becomes unified and consciously right superior and happy."[19] War was another method, though the pacifist James insisted that one needed only war's "moral equivalent" to breed "the martial type of character" and "civic

[16] Susanna Barrows, *Distorting Mirrors: Visions of the Crowd in Late Nineteenth-Century France* (New Haven, CT: Yale University Press, 1981), 11–16, 170; Robert A. Nye, *The Origins of Crowd Psychology: Gustave Le Bon and the Crisis of Mass Democracy in the Third Republic* (London: Sage Publications, 1975), 72–73.

[17] Le Bon, *The Crowd*, 61; Barrows, *Distorting Mirrors*, 174.

[18] William James, *The Varieties of Religious Experience: A Study in Human Nature* (New York: Longmans, Green, 1902), 176.

[19] *Ibid.*, 189.

passion."[20] Many other causes could bring about regeneration: "The new birth," James wrote, "may be produced by the irruption into the individual's life of some new stimulus or passion, such as love, ambition, cupidity, revenge, or patriotic devotion." All that mattered was that the experience be emotional rather than rational: "This added dimension of emotion, this enthusiastic temper of espousal, . . . redeems and vivifies an interior world which otherwise would be an empty waste."[21]

Accordingly, James disagreed strongly with Le Bon about the value of charismatic followership. Though he praised Le Bon for producing "the first scientific attempt to treat a subject of supreme importance," James criticized the resulting book's "grave defects," particularly the idea that crowds were dangerous and animalistic as a rule.[22] "To a reader even half-respectful of the socialistic ideals of the present generation," James wrote, "it seems rather a *reduction ad absurdum* of the pretension of Science to look down upon all such ways of thinking as essentially crazy, to find that her own last word of practical wisdom about human life is to advise her votaries to dwell on the frontier and have bonds invested in many countries, so that when that insane beast Man 'breaks out' in one they may get into another escape." Le Bon's arguments, James concluded, amounted to nothing less than a rejection of religion and of the type of regeneration James himself advocated.[23]

The argument between Le Bon and James reflected a shift in the history of American charismatic discourse. While James and Le Bon disagreed about magnetism's moral value, they shared with many Americans a real interest in the ability of the charismatic relationship to change society. Gone was the mid-nineteenth-century fear of sexual and financial exploitation by charismatic leaders; gone, except for Watterson and a few other aging Emersonian individualists, was the notion that charisma was meaningless flimflam, or that personal magnetism should be lampooned in defense (in the *Cleveland Plain Dealer*'s words) of "brains against boodle."[24] Instead, Americans engaged in sober debate concerning the social consequences of the charismatic relationship. Charismatic

[20] William James, "The Moral Equivalent of War," Leaflet no. 27 (New York: American Association for International Conciliation, 1910), 15, 16, 18.

[21] James, *Varieties of Religious Experience*, 48.

[22] William James, review of Le Bon, *The Crowd*, *Psychological Review*, Vol. 4 (May 1897), 313.

[23] *Ibid.*, 314–315; italics in original.

[24] *Cleveland Plain Dealer*, November 5, 1894.

movements on a national scale, many now believed, could change the minds of millions by molding Americans into a great mass of followers – or they could change public policy by transforming those followers into an activist army dedicated to a leader's social or political platform.

For the time being, relatively few American thinkers shared Le Bon's view that the leader–follower relationship was a nasty, cynical business. Instead, many hoped that magnetism could be channeled into social and political movements that would benefit all Americans. "Have we 'Liberals' ... ever devised anything so well adapted as this to the needs of average mortals struggling with the ordinary troubles of life?" asked James Parton in an 1890 essay on Henry Ward Beecher.[25] "The men and the organizations that have had in charge the moral interests of the people of the United States for the last fifty years have not been quite equal to their trust." During that time, a diverse set of civic problems had disordered American society. "There seems great need of something that shall have power to spiritualize mankind, and make head against the reinforced influence of material things," Parton concluded. "It may be that the true method of dealing with the souls of modern men has been, in part, discovered by Mr. Beecher, and that it would be well for persons aspiring to the same vocation to *begin* their preparation by making a pilgrimage to Brooklyn Heights."[26]

Parton's view of charismatic leadership as a powerful tool for improving society was a popular one, but it raised a more troubling question: who would control these charismatic movements, and what sorts of changes would they bring? Americans of the period had many answers – and not all of them could be right.

* * *

At first glance, the letter seemed to be just one more statement of appreciation from an eager Theodore Roosevelt supporter. Like other pieces of correspondence received by Roosevelt on October 23, 1912, the letter expressed relief that the former president had survived an assassination attempt nine days earlier. Like other letters, it was scrawled in a heavy, almost illegible hand. And like much of the president's other mail, the letter waxed poetic about Roosevelt's distinctively charismatic leadership style. "I cannot forbear to add my congratulations on your extraordinary

[25] James Parton, *Famous Americans of Recent Times* (Boston: Houghton, Mifflin, 1890), 369.

[26] *Ibid.*, 371–372; italics in original.

escape and your release from danger," it read. "We were all of us very grateful that the leader whom we love & admire so much was not taken away." In most ways – including its gushing regard for Roosevelt – the note resembled nothing more than an ordinary missive from one of the ex-president's many charismatic followers.[27]

What made the letter unusual was the identity of its author. It was written not by an ordinary voter or low-level campaign operative, but by America's foremost progressive philosopher. Three years earlier, Herbert David Croly had penned *The Promise of American Life*; the book had been an instant success and had catapulted Croly into the first rank of American thinkers. Croly's subject had been the nebulous, almost undefinable concept of progressivism. He had been the first intellectual to codify progressive principles in a way that nearly all self-identified progressives found compelling. "Herbert Croly, in 'The Promise of American Life,'" Roosevelt wrote later, "has set forth the reasons why our individualistic democracy ... necessarily produced the type of business man who sincerely believed, as did the rest of the community, that the individual who amassed a big fortune was the man who was the best and most typical American."[28] That was only part of what *The Promise* had done. In addition to describing progressive ideals, Croly had created a blueprint for realizing those ideals through political action. The linchpin of Croly's plan lay in the adoption of charismatic leadership for political purposes. When Croly called Roosevelt "the leader I love & admire so much," he was not just praising the president's leadership style – he was linking that style to the realistic achievement of progressive goals.

Considering his importance in the history of American charisma, Croly (born January 23, 1869) was remarkably free of personal magnetism. It was not the fault of his parents; David Goodman Croly and Jane Cunningham Croly, both journalists, were highly magnetic in their own right. David was "warm, friendly, leisurely, and full of wit," noted Herbert's biographer.[29] Jane, who wrote under the pseudonym "Jennie June," "is entirely free from affectation, is always blithe and natural and kind and wins all by her personal magnetism," reported the *New Orleans Picayune* in 1887.[30] Herbert could not have been more different from his

[27] Herbert Croly to Theodore Roosevelt, October 23, 1912, microfilm: reel 154, Theodore Roosevelt Papers, Library of Congress.

[28] Theodore Roosevelt, *An Autobiography* (New York: Scribner, 1913), 77–78.

[29] David W. Levy, *Herbert Croly of* The New Republic*: The Life and Thought of an American Progressive* (Princeton: Princeton University Press, 1985), 18.

[30] "Our Jenny June," *New Orleans Daily Picayune*, November 13, 1887, 10.

gregarious parents, however. "It was never easy for him to deal with people," remembered Croly's friend Edmund Wilson, "and if the visitor himself were at all diffident, he would be likely to find the conversation subsiding into a discontinuous series of remarks ... At last the visitor would lose heart and stop, and a terrible silence would ensue."[31] Croly's shyness made it difficult for him to make friends or speak in public, yet he would become one of the keenest interpreters of the charismatic abilities he himself did not possess.

No son of David Croly could be anything but a philosopher at heart. David was a devoted follower of Auguste Comte's positivist theories, and he impressed his own convictions upon Herbert from boyhood. Comte argued that absolute truth could be discovered through scientific endeavor and that society should be ordered according to scientific studies and rational laws. Despite positivism's extreme focus on reason, however, Comte also fancied himself the leader of a powerful social movement, and David and other positivists often resembled fervent charismatic followers.[32] The perceptive Herbert may well have recognized the contradiction between his father's rationalist philosophy and David's emotional connection with his own hero – a connection to which, Herbert wrote later, David clung "with all the force of religious conviction."[33] Meanwhile, in college at Harvard, Herbert discovered a new series of influences in members of the philosophy faculty, including Josiah Royce and William James. Herbert's college years culminated in a full-scale rebellion against positivism and an embrace of the Harvard professors. Though Croly became especially attached to Royce, he also imbibed James' philosophy, with its emphasis on the spiritual "regeneration" of humankind.[34]

For Croly, as for Henry Ward Beecher, developing his own philosophy meant a never-ending battle with his overbearing father. Herbert's shy, enigmatic personality made it difficult for him to counter David's badgering letters. David Croly disliked James, Royce, and the other Harvard philosophers; he feared his son's growing attachment to religious values; he regaled Herbert with descriptions of "your shortcomings"; most of all,

31 Edmund Wilson, "H. C.," *The New Republic*, July 16, 1930, 266; Levy, *Herbert Croly of* The New Republic, xii.

32 Levy, *Herbert Croly of* The New Republic, 31–33.

33 Herbert David Croly, "In Memoriam: David Goodman Croly – Estimates of the Man, His Character, and His Life's Work," *Real Estate Record and Builder's Guide* (May 18, 1889), 7.

34 *Ibid.*, 50, 57, 66.

he worried that his son was slipping away from him.[35] David died in 1889 believing that his son had deserted his ideas – as Herbert put it, that "Part of his life work had failed."[36] Partly because of such crushing expectations, Croly's early years were largely devoid of success. He dropped in and out of Harvard repeatedly, ultimately failing to earn a degree; through bouts of gloom and ill health and a job editing the *Architectural Record*, he wrote little about government or social organization and expressed few ideas about political philosophy.[37] Herbert, it seemed, was destined for an obscure journalistic career that would frustrate his father's lofty aspirations for him.

In 1900, however, Croly had a spark of inspiration while reading a newly published work of fiction. "The idea which lies at the basis of 'The Promise of American Life,' " he wrote in 1910, "first occurred to me about ten years ago, during a reading of Judge Robert Grant's novel, 'Unleavened Bread.' In that story the author has ingeniously wrought out the contradiction subsisting between certain aspects of the American democratic tradition and the methods and aspirations which dominate contemporary American intellectual work."[38] Many aspects of *Unleavened Bread* might have struck Croly's fancy. Grant's 1900 volume skewered a number of facets of American culture, including social climbing, divorce, rampant individualism, political corruption, and the commercialization of art.[39] Though Croly did not indicate interest in any particular character in the book, he may have been especially fascinated by James O. Lyons. In Grant's narrative, Lyons is a charismatic leader, politician, senator, and governor, "a large, full-bodied man ... impressive and slightly pontifical; his voice resonant and engaging."[40] Like Beecher, Blaine, and other charismatic orators, Lyons knows how to win over a crowd: "His speech flowed with the musical sweep of a master of platform oratory ... The audience listened in absorbed silence, spell-bound by the magnetism of his delivery."[41] Lyons' speeches are

[35] *Ibid.*, 58–59, 64; David Goodman Croly to Herbert Croly, February 13, 1888, quoted in *Ibid.*, 69.

[36] Croly, "In Memoriam," 7; Levy, *Herbert Croly of* The New Republic, 66.

[37] Levy, *Herbert Croly of* The New Republic, 84.

[38] Herbert Croly, "Why I Wrote My Latest Book: My Aim in 'The Promise of American Life'," *The World's Work*, Vol. 20 (June 1910), 13086.

[39] Christopher P. Wilson, " 'Unleavened Bread': The Representation of Robert Grant," *American Literary Realism, 1870–1910*, Vol. 22, No. 3 (Spring 1990), 26–33; Charles Forcey, *The Crossroads of Liberalism: Croly, Weyl, Lippmann, and the Progressive Era, 1900–1925* (New York: Oxford University Press, 1961), 22–23.

[40] Robert Grant, *Unleavened Bread* (New York: Scribner, 1900), 85.

[41] *Ibid.*, 282.

particularly strong in their nationalism, demonstrating "an abiding faith in the superiority of everything American."[42] But Lyons is as corrupt as he is charismatic. "Instead of fighting corporations," Lyons is "now the close adviser of a score of them ... the confidential attorney ... consulted in regard to their vital interests, and who charged them liberal sums for his services."[43] Just as with James Blaine, corruption and charismatic abilities seem to go hand in hand in Lyons' character.

Though Grant's writing is subtle, *Unleavened Bread* makes its condemnation of Lyons clear. At the climax of the book, a political opponent reveals that Lyons has accepted corporate bribes; the sly Lyons avoids public censure by voting against the corporation's interests, breaking his word to the corporation in order to appear honest to the voters. At the end of the book, Lyons has been elected to the Senate. He addresses a cheering crowd with a visage bearing "the effect of a patriarch, or of one inspired." "Your past has been ever glorious," Lyons tells his followers; "your future looms big with destiny ... I take up the work which you have given me to do, pledged to remain a democrat of the democrats, an American of the Americans."[44] Croly was horrified: "It struck me as deplorable that American patriotic formulas could be used with even the slightest plausibility to discourage competent and specialized individual intellectual effort, and I began to consider the origin and meaning of this contradiction, and the best method of overcoming it without doing violence to that which was best in the American democratic tradition."[45]

The Promise of American Life (1909), Croly's book-length response to Grant, was in a sense Croly's explanation for why the likes of James O. Lyons could hoodwink honest American citizens.[46] Croly began by charging that Americans suffered from a bad case of civic laziness. The time had come for people to stop thinking of their national promise as something that would just *happen* without any effort on their part, and to start considering it "instead a responsibility, which requires for its fulfillment a certain kind of behavior ... laborious,

[42] *Ibid.*, 284. [43] *Ibid.*, 285. [44] *Ibid.*, 430–431.

[45] Croly, "Why I Wrote My Latest Book," 13086.

[46] For alternate views, see Forcey, *The Crossroads of Liberalism*, 22–51; Levy, *Herbert Croly of* The New Republic, 96–131; and Edward A. Stettner, *Shaping Modern Liberalism: Herbert Croly and Progressive Thought* (Lawrence, KS: University Press of Kansas, 1993), 33–76.

single-minded, clear-sighted, and fearless work."[47] "The redemption of the national Promise," he declared, "has become a cause for which the good American must fight."[48] What must happen for this promise to be redeemed? Here Croly outlined a variety of traditional progressive solutions: "The existing concentration of wealth and financial power in the hands of a few irresponsible men" must end; corporations must fall under government regulation; bosses and special interests must exit the political sphere; "unscrupulous unionism" must sacrifice its own interests for the good of all Americans; lawyers and judges must consider social needs, not just narrow legalism, in their decisions; workers must "obtain ... a constantly higher standard of living" through government intervention.[49] These things should be brought about by the centralization of power in the hands of the federal government, particularly in the executive branch.

Croly stated this policy platform cogently and fitted it with some inventive historical trappings – progressivism was the philosophy of Alexander Hamilton, he wrote, while *laissez-faire* attitudes harkened back to Thomas Jefferson.[50] Few of Croly's policy positions were in any way controversial to most progressives. Accordingly, his contemporaries may be forgiven for praising his platform while largely ignoring the more innovative elements of his argument. Croly's protégé Walter Lippmann spoke for many other progressives when he wrote, "I should say that 'The Promise of American Life' was the political classic which announced the end of the Age of Innocence with its romantic faith in American destiny and inaugurated the process of self-examination."[51] Had it done merely that, *The Promise* would have been only a synthesis of what progressives had been advocating for years. But Croly did more than simply outline a program that could remove the corrupt James O. Lyonses from the political scene; he also explained how the charismatic relationship could make that program a reality.

Croly recognized that neither policies nor exhortations were enough to alter the course of American society. Instead, "Democracy must stand or fall on a platform of possible human perfectibility."[52] The changes he

[47] Herbert Croly, *The Promise of American Life* (New York: Macmillan, 1909), 4, 6.

[48] *Ibid.*, 21. [49] *Ibid.*, 23, 111, 113, 117, 128, 134, 206.

[50] *Ibid.*, 29; Jacob Kramer, *The New Freedom and the Radicals: Woodrow Wilson, Progressive Views of Radicalism, and the Origins of Repressive Tolerance* (Philadelphia: Temple University Press, 2015), 40.

[51] Walter Lippmann, "Notes for a Biography," *The New Republic*, July 16, 1930, 250; Levy, *Herbert Croly of* The New Republic, 132–135.

[52] Croly, *The Promise of American Life*, 400.

advocated could only come to pass through a tectonic shift in popular consciousness. To explain this shift, Croly expanded William James' concept of personal regeneration to encompass the American nation as a whole. "The task of individual and social regeneration," he wrote, "must remain incomplete and impoverished, until the conviction and feeling of human brotherhood enters into possession of the human spirit. The laborious work of individual and social fulfillment may eventually be transfigured by an outburst of enthusiasm … the finer flower of an achieved experience and a living tradition."[53] The task could only be completed, he reiterated, if some external force "will reveal to men the path whereby they may enter into spiritual possession of their individual and social achievements, and immeasurably increase them by virtue of personal regeneration."[54]

Croly was a synthetic thinker, and his introduction of religious regeneration into a progressive political argument was not new; Croly's contemporaries, the progressive theologians of the "Social Gospel," had made substantially the same argument. Where James had seen personal regeneration as a means of unlocking the power of the individual, Social Gospel minister Walter Rauschenbusch argued in *Christianity and the Social Crisis* (1907) that that power should extend across a whole nation. "If … the old [religious] enthusiasm is now directed toward the moral regeneration of society," Rauschenbusch wrote, "it would mean a new era for humanity … The moral forces latent in Christian society can be aroused and mobilized for the progressive regeneration of social life."[55] The simultaneous regeneration of masses of people could give Americans the means to reorder society in precisely the ways Rauschenbusch and Croly advocated. Croly moved beyond Rauschenbusch, however, by devising a mechanism to create this nationwide regeneration. Where Rauschenbusch relied on religious exhortation to regenerate Americans, Croly turned to a timelier and more powerful force: charismatic leadership.

Croly's plan recalled James O. Lyons and his magnetic hold over his followers. The problem with Lyons, Croly argued, was not that his power was dangerous, but that he himself was unscrupulous; not Lyons, but someone animated by true national purpose, should be wielding magnetic power and shaping the populace. "The American people are absolutely

[53] *Ibid.*, 452. [54] *Ibid.*, 453–454.

[55] Walter Rauschenbusch, *Christianity and the Social Crisis* (New York: Macmillan, 1907), 205, 344.

right in insisting that an aspirant for popular eminence shall be compelled to make himself interesting to them," Croly insisted. "And if the aspiring individual accepts this condition as tantamount to an order that he must haul down the flag" of his ideals "in order to obtain popular appreciation and reward, it is he who is unworthy to lead, not they who are unworthy of being led." Certainly men such as Lyons might possess more charismatic ability than civic-mindedness, or noble leaders might be devoid of magnetism. "But better the risk ... than sham battles and unearned victories."[56]

Then, in a remarkable passage, Croly launched into a full-throated defense of the charismatic relationship as an organizing principle of society. "The common citizen can become something of a saint and something of a hero," he wrote, paraphrasing Harvard philosopher George Santayana, "not by growing to heroic proportions in his own person, but by the sincere and enthusiastic imitation of heroes and saints, and whether or not he will ever come to such imitation will depend upon the ability of his exceptional fellow-countrymen to offer him acceptable examples of heroism and saintliness."[57] "There is only one way," he continued, "in which popular standards and preferences can be improved. The men whose standards are higher must learn to express their better message in a popularly interesting manner. The people ... will rally to the good thing, only because the good thing has been made to look good to them."[58]

Croly was again drawing on already-extant ideas, including a deep connection between personal magnetism and political regeneration that dated back to the early French mesmerists of the 1780s.[59] Similarly, Croly's suggestion that progressive policies should be "made to look good" to voters echoed the style of advertised politics popularized by William McKinley, Mark Hanna, and others. There was a difference, however: Croly believed the leader himself, not his campaign apparatus, could best promote progressivism through his charismatic connection with followers. Croly compared such leadership to the job of an architect who improves public artistic tastes by popularizing a more cultivated aesthetic style; similarly, a leader who could trigger regeneration in a mass of people could bring about the whole progressive program at a stroke.[60] Piecemeal progressive legislation was designed to prepare

[56] Croly, *The Promise of American Life*, 443. [57] *Ibid.*, 454. [58] *Ibid.*, 442–443.

[59] Robert Darnton, *Mesmerism and the End of the Enlightenment in France* (Cambridge, MA: Harvard University Press, 1968), 124.

[60] Croly, *The Promise of American Life*, 445–447.

followers for their "moral conversion" so that "some democratic evangelist – some imitator of Jesus" could bring about their full regeneration: "[N]ot until the [social] reorganization has been partly accomplished, and the individual released, disciplined and purified, will the soil be prepared for the crowning work of some democratic Saint Francis."[61] In the meantime, every "exceptional individual" should learn "to impose himself on the public"; the techniques of charismatic speech were available to anyone with the desire and ability to use them.[62] In Croly's vision, just as in Henry Ward Beecher's, charismatic oratory was a universal goal. The difference was that Beecher sought magnetic power in order to save souls; Croly wanted it to transform American politics.

Of course, Croly was now dangerously close to endorsing the behavior of the fictional Lyons. What would prevent the misuse of the charismatic relationship by unscrupulous operators? "The kind of leadership we have postulated above," he admitted, "is by its very definition and nature liable to become perverse and distracting."[63] Walter Lippmann and other progressives attempted to solve this problem by creating an absolute division between political leaders, who might wield charismatic power, and scientific experts, who must be guided by rational discourse.[64] But the dividing line quickly broke down; when scientists such as forester Gifford Pinchot and mining engineer Herbert Hoover crossed over to become charismatic politicians, most progressives applauded them for doing so. Croly's answer to the problem was more intellectually honest. The safety of the charismatic relationship would always be a process of negotiation and suspicion, he recognized. Leaders must remember that leadership was "a dangerous temptation ... and just because a leader cannot wholly trust himself to his following, so the followers must always keep a sharp lookout lest their leaders be leading them astray."[65] Only vigilance on both sides could empower a democratic St. Francis while protecting against men such as Lyons.

Because of this checking mechanism, Croly believed even an imperfect leader could safely bring about regeneration. His ideal St. Francis was Abraham Lincoln, who "always regarded other men and acted towards

[61] *Ibid.*, 453. [62] *Ibid.*, 447. [63] *Ibid.*, 449.

[64] James T. Kloppenberg, *Uncertain Victory: Social Democracy and Progressivism in European and American Thought, 1870–1920* (New York: Oxford University Press, 1986), 382–384; Walter Lippmann, *Drift and Mastery: An Attempt to Diagnose the Current Unrest* (New York: Kennerley, 1914), 282.

[65] Croly, *The Promise of American Life*, 449.

them … as human beings, capable of better things; and consequently all of his thoughts and actions looked in the direction of a higher level of human association … Democracy meant to him more than anything else the spirit and principle of brotherhood."[66] Croly understood, however, that another Lincoln would likely not be forthcoming. Accordingly, he turned his attention to contemporary reformers. For the most part, he found them sorely lacking in the abilities he sought. He castigated the charismatic William Jennings Bryan for being a wrongheaded and mediocre thinker who "stands for the sacrifice of the individual to the popular average."[67] He dismissed New York City District Attorney William Travers Jerome as insufficiently versed in state and national political issues.[68] And he attacked corrupt publisher and politician William Randolph Hearst as either "a fanatic" or "the sheerest demagogue."[69]

Croly paused, however, before the figure of Theodore Roosevelt, in 1909 the nation's most popular politician. Roosevelt was different from the other reformers, Croly felt; his "work has tended to give reform the dignity of a constructive mission … More than any other American political leader, except Lincoln, his devotion both to the national and to the democratic ideas is thorough-going and absolute."[70] Nevertheless, Roosevelt was far from perfect. "Mr. Roosevelt has done little to encourage candid and consistent thinking … In his own career his intelligence has been the handmaid of his will." Roosevelt's problem, according to Croly, was that he lacked the fine character "balance" of a Lincoln; instead, "He may be figured as a Thor wielding with power and effect a sledge-hammer in the cause of national righteousness."[71] In any case, Roosevelt would have to do for the time being. "Mr. Roosevelt and his hammer must be accepted gratefully, as the best available type of national reformer; but the day may and should come when a national reformer will appear who can be figured more in the guise of St. Michael, armed with a flaming sword and winged for flight."[72]

The Promise of American Life not only heralded Croly's arrival on the national scene as a major progressive intellectual; it also marked a major development in American ideas about charisma. More clearly than anyone before him, Croly had outlined a connection between the charismatic relationship and practical sociopolitical change. Charisma, he believed,

[66] *Ibid.*, 94. [67] *Ibid.*, 160. [68] *Ibid.*, 161–162. [69] *Ibid.*, 165. [70] *Ibid.*, 167, 170. [71] *Ibid.*, 174. [72] *Ibid.*, 175.

could serve as a powerful engine of social or political reform; it could be harnessed consciously and used to great effect. In 1909, Croly was virtually the only progressive to make this connection, though his faith in charisma as an agent of national regeneration would bear political fruit soon enough. At the time, however, another man shared many of Croly's insights about the charismatic relationship. Ironically, that man had more in common with P. T. Barnum, or even with James O. Lyons, than with Herbert David Croly.

* * *

In May 1914, as Croly was finishing his second book on progressive economic policies, the writer, publisher, and self-promoter Elbert Hubbard eagerly volunteered his services to help John D. Rockefeller, Jr., crush a striking labor union. "It seems to me that your stand is eminently right, proper, and logical," wrote Hubbard. Rockefeller's "stand" involved ordering fifteen striking Colorado miners shot dead in the April 20 "Ludlow Massacre," but that was of no consequence to Hubbard; the important thing was "showing this country, if possible, that we are drifting at present in the direction of I. W. W. socialism." Hubbard offered to write an essay making these points if Rockefeller would commit to "distributing a certain number of copies of the Fra [Hubbard's magazine] containing my article."[73] The following month, he prodded Rockefeller again, hinting pointedly that the businessman's father supported Hubbard's project. "I had a delightful game of golf with your father on Saturday," Hubbard wrote. "How fine and brown and well and strong he is."[74]

When Rockefeller still would not commit to distributing copies, Hubbard went ahead and wrote the article anyway. "That Mr. Rockefeller is guilty of murder because his men have successfully defended his property against assaults is one of the curious fallacies of anarchistic reasoning," Hubbard argued. "This strike was the work of the agitator, not the worker ... The dangers of secession are as nothing to the villainous attack by these conspirators on the Red, White, and Blue!"[75] After seeing the essay,

[73] Elbert Hubbard to John D. Rockefeller, Jr., May 3, 1914, quoted in Commission on Industrial Relations, *Industrial Relations: Final Report and Testimony*, Vol. VII (Washington, DC: Government Printing Office, 1916), 6676.

[74] Elbert Hubbard to John D. Rockefeller, Jr., June 8, 1914, quoted in Commission on Industrial Relations, *Industrial Relations*, 6676.

[75] Elbert Hubbard, "The Colorado Situation," *The Fra*, Vol. XIII, No. 5 (August 1914), 153–155.

Rockefeller agreed to distribute a thousand copies to influential Coloradans. "Every time some sane unbiased man presents the facts regarding this situation," he wrote Hubbard, "something worth while has been accomplished."[76] Hubbard responded by penning a second, more vituperative article on the strike. In it, he implied that the elderly "Mother" Jones was little more than a prostitute: "Mother Jones is not a working woman ... her profession is something else." The goal of Jones and the other strikers, Hubbard declared, was simply "to intimidate, coerce and finally murder men who wish to work, and destroy the property of employers."[77]

The apparent quid pro quo between Hubbard and Rockefeller scandalized many Americans. The arrangement led to a hearing by the federal Commission on Industrial Relations and, in 1920, a denunciation by the Socialist writer Upton Sinclair.[78] Hubbard, wrote Sinclair with white-hot anger, was a "sacred worm" whose "wriggling carcass ... all Capitalist Journalism venerated." Sinclair summed up Hubbard's behavior toward strikers and the poor: "This poisonous worm came crawling over their faces and ate out their eyes."[79] Yet that same "poisonous worm," that inveterate huckster, shared with Croly a strong and cogent advocacy of charisma as a social force. The fact that men as politically and personally different as Hubbard and Croly agreed substantially on this issue demonstrated charisma's breadth of support and helped to ensure the phenomenon's importance during the early twentieth century.

It all began with soap. Sixteen years after Hubbard's birth on June 19, 1856, he became a traveling soap salesman first for J. Weller & Co. and then, after a corporate split, for the Larkin Company.[80] Hubbard excelled at his trade and mastered some charismatic techniques in the process. "My smile was contagious, also infectious, as well as fetching," he remembered. "When I arrived in a town everybody smiled, and invited others to smile ... I scattered smiles, lilac-tinted stories, patchouli

[76] John D. Rockefeller, Jr., to Elbert Hubbard, August 3, 1914, box 10, Elbert Hubbard Papers, Harry Ransom Center, University of Texas at Austin; Commission on Industrial Relations, *Industrial Relations*, 6707.

[77] Elbert Hubbard, "In Colorado," *The Fra*, Vol. XIV, No. 4 (January 1915), 98, 100.

[78] Committee on Industrial Relations, *Industrial Relations*, 6707, 6720.

[79] Upton Sinclair, *The Brass Check: A Study of American Journalism* (Pasadena, CA: Upton Sinclair, 1920), 314.

[80] Robert L. Beisner, " 'Commune' in East Aurora," *American Heritage*, Vol. 22, No. 2 (February 1971), 73.

persiflage, good cheer, and small silver change all over the route ... And I sold the goods."[81]

After Hubbard's brother-in-law John Larkin offered him a one-third partnership in the business, Hubbard began to learn the principles of charismatic organization.[82] Hubbard was an innovative advertiser who quickly built the company into a successful enterprise.[83] Among his schemes was an ingenious plan to turn Larkin Soap's customers into salesmen themselves. Eliminating grocery stores and traveling agents from Larkin's business model, Hubbard mailed large packages of soap directly to customers who agreed to form "Larkin Clubs of Ten" and resell the soap to nine other families.[84] Without quite realizing it, Hubbard was selling soap in the same way charismatic preachers such as Billy Sunday sold salvation: the Larkin Clubs, like the Billy Sunday Clubs, allowed an energized community to "convert" others to the cause in the absence of a charismatic leader.

When Hubbard bolted Larkin Soap in 1893 to begin a career in "the realm of thought," he began to emphasize his charismatic abilities more strongly.[85] At the age of thirty-seven, Hubbard transformed himself into his own unique brand of magnetic man, bent on marketing himself just as he had previously advertised soap. "All live men are advertisers," he asserted, "and the only man who should not advertise ... is a dead one, whether he knows it or not."[86] He shaved off his salesman's moustache and grew his hair long; topping off the look with a wide-brimmed felt hat, he resembled the young William Jennings Bryan.[87] He built the Roycroft publishing commune at East Aurora, New York, and began churning out books and three monthly magazines (the aesthetic *Philistine*, the pro-business *Fra*, and the inspirational *Little Journeys to the Homes of the Great*) with the zeal of a born promoter. He embraced the quasi-

81 [Elbert Hubbard], "The Traveling Man," *The Philistine: A Periodical of Protest*, Vol. 39, No. 4 (September 1914), 110–111.

82 Howard R. Stanger, "From Factory to Family: The Creation of a Corporate Culture in the Larkin Company of Buffalo, New York," *Business History Review*, Vol. 74, No. 3 (Autumn 2000), 411.

83 See Milton Fuessle, "Elbert Hubbard: Master of Advertising and Retailing," *The Advertising World*, Vol. 20, No. 3 (August–September 1915), 139–144.

84 Stanger, "From Factory to Family," 415–416; Beisner, " 'Commune' in East Aurora," 74.

85 Elbert Hubbard to Juliana Hubbard, quoted in Freeman Champney, *Art & Glory: The Story of Elbert Hubbard* (New York: Crown Pub., 1968), 41.

86 Quoted in Fuessle, "Elbert Hubbard," 142; William Leach, *Land of Desire: Merchants, Power, and the Rise of a New American Culture* (New York: Pantheon, 1993), 42.

87 Charles F. Hamilton, *As Bees in Honey Drown: Elbert Hubbard and the Roycrofters* (South Brunswick, UK: A. S. Barnes, 1973), 57; Champney, *Art & Glory*, 30.

religious title of "Fra Elbertus," or "Brother Elbert." No shrinking violet, he hung a likeness of himself in every room at Roycroft.[88] In 1909, he even spent twenty weeks on the vaudeville circuit with Major Pond.[89] Hubbard's new personality, like Beecher's, was equal parts natural and artificial. "Mr. Hubbard is the only one of us who wears his make-up on the street," quipped a fellow vaudevillian.[90] Finally, Hubbard adapted his successful soap-selling technique to his new charismatic enterprise: the "Society of the Philistines" and the "American Academy of Immortals" solicited membership dues while enticing subscribers to purchase more Roycroft products.[91]

In some ways, charismatic performance bore dividends for Hubbard. "Dozens write me," he claimed after his vaudeville tour, "saying they saw me and heard me and that I have benefited them and helped them to live and face the duties of the day."[92] Yet Fra Elbertus never quite achieved a bona fide charismatic following. He was too brash, too argumentative, too salesmanlike, and too atheistic for many Americans to take seriously. Listeners were more likely to laugh at his antics than to venerate him as a leader. In Cincinnati, the vaudeville audience booed him off the stage; a year later, vaudeville managers in that city were still joking that they hoped audiences did not "Elbert Hubbardize" their clients.[93] Frustrated in his ambition to become a charismatic leader, Hubbard had to settle for being a public intellectual. In that role, at least, he was wildly successful.

Hubbard's philosophy was a unique mixture: a pinch of union-busting, a dash of self-help, a hefty serving of the Arts and Crafts movement's emphasis on meaningful work, all soaked in a marinade of Phineas Quimby's New Thought ideals.[94] In addition, despite Hubbard's failed charismatic career, personal magnetism and charismatic leadership held starring roles in his intellectual output. Hubbard especially

88 Fuessle, "Elbert Hubbard," 143. 89 Champney, *Art & Glory*, 139–140.

90 Beisner, " 'Commune' in East Aurora," 106.

91 Bruce A. White, *Elbert Hubbard's* The Philistine: A Periodical of Protest *(1895–1915)* (Lanham, MD: University Press of America, 1989), 25; *Ibid.*, 106.

92 Elbert Hubbard, *In the Spotlight: Personal Experiences of Elbert Hubbard on the American Stage*, comp. John T. Hoyle (East Aurora, NY: The Roycrofters, 1917), 90.

93 Felix Shay, *Elbert Hubbard of East Aurora* (New York: William H. Wise, 1926), 472; Champney, *Art & Glory*, 139; unpublished manager's review of Princess Baratoff, October 9, 1911, Report Book 12, 155, Keith/Albee Collection, University of Iowa Library. Thanks to M. Alison Kibler for this last reference.

94 Nancy Ann McCowan Sumner, "Orison Swett Marden: The American Samuel Smiles" (Ph.D. diss., Brown University, 1981), 203.

emphasized charismatic qualities in the short, reverent biographies that made up his *Little Journeys to the Homes of the Great*. Hubbard wrote the *Little Journeys* in part to bring him financial success by inducing his biographical subjects to buy reprints of his publications. In July 1909, for instance, Hubbard sent Andrew Carnegie proofs of a *Little Journey* about the Scottish magnate and convinced Carnegie to purchase a hundred copies of the finished product.[95] More important, the *Little Journeys* took part in a tradition of inspirational serial biographies that championed obedience and hard work as the necessary requisites for success. The English author Samuel Smiles popularized this form in the United States with *Self-Help* (1859), and motivational writers such as Orison Swett Marden perpetuated the idea.[96] Even Theodore Roosevelt and Henry Cabot Lodge got into the heroic biography business with their *Hero Tales from American History* (1895). "It is a good thing for all Americans," Lodge and Roosevelt wrote, "... to keep in mind the feats of daring and personal prowess done in time past by some of the many champions of the nation in the various crises of her history ... No people can be really great unless they possess also the heroic virtues which are as needful in time of peace as in time of war."[97] Hubbard went further than had these earlier writers, however. Having failed as a charismatic leader, Hubbard now envisioned himself as the organizer of a sort of charismatic relationship between reader and biographical subject. The historical figures depicted in the *Little Journeys*, he hoped, would rise from the printed page as idealized charismatic leaders who would teach wholesome values to their reader-followers.

Hubbard's series of *Little Journeys to the Homes of Eminent Orators* made explicit his interest in charisma. "Oratory is the impassioned outpouring of a heart – a heart full to bursting," he wrote in an essay on Girolamo Savonarola; "it is the absolute giving of soul to soul ... Oratory is the ability to weld a mass of people into absolutely one mood ... [The orator's] theme must always be an appeal for humanity." He echoed Le Bon's gendering of the masculine leader and feminine crowd: "The audience is the female element – the orator the male, and

95 Andrew Carnegie to Elbert Hubbard, July 3, 1909, box 9, Elbert Hubbard Papers.

96 Sumner, "Orison Swett Marden," 18; Samuel Smiles, *Self-Help, with Illustrations of Character and Conduct* (London: John Murray, 1859); Orison Swett Marden, *Little Visits with Great Americans* (New York: The Success Company, 1903).

97 Henry Cabot Lodge and Theodore Roosevelt, *Hero Tales from American History* (New York: Century, 1895), ix.

love is the theme."[98] In another essay, Hubbard described Patrick Henry's first public address in terms that echoed James' concept of regeneration: "In great oratory the appearance of the man is always changed . . . The idea of 'Cosmic Consciousness' – being born again – is not without its foundation in fact: the soul is in process of gestation, and when the time is ripe the new birth occurs, and will occur again and again."[99] Finally, Hubbard paid special attention to that great charismatic innovator, Henry Ward Beecher. "Such a specimen of mental, spiritual, and physical manhood," he wrote, "nature produces only once a century."[100] Beecher, he felt, had grasped charisma's real purpose: "The business of the orator is to inspire other men to think and act for themselves."[101] In an introduction to a textbook on oratory, Hubbard further emphasized these themes. He praised the orator's ability "to subdue the audience and blend mind with mind"; the orator, he declared, "through love lifts up humanity and sways men by a burst of feeling that brooks no resistance ... Oratory is an exercise of power."[102]

At first, Hubbard's writings drew only a modest following, but Hubbard's fortunes changed in 1899. In that year, an essay Hubbard had written to fill space in *The Philistine* came to the attention of the New York Central Railroad's "demon passenger agent" George H. Daniels. The "pudgy, chin-whiskered" Daniels (according to one railroad historian) was an interesting character in his own right and, like Hubbard, an innovative advertising pioneer. Daniels sold railway tickets by creating a mystique of comfort and fine living surrounding the New York Central. He chartered faster, more glamorous trains, improved dining car service, installed a team of "redcap" porters on every train to help passengers with their bags, and pioneered a new visual advertising idiom of comfort and leisure. In addition, Daniels conceived the idea of writing and distributing free reading material on the New York Central lines to advertise the railroad – the travel brochure *Health and Pleasure on America's Greatest Railroad*, the monthly travel magazine *Four-Track News*, and the *Four-Track Series*

98 Elbert Hubbard, *Little Journeys to the Homes of Eminent Orators* (New York: G. P. Putnam/Knickerbocker Press, 1907), 113–114.

99 Hubbard, *Little Journeys to the Homes of Eminent Orators*, 384.

100 *Ibid.*, 474.

101 *Ibid.*, 457.

102 Elbert Hubbard, "Introduction," in Henry Dickson, *Dickson's How to Speak in Public*, 3rd ed. (Chicago: Dickson School of Oratory, 1911), 5.

of pamphlets.[103] Daniels was not merely a master advertiser himself; like Hubbard, he was a vocal advertising advocate. "Without advertising no business can be successful," Daniels told the New York Sphinx Club in 1901. "A merchant who does not advertise is like a man winking at a pretty girl in the dark – he knows what he is doing, but no one else does."[104]

When Daniels opened the March 1899 *Philistine*, he recalled later, "The title 'A Message to Garcia,' struck me as peculiar, and I felt confident that underneath it would be found something of unusual interest." The article concerned an incident in the Spanish-American War in which an American army captain, Andrew Summers Rowan, successfully carried a message behind enemy lines to Cuban rebel leader Calixto Garcia. "That," Daniels told his secretary after reading the essay, "is the finest thing of its kind I have ever read."[105] "Charlie," he continued, "that's good. We know lots of folks who need to read that. Let's ask Hubbard to print us one thousand of them to send around."[106] One thousand became two, and then three – and then Daniels asked Hubbard to quote him the price for 100,000 copies. Hubbard was stunned: a *hundred thousand* copies? He gave Daniels permission to print the piece on his own.[107] Daniels added *A Message to Garcia* to the *Four-Track Series* and began printing copies a million at a time – and Hubbard's career as a public intellectual was launched.[108] Letters poured in to East Aurora asking for copies of *A Message to Garcia* faster than the Roycroft presses could produce them. Booker T. Washington ran the essay in the *Tuskegee Student*.[109] Even Billy Sunday read and appreciated the piece.[110] By the end of the year, the essay had been reprinted over seven million times; by Hubbard's death, according to one estimate, nearly forty million copies had appeared.[111]

103 Alvin F. Harlow, *The Road of the Century: The Story of the New York Central* (New York: Creative Age Press, 1947), 405, 409, 412; Edward Hungerford, *Men and Iron: The History of the New York Central* (New York: Thomas Y. Crowell, 1938), 376.

104 Quoted in "Advertising a Nation," *Lexington Morning Herald*, October 21, 1901, 2.

105 George H. Daniels, " 'A Message to Garcia': How It Came to Be Written and Why a Million Copies of It Are Being Printed," speech in New York, May, 22, 1899.

106 "That 'Message to Garcia'," *New York Sun*, December 3, 1899, 6.

107 Shay, *Elbert Hubbard of East Aurora*, 160.

108 Beisner, " 'Commune' at East Aurora," 108.

109 Booker T. Washington to Elbert Hubbard, June 21, 1899, box 10, Elbert Hubbard Papers.

110 W. A. Sunday to Elbert Hubbard II, May 7, 1930, box 12, Elbert Hubbard Papers.

111 "That 'Message to Garcia' 6"; Fuessle, "Elbert Hubbard," 143.

At first glance, *A Message to Garcia* seemed a typical pro-business screed. It praised the obedient worker and criticized subordinates who asked too many questions or refused to carry out arduous tasks. "It is not book-learning young men need," Hubbard wrote, "nor instruction about this and that, but a stiffening of the vertebrae which will cause them to be loyal to a trust, to act promptly, concentrate their energies: do the thing – 'Carry a message to Garcia!' "[112] Men such as Rowan were rare, Hubbard insisted: "Slip-shod assistance, foolish inattention, dowdy indifference, & half-hearted work seem the rule; and no man succeeds, unless by hook or crook, or threat, he forces or bribes other men to assist him."[113] Many readers likely interpreted *Garcia* as a simple exhortation to workers: shape up and follow orders! After reading the essay, the editor of the *Chicago Evening Journal* wrote to Daniels lamenting "the grinding monotony of dragooning a lot of mentally knock-kneed employes [*sic*] day after day, into doing the work they are paid to do, and the lying awake nights wondering if the latest blockhead that was intrusted with a piece of work did it or did something else his wandering mind thought was it." The editor blasted such employees as "cheats ... They are not entitled to much, and they don't get much ... There is a golden prize hung up for the young man of to-day who can learn just simply to carry out orders."[114]

A closer look at *Garcia*, however, suggests that the essay's message is more complex. Rowan's character in particular shows some qualities of both a charismatic leader and a follower. Like charismatic followers, Hubbard's Rowan demonstrates commitment to both his nationalist cause and his military superior and displays unusual energy and dedication to the task at hand; his ability "to be loyal to a trust," to "concentrate [his] energies," and his "... capacity for independent action" could describe any devotee of a charismatic figure. More important, Hubbard intended Rowan to serve as a model for real-life workers – to forge a similar bond with charismatic reader-followers as did the subjects of the *Little Journeys*. "By the Eternal!" he wrote, "there is a man whose form should be cast in deathless bronze and the statue placed in every college of the land."[115] "The hero," he explained later, "is the man who does the thing – does his work – carries the message."[116] In Hubbard's innovative

[112] Elbert Hubbard, *A Message to Garcia: Being a Preachment* (East Aurora, NY: The Roycrofters, 1899), 2–3.

[113] *Ibid.*, 3. [114] Quoted in Daniels, "'A Message to Garcia'," 7–8.

[115] Hubbard, *A Message to Garcia*, 2. [116] Shay, *Elbert Hubbard of East Aurora*, 159.

written model of the charismatic relationship, Rowan was the hero, American workers his admiring followers.

In his full-length biography of Jesus, *The Man of Sorrows* (1905), Hubbard brought all these pieces together in an impassioned defense of the charismatic relationship. "We need Messiahs now just as much as they did two thousand years ago – and more," he wrote. "Let a man arise who believes in his own divinity; who is filled with the spirit of love; who has the yearning heart and unselfish soul, and men will everywhere flock to his standard."[117] The son of God was an unusual biographical subject for a proud atheist, but Hubbard, drawing on New Thought teachings about the mind's power over the body, argued that Christ worked miracles through charismatic power rather than divine ability. "This ecstasy of faith, hope, uplift and sublime strength is highly contagious," he explained, "and sick people – those with nervous disorders – coming under its influence, are often made . . . well. Thoughtful physicians know and admit the wonderful effects of mind on mind, and of mind over matter."[118] The key to obtaining this religious ecstasy, Hubbard concluded, lay in the obedience he had counseled in *Garcia*: "The Kingdom must be gained, not by making war on the established order, but by accepting it, paying taxes to Caesar, making the best of outward environment by submitting to it, and then conquering through this sublime ecstasy of the soul that raises one clear above the dross of earth and the rust and dust of time."[119]

Here, in *The Man of Sorrows*, lay the main argument of Hubbard's charismatic thought. Hubbard agreed with Croly that the charismatic relationship was beneficial to followers and that it was a key part of the American social structure. The two men differed, however, in their expectations for how charismatic movements would influence society. Croly predicted that charisma would transform followers into agents of social change who would demand national regeneration. Hubbard, by contrast, saw the leader–follower relationship both as a way of training Americans to "accept . . . the established order" and as a reward for their doing so.[120] Hubbard's leaders were Horatio Alger types, polite and hardworking; even Jesus was "brought . . . up to be useful; to wait

117 Elbert Hubbard, *The Man of Sorrows: Being a Little Journey to the Home of Jesus of Nazareth* (East Aurora, NY: The Roycrofters, 1908), 41.

118 *Ibid.*, 33. 119 *Ibid.*, 35.

120 Eileen Boris, *Art and Labor: Ruskin, Morris, and the Craftsman Ideal in America* (Philadelphia: Temple University Press, 1986), 146.

on himself; to respect his elders and to do good work."[121] Learn from your leaders to accept the inequalities inherent in society, Hubbard argued, and you could reap the rewards of charismatic self-transformation. Croly and Hubbard also located follower agency in different activities. Where Croly's followers made choices about which leaders and causes to support, Hubbard's workers expressed their individuality in the methods they chose to carry out their assigned tasks. A man who accepted the established order could carry a message to Garcia in any way he chose; obedience made work meaningful and opened the door to a world of endless creativity. As Russell Herman Conwell, a popular Chautauqua orator, put it, "Greatness consists not in the holding of some future office, but really consists in doing great deeds with little means and the accomplishment of vast purposes from the private ranks of life."[122]

Hubbard spoke for a wide swath of American business leaders when he voiced these sentiments. "You would take the prize if one were awarded to the one who could make the most out of the least," Carnegie wrote to Hubbard. "You have a style of your own and hit the nail in the most unexpected fashion."[123] Carnegie himself developed a Hero Fund that he asked Hubbard to promote; the fund honored ordinary Americans who were injured or killed while helping others.[124] In another era, men such as Carnegie and Rockefeller might have opposed charismatic movements as a threat to order and a dangerous tool of the masses. In the wake of the magnetism craze, however, they saw the charismatic relationship as one that could be used to stabilize society and preserve their interests. "We live in a heroic age," Carnegie explained.[125] This conservative interpretation of charisma, they stressed, benefited workers as well as employers. "The man who can carry a message to Garcia," Hubbard wrote, "... is so rare that no employer can afford to let him go ... Anything such a man asks shall be granted."[126]

121 Hubbard, *The Man of Sorrows*, 21.
122 Russell Herman Conwell, *Acres of Diamonds* (New York: Harper & Brothers, 1915), 58–59.
123 Carnegie to Hubbard, July 3, 1909, Elbert Hubbard Papers.
124 Hubbard made only a passing reference to the Fund in his *Little Journey* on Carnegie. *Ibid.*; Elbert Hubbard, *Little Journeys to the Homes of Great Business Men: Andrew Carnegie* (East Aurora, NY: The Roycrofters, 1909), 66.
125 Andrew Carnegie, "Deed of Trust – Carnegie Hero Fund Commission," in *Annual Report of the Carnegie Hero Fund Commission* (Pittsburgh, PA: Carnegie Hero Fund Commission, 1930), 9–11, quoted in Peter N. Stearns, *American Cool: Constructing a Twentieth-Century Emotional Style* (New York: New York University Press, 1994), 72.
126 Hubbard, *A Message to Garcia*, 10–11.

Furthermore, Hubbard's connection with George Daniels underscored the connection between conservative charisma and advertising. Like Mark Hanna and other pioneers of advertised politics, Hubbard believed the essential appeal of leaders could be transmitted through the printed page; accordingly, his brand of charismatic influence was aligned, for the time being, with the interests of advertisers such as Daniels. Advertising, Hubbard felt, could marshal charismatic techniques to influence readers or viewers. Unlike political advertisers, though, Hubbard sought not votes or sales but internal charismatic transformations within his readers. He had come a long way from "selling the goods" as a young soap salesman; now, he sought to sell workers on a new vision of themselves, laboring harmoniously within a fulfilling and prosperous America.

When Elbert Hubbard went down with the *Lusitania* on May 7, 1915, his family received hundreds of condolence letters from prominent figures.[127] Americans as disparate as the populist William Jennings Bryan and the conservative Elihu Root, the industrialist J. Ogden Armour and the labor leader Terence Powderly, took the opportunity to eulogize Fra Elbertus; even Billy Sunday sent a letter of sympathy.[128] Hubbard left behind a varied legacy in the fields of advertising, publishing, performance, craftsmanship, and philosophy, but one of his most important contributions was in the field of charismatic thought. There is no evidence that Hubbard's written descriptions of charismatic leaders actually induced charismatic followership among American workers. Nevertheless, more clearly than any other intellectual, Hubbard articulated a notion of charisma that was compatible with American conservatism. His political views differed greatly from Croly's, but the two men shared a respect and appreciation for the charismatic relationship as an important and beneficial social force. Nor were they the only thinkers to integrate charisma into their visions of society. Perhaps the most surprising turn-of-the-century defense of charismatic movements came from the radical edge of the political spectrum – from the very "agitators" Hubbard had excoriated in Ludlow.

* * *

They wrote a song about Joe Hill: "I dreamed I saw Joe Hill last night / Alive as you and me. / Says I, 'But Joe, you're ten years dead.' / 'I never

[127] Champney, *Art & Glory*, 195.

[128] Elbert Hubbard II, ed., *In Memoriam: Elbert and Alice Hubbard* (East Aurora, NY: The Roycrofters, 1915), 105, 182, 208, 221, 342.

died,' says he. / 'I never died,' says he."[129] The lyrics, penned by Alfred Hayes in 1934, explain that Hill "didn't die" because "What they could never kill / Went on to organize . . . / Where workers strike and organize / It's there you'll find Joe Hill."[130] But Hill lived on in more tangible ways, too. After the state of Utah executed Hill on November 19, 1915, for a murder he likely did not commit, the Industrial Workers of the World songwriter received no fewer than three lavish funerals. Thousands of workers attended a service for Hill at a Salt Lake City mortuary; most had to stand outside after the tiny chapel reached capacity.[131] Five thousand more filled the West Side Auditorium in Chicago to pay their respects, while "the sidewalks outside the building were jammed solidly for three blocks" by 30,000 additional mourners.[132] The IWW "Wobblies," as they were called, held a third service at Chicago's Graceland Cemetery; this time, the crowd so overflowed the chapel that the proceedings had to be moved outside to a grassy field. Hill's body was cremated, but the rituals continued. A year later, IWW president William "Big Bill" Haywood distributed 150 packages of Hill's ashes to union members and instructed them to scatter Hill's remains all over the country and the world.[133] One packet got lost in the mail and was rediscovered in 1986. The surviving IWW members asked for custody, and in June 1989 Joe Hill had one more funeral in Lafayette, Colorado, where hundreds of people witnessed the final scattering of his remains.[134]

It was a bizarre end for the iconic Wobbly songwriter, considering Hill's own views on hero-worship and charismatic leadership. Hill's most famous song, "The Preacher and the Slave," skewered the evangelical Holiness movement for inspiring people to pray for salvation when they could be fighting for a living wage. "Work and pray, live on hay, / You'll get pie in the sky when you die," mocked Hill, coining a phrase that endures to this day.[135] Other radicals made the connection between charismatic leadership and oppression more explicit. Wobblies, for

[129] Alfred Hayes and Earl Robinson, "Joe Hill" (1936), quoted in William M. Adler, *The Man Who Never Died: The Life, Times, and Legacy of Joe Hill, American Labor Icon* (New York: Bloomsbury, 2011).

[130] *Ibid.*, 19, 20. [131] Adler, *The Man Who Never Died*, 335.

[132] *Ibid.*, 339; "Red Flag Waves as I. W. W. Chiefs Praise Joe Hill," *Chicago Tribune*, November 26, 1915, 13.

[133] *Ibid.*, 340. [134] *Ibid.*, 348–349.

[135] Joe Hill, "The Preacher and the Slave," quoted in William Kostlevy, *Holy Jumpers: Evangelicals and Radicals in Progressive Era America* (New York: Oxford University Press, 2010), 3–4, 6–7.

instance, removed the words "leader" and "Great Commander" from a popular song before repurposing it as a labor ballad.[136]

The charismatic Billy Sunday, in particular, was a frequent whipping boy for labor radicals. Poet Carl Sandburg led the charge against Sunday: "There is terrific tragedy of the individual and of the crowd in and about Billy Sunday. He is the most conspicuous single embodiment in this country of the crowd leader or crowd operative who uses jungle methods, stark voodoo stage effects, to play hell with democracy."[137] The *Industrial Worker* agreed, attacking Sunday in 1909 as a hypocrite and a traitor: "The people who followed Christ for loaves were not up to the standard of Sunday. How much better to follow Christ to some purpose – for thousands of dollars, for instance ... He must have taken a post-graduate course on the life of Judas Iscariot and Ananias."[138] Eugene Debs reported rhetorically stripping Sunday "stark naked and the great crowd went wild as I showed him up for the fraud & charlatan he is."[139] "Do you know," remarked the painter and sometime Socialist George Wesley Bellows in 1917, "I believe Billy Sunday is the worst thing that ever happened to America?"[140] As the attacks on Sunday showed, American radicals saw charismatic leadership – or really, any leadership at all – as trickery designed to lead the masses into false consciousness and distract them from their true needs. So why did the Wobblies make such a fuss over Joe Hill?

As it happened, there were two types of charismatic figure whom many radicals accepted as compatible with their ideology. Hill belonged to the first type: the martyr. Since heroes were only dangerous when they could use their influence to manipulate their followers, deceased radicals were generally safe to admit into the pantheon. The Wobblies found Hill useful in death precisely because their hero-worship could not inflate his ego or steer him toward bourgeois pretensions; he could inspire working people without any fear that their loyalty to him might lead them away from radicalism. Elaborate funerals for the martyred and not-quite-martyred

136 Donald E. Winters, Jr., *The Soul of the Wobblies: The I. W. W., Religion, and American Culture in the Progressive Era, 1905–1917* (Westport, CT: Greenwood Press, 1985), 46.

137 Carl Sandburg to Alfred Harcourt, 1916, quoted in Sandburg, *The Letters of Carl Sandburg*, ed. Herbert Mitgang (New York: Harcourt, Brace and World, 1968), 108; Winters, *The Soul of the Wobblies*, 71–72.

138 "Billy Sunday," *Industrial Worker*, March 18, 1909, 2.

139 Eugene V. Debs to Theodore Debs, March 3, 1917, reel 2, Debs Collection, Indiana State University, Terre Haute, Indiana.

140 "The Big Idea: George Bellows Talks about Patriotism for Beauty," *The Touchstone*, Vol. 1, No. 3 (July 1917), 270.

were a staple of radical unionist culture. "Big Bill" Haywood, for instance, died dissolute and friendless in a Moscow hotel, not heroically at the hands of his oppressors as Hill did. Nevertheless, Haywood's fellow Communists held impressive parades for him and buried his ashes with great ceremony in both Moscow and Chicago.[141] Despite their anticlericalism, radicals used the figure of Jesus Christ in a similar way. Writers such as George Lippard, George Herron, and Bouck White – the latter two Christian Socialist ministers – presented Jesus as a radical leader of workingmen martyred for his cause.[142]

To swell their numbers and rouse the masses to action, however, radicals needed more than just memories of dead heroes. At such times, there was a second type of charismatic leader they could call upon. Haywood identified the type in a 1902 editorial. "The agitator," he wrote, "is the advance agent of social improvement . . . His presence is always required, as ... without the agitator the work would only be partly done and much of the value of organization be lost ... A labor union without an agitator is like a quartz mill without a piece of machinery of the same name."[143] The job of an agitator – the union one, not the mechanical one – was to make people think about the economic conditions in which they found themselves: "He never tires of stirring up questions and problems that are not always in his province to settle, but without him would never have come to the surface."[144] Labor editor John Swinton had made a similar argument in an 1885 editorial, but substituting the term "orator" for "agitator." "We need a great orator for this people's battle against capitalism," Swinton had insisted then – "a man of superlative eloquence ... ready to sacrifice himself and all the prizes of life for the cause." It was no surprise that Swinton turned to the memory of Jonathan Barber's greatest student for inspiration: "Oh, for another Wendell Phillips!"[145]

[141] Peter Carlson, *Roughneck: The Life and Times of Big Bill Haywood* (New York: W. W. Norton, 1983), 325, 327.

[142] Dan McKanan, *Prophetic Encounters: Religion and the American Radical Tradition* (Boston: Beacon Press, 2011), 112–113; David Burns, *The Life and Death of the Radical Historical Jesus* (New York: Oxford University Press, 2013), 62–63, 86–90; Herbert G. Gutman, "Protestantism and the American Labor Movement: The Christian Spirit in the Gilded Age," *American Historical Review*, Vol. 72, No. 1 (October 1966), 85–86.

[143] William D. Haywood, "The Agitator," *The Miners' Magazine*, Vol. 3 (February 1902), 6.

[144] *Ibid.*, 6.

[145] "Wanted – An Orator," *John Swinton's Paper*, July 19, 1885; Kenneth G. Hance, H. O. Hendrickson, and Edwin W. Schoenberger, "The Later National Period, 1860–1930,"

Agitators often used charismatic methods to win workers over to their cause. William Z. Foster recalled his conversion to Socialism under the influence of a radical street orator: "I listened entranced by what the speaker said ... His arguments and analysis seemed to give real meaning to all my experience in the class struggle ... The speaker was a good one and I drank in his words eagerly. I left the meeting in great enthusiasm ... That street meeting indeed marked a great turning point in my life."[146] Agitators' transient role distinguished them from traditional charismatic leaders, however. Just as in a quartz mill, an agitator was a tool: he or she converted listeners in a single meeting, then melted back into the radical machinery so the newly converted could choose their own courses of action. Foster never again saw the street orator who was so influential in his life; he could not even recall his name. In this way, Foster and other converts were safe from the reactionary backsliding that could so easily bedevil charismatic figures.

That was the theory, at any rate. In reality, agitators had an unnerving habit of sticking around past their expiration dates – and radicals tended to ignore or even celebrate the permanence of such figures. Haywood was a good example. Wobblies and labor supporters united in their admiration for the oratorical skills of the rangy, one-eyed agitator. "He had tremendous magnetism," labor reporter Art Shields noted. "Huge frame, one blazing eye, voice filling the hall ... like a clap of thunder."[147] "He had a personal and physical magnetism that nobody could resist," recalled union member Mary Gallagher. "It was something inborn in his personality that made him such a great leader."[148] "He is a torch amongst a crowd of uncritical and credulous workmen," agreed British Labour politician Ramsay MacDonald. "I saw him addressing a crowd in England ... He made them see things, and their hearts bounded to be up and doing."[149] Haywood spoke to tens of thousands in Chicago, Milwaukee, and New York; crowds

in William Norwood Brigance, ed., *A History and Criticism of American Public Address*, Vol. 1 (New York: McGraw-Hill, 1943), 147.

146 William Z. Foster, *From Bryan to Stalin* (New York: International Publishers, 1937), 23.

147 Quoted in Len De Caux, *The Living Spirit of the Wobblies* (New York: International Publishers, 1978), 35; Carlson, *Roughneck*, 147.

148 Willa K. Baum, Oral History of Mary E. Gallagher, 1955, Bancroft Library, University of California, Berkeley, quoted in Melvyn Dubofsky, *"Big Bill" Haywood* (New York: St. Martin's Press, 1987), 1.

149 J. Ramsay MacDonald, *Syndicalism: A Critical Examination* (London: Constable & Co., 1912), 36–37; Dubofsky, *"Big Bill" Haywood*, 1.

spontaneously acclaimed him as presidential timber.[150] Haywood's Chicago speech seared itself into the memory of Wobbly artist Ralph Chaplin. "Few who ever heard Bill's voice can ever forget it," Chaplin commented. "Speaking was his special gift."[151] Even the hostile *Paterson Press* admitted to being impressed with Haywood's "magnetic power."[152]

That power was not so much a "special gift" or "inborn in his personality" as it was the result of practice and calculation. What leaders such as Bryan and Beecher learned through elocution courses, Haywood gleaned from years of organizing and observing. At a 1912 strike in Lawrence, Kansas, union organizers Elizabeth Gurley Flynn and Carlo Tresca learned from Haywood how to replicate the leader's powerful connection with immigrant workers whose command of English might be limited. Haywood taught Flynn "to use short words and short sentences, to repeat the same thought in different words if I saw that the audience did not understand … never to reach for a three-syllable word if one or two would do."[153] When audiences lacked even basic English skills, Haywood resorted to purely physical orations. "He would hold over the crowd his huge, powerful hand," Tresca recalled. "He would seize one finger after the other with his other hand, saying to his audience: '… Every finger by itself has no force. Now look' – He would bring the fingers close together, close them into a bulky, powerful fist, lift that fist in the face of the crowd, saying, 'See that? That's IWW.' The mass would go wild."[154] Firmly ensconced in leadership positions, intimately acquainted with magnetic speaking techniques, Haywood was a charismatic leader in all but name – yet his eager followers never saw the contradiction between his popularity and their criticism of "bourgeois" charismatic leaders such as Sunday.

More problematic even than Haywood was Eugene V. Debs. "Tall, blue-eyed, pale, smooth-shaven and inclined to baldness," according to *Yenowine's Illustrated News*, Debs was universally acclaimed as a magnetic man and a great orator.[155] Foster called him "the greatest agitator of the American revolutionary movement"; Flynn remembered

[150] Dubofsky, *"Big Bill" Haywood*, 50–51; Carlson, *Roughneck*, 145; "10,000 Turn Out to Greet Haywood," *New York Times*, January 18, 1908, 2.

[151] Quoted in Carlson, *Roughneck*, 146. [152] *Ibid.*, 203.

[153] Elizabeth Gurley Flynn, *The Rebel Girl: An Autobiography, My First Life (1906–1926)* (New York: International Publishers, 1973), 131.

[154] Quoted in Carlson, *Roughneck*, 165.

[155] "A True Picture of Debs," *Yenowine's Illustrated News*, July 21, 1894, 4.

FIGURE 4.1 Eugene V. Debs' passionate oratory and "magnetic hands" made him a powerful charismatic speaker.
Source: Photo of Eugene V. Debs, Chicago, 1912, courtesy of the Department of Special Collections, Cunningham Memorial Library, Indiana State University.

him bursting with "eloquence such as I had never heard."[156] "He has always meant to me the one great inspiring force in the spiritual desert of the United States," Emma Goldman wrote.[157] Newspapers noted Debs' "wonderful personal magnetism, so that scarcely any one who has met him has failed to come under the spell of his affable and persuasive manners."[158] Frederic O. MacCartney, nominating Debs for president at the 1900 Socialist convention, dubbed him "a liberator of his kind … the knight errant of the new chivalry which will mean the emancipation of our land."[159] To all of them, Debs seemed the one man whose charismatic speaking could unite all the radical factions into a unified movement and lead that movement to victory.

156 Foster, *From Bryan to Stalin*, 142; Flynn, *The Rebel Girl*, 121.
157 Emma Goldman to Theodore Debs, February 6, 1928, reel 5, Debs Collection.
158 "Who Debs Is," *New York Recorder*, quoted in *Galveston Daily News*, July 13, 1894.
159 *Social Democratic Herald*, March 17, 1900, quoted in Nick Salvatore, *Eugene V. Debs: Citizen and Socialist*, 2nd ed. (Urbana, IL: University of Illinois Press, 2007), 175.

Unlike Haywood, Debs had begun his career as a mainstream politician. Accordingly, though he adopted some of Haywood's gestural speaking techniques when facing multilingual audiences, Debs was more comfortable using traditional charismatic methods.[160] Debs "in his youth trained himself in the art of public speaking," wrote IWW activist Alexander Trachtenberg; the young orator's models included Robert Ingersoll and William Jennings Bryan.[161] Ralph Korngold, an activist and writer, explained Debs' techniques for holding his listeners' attention: "Walking back and forth on the platform, a little bent, his arm outstretched, pointing or shaking his finger, he seemed to be addressing each member of his audience separately."[162] "There was magic in his choice of words and tone of voice, in his outstretched appealing hands, his bent body," recalled Shubert Sebree. "He felt every emotion his words portrayed and he had the remarkable power of compelling others to fully share in this emotion."[163]

While he bragged about stripping Billy Sunday "stark naked" before an audience, Debs adopted prophetic Christian imagery similar to Sunday's in order to inspire his followers.[164] "Debs on the platform was more the evangelist," Trachtenberg reported. "He appealed to his audience rather than reasoned with it. He always tried to convert."[165] Like Elbert Hubbard before him, Debs repurposed Jesus Christ as a charismatic leader who would have supported the orator's own cause. "The martyred Christ of the working class," he wrote in a 1914 essay, "the inspired evangel of the downtrodden masses, the world's supreme revolutionary leader, ... had the majesty and poise of a god, the prophetic vision of a seer, the great, loving heart of a woman, and the unaffected innocence and simplicity of a child."[166] Debs also adapted the rhetoric of masculinity to advance his argument: "No man can rightly claim to be a man unless he is free," he

[160] Salvatore, *Eugene V. Debs*, 231.

[161] Alexander Trachtenberg, *Heritage of Gene Debs* (New York: International Publishers, 1928), 22.

[162] Ralph Korngold, "The Debs I Knew," in J. Robert Constantine, ed., *Debs Remembered: A Collection of Reminiscences* (Terre Haute, IN: Indiana State University (unpublished), 1981), reel 5, Papers of Eugene V. Debs microfilm edition.

[163] Shubert Sebree, "Gene Debs, My Beloved Comrade," in Constantine, ed., *Debs Remembered.*

[164] Salvatore, *Eugene V. Debs*, 65.

[165] Trachtenberg, *Heritage of Gene Debs*, 22–23; *Ibid.*, 231.

[166] Eugene V. Debs, "Jesus, The Supreme Leader," *Coming Nation*, March 1914, reprinted in Debs, *Labor and Freedom: The Voice and Pen of Eugene V. Debs* (St. Louis: Phil Wagner, 1916), 29.

told audiences as he urged them to fight for better treatment.[167] Finally, Debs incorporated mainstream American ideals of individualism and civic republicanism into his Socialist rhetoric.[168]

From a Socialist perspective, much of Debs' philosophy likely came across as bourgeois and counterrevolutionary – but few radicals seemed to mind. "The people are wild with enthusiasm," Debs wrote to his parents after an 1896 speech in Chicago. "Such exhibition of love & emotion, men & women & children I never witnessed."[169] Letters poured in from adoring followers declaring Debs a hero and, after his 1918 imprisonment, a martyr. Many recalled that Debs' magnetic presence, not his arguments, had converted them to Socialism. A veteran Socialist explained to Heywood Broun the secret of Debs' appeal: "That old man with the burning eyes actually believes that there can be such a thing as the brotherhood of man ... As long as he's around I believe it myself."[170] The poet William Ellery Leonard made clear how far the radical conception of Debs had drifted from the limited role of the agitator. "It is this that makes Debs mean so much to me," Leonard wrote: "[H]e realizes my boyhood visions of the Heroic Americans, the man firmly planted in his Instincts, unmoved by Opinion, and unafraid before Authority, in the assertion of his own inviolable integrity."[171] In a striking letter, R. J. Young explained his followership of Debs in terms borrowed explicitly from Carlyle. "The world has always had heroes – has always needed them – never more so than now," he wrote; "all progress has been due to those great souls to whom nothing mattered but Truth! – As you know, Carlyle said we are all hero worshippers, and I am only offering my wreath of laurel, while my hero is yet in the flesh and can breathe in the fragrance with which I would endow it, had I the power."[172]

In theory, radicals were opposed to the charismatic relationship. "Too long have the workers of the world waited for some Moses to lead them out of bondage," Debs himself argued in 1905. "I would not lead you out if I could; for if you could be led out, you could be led back

167 Eugene V. Debs, "Unity and Victory," speech before State Convention of American Federation of Labor, Pittsburg, Kansas, August 12, 1908, reprinted in Debs, *Labor and Freedom*, 128–129; *Ibid.*, 228.

168 Salvatore, *Eugene V. Debs*, 172.

169 Eugene V. Debs to Jean Daniel and Marguerite Debs, October 12, 1896, reel 1, Debs Collection.

170 Quoted in Broun, "The Miracle of Debs," 38; Salvatore, *Eugene V. Debs*, 225.

171 William Ellery Leonard, quoted in Ruth Le Prade, ed., *Debs and the Poets* (Pasadena, CA: Upton Sinclair, 1920), 70.

172 R. J. Young to Eugene V. Debs, April 7, 1920, reel 2, Debs Collection.

again."[173] In reality, however, radicals' acceptance of the charismatic figures of agitator and martyr flung the door wide open to figures such as Debs and Haywood. The same activists who lampooned Billy Sunday's charismatic speeches could describe Debs as a "Heroic American" or, like Sara Cleghorn, beg for a piece of his coat. Socialists even began to hold revivalist camp meetings in direct imitation of their religious opponents.[174] Early in Debs' career, a union colleague excoriated the leader for encouraging "hero-worship ... Does any sane man imagine for a moment that there is any other purpose behind all this than a desire to pose as a Sir Anthony Absolute, to be recognized as the great 'I Am,' and reverenced accordingly."[175] This position accorded with radical ideology, but Debs' antagonist was virtually alone in his criticism. Generally speaking, radicals seemed just as happy with their charismatic leaders as did progressives and conservatives.

* * *

From radical to moderate, from progressive to conservative, a broad spectrum of Americans believed the charismatic relationship was a beneficial agent of change by 1910. In the end, even the curmudgeonly Henry Watterson could not escape the clutches of charismatic followers; many insisted that Watterson himself exuded the personal magnetism he claimed to despise. "A Napoleon among the editorial writers and ... an orator of irresistible force," gushed the *Milwaukee Journal* in 1896, "he exerts a personal magnetism by the affability and cordiality that mark the whole-souled man."[176] In the same year, former Indianapolis mayor John P. Hopkins tried to convince Watterson to run for president as a third-party candidate because the campaign "requires a man with that personal magnetism that wins people to him."[177]

Watterson's paradox nicely represented the charismatic conundrum of turn-of-the-century America. Many people claimed to agree with Le Bon that charismatic leadership was a cynical but necessary response to crowd

173 Eugene V. Debs, *Industrial Unionism*, speech delivered December 10, 1905 (New York: New York Labor News Co, 1906), 3.

174 Salvatore, *Eugene V. Debs*, 236.

175 T. P. O'Rourke, letter in *Locomotive Fireman's Magazine*, Vol. 14 (March 1890), 251–252, quoted in *Ibid.*, 94–95.

176 "Henry Watterson, Prophet," *Milwaukee Journal*, June 25, 1896, 4.

177 "The Watterson Boom Being Carefully Nursed by John P. Hopkins," *Associated Press*, reprinted in *New Orleans Daily Picayune*, August 31, 1896.

hysteria, or with Watterson that charismatic phenomena had no social benefits and should be avoided altogether. At the same time, though, many of those same Americans accepted or even welcomed charismatic movements that served their own candidates or policy platforms. Herbert Croly and Elbert Hubbard were unusual in their frank support for charismatic techniques. Many more Americans resembled the radical unionists: contemptuous of personal magnetism except when it stemmed from their own beloved charismatic leaders.

Croly's "democratic Saint Francis," Hubbard's "man with the message," and the unionists' "agitator" formed a curiously powerful triumvirate. Each archetype represented a broad vision for how charisma could and should remake American society. Croly and progressives wanted to bring economic equality and spiritual regeneration to the nation; Hubbard and conservatives wanted to consecrate the working class to an established order newly infused with meaning; radicals wanted to rebuild society in the image of social justice. These charismatic philosophers were not working in the abstract, nor did they expect their visions would take long to reach fruition. Indeed, each archetype seemed to fit ready-made charismatic saviors near at hand: Theodore Roosevelt for Croly, the captains of industry for Hubbard, Debs and Haywood for the radicals. The three visions united many disparate Americans in the belief that charismatic movements could motivate followers and enact social change on a national scale. Each group, however, expected that the power of the charismatic relationship would vindicate the group's own model of American society. As the twentieth century's second decade began, Croly's progressives would get the first chance to prove charismatic techniques compatible with their ideal social vision. The stage was set for a series of confrontations over charisma – confrontations that would play out in the most public of arenas, with dramatic consequences for American culture.

5

Changing Society

The Rise and Fall of Progressive Charisma, 1910–1920

On Monday, August 5, 1912, thirty-one-year-old attorney Donald Richberg arrived at the Chicago Coliseum to attend the national convention of the new Progressive Party. Sixteen years earlier, William Jennings Bryan had electrified the Coliseum with his "Cross of Gold" speech. The old Coliseum had burned down in 1897, though the new location sported the same semicircular seating arrangement that had greeted Bryan as he ascended the rostrum.[1] Just as the Coliseum was different, American politics had changed, too. Bryan's 1896 listeners had come to the convention as dispassionate observers and left as converts, but Richberg and his fellow 1912 Progressive delegates were already charismatic followers when they arrived in Chicago. In the same building six weeks earlier, many of them had watched progressive ex-president Theodore Roosevelt lose the Republican presidential nomination to his successor William Howard Taft. Roosevelt, enraged, had walked out of the Republican convention and declared himself an independent candidate. "We stand at Armageddon," he had proclaimed, "and we battle for the Lord." At the time, the skeptical Richberg had wished Roosevelt would "leave the Bible and the Lord out of this row," but by August 5 he and others had fully embraced Roosevelt's sacralization of politics.[2]

[1] Moffett Studio and Kaufmann, Weimer & Fabry Co., *National Progressive Convention, Chicago, August 6, 1912*, photograph, August 6, 1912, PLC-USZ62-116075, Prints and Photographs Division, Library of Congress; *Chicago Daily News*, *[Progressive Party National Convention of 1912, Coliseum Hall Filled with People]*, photograph, August 6, 1912, Prints and Photographs Division, Library of Congress, accessed December 28, 2012, http://hdl.loc.gov/loc.ndlpcoop/ichicdn.n059374.

[2] Donald Richberg, *Tents of the Mighty* (New York: Willett, Clark & Colby, 1930), 30.

They plunged headlong into the convention as if it were a religious movement.

"The progressive national convention," Richberg wrote later, "was a great revival meeting."[3] Delegates burst into spontaneous renditions of "The Battle Hymn of the Republic," "Onward, Christian Soldiers," and the "Doxology"; singing "Follow, Follow, We Will Follow Jesus," they replaced "Jesus" with "Roosevelt."[4] Journalists "who had been sent to the convention to scoff," reported Correspondent Richard Harding Davis, "remained to pray."[5] The event, wrote party secretary Oscar King Davis, "was marked by a fervor almost religious in character ... The atmosphere was charged with emotion akin to prayer."[6] "It was a Methodist camp meeting done over into political terms," agreed the *New York Times*.[7] "The occasion," remembered journalist and Roosevelt backer William Allen White, "had all of the psychological trappings and habiliments of a crusade. We were indeed Christian soldiers 'marching as to war' – and rather more than mildly mad."[8] When Roosevelt ascended the platform to deliver his appropriately titled "Confession of Faith," the applause lasted for fifty-three minutes – over twice as long as had the ovation following Bryan's "Cross of Gold" address.[9] "This was a much more emotional assemblage," Edward G. Lowry concluded in *Harper's Weekly*, "than any other that has gathered for political reasons in the United States this year."[10] Campaign chronicler George Henry Payne put it more poetically: "From a mass of men and women ... that great convention ... became one. It spoke, it lived, it breathed ... It was an army, it was

[3] *Ibid.*, 35.

[4] John Allen Gable, *The Bull Moose Years: Theodore Roosevelt and the Progressive Party* (Port Washington, NY: Kennikat Press, 1978), 75; Amos Pinchot, *History of the Progressive Party 1912–1916*, ed. Helene Maxwell Hooker (Washington Square, NY: New York University Press, 1958), 170.

[5] Richard Harding Davis, "The Men at Armageddon," *Collier's*, August 24, 1912, 11.

[6] Oscar King Davis, *Released for Publication: Some Inside Political History of Theodore Roosevelt and His Times, 1898–1918* (Boston: Houghton Mifflin, 1925), 327.

[7] "Hail New Party in Fervent Song," *New York Times*, August 6, 1912, 1; Gable, *The Bull Moose Years*, 75.

[8] William Allen White, *The Autobiography of William Allen White* (New York: Macmillan, 1946), 484.

[9] Davis, "The Men at Armageddon," 10; Richard Franklin Bensel, *Passion and Preferences: William Jennings Bryan and the 1896 Democratic National Convention* (New York: Cambridge University Press, 2008), 235.

[10] Edward G. Lowry, "With the Bull Moose in Convention," *Harper's Weekly*, August 17, 1912, 9.

a new party, in the parlance of the day; it was a force in the history of the world."[11]

In his autobiography, Richberg explained the delegates' charismatic fervor. "My generation," he wrote, "was spoiling for a fight with the ancient enemies of progress ... It wanted to get religion, but not in churches patronized by thieves. So when T. R. located Armageddon and the band played marching hymns, we put on shining armor and went out to battle for the Lord."[12] Roosevelt's progressivism, Richberg concluded, "was based on what the Colonel well called a 'confession of faith.' It had a creed. You accepted it and joined the church."[13] Amos Pinchot, the younger brother of one of Roosevelt's closest friends, described the delegates' motivation in similar terms. The "nondescript army" of delegates, he wrote, "was miraculously kept united by the magnetism of one electric personality, and the pervasive thought that somehow something worth while and exciting was about to eventuate through their chief's magic." These followers were certain that "the Progressive party, under Roosevelt, was going to free the United States not only from political and economic but from spiritual night. It was to rout Taft's Republican hosts, but this was merely a prelude to routing all the hosts of darkness." Accordingly, the delegates were more interested in the emotions of followership than in devising a concrete platform of action. "In the innocence of our hearts we believed that all that was required to reach the holy city of our dreams was to huddle ourselves and our aspirations under one great umbrella and to advance, saint and sinner, patriot and politician, with arms entwined and voices raised in song."[14] Writer Joel Springarn summed up this charismatic sentiment in verse: "Like the Moslem home from Mecca, we have seen the sacred shrine; / We have made a pilgrim's journey and bring back the word divine. / We have tiptoed to the altar, we have opened up the door; / Oh, the world will never seem to us the world it was before!"[15]

The 1912 "Bull Moose" Progressive Party convention marked the arrival of progressive charisma on the national stage. Where charismatic leadership had once been the province of ministers, philosophers, Chautauqua lecturers, and cultural commentators as well as politicians, by 1910 progressives and their political agenda of middle-class reform dominated

[11] George Henry Payne, *The Birth of the New Party, or Progressive Democracy* (Napierville, IL: H. E. Rennels, 1912), 66.
[12] Richberg, *Tents of the Mighty*, 32. [13] *Ibid.*, 35.
[14] Pinchot, *History of the Progressive Party 1912–1916*, 170.
[15] Quoted in Mark Sullivan, "Armageddon in Chicago," *Collier's*, August 24, 1912, 13.

charismatic discourse. Many magnetic leaders found success during the 1910s – Billy Sunday drew his largest crowds in that decade, Eugene Debs his strongest vote totals – but progressives boasted an outsize contingent of prominent charismatic orators. Figures such as Indiana senator Albert Beveridge, Wisconsin senator Robert La Follette, and California governor Hiram Johnson electrified audiences on the Chautauqua circuit and the campaign trail with charismatic speeches on progressive subjects. In an April 1912 article on political oratory, journalist William Bayard Hale identified twenty-eight leading American political speakers; well over half were avowed progressives.[16] At the same time, few charismatic enterprises matched progressivism for raw ambition. Even William Jennings Bryan had hoped merely to win an election and to give the common man a fair shake, but the progressives sought something more: to put the charismatic relationship in service of a reorganization of American society and, by 1917, of the whole world. "The crowning work," Herbert Croly had called it – and by 1912 the progressives, "armed with a flaming sword and winged for flight," were ready to perform their task of regeneration.

The fractious progressive movement, never able to agree on a universal policy platform or approach to government, united under the leadership of two larger-than-life figures: Roosevelt, who overcame his earlier distaste for charismatic oratory to become the "electric personality" of the Bull Moose convention, and Woodrow Wilson, who served as president for most of the decade. Closely entwined with a variety of progressive campaigns, charismatic leader–follower relationships were more ubiquitous and relevant than ever. Yet while progressives won numerous elections and enacted much of their platform during the 1910s, their leaders seemed strangely unable to grasp the finer points of charismatic techniques or to use them effectively in political campaigns. The magnetic presence with which Bryan had sent a tremor through establishment politics never achieved a comparable result in progressive hands. The failure of the Bull Moosers and, later, the Wilsonians to fulfill their own charismatic hopes revealed much about the contradictions of progressivism as a philosophy. Simply put, many progressives misunderstood the charismatic relationship in the same ways they misread American culture. Accordingly, while progressive charisma played a leading role in national politics during the 1910s, it failed to fulfill Croly's hopes for widespread social transformation. Despite the hymns

[16] William Bayard Hale, " 'Friends and Fellow-Citizens': Our Political Orators of All Parties, and the Ways They Use to Win Us," *The World's Work*, April 1912, 673–680.

and the shining armor, progressive charisma ultimately had little to show for its stand at Armageddon.

* * *

The letter was everything Herbert Croly could have hoped for. Croly and his friend Judge Learned Hand had plotted in early 1910 to provide Theodore Roosevelt with a copy of *The Promise of American Life* and, in so doing, induce the ex-president to run for the White House again using Croly's ideas as his political platform.[17] Now Roosevelt had read the book, and read it carefully – journalist Ray Stannard Baker spotted *The Promise* in Roosevelt's library, "with many passages heavily scored & pages on the fly-leaf with references."[18] On July 31, Croly found a letter from Roosevelt waiting in his mail. "I do not know when I have read a book which I felt profited me as much as your book on American life," Roosevelt wrote; he promised to "use your ideas freely in speeches I intend to make."[19] True to his word, Roosevelt gave a speech exactly a month later in Osawatomie, Kansas, in which he endorsed Croly's ideas in their entirety. Even the buzzword by which the ex-president described his new platform – the "New Nationalism" – was a direct borrowing from Croly.[20] Ultimately, Roosevelt did in fact use Croly's ideas as a platform for a presidential campaign.[21]

"Mr. Roosevelt and his hammer," Croly had written in *The Promise*, constituted "the best available type of national reformer" – the ideal charismatic leader bent on enacting a progressive vision of society. Some observers, however, questioned whether Roosevelt was a charismatic figure at all. "I can not myself understand why Mr. Roosevelt should be described as 'magnetic,' " British journalist R. A. Scott-James wrote in the

[17] Charles Forcey, *The Crossroads of Liberalism: Croly, Weyl, Lippmann, and the Progressive Era, 1900–1925* (New York: Oxford University Press, 1961), 123–125.

[18] Ray Stannard Baker, Diary, Container 121, Notebook K, 151–153, Ray Stannard Baker Papers, Library of Congress, quoted in David W. Levy, *Herbert Croly of* The New Republic*: The Life and Thought of an American Progressive* (Princeton: Princeton University Press, 1985), 139.

[19] Herbert Croly to Learned Hand, August 1, 1912, Learned Hand Papers, Law School Library, Harvard University, quoted in Levy, *Herbert Croly of The New Republic*, 137–138.

[20] Theodore Roosevelt, "The New Nationalism," speech at Osawatomie, KS, August 31, 1910, in Roosevelt, The Works of Theodore Roosevelt, memorial ed., Vol. 19: *Social Justice and Popular Rule*, ed. Hermann Hagedorn (New York: Scribner, 1926), 27; Herbert Croly, *The Promise of American Life* (New York: Macmillan, 1909), 169.

[21] John Milton Cooper, Jr., *The Warrior and the Priest: Woodrow Wilson and Theodore Roosevelt* (Cambridge, MA: Belknap Press of Harvard University Press, 1983), 153.

North American Review. "His art of impressing lacks the subtlety and depth which we should associate with the word."[22] At the same time, Roosevelt's oratory did not conform to the charismatic style outlined by James Rush and Jonathan Barber. Where speakers such as Beecher and Bryan, trained in Rush's elocution techniques, were famous for their sonorous voices and fluid motions on the podium, Roosevelt's speech was oddly high-pitched and his gestures jerky and off-putting – "terrible," William Allen White called them.[23] "He leaned toward the audience," remembered G. N. Keniston, "using fist and index finger gestures – flashing eyes and snapping teeth."[24] Roosevelt was "tiring to listen to," reported William Bayard Hale, because he "grimaces constantly and gesticulates continually."[25] While other charismatic figures followed Charles Finney's advice and spoke extemporaneously, allowing their words to ebb and flow with the emotions of the audience, Roosevelt carefully crafted, dictated, and revised his speeches. He then sought criticism of the drafts from as many people as possible; O. K. Davis remembered one instance in which Roosevelt, traveling by train to a speaking engagement, changed a key passage of his speech on the advice of the brakeman.[26] The resulting addresses contained much detail but lacked emotional punch, at least on the printed page. Accordingly, some commentators have concluded that Roosevelt was not much of an orator, charismatic or otherwise.[27]

The reality of Roosevelt's appeal was more complicated. While avoiding traditional charismatic speaking techniques, the Rough Rider

[22] R. A. Scott-James, "An English Journalist's Impression of Roosevelt," *North American Review*, reprinted in *Dallas Morning News*, October 12, 1912, 10.

[23] William Allen White to William Auburn Behl, April 12, 1941, quoted in Behl, "The Speaking and Speeches of Theodore Roosevelt" (Ph.D. diss., Northwestern University, 1942), 391; H. W. Brands, "Politics as Performance Art: The Body English of Theodore Roosevelt," in Leroy G. Dorsey, ed., *The Presidency and Rhetorical Leadership* (College Station, TX: Texas A&M University Press, 2002), 115.

[24] G. N. Keniston to William Auburn Behl, April 2, 1941, quoted in Behl, "The Speaking and Speeches of Theodore Roosevelt," 391.

[25] Hale, " 'Friends and Fellow-Citizens'," 676.

[26] Davis, *Released for Publication*, 265; William Norwood Brigance, "In the Workshop of Great Speakers," *American Speech*, Vol. 1 (August 1, 1926), 589–590; William Auburn Behl, "Theodore Roosevelt's Principles of Speech Preparation and Delivery," *Speech Monographs*, Vol. 12, No. 1 (1945), 119; Richard Murphy, "Theodore Roosevelt," in Marie Kathryn Hochmuth, ed., *A History and Criticism of American Public Address*, Vol. 3 (New York: Longmans, Green, 1955), 332–336.

[27] Behl, "Theodore Roosevelt's Principles of Speech Preparation and Delivery," 112; Murphy, "Theodore Roosevelt," 360; Brands, "Politics as Performance Art," 115.

forged a unique connection with his supporters through his self-presentation as an ideal of romantic manhood. Roosevelt's embrace of charismatic leadership as a form of masculinity reflected his persistent approach to politics and, indeed, to his own life history. The ex-president, born in New York City on October 28, 1857, presented his early life as an arduous struggle for strength and achievement. "Having been a sickly boy, with no natural bodily prowess," he wrote in his 1913 autobiography, "I was nervous and timid." Following a series of asthma attacks and an encounter with two teenaged bullies who manhandled him with "easy contempt," Roosevelt determined to make himself into a physical specimen. He took up boxing, wrestling, archery, horseback riding, and marksmanship, all in an effort to build a strong, athletic body.[28] Roosevelt viewed his self-forged masculinity with pride; beginning in his college years, he often had himself photographed shirtless or astride a horse, flexing his muscles or carrying a rifle.[29] Later, he transformed his personal success into a philosophy of national renewal. "The doctrine of the strenuous life," he declared in 1899, held that Americans should disdain "a life of slothful ease." Instead, they should pursue "the life of toil and effort ... to dare and endure and to labor ... to wrest triumph from toil and risk."[30] Throughout his life, Roosevelt embedded his own actions within a narrative of masculine struggle against long odds; in so doing, he reflected the desires of his followers for individual and social regeneration.[31]

Roosevelt developed his speaking style in the same way he had built his body: on his own, through struggle and methodical practice. During his college years at Harvard, he wrote later, "I had ... no idea of going into public life, and I never studied elocution or practiced debating."[32] He did, however, gain insights into public speaking from his favorite college instructor, the rhetorician Adams Sherman Hill. Hill's 1893 book *Principles of Rhetoric and Their Application* suggests the

[28] Theodore Roosevelt, *An Autobiography* (New York: Macmillan, 1913), 32–36; Kathleen Dalton, *Theodore Roosevelt: A Strenuous Life* (New York: Knopf, 2002), 35, 52.

[29] John F. Kasson, *Houdini, Tarzan, and the Perfect Man: The White Male Body and the Challenge of Modernity in America* (New York: Hill and Wang, 2001), 4–5.

[30] Theodore Roosevelt, "The Strenuous Life," in Roosevelt, *The Strenuous Life: Essays and Addresses* (New York: Century, 1900), 1, 3.

[31] Sarah Watts, *Rough Rider in the White House: Theodore Roosevelt and the Politics of Desire* (Chicago: University of Chicago Press, 2003), 1–7.

[32] Roosevelt, *An Autobiography*, 27.

professor's negative attitude toward charismatic oratory. "Our feelings ought to be regulated by the facts which excite them," Hill wrote. He cautioned that speakers should avoid direct displays of emotion and should instead use a variety of rhetorical tactics to induce emotions in their audiences. Even "in periods of great religious or political excitement," Hill warned, "if there are any cool heads in the hall, it will be well to study moderation."[33] Hill's advice, ill-suited to a charismatic era, was the only formal training Roosevelt received in public speaking, and it showed, at least during Roosevelt's college years. "He had then almost a defect in his speech," wrote classmate Charles G. Washburn, "which made his utterance at times deliberate and even halting ... In his excitement he would sometimes lose altogether the power of articulation."[34] "He still had difficulty in enunciating clearly or even in running off his words smoothly," William Roscoe Thayer recalled. "At times he could hardly get them out at all, and then he would rush on for a few sentences, as skaters redouble their pace over thin ice."[35]

Roosevelt eventually overcame his youthful struggles with public speaking, but he retained an idiosyncratic style that often transfixed listeners through sheer force of personality rather than impressive technique. Though Roosevelt would have disliked the comparison, charismatically he was more Blaine than Beecher – more apt to win followers through his bearing and persona than through a mastery of elocutionary form.[36] "When he came into a room," White remembered, "he changed all relations in the room because perhaps all minds and hearts turned to him."[37] Schuyler Merritt, later a congressman from Connecticut, recalled how Roosevelt transformed the dull texts of his speeches into successful charismatic theater: "At the end of each topic," Merritt reported, "he would either say something which would bring the audience to its feet in applause, or say something humorous, which

[33] Adams Sherman Hill, *The Principles of Rhetoric and Their Application* (New York: Harper and Brothers, 1893), 238–240.

[34] Charles G. Washburn, *Theodore Roosevelt: The Logic of His Career* (Boston: Houghton Mifflin, 1916), 5.

[35] Quoted in Edmund Morris, *The Rise of Theodore Roosevelt* (New York: Coward, McCann and Geoghegan, 1979), 109; Robert V. Friedenberg, *Theodore Roosevelt and the Rhetoric of Militant Decency* (New York: Greenwood Press, 1990), 6–7.

[36] David Greenberg, *Republic of Spin: An Inside History of the American Presidency* (New York: W. W. Norton, 2016), 41–42.

[37] White, *The Autobiography of William Allen White*, 490.

FIGURE 5.1 Theodore Roosevelt (shown here in 1902) had a charismatic, if idiosyncratic, speaking style; running for president ten years later, however, he was unable to deploy his charismatic techniques effectively.
Source: Photo of Theodore Roosevelt, Asheville, North Carolina, September 9, 1902, courtesy of the Houghton Library, Harvard University, 560.51 1902-156.

would cause them to laugh."[38] Roosevelt, observers noticed, connected with his audience members primarily during these more extemporaneous moments.[39]

Though the prepared speeches themselves were a weak point for Roosevelt, the president mastered other charismatic techniques that relied more on hard work than melodious oratory. Beginning with the Blaine campaign in 1884, Roosevelt served as one of the Republican "spellbinders" who traveled the country every four years speaking on behalf of the presidential ticket.[40] Roosevelt perfected the "special train" method of campaigning during his 1898 gubernatorial race, a full decade before Debs boarded the "Red Special." "In the campaign of 1898," journalist Luther M. Little wrote two years later, "he accomplished a task of campaigning which has seldom been equaled ... Theodore Roosevelt is a marvel as a campaigner, more from his tremendous strength, energy, force, and endurance than from finish and grace of delivery or diction."[41] Promoted to "chief spellbinder" as McKinley's 1900 running mate, Roosevelt matched the skillful Bryan speech for speech. "I am as strong as a bull moose and you can use me up to the limit," Roosevelt told his campaign manager; by Election Day, he had spoken to three million people at a total of 673 stops.[42] During and after his presidency, he regularly addressed crowds of up to 100,000 people, and his handshaking prowess was legendary.[43]

Roosevelt's contemporaries also noticed quasi-religious elements of the president's speaking style.[44] "Mr. Roosevelt keeps a pulpit concealed on his person," wrote an early critic.[45] The president was "a veritable

38 Quoted in Frederick S. Wood, *Roosevelt as We Knew Him* (Philadelphia: John C. Winston, 1927), 324.

39 Oscar S. Straus, *Under Four Administrations: From Cleveland to Taft* (Boston: Houghton Mifflin, 1922), 208–209; Friedenberg, *Theodore Roosevelt and the Rhetoric of Militant Decency*, 16.

40 Kenneth Cmiel, *Democratic Eloquence: The Fight over Popular Speech in Nineteenth-Century America* (New York: William Morrow, 1990), 248.

41 Luther M. Little, "Campaign Orators," *Munsey's Magazine*, Vol. 24, No. 2 (November 1900), 284.

42 Murphy, "Theodore Roosevelt," 316–317; "Roosevelt Ends His Tour," *New York Times*, November 3, 1900, 2.

43 Behl, "The Speaking and Speeches of Theodore Roosevelt," 70; "The Popular Greeting," *The Outlook*, June 25, 1910, 353; Michael McGerr, *A Fierce Discontent: The Rise and Fall of the Progressive Movement in America, 1870–1920* (orig. pub. The Free Press, 2003; New York: Oxford University Press, 2005), 182.

44 "Our Preacher President," *The Independent*, Vol. 61 (December 13, 1906), 1431.

45 Quoted in Carleton Putnam, *Theodore Roosevelt: The Formative Years, 1858–1886* (New York: Scribner, 1958), 288; Friedenberg, *Theodore Roosevelt and the Rhetoric of Militant Decency*, 9.

preacher of social righteousness," declared Jane Addams, "with the irresistible eloquence of faith sanctified by work." Roosevelt's aide Gifford Pinchot proclaimed his friend "the greatest preacher of righteousness in modern times . . . There was no man beyond the reach of his preaching and example."[46] Roosevelt embraced these descriptions by declaring the presidency a "bully pulpit" from which he could influence Americans.[47] "I want to preach," he told O. K. Davis in 1909. "I have a good many sermons in me that I want to deliver."[48]

Ultimately, most observers concluded that Roosevelt possessed a great deal of his own unique brand of personal magnetism. "Bryan had magic," remembered journalist Julian Street, and "he sort of hypnotized his hearers"; Roosevelt, by contrast, "wasn't a great speaker but one felt the force and magnetism of his personality and . . . his great honesty and genuineness."[49] Richberg made a similar evaluation of Roosevelt's merits relative to those of other charismatic progressives. Comparing the president's style to "the vague generalizations of the evangelic Bryan, the close reasoning of the uncompromising La Follette, [and] the erudite radicalism of Wilson," Richberg concluded that " 'Roosevelt progressivism' expressed more accurately the mass sentiment of my generation."[50] "He is not an orator, this man Roosevelt," wrote George Henry Payne, "but he was the leader, he was the mighty force" behind progressivism.[51] "For a decade I had noticed something magnetic about him," White remembered.[52] "Vigor, intelligence, friendliness radiated from him," recalled political scientist and Bull Moose Party member Charles Edward Merriam, "and gave him a wide circle of personal followers."[53]

Charismatic leadership, of course, required more than simply deploying magnetic techniques and mesmerizing the masses; it involved an instinctive understanding of the connection between leaders and

[46] Quoted in Christian F. Reisner, *Roosevelt's Religion* (New York: Abingdon Press, 1922), 205.

[47] Lyman Abbott, *Silhouettes of My Contemporaries* (Garden City, NY: Doubleday, Page, 1922), 310; Friedenberg, *Theodore Roosevelt and the Rhetoric of Militant Decency*, 9–10.

[48] Davis, *Released for Publication*, 139.

[49] Julian Street to William Auburn Behl, April 11, 1941, quoted in Behl, "The Speaking and Speeches of Theodore Roosevelt," 392 n. 3.

[50] Richberg, *Tents of the Mighty*, 34. [51] Payne, *The Birth of the New Party*, 67.

[52] White, *The Autobiography of William Allen White*, 490.

[53] Charles Edward Merriam, *Four American Party Leaders* (New York: Macmillan, 1926), 93; Helene Maxwell Hooker, "Biographical Introduction," in Pinchot, ed., *History of the Progressive Party 1912–1916*, 45.

followers. By some measures, Roosevelt was particularly skilled in this regard. "Fellows," Progressive Party vice chair Medill McCormick told the convention's platform committee, "we must remember that T. R. is great because he understands the psychology of the mutt."[54] In late August 1910, Roosevelt and Davis were talking aboard a train when they saw a woman watching them in the rain outside, holding a baby in her arms. Roosevelt "jumped to the rear platform and waved his hand to the woman," Davis wrote. "She saw him, and with both hands lifted the baby up toward the Colonel." Roosevelt was deeply moved by the experience. "By George!" he exclaimed, "[a] thing like that gives you a lump in the throat. It makes me feel like a great calf. These people have such trust and confidence, and so often they think a man can do all sorts of things that no one can do."[55] Roosevelt's emotional reaction to the support of his followers was a driving force in his political career. During his tenure as governor of New York, for instance, Roosevelt declared that his strategy for defeating political bossism was "by making a direct appeal to the mass of voters themselves."[56] At times, Roosevelt's connection with his followers raised his usually workmanlike oratory to new heights of eloquence. "Oh, my friends," he burst out during a Kansas City speech just a few days after the incident on the train, "I beg of you so to live and so to see that your country is governed that this Nation may always be in very truth the door of golden hope to the oppressed and downtrodden of all the world!"[57]

If Roosevelt's own words are to be believed, in fact, his main reason for seeking a third term was to fulfill the expectations of his massive charismatic following. "There is a good deal of honest feeling for me," he wrote *Outlook* editor William Bailey Howland in December 1911, "among plain simple people who wish leadership, but who will not accept leadership unless they believe it to be sincere, fearless, and intelligent." Given these circumstances, running in 1912 was "a duty which I could not shirk."[58] In a conversation with banker Otto H. Kahn several years later, Roosevelt reiterated that an organic popular movement had called him to leadership. "During my administration," he told Kahn, "[t]he masses of

54 Richberg, *Tents of the Mighty*, 34.
55 Quoted in Davis, *Released for Publication*, 207–208.
56 Quoted in Behl, "The Speaking and Speeches of Theodore Roosevelt," 67.
57 Quoted in Davis, *Released for Publication*, 214.
58 Theodore Roosevelt to William Bailey Howland, December 23, 1911, in Harold Howland, *Theodore Roosevelt and His Times: A Chronicle of the Progressive Movement* (New Haven, CT: Yale University Press, 1921), 207.

the people supported me and hailed me as a deliverer." After his retirement in 1909, "[t]housands, hundreds of thousands, called to me to come to the rescue." Despite Roosevelt's reluctance to bolt the Republican Party after his convention defeat, the people had demanded that he do so. "They looked to me as their leader ... They now called upon me to head an independent movement ... Through the mouth of spokesman after spokesman they insisted. They were aflame with a fine, exalted, passionate aspiration." Roosevelt could not disappoint such followers. "In loyalty, honor, and duty, there was nothing for me to do but to heed their call and make the race with all my might."[59]

Roosevelt's emphasis on the insistence of his followers may have been self-serving, but it also honestly reflected the ex-president's masculinized understanding of the charismatic relationship. For Roosevelt, charismatic leadership represented the "call" of "loyalty, honor, and duty" to wage a great struggle on behalf of the people. Accordingly, he declared in 1912 that the central issue of his campaign was "the right of the people to rule." "In order to succeed," he declared in a March 20 speech at Carnegie Hall, "we need leaders of inspired idealism, leaders to whom are granted great visions, who dream greatly and strive to make their dreams come true; who can kindle the people with the fire from their own burning souls." The leader himself, however, "is but an instrument, to be used until broken and then to be cast aside."[60] Roosevelt reiterated this interpretation of charisma in his "Confession of Faith" at the Progressive convention. "Our cause is based on the eternal principles of righteousness," he told the assembled delegates. Then, he repeated his peroration from the Republican convention six weeks earlier. "Now to you men, who, in your turn, have come together to spend and be spent in the endless crusade against wrong ... I say ...: We stand at Armageddon, and we battle for the Lord."[61]

By 1912, Roosevelt was the most popular charismatic figure in public life.[62] "His immense personal prestige with the people," declared

[59] Quoted in Wood, *Roosevelt as We Knew Him*, 253.

[60] Theodore Roosevelt, "The Right of the People to Rule," speech at Carnegie Hall, New York City, March 20, 1912, in Roosevelt, "The Works of Theodore Roosevelt," memorial ed., Vol. 19: *Social Justice and Popular Rule*, ed. Hermann Hagedorn (New York: Scribner, 1926), 222–223; Sidney M. Milkis, *Theodore Roosevelt, the Progressive Party, and the Transformation of American Democracy* (Lawrence, KS: University Press of Kansas, 2009), 60–61.

[61] Theodore Roosevelt, "A Confession of Faith," in Roosevelt, *The Works of Theodore Roosevelt*, memorial ed., Vol. 19, 410–411.

[62] Kathleen Dalton, "Why America Loved Theodore Roosevelt: Or Charisma is in the Eyes of the Beholders," *Psychohistory Review*, Vol. 8 (Winter 1979), 16–17, 20–21.

reformer Delos F. Wilcox, made him appear to established interests "the most dangerous of all leaders."[63] "There is no other person who has anything like [his] hold upon all the people," agreed the *Hamilton Daily Republican-News*. "The people would follow him further and more willingly than they would follow anyone else, and more willingly than they would follow any party."[64] This belief that Roosevelt's charismatic authority could trump party loyalty among American voters was what motivated Roosevelt to lead his supporters out of the Republican Party into a movement centered on his personality. In doing so, Roosevelt and his supporters joined a great battle, an Armageddon, in the fight between American progressives and conservatives. The resulting election, they believed, would decide the fate of progressivism in American life. It would also put the charismatic relationship to its greatest test. Achieving electoral victory without a national campaign organization or entrenched party loyalties would prove charisma an unstoppable force in American society.

Henry Watterson recognized the charismatic stakes. Since Roosevelt's return from Europe in 1910, the irascible "Marse Henry" had kept up a steady drumbeat of attacks on the ex-president from the editorial page of the *Louisville Courier-Journal*. Dubbing Roosevelt "the ogre at Oyster Bay" and comparing him to Napoleon, Watterson insisted that Roosevelt wanted nothing less than to "Bryanize the Republican Party."[65] "Hero worship has done infinite mischief in the world," Watterson insisted, "from Caesar to Napoleon, from Tamerlane to Teddy!"[66] Now in his seventies, the aging opponent of charismatic movements still felt that magnetism was antithetical to a well-ordered society. "Good government can never be, has never been, the offspring of hysterical screaming," he wrote in another editorial, renewing his gendered attacks on charismatic leaders and followers. "It is the child of reason and virtue, the emanation of intelligent discussion, the result of calm and patriotic

[63] Delos F. Wilcox, "The New Irrepressible Conflict," *The Independent*, June 13, 1912, 1309.

[64] "Roosevelt's Name is a Great Asset," *Hamilton Daily Republican-News*, January 8, 1910, 10.

[65] Quoted in "A Review of the World," *Current Literature*, Vol. 49, No. 4 (October 1910), 349; Henry Watterson, "The Ogre at Oyster Bay," undated editorial, *Louisville Courier-Journal*, microfilm: reel 3, Henry Watterson Papers, University of Louisville; *Louisville Courier-Journal*, reprinted in "Roosevelt and Monarchism," *Springfield Republican*, April 9, 1910, 10.

[66] Henry Watterson, "Munich and the Tyrol," *Louisville Courier-Journal*, May 22, 1905, reel 3, Henry Watterson Papers.

deliberation."[67] Watterson took solace in predicting that Roosevelt could not win based on charismatic oratory alone. "The history of American politics," he declared, "going back to Henry Clay and coming down to James G. Blaine is conclusive upon the point that personality spread out over the continent spreads exceedingly thin."[68]

Could Roosevelt's odd charismatic blend successfully replace the entire local and national organization that formed a political party? The delegates singing hymns for Teddy in the Chicago Coliseum believed that it could. The ensuing campaign would determine whether they were right.

* * *

Just after noon on Friday, October 18, 1912, California governor and Progressive Party vice presidential nominee Hiram Johnson stormed into the party's New York headquarters and confronted national secretary Oscar King Davis in his office. The Progressive campaign was going terribly, Johnson informed the stunned party operative, and the blame lay squarely on Davis' shoulders. It was Davis' job to coordinate the national speaking tours of party orators, including Johnson, Roosevelt, and Beveridge. Johnson, Davis wrote later, charged angrily that the speaking program thus far had been a disaster. "The campaign had been mismanaged, or not managed at all, from the start ... The publicity work was wretched. Wholly inadequate preparation for it had been made, and advance effort, especially where he had been concerned, had been omitted until he secured his own man to attend to it." The result, Johnson continued, was that he was speaking ten to fifteen times a day, often to nearly empty gatherings and inadequately prepared audiences. "It was ridiculous to ask a candidate to make most of the meetings he had been forced to make," he concluded, "with no proper preliminaries, no assurance of crowds, and no publicity groundwork."[69]

Once he had recovered his composure, Davis too became angry. For over two months he had put up with Johnson's complaining letters from the campaign trail, his refusal to vary the themes of his speeches to generate local press coverage, and his unwillingness to change his schedule

[67] Henry Watterson, "The Tyranny of Majorities," undated editorial, *Louisville Courier-Journal*, reel 3, Henry Watterson Papers.

[68] Henry Watterson, "Can Roosevelt Come Back?" *Louisville Courier-Journal*, February 29, 1912, reprinted in "Watterson Discusses T. R.," *Kansas City Star*, February 29, 1912, 3.

[69] Davis, *Released for Publication*, 400.

to coordinate with the national campaign.[70] If Johnson wanted to take a larger role in the speaking program, Davis told the governor, "He would have a good many more short stops to make than he had been making, when he would have to greet crowds from the rear platform of his car, and would be expected to make little five- or ten-minute talks to them ... This would involve, I said, considerably more than he had been doing." Johnson was incredulous: "Well ... what do you think I have been doing?" "I think you have been making two meetings a day," Davis replied curtly, "and delivering the same speech too frequently for good publicity."[71]

Writing thirteen years later, Davis framed the confrontation between himself and Johnson as a clash of personalities. Johnson considered Davis incompetent; Davis thought Johnson lazy and self-absorbed. In truth, the loyal partisan Davis and the famously hardworking Johnson were both doing their best to achieve a Progressive victory in November. Instead, the argument between the two political veterans represented a conflict between competing models of charismatic organization. The difference between Davis and Johnson's views of an ideal speaking campaign demonstrated the gulf between the Progressive Party's approach to charisma and that which had worked for charismatic leaders in the past – and spelled trouble for the Party's ambitious charismatic project.

The Progressives faced many structural obstacles in the campaign – a lack of party organization, hostility from voters loyal to other parties, the antipathy of the partisan press – but they also created difficulties of their own. For one thing, the movement had trouble attracting support beyond the middle-class professionals who made up its core. The problem was evident even at the convention. Looking around the Coliseum, White noticed striking similarities among the delegates. "Here," he wrote, "were the successful middle-class country-town citizens, the farmer whose barn was painted, the well paid railroad engineer, and the country editor. It was a well dressed crowd." White recognized these people as members of "our own kind" – the middle class. "Looking over the crowd," he continued, "judging the delegates by their clothes, I figured that there was not a man or woman on the floor who was making less than two thousand a year, and not one, on the other hand, who was topping ten thousand."[72] Amos Pinchot also remarked on the delegates' middle-class characteristics. "There was a large number of superior, intelligent, and deeply earnest

[70] *Ibid.*, 349–351. [71] *Ibid.*, 402.
[72] White, *The Autobiography of William Allen White*, 483.

people," he wrote. "They were public-spirited businessmen, farmers, lawyers, college professors, instructors, students, schoolteachers, social workers, inconspicuous Insurgent politicians, editors ... radical thinkers ... socialists ... and a sprinkling of rash, liberal-minded clergymen."[73] Such figures were advance agents of an ideal progressive society, but they did not constitute an electoral majority. To win, Roosevelt would also need to attract the masses – laborers, poor farmers, struggling clerks, the unemployed.

Charismatic leaders could certainly appeal to poorer Americans; indeed, Bryan, Haywood, and Debs had crafted successful movements out of just such a strategy. Tellingly, though, the Bull Moosers derided these efforts to adapt charismatic techniques for the lower classes. Roosevelt himself had savaged Bryan in 1896 as a "demagogue" worthy of "contemptuous pity," one of those figures whose "heads are turned by the applause of men of little intelligence" and whose statements induced "hysteria."[74] Roosevelt's friend Owen Wister was equally harsh. "Bryan was a true politician," Wister wrote, "a sham statesman, offering quack remedies with the persuasion that appeals to ignorance ... [Bryan's free-silver slogan] 'Sixteen-to-one' held a magic more popular with multitudes than the appeal to reason."[75] The supporters of such candidates, White wrote, were "the ne'er-do-wells, the misfits – ... neurotics full of hates and ebullient, evanescent enthusiasms."[76] Among the Bull Moosers, only Charles Merriam understood the flaw in this line of reasoning. "What [Bryan's] enemies could not understand," Merriam explained in 1926, "was that the people are as much interested in knowing about their leader's heart as in knowing about his head, and that sympathy no less than intelligence plays its part in the great process of popular control."[77]

The result of this disdain for populist approaches to charisma was that the convention delegates found Roosevelt more charismatic than did ordinary voters. Urban reformer Jacob Riis, "a hero worshipper of the most pronounced type" according to the *Duluth News-Tribune*, "talks Roosevelt, thinks Roosevelt, dreams Roosevelt; ... and reforms make him

[73] Pinchot, *History of the Progressive Party 1912–1916*, 170–171.

[74] Theodore Roosevelt, "The Menace of the Demagogue," speech in Chicago, October 15, 1896, in Roosevelt, *The Works of Theodore Roosevelt*, memorial ed., Vol. 14: Campaigns and Controversies, ed. Hermann Hagedorn (New York: Scribner, 1926), 258.

[75] Owen Wister, *Roosevelt: The Story of a Friendship* (New York: Macmillan, 1930), 53.

[76] White, *The Autobiography of William Allen White*, 483.

[77] Merriam, *Four American Party Leaders*, 83–84.

rejoice because of Roosevelt. To him Mr. Roosevelt is the greatest man of the age."[78] After seeing Roosevelt in person for the first time, White pronounced himself "afire with the splendor of the personality that I had met."[79] His newspaper articles during the 1912 campaign "were well loaded with Roosevelt faith, for I was burning up for the cause."[80] Author Hamlin Garland wrote to Roosevelt that the Progressive convention had "stirred my fighting blood."[81] Even the normally reserved Croly wrote of voting for Roosevelt as "an affirmation of faith – a dedication to personal service."[82] Roosevelt certainly relied on the support of such figures, but electorally speaking they were no substitute for a true popular following. For all Roosevelt's talk of the "honest feeling for me among plain simple people," he was unwilling to present himself to the masses in a way that maximized his charismatic appeal.

The Progressive approach to campaign speaking reflected and compounded Roosevelt's difficulties with charismatic self-presentation. At first glance, the speaking program closely resembled the charismatic tours of Bryan's campaigns or Roosevelt's 1900 vice presidential candidacy. Roosevelt and Johnson traveled constantly; the Bull Moose himself eventually delivered over 150 speeches in thirty-two states, with Johnson speaking at over three times as many engagements.[83] The volume of Roosevelt's speeches was much smaller than in previous elections – Roosevelt and Bryan had each spoken around 600 times during the 1900 campaign, for instance – but there was an even more important difference between the Roosevelt and Bryan charismatic campaigns. Because Bryan understood the central role of oratory in creating charismatic followers, he designed his speaking tours so as to meet and inspire as many potential followers as possible. The goal of a Bryan tour was to create Bryan voters at the train platform or in the hall, where charismatic techniques such as musical preparation, elocutionary performance, and handshakes could convert followers with maximum effect.

78 "T. R. is Idol of Jacob Riis," *Duluth News-Tribune*, March 19, 1910, 9.

79 White, *The Autobiography of William Allen White*, 297. 80 *Ibid.*, 460.

81 Hamlin Garland to Theodore Roosevelt, August 7, 1912, microfilm: reel 150, Theodore Roosevelt Papers, Library of Congress.

82 Herbert Croly, "A Test of Faith in Democracy," *The American Magazine*, Vol. 74, No. 1 (November 1912), 22.

83 Gable, *The Bull Moose Years*, 111; George E. Mowry, *The California Progressives* (Berkeley, CA: University of California Press, 1951), 192; Francis L. Broderick, *Progressivism at Risk: Electing a President in 1912* (New York: Greenwood Press, 1989), 150–151.

Roosevelt, by contrast, seemed determined to rerun the McKinley campaign of 1896. Mark Hanna's advertised campaign had relied not on the candidate's in-person oratorical prowess, but on the power of his printed speeches distributed across the country to local campaign organizations. Roosevelt, too, had a publicity bureau for distributing speeches, but with little money and less organization the Progressives had to rely on newspaper coverage to carry Roosevelt's addresses to voters. Accordingly, the Roosevelt tours placed little emphasis on reaching audiences and more on attracting the local and national press.[84] The Progressives' choice of a journalist, O. K. Davis, to head up the campaign travel program was telling. Where Bryan cared little about press coverage and often delivered similar speeches to each audience he encountered, Davis at one point yanked Roosevelt from the campaign trail because "the Colonel was going stale, and was rehashing old stuff to such an extent that there was difficulty in getting away news stories that the papers would carry."[85] At the same time, Davis complained about "the way in which towns and committees along the route would insist on stops that had not been scheduled" – the very follower-generated stops Bryan would have seen as integral to his charismatic goals.[86] In making these choices, Davis was not acting alone. It was Roosevelt himself who, in 1911, had written to his sister that he hoped "never to speak" unless he could "render the speech one not really to the audience addressed, but to a National audience."[87]

McKinley had succeeded with this print-distribution strategy because he was not seeking a charismatic following; his organization, flush with cash and local partisan organization, could get by comfortably with a politics of advertising. The Progressives, however, were relying on the charismatic relationship to make up for enormous deficiencies in money, organization, and local support. As a charismatic strategy, the Davis approach was destined to fail. Notwithstanding Elbert Hubbard and his *Little Journeys*, no charismatic figure had ever convinced large numbers of followers to consecrate themselves to the cause by focusing on a literature campaign. To be sure, Sunday's printed sermons ran in local newspapers, while Bryan ran a weekly publication for supporters; in both cases,

84 Michael E. McGerr, *The Decline of Popular Politics: The American North, 1865–1928* (New York: Oxford University Press, 1986), 161.

85 Davis, *Released for Publication*, 353–354. 86 *Ibid.*, 352–353.

87 Theodore Roosevelt to Anna Roosevelt Cowles, June 29, 1911, in Theodore Roosevelt, *Letters from Theodore Roosevelt to Anna Roosevelt Cowles, 1879–1918* (New York: Scribner, 1924), 291; Murphy, "Theodore Roosevelt," 338.

however, the overwhelming majority of their charismatic correspondents converted under the influence of oratory, not reading. For a candidate such as Roosevelt whose prepared speeches lacked charismatic effect and were the weakest part of his performance, the choice to foreground the prepared texts was disastrous.

Of all the Progressives involved in the campaign, only Hiram Johnson seemed to understand the problems with this approach. Stumping across California in an automobile two years earlier, the little-known attorney had won the state governorship primarily through his magnetic speaking style.[88] Johnson did not have the traditional melodious speech of a Bryan or a Blaine. "His voice sounds just as an east wind feels," one journalist remarked. "It grates and snarls and pierces, and puts you all on edge."[89] Another writer agreed that Johnson's speech "sounds like a ripsaw going through a hard knot."[90] Despite his unappealing voice, however, Johnson consistently inspired charismatic reactions in his listeners.[91] Johnson produced "a moral fervor," wrote Edmund Norton, "fusing the assemblies into almost a spiritual frenzy for a few seconds; a mass phenomenon … rarely or never witnessed outside of religious meetings."[92] Other journalists described him as a "political revivalist" whose speeches resembled "the inspiring appeals of some prophet or crusader of the delivered truth."[93] San Francisco editor Fremont Older recalled hearing Johnson address an audience "in a low, intimate, earnest tone, as if each one was a personal friend. I have never before or since seen an audience so moved by a political speaker."[94] More important, Johnson was a master of charismatic organizing. During his gubernatorial campaign, he had recruited local committees to prepare audiences in advance of his speeches, secured free advertising from newspapers, and even attached cowbells to his car to attract audience members as he

88 "Hiram Johnson, Political Revivalist," *American Review of Reviews*, September 1912, 308.

89 Editorial in *Current Literature*, quoted in "Hiram Johnson, Political Revivalist," 308.

90 "Johnson of California: A Progressive in a Hurry," *Current Literature*, August 1912, 156, quoted in Michael A. Weatherson and Hal W. Bochin, *Hiram Johnson: Political Revivalist* (Lanham, MD: University Press of America, 1995), 53.

91 Mowry, *The California Progressives*, 113.

92 Quoted in *Current Literature*, August 12, 1912, 156–157, quoted in Weatherson and Bochin, *Hiram Johnson*, 32.

93 "The World We Live in," *McClure's*, Vol. 38 (1911–1912), 480, and *Riverside Daily Press*, October 29, 1910, quoted in Weatherson and Bochin, *Hiram Johnson*, 31–32.

94 Quoted in Weatherson and Bochin, *Hiram Johnson*, 32.

approached his destination.[95] The pugnacious Johnson knew a flawed charismatic strategy when he saw one – yet Davis and the other Progressives largely ignored his warnings.

Roosevelt's letters from voters during the campaign reveal just how dearly the Progressives' literature-first strategy cost the party. Roosevelt did receive a few letters that reflected the familiar elements of charismatic followership; aside from a few namesake letters, however, virtually all of this correspondence came from Americans who had seen the ex-president in person.[96] Margaret Shaw Graham, a Louisville suffrage activist, had been opposed to Roosevelt until she heard him speak. "I wanted to hear you," she wrote Roosevelt, "to get even closer in spirit than I had thru your writings ... Well, I began to return after the spirit of that night got to work tho I didn't realize how much of a 'Teddyite' I am till yesterday ... I wish I could shake hands [with you]."[97] Scottish immigrant David Carver had a similar reaction to hearing a Roosevelt speech. "The honest intelligent way you spoke," he wrote, "to me it seemed a heart to heart talk, the sane, solid principles you expounded convinced me that you and you alone were worthy of support. Since then, every chance I get I have been advocating the principles of the Progressive Party."[98] George B. Wells wrote that he had shaken hands with Roosevelt on four separate occasions; during their fourth handshake, "[t]he hearty whole souled laugh with which you responded sir still rings in my ears."[99] William Ruddicks, Jr., wrote simply to express his disappointment at having missed a Roosevelt appearance. "Dear Honored Sir," he wrote, "I got up at five o'clock and went nine miles to Steubenville to see you and you may bet I was sorry not to see you ... I have wanted to see you ever since I read one of your books. Will you please let me know when I will have the chance to see you in Steubenville[?]"[100]

95 Weatherson and Bochin, *Hiram Johnson*, 28; "Hiram Johnson, Political Revivalist," 308.

96 Oscar P. Dobrovolsky to Theodore Roosevelt, August 9, 1912, reel 151, Theodore Roosevelt Papers; Julius J. Eyring to Theodore Roosevelt, August 22, 1912, reel 151, Theodore Roosevelt Papers; F. A. Anderson to Theodore Roosevelt, ca. November 5, 1912, reel 156, Theodore Roosevelt Papers.

97 Margaret Shaw Graham to Theodore Roosevelt, August 12, 1912, reel 151, Theodore Roosevelt Papers, underscore in original.

98 David Carver to Theodore Roosevelt, August 26, 1912, reel 152, Theodore Roosevelt Papers.

99 George B. Wells to Theodore Roosevelt, August 23, 1912, reel 151, Theodore Roosevelt Papers.

100 William Ruddicks, Jr., to Theodore Roosevelt, February 21, 1912, reel 130, Theodore Roosevelt Papers.

Followers who had merely read Roosevelt's speeches or followed his campaign in the papers, meanwhile, were more cordial than charismatic. "I have just read the full text of your Columbus address," wrote A. J. Gilbert after Roosevelt announced his candidacy, "and feel that I cannot constrain my desire to heartily congratulate you upon your splendid effort. The address is not only timely but a veritable philippic."[101] Charles McCarthy described the same speech as "thoroughly sound and full of irresistible logic ... the people of this country will soon recognize it as such."[102] Joseph Allen asked his son to read him "every word" of the address; afterward, he wrote Roosevelt to "congratulate you on that Noble speech ... It was one of the greatest speeches I have ever heard since the days of Lincoln."[103] After the Bull Moose convention, Charles A. Vaultine wrote "simply to say that I have carefully read your [convention] address and the platform of the Progressive Party, and that I like them both – like them very much."[104] Despite the enthusiasm of such letters, their lack of sacralization and religious allusions formed a striking contrast with Bryan's correspondence; few writers compared the Bull Moose candidate to Moses or begged him to free them from oppression.[105]

The flaws in Roosevelt's charismatic campaign became evident in the aftermath of a dramatic assassination attempt. On October 14 in Milwaukee, John Schrank shot the ex-president in the chest while Roosevelt was on his way to deliver a speech.[106] Luckily for Roosevelt, his glasses case and the folded manuscript of his speech deflected the shot

[101] A. J. Gilbert to Theodore Roosevelt, February 22, 1912, reel 130, Theodore Roosevelt Papers.

[102] Charles McCarthy to Theodore Roosevelt, February 23, 1912, reel 130, Theodore Roosevelt Papers.

[103] Joseph Allen to Theodore Roosevelt, February 22, 1912, reel 130, Theodore Roosevelt Papers.

[104] Charles A. Vaultine to Theodore Roosevelt, August 8, 1912, reel 150, Theodore Roosevelt Papers.

[105] Rare exceptions include George Zitzman to Theodore Roosevelt, June 22, 1912, reel 146, Theodore Roosevelt Papers; H. C. Bowers to Theodore Roosevelt, August 13, 1912, reel 151, Theodore Roosevelt Papers; and Julius C. Lowe to Theodore Roosevelt, October 17, 1912, reel 153, Theodore Roosevelt Papers.

[106] Stan Gores, "The Attempted Assassination of Teddy Roosevelt," *The Wisconsin Magazine of History*, Vol. 53, No. 4 (Summer 1970), 269; Joseph L. Gardner, *Departing Glory: Theodore Roosevelt as Ex-President* (New York: Scribner, 1973), 272; Patricia O'Toole, *When Trumpets Call: Theodore Roosevelt After the White House* (New York: Simon & Schuster, 2005), 217; Gerard Helferich, *Theodore Roosevelt and the Assassin: Madness, Vengeance, and the Campaign of 1912* (Guilford, CT: Lyons Press, 2013), 172–176.

from what would have been a fatal trajectory. Realizing that he was not mortally wounded, Roosevelt insisted on delivering his speech as planned. "This is my big chance," he told Davis and his other aides, "and I am going to make that speech if I die doing it."[107] Roosevelt followed through on this promise in theatrical fashion. "Friends," he announced, revealing his bloodstained shirt to the shocked audience, "I shall ask you to be as quiet as possible. I don't know whether you fully understand that I have just been shot; but it takes more than that to kill a bull moose." He spoke for over an hour before finally consenting to leave for the hospital.[108]

Roosevelt saw the performance as his "big chance" because he believed the whole nation was watching him on that Milwaukee stage; all of America, he felt, would become at a stroke his devoted charismatic followers. Once again, however, Roosevelt's incomplete understanding of charisma impeded his goals. After the assassination attempt, his correspondents appeared concerned, angry, and perhaps slightly more aware of the stakes of the election – but because they had not seen the event in person, their responses still lacked the emotional heft of charismatic missives. "My dear sir," Thomas Thompson wrote in a typical letter, "you have my sympathy and my prayers for your speedy recovery from the dastardly assault on your life."[109] "Will you convey to Colonel Theodore Roosevelt," wrote Maud Cripster Rankin to the candidate's wife Edith, "my deep sympathy for him, of the dastardly attempt upon his life. I was stricken to the heart at the news."[110] "How my heart ached to think of such a brave and wonderful leader having been assassinated," schoolgirl Irena Farr remarked.[111] "I was vary [sic] sorrow that you was shot," wrote Edward Johnston in a grammatically challenged missive; "it makes me feel vary sad I did not sleep last night for thinking about it."[112] An occasional letter seemed more touched with charismatic enthusiasm than the rest. "We all love Mr. Roosevelt, and have for years," wrote Mrs. R. L. Bocock to Edith Roosevelt. "He is the greatest man we have in history, or ever will have, and he can have any thing he asks for, even to

107 Davis, *Released for Publication*, 379. 108 Gardner, *Departing Glory*, 274–275.

109 Thomas Thompson to Theodore Roosevelt, October 16, 1912, reel 153, Theodore Roosevelt Papers.

110 Maud Cripster Rankin to Theodore Roosevelt, October 15, 1912, reel 153, Theodore Roosevelt Papers.

111 Irena Farr to Theodore Roosevelt, October 15, 1912, reel 153, Theodore Roosevelt Papers.

112 Edward Johnston to Theodore Roosevelt, October 16, 1912, reel 153, Theodore Roosevelt Papers; spelling errors in original.

Mexico." "What you said about the man that shot you," commented Walter Dole, "made me feel that you are like Jesus Christ." Once again, however, these authors had had personal contact with the candidate: Dole had seen Roosevelt speak, and Bocock's daughter had shaken hands with the Bull Moose.[113]

"If every tear for you," Martha S. Fuller wrote to Roosevelt after the assassination attempt, "every sigh every heart ache every prayer were a vote you would go into the Presidential chair, all right."[114] Unfortunately for Roosevelt, Fuller's prophecy was not enough for an electoral victory. On November 5, 1912, Democrat Woodrow Wilson won a clear electoral majority with nearly 42 percent of the national popular vote. Roosevelt came in second with 27 percent, just ahead of Taft's 23 percent. Meanwhile, Debs scored by far his best electoral performance, doubling his previous high of 3 percent.[115] Henry Watterson was outraged: even a second-place showing, he felt, was too good for Roosevelt. "It is certainly true that each one of those who in 1912 voted for Theodore Roosevelt did by his act commit treason to the spirit of our institutional freedom," he wrote after the election. "That more than four millions of these restless beings . . . voted in 1912 to return Theodore Roosevelt to the head of the Nation proves conclusively the existence of an epidemic of hysteria. To that extent it is equally conclusive that at least four millions are wholly unfit for self-government."[116]

Notwithstanding Watterson's ire, the election results left the Bull Moosers little to celebrate. Despite Roosevelt's charismatic efforts, only 59 percent of eligible voters cast presidential ballots – the worst turnout in seventy-six years, and a full twenty points less than in the Bryan-McKinley race of 1896.[117] Twenty-seven percent of an apathetic electorate was not going to bring about a progressive society or even a partisan realignment; indeed, it meant the death of the Bull Moose Party as an organized movement. The down-ticket Progressive candidates had run so far behind Roosevelt that they hardly registered

[113] Mrs. R. L. Bocock to Edith Roosevelt, October 16, 1912, reel 153, Theodore Roosevelt Papers, underscore in original; Walter Dole to Theodore Roosevelt, October 17, 1912, reel 153, Theodore Roosevelt Papers.

[114] Martha S. Fuller to Theodore Roosevelt, October 19, 1912, reel 153, Theodore Roosevelt Papers; underscore in original.

[115] Lewis L. Gould, *Four Hats in the Ring: The 1912 Election and the Birth of Modern American Politics* (Lawrence, KS: University Press of Kansas, 2008), 176.

[116] Henry Watterson, "Our Wandering Minstrel" and "The Ogre at Oyster Bay," *Louisville Courier-Journal*, undated editorials, reel 3, Henry Watterson Papers.

[117] McGerr, *The Decline of Popular Politics*, 185.

in the final results.[118] The Progressives recognized the magnitude of the defeat. Out of the ticket's four million votes, White wrote to Roosevelt, one million came from "the leaders of thought in the community," more than that from "the 'sheep vote,' " and "a million, perhaps not quite so many, Teddy votes – votes of men who had confidence in you personally without having any particular intelligent reason to give why." This showing was likely the best the movement could hope for, White concluded; in the future, "We are going to lose the sheep votes and the Teddy votes."[119]

Even the normally ebullient Roosevelt could not hide his disappointment. "There is no use disguising the fact that the defeat at the polls is overwhelming," he admitted to Arthur Lee on the night of the election. "I had expected defeat, but I had expected that we would make a better showing."[120] "It would be a mistake to nominate me [again for president]," he declared, "unless the country has in its mood something of the heroic."[121] After beating back a libel suit in 1915, Roosevelt mused on the power and limitations of charismatic leadership. During the trial, he was able to win over the jurors only "because I could reach them personally," he noted. "But it is of course impossible for me to reach more than the smallest fraction of our people in such fashion."[122]

As Roosevelt belatedly recognized, even a perfect charismatic campaign would have been unlikely to secure victory. The charismatic relationship was a valuable organizational tool because it turned casual followers into tireless activists by offering them power, agency, and an intimate connection with their leaders. Despite some instances of success, however, there was little evidence that charismatic efforts could deliver any particular number of votes for a candidate or platform. Even Bryan, a master of popular appeal who controlled a national party apparatus,

[118] George E. Mowry, *Theodore Roosevelt and the Progressive Movement* (New York: Hill and Wang, 1946), 281–282.

[119] William Allen White to Theodore Roosevelt, September 24, 1913, in William Allen White, *Selected Letters of William Allen White*, ed. Walter Johnson (New York: Henry Holt, 1947), 144–145.

[120] Theodore Roosevelt to Arthur Hamilton Lee, November 5, 1912, in Roosevelt, *The Letters of Theodore Roosevelt*, Vol. 7, ed. Elting E. Morison (Cambridge, MA: Harvard University Press, 1954), 633.

[121] Quoted in "Roosevelt's Hat Again in the Ring," *New York Times*, March 10, 1916; Murphy, "Theodore Roosevelt," 343.

[122] Theodore Roosevelt to unnamed correspondent, June 3, 1915, in Joseph Bucklin Bishop, *Theodore Roosevelt and His Time, Shown in His Own Letters*, Vol. 2 (New York: Scribner, 1920), 381–382; Murphy, "Theodore Roosevelt," 343.

had failed three times to win the presidency; expecting Roosevelt to do better with little financial support and no established political organization was probably unrealistic. The Bull Moosers viewed things differently, however. As they saw it, they had put their trust in the charismatic movement as a political strategy, and it had failed them. Accordingly, many of Roosevelt's demoralized associates blamed the charismatic relationship itself for the loss. "The lesson taught by the Progressive incident," wrote Amos Pinchot, "seems simply to be the familiar one: that a party cannot be founded ... solely upon the personality of an individual."[123] O. K. Davis was blunter. The people, he told Roosevelt in 1914, "don't know enough to rule. They don't pay enough attention to their own affairs to have any right to govern the affairs of others. They won't see and they won't learn." For Davis, charismatic movements were untrustworthy because the people themselves could not be trusted. "The right of the people to rule," he concluded, "is bunk."[124]

* * *

On April 2, 1880, two University of Virginia students faced one another in the University's Jefferson Hall to begin the Jefferson Literary and Debating Society's final debate of the season. Twenty-year-old William Cabell Bruce, later a U.S. senator from Maryland, towered over his rival. "Tall and sparely built," recalled one observer, Bruce had "the face of a poet, the head of a statesman, and [was] rather fiery in his elocution." Bruce's rival Thomas Woodrow Wilson, also twenty, was "much lower of stature, but erect and firm on his feet, and displaying an iron jaw and searching eyes"; he "suggested a mighty force which found expression in masterful logic and faultless periods."[125] Both Bruce and Wilson sought the Debater's Medal for the season's best speaker, and each performed well. Nevertheless, the audience quickly noticed a difference in style between the two men. Bruce, following the elocutionary recommendations of James Rush, "was all action, action, action," remembered a classmate. "Graceful gestures. Sweep of arms. Step forward. Step backward. Action suited to words." Wilson, by contrast, "adopted the English style. Stand still and talk. No gestures. No step forward. No raising of

[123] Pinchot, *History of the Progressive Party 1912–1916*, 226.

[124] Davis, *Released for Publication*, 431.

[125] University [of Virginia?] Magazine, Vol. 20 (October 1880[?]), 50–52, quoted in William Cabell Bruce, *Recollections* and *The Inn of Existence* (orig. pub. 1936; rev. ed. Baltimore, MD: Gateway Press, 1998), 70.

arm. I think he raised his hand once or twice."[126] At the end of the debate, the faculty judges sided with Bruce. Devastated, Wilson at first refused to accept the second-place prize; he had to be coaxed by his friends to appear at the medal ceremony.[127]

It was a pattern of events that recurred more than once in Wilson's career. Critics frequently argued that Wilson's speaking style, while polished, lacked Roosevelt's warmth or Bryan's emotion. "When I met him," William Allen White wrote, "he seemed to be a cold fish ... The hand he gave me to shake felt like a ten-cent pickled mackerel in brown paper – irresponsive and lifeless ... When he tried to be pleasant he creaked."[128] "He wanted to speak for the common crowd," recalled editor James Kerney, "but in private he frequently found it difficult to tolerate them."[129] For their part, Wilson's supporters often noted the same characteristics with approval. "His very nature resisted outbursts of popular passion, which he never considered the sober thought of the people," Secretary of State Robert Lansing recalled. "He had the faculty of remaining impervious to such influences, which so often affect the minds of lesser men."[130] Watterson compared Wilson favorably to Henry Clay, Stephen Douglas, Blaine, and Bryan, "magnetic men, whose lodestones at the supreme point failed them." Wilson, he concluded happily, "resembles no one of them."[131]

Wilson's dissimilarity to Bruce and others like him was neither coincidental nor caused by a lack of oratorical skill. While Roosevelt's inability to maximize his charismatic appeal stemmed largely from misunderstanding, Wilson's speaking style was a carefully considered choice. In fact, Wilson possessed a more thoroughly developed philosophy of oratory than any charismatic figure since Beecher. Drawing on sources including his own preacher father, the French rhetorician Abbé Louis

[126] Baxter Gipson to Henry Bragdon, January 23, 1942, box 62, Henry Wilkinson Bragdon Collection of Reminiscences, Princeton University, quoted in Robert Alexander Kraig, *Woodrow Wilson and the Lost World of the Oratorical Statesman* (College Station, TX: Texas A&M University Press, 2004), 41.

[127] Quoted in A. W. Patterson, *Personal Recollections of Woodrow Wilson* (Richmond, VA: Whittet & Shepperson, 1929), 15.

[128] White, *The Autobiography of William Allen White*, 479.

[129] James Kerney, *The Political Education of Woodrow Wilson* (New York: Century, 1926), xiii.

[130] Robert Lansing, *War Memoirs of Robert Lansing* (Indianapolis, IN: Bobbs-Merrill, 1935), 349.

[131] Henry Watterson, "Buchanan–Douglas–Wilson," undated editorial, *Louisville Courier-Journal*, reel 2, Henry Watterson Papers.

Bautain, and the English writers Edmund Burke, Oliver Goldsmith, and Henry W. Lucy, Wilson entered college with definite ideas about public speaking.[132] The talented and desperately ambitious Wilson believed that oratory was the key to power and leadership, and that moral character and training were in turn the key to oratory. Accordingly, while the collegiate Roosevelt spent his free time hunting and fishing, Wilson practiced his speaking skills in Princeton's Potter's Woods and in the empty nave of his father's church.[133] While Roosevelt shrugged off his lack of oratorical training at Harvard, Wilson railed in the school newspaper that "we view oratory in an entirely wrong light in Princeton."[134] While Roosevelt dreamed of training as a scientist, Wilson knew early on that he wanted to become an orator.

Wilson's views on public speaking bore some similarities to the charismatic theories promoted by Finney, Beecher, Croly, and others. Wilson agreed with advocates of charismatic movements that public speakers should work to sway the masses. The "object of oratory," he wrote while in college in 1877, "is persuasion and conviction – the control of other minds by a strange personal influence and power."[135] Oratory was, he explained seven years later to his fiancée Ellen Axson, "the art of putting things so as to appeal irresistibly to an audience."[136] Wilson recognized, too, that successful public speakers required a grasp of mass psychology. "Men in the mass differ from men as individuals," Wilson wrote in an 1890 address. "The leader of men must have such sympathetic and penetrative insight as shall enable him to discern quite unerringly the motives which move other men *in the mass* ... [He] need only know what it is that lies wanting to be stirred in the minds and purposes of groups and masses of men."[137]

Wilson disagreed with charismatic advocates, however, about both the style and the purpose of public speaking. "The orator who maintains

[132] Kraig, *Woodrow Wilson and the Lost World of the Oratorical Statesman*, 14, 18–19.

[133] *Ibid.*, 23–24.

[134] X [Woodrow Wilson], untitled editorial, *The Princetonian*, Vol. 2, No. 4 (June 7, 1877), 43; Ray Stannard Baker, *Woodrow Wilson: Life and Letters*, Vol. 1 (Garden City, NY: Doubleday, Page, 1927), 92.

[135] X [Woodrow Wilson], untitled editorial, *The Princetonian*, Vol. 2, No. 4 (June 7, 1877), 43.

[136] Woodrow Wilson to Ellen Louise Axson, January 16, 1884, quoted in Baker, *Woodrow Wilson*, Vol. 1, 186.

[137] Woodrow Wilson, "Leaders of Men," speech at University of Tennessee, Knoxville, June 17, 1890, in Arthur S. Link, ed., *The Papers of Woodrow Wilson*, Vol. 6 (Princeton: Princeton University Press, 1969), 649, 650–651; italics in original.

complete sovereignty over his emotions," he declared in a college speech, "is a thousandfold more powerful than he who 'saws the air' and 'tears a passion to tatters.' Emotional demonstrations should come from his audience, not from the orator himself." Instead, Wilson advocated a speaking style that lacked gesture and vocal modulation, but that contained a powerful concealed emotion – "the calmness of white heat."[138] The ideal orator, he felt, should be suffused with the fervor of his message so as to move the audience by the power of his belief alone. "What kindles an audience is no such enigmatical thing as 'personal magnetism,' " he wrote to Ellen Axson in 1884, "though it is something quite as mysterious, perhaps: it is contact with the orator's own inmost life – with his very soul. They have seen and touched his spirit; they have for the moment partaken of his power. His heart has gone out into theirs, and the life of their sympathy has entered into him."[139] Accordingly, Wilson criticized not only charismatic speakers such as Bruce who relied on elocutionary techniques, but also those such as Bryan who told audiences what they wanted to hear rather than trying to change their listeners. Education and uplift, "persuasion and conviction," were his goals. Like Beecher and Bryan, Wilson wanted to change America through oratory; but rather than rallying the people to reform their society, the future professor and college president sought to change institutions by reforming the people themselves.[140]

Thus it happened that on January 13, 1885, Wilson went to hear a lecture by the greatest charismatic orator of the age, Henry Ward Beecher – and came away unimpressed. "He sent through [his speech] a stream of strong, shallow, noisy, irregular, evident, picturesque, taking talk," Wilson wrote to Ellen Axson. "Nobody wanted him to stop; nobody failed to admire the skill and popular force of the man; nobody carried away much instruction." To Wilson, Beecher's performance was shallow and self-serving; Beecher had achieved a charismatic hold over his audience, but without changing any minds. "He proved," Wilson concluded, only "that dilute sense may fill a hall with intent listeners … Dan'l Webster could have had as great success, but Beecher paid much less

[138] Woodrow Wilson, "John Bright," speech at University of Virginia, March 1880, in Wilson, *The Public Papers of Woodrow Wilson*, Vol. 1, ed. Ray Stannard Baker and William E. Dodd (New York: Harper & Brothers, 1925), 50.

[139] Woodrow Wilson to Ellen Louise Axson, April 20, 1884, in Arthur S. Link, ed., *The Papers of Woodrow Wilson*, Vol. 3 (Princeton: Princeton University Press, 1967), 138.

[140] Kraig, *Woodrow Wilson and the Lost Art of the Oratorical Statesman*, 31.

for his."[141] In 1897 Wilson denounced William Jennings Bryan in similar terms. "We might have had Mr. Bryan for President," he lamented, simply "because of the impression which may be made upon an excited assembly by a good voice and a few ringing sentences."[142]

Throughout his political career, Wilson frequently encountered charismatic speakers such as Beecher, Bryan, and Bruce. Each time, he decried their shallowness and demagoguery, belittled their rhetorical abilities, and criticized them for playing to the baser instincts of their audiences. Despite winning two presidential elections, however, Wilson ultimately paid a political price for his intellectual elitism concerning charisma. He was unwilling to accept what was obvious to observers at the Jefferson Society debate: the William Cabell Bruces of the world, with their emotional delivery and populist rhetoric, could connect with the American people in a way Wilson could not.

* * *

Notwithstanding his complex relationship with charisma, Wilson had become an impressive public speaker by the time he assumed the presidency in 1913. Though Wilson still spoke in the restrained style to which he was accustomed – keeping his hands in his coat pockets, removing his right hand only occasionally for a momentary gesture – his performance frequently stirred his listeners.[143] "Purity of diction, logical order, clearness and simplicity of statement" characterized Wilson's addresses, noted New Jersey politician John W. Westcott. Wilson "easily caught, dominated and convinced all minds" because he avoided every "trick of language, brilliant sophistry, or impassioned manner" and instead spoke with "truth, supported by resistless moral energy."[144] "There was a naturalness in his voice and manner," recalled young Princeton instructor Hardin Craig, "a restrained skill in his use of gestures, and a perfection in his articulation." After one of Wilson's speeches at Princeton, "We concluded, and not wrongly,

[141] Woodrow Wilson to Ellen Louise Axson, January 14, 1885, in Link, ed., *The Papers of Woodrow Wilson*, Vol. 3, 608.

[142] Woodrow Wilson, "The Making of the Nation" (1897), in Arthur S. Link, ed., *The Papers of Woodrow Wilson*, Vol. 10 (Princeton: Princeton University Press, 1971), 233.

[143] George C. Osborn, "Woodrow Wilson as a Speaker," *Southern Speech Journal*, Vol. 22, No. 2 (1956), 70.

[144] John W. Wescott, *Woodrow Wilson's Eloquence* (Camden, NJ: I. F. Huntzinger, 1922), 27–28.

that we had listened to the words of one of the world's great orators."[145]

Writing in 1911, William Bayard Hale explained how Wilson won over his audiences. "The members of a Democratic Club at an annual dinner," Hale admitted, "are at first a little puzzled to listen to an exposition such as Origen, Augustine, or Hegel might make." But Wilson slowly gained their attention, and then, through his "conclusions which at last shine out white-hot in the fire of moral conviction, it is with a tempest of enthusiasm that they shout their understanding." Wilson spoke in "a new language – but one for which the people have an instinctive, Pentecostal understanding." No one, Hale concluded, "can listen to Woodrow Wilson and see the emotions of the audiences of earnest men who hang upon his words, without feeling that he is witnessing the beginning of a political revolution, and that its prophet and captain stands before him."[146]

Furthermore, despite Wilson's rejection of the magnetic speaking style, the emotional reactions of his followers showed that Wilson had developed some charismatic characteristics of his own. Journalist Ellery Sedgwick, "a young man in search of a hero," heard Wilson speak in 1905 and came away "a burning disciple ... I shouted upstairs to my wife, 'I have been listening to a great man. I know it! I know it! Wilson will be famous.' "[147] Joseph P. Tumulty, who later became Wilson's press secretary and advisor, recalled his first taste of Wilsonian oratory in similar terms. "The personal magnetism of the man ... held the men in the Convention breathless under their mystic spell," he wrote. "Men stood about me with tears streaming from their eyes ... It seemed as if they had been lifted out of the selfish miasma of politics, and, in the spirit of the Crusaders, were ready to dedicate themselves to the cause."[148] These charismatic follower responses continued well into Wilson's presidency. Reporter Rodney Bean, accompanying Wilson on a brief speaking tour in 1916, noticed charismatic reactions among Wilson's listeners. "Men told me as they left the meeting [at Milwaukee]," Bean wrote, "that it was the most impressive moment in their lives. The President had reached the

[145] Hardin Craig, "Woodrow Wilson as an Orator," *Quarterly Journal of Speech*, Vol. 38 (April 1952), 146–147.

[146] William Bayard Hale, "Woodrow Wilson: Possible President," *The World's Work*, May 1911, 14351–14352.

[147] Ellery Sedgwick, *The Happy Profession* (Boston: Little, Brown, 1946), 179.

[148] Joseph P. Tumulty, *Woodrow Wilson as I Know Him* (Garden City, NY: Doubleday, Page, 1921), 21–22.

people and had stirred their deepest emotions."[149] Meanwhile, like Bryan before him, Wilson had his share of namesakes whose eager parents sent letters and photos in the mail; one family even named their twin sons Woodrow and Wilson.[150]

Though it was Theodore Roosevelt who first described the presidency as a "bully pulpit," Wilson used the presidential speaking prerogative in a more expansive fashion than had any of his predecessors; his frequent public addresses created what scholars have termed the modern "rhetorical presidency."[151] He began the practice of regular presidential press conferences and defied a century of tradition to deliver over a hundred speeches directly to Congress.[152] Despite Wilson's effectiveness on the platform, however, the president was reluctant to undertake speaking tours of the country, either for campaign purposes or to promote legislation. During both his 1910 campaign for governor of New Jersey and the 1912 presidential race, his advisors virtually had to force him to undertake rigorous campaign swings.[153] As late as early October of his 1916 reelection campaign, Wilson was still resorting to the McKinley strategy of front-porch oratory rather than embarking on a national tour.[154]

149 Rodney Bean, "The President among the People," *The World's Work*, April 1916, 614.

150 Moisse Schwartz to Woodrow Wilson, November 7, 1912, microfilm: reel 32, Woodrow Wilson Papers, Library of Congress; Porter Myers to Woodrow Wilson, November 3, 1916, reel 83, Woodrow Wilson Papers; Erwin Fisher to Woodrow Wilson, November 4, 1916, reel 83, Woodrow Wilson Papers; A. J. Folsom to Woodrow Wilson, November 4, 1916, reel 83, Woodrow Wilson Papers; Addie Seas to Woodrow Wilson, March 24, 1917, reel 86, Woodrow Wilson Papers; Mr. and Mrs. Frank Sperling to Woodrow Wilson, April 2, 1917, reel 86, Woodrow Wilson Papers; Otis Wingo to Woodrow Wilson, April 4, 1917, reel 86, Woodrow Wilson Papers; Ivan Kelly to Woodrow Wilson, undated letter (received April 9, 1917), reel 86, Woodrow Wilson Papers; S. A. and Della Starkey to Woodrow Wilson, September 6, 1919, reel 105, Woodrow Wilson Papers; Mrs. J. L. Belk to Woodrow Wilson, September 22, 1919, reel 105, Woodrow Wilson Papers; Mr. and Mrs. William Howard to Woodrow Wilson, October 6, 1919, reel 105, Woodrow Wilson Papers; Martin V. Hall to Woodrow Wilson, October 7, 1919, reel 105, Woodrow Wilson Papers.

151 Jeffrey K. Tulis, *The Rhetorical Presidency* (Princeton: Princeton University Press, 1987), 4, 118; Daniel Stid, "Rhetorical Leadership and 'Common Counsel' in the Presidency of Woodrow Wilson," in Richard J. Ellis, ed., *Speaking to the People: The Rhetorical Presidency in Historical Perspective* (Amherst, MA: University of Massachusetts Press, 1998), 164–168, 178.

152 Henry A. Turner, "Woodrow Wilson and Public Opinion," *Public Opinion Quarterly*, Vol. 21, No. 4 (Winter 1957–1958), 509, 512.

153 Kerney, *The Political Education of Woodrow Wilson*, 65; Kraig, *Woodrow Wilson and the Lost World of the Oratorical Statesman*, 113, 124.

154 Arthur S. Link, *Wilson: Campaigns for Progressivism and Peace,1916–1917* (Princeton: Princeton University Press, 1965), 103; August Heckscher, *Woodrow Wilson*

Similarly, during the legislative session, Wilson rarely carried out his threats to appeal to the people "over the heads" of their representatives. In February 1916, Wilson finally delivered fifteen speeches across six states in support of a military preparedness bill. Despite favorable press coverage and appreciative audiences, however, the president quickly retreated to a compromise position on preparedness; his frustrated secretary of war resigned in protest.[155]

Wilson's preference for keeping his bully pulpit at home in Washington reflected above all the influence of Colonel Edward Mandell House. The wily Texan had insinuated himself into Wilson's inner circle during the 1912 campaign and soon became the president's chief advisor and closest intimate.[156] House's pseudonymously published novel *Philip Dru: Administrator* (1912), which Wilson read carefully, offered a clear statement of House's views on charismatic campaigns. The novel's hero, Philip Dru, becomes a benevolent and popular dictator not by touring the country as a traveling orator, but by speaking eloquently before small groups of American leaders. At one early meeting, Dru wins over audience members through a platform personality similar to Wilson's: "In a voice like a deep-toned bell, he spoke with such fervor and eloquence that one who was present said afterwards that he knew the hour and the man had come."[157] Later, after Dru becomes dictator, he delivers an eloquent address before a meeting of revolutionary leaders. Afterward, "Each member went home a believer in Dru and the policy he had adopted. They, in turn, converted the people to their view of the situation, so that Dru was able to go forward with his great work, conscious of the support and approval of an overwhelming majority of his fellow countrymen."[158] This was House's, and by extension Wilson's, preferred method of charisma: turn leaders and legislators into followers in Washington, and

(New York: Scribner, 1991), 412, 414; William F. McCombs, *Making Woodrow Wilson President*, ed. Louis Jay Lang (New York: Fairview, 1921), 90; McGerr, *The Decline of Popular Politics*, 161, 166.

155 John Milton Cooper, Jr., *Woodrow Wilson: A Biography* (New York: Knopf, 2009), 309, 311.

156 Godfrey Hodgson, *Woodrow Wilson's Right Hand: The Life of Colonel Edward M. House* (New Haven, CT: Yale University Press, 2006), 6–7; Arthur D. Howden Smith, *Mr. House of Texas* (New York: Funk and Wagnalls, 1940), 42–45; Charles E. Neu, *Colonel House: A Biography of Woodrow Wilson's Silent Partner* (New York: Oxford University Press, 2015), 67–68.

157 [Edward Mandell House], *Philip Dru: Administrator* (New York: B. W. Huebsch, 1912), 106.

158 *Ibid.*, 157.

they would return home to spread the message among the people of their districts. It was an effective method in some ways, but it also reflected an elitist sensibility; by interacting primarily with other leaders, Wilson never had to bring his case directly to ordinary Americans.

Wilson's aversion to speaking tours dismayed Herbert Croly. Banished from political influence after Roosevelt's defeat, Croly used his new journalistic pulpit at *The New Republic* to continue his advocacy for charismatic leadership. After Wilson retreated on the preparedness issue, Croly blasted the president for his fear of charismatic speaking tours. "During the hulabaloo [*sic*] of Mr. Wilson's political pilgrimage through the Middle West," Croly wrote, "it looked as if the President ... would rise to his extraordinary opportunity of leadership and rally to his support the aggressive part of American public opinion. That hope and expectation must now be abandoned." Wilson "seems unable to hold a sustained course. He alternates helplessly between energy and inertia, between fighting and yielding, between leading his country and allowing his party to lead him." Wilson's unwillingness to speak directly to the people showed a fundamental lack of leadership. "There will be moments," Croly concluded, "in which he will look and talk like a real leader, who understands that the power of the Presidential office depends on the direct personal contact of its incumbent with popular opinion"; ultimately, however, Wilson "is not up to his job."[159] As the nation drifted toward war with Germany, Wilson's charismatic reticence continued to disappoint Croly. On January 22, 1917, Wilson borrowed a phrase from Croly and delivered a speech touting "peace without victory." Croly was thrilled by the address; it was, he told Colonel House, "the greatest event of his own life."[160] He immediately urged Wilson to follow up his speech with a national charismatic tour. "Would it not be well after Congress adjourns," he asked, "to make a certain number of speeches throughout the country appealing directly to the people?"[161] Predictably, however, Wilson took no action on the idea.

The peace tour became moot less than three months later; after German submarines resumed unrestricted bombing of American ships, Wilson asked Congress to declare war. With the nation

159 "A Costly Resignation," *The New Republic*, February 19, 1916, 56–57.

160 Edward Mandell House to Woodrow Wilson, January 22, 1917, quoted in Forcey, *The Crossroads of Liberalism*, 267.

161 Herbert Croly to Woodrow Wilson, January 23, 1917, reel 85, Woodrow Wilson Papers.

embarked on a conflict that would send two million soldiers overseas and claim over 50,000 American lives in battle, Wilson needed to rally support for U.S. participation.[162] Again, however, the president avoided the sort of speaking tour Croly advocated. Instead, he chose a strategy that carried to an extreme the Philip Dru method of creating followers. No longer need the president inspire even the leaders of public opinion directly, as the fictional Dru had done; with a war on, pure patriotism could do that. The key lay in encouraging those leaders to convert ordinary Americans to the cause. To coordinate this effort, Wilson chartered America's first propaganda bureau: the Committee on Public Information (CPI).

Wilson chose George Creel, an enthusiastic and loyal progressive journalist from Denver, as chief of the new organization.[163] Creel's public statements identified him as an opponent of charisma. In an attack on Theodore Roosevelt written for Wilson's reelection campaign, Creel decried Roosevelt's magnetism as "a destructive, disintegrative force" and remarked that the ex-president's Progressive Party record proved the failure of his leadership style. "People have learned the lesson," he wrote, "that the safety of democratic institutions is best conserved by devotion to principles rather than devotion to personalities."[164] Defending the CPI in 1918, Creel likewise declared himself opposed to emotional appeals to the masses. "I do not believe that public opinion has its rise in the emotions," he insisted. "I feel ... that it has its base in reason, and that it expresses slow-formed convictions rather than any temporary excitement or any passing passion of the moment ... We have never made any appeal to the emotions."[165]

Creel's claim that his propaganda was emotionless is difficult to believe; indeed, the Committee's sprawling activities – including posters, pamphlets, films, cartoons, exhibits, advertising and speakers' bureaus, a press service, and foreign propaganda departments – were designed

[162] Edward M. Coffman, *The War to End All Wars: The American Military Experience in World War I* (New York: Oxford University Press, 1968), 230, 363.

[163] George Creel, *Rebel at Large: Recollections of Fifty Crowded Years* (New York: G. P. Putnam's Sons, 1947), 157–158; Alan Axelrod, *Selling the Great War: The Making of American Propaganda* (New York: Palgrave Macmillan, 2009), 64–67; J. Michael Sproule, *Propaganda and Democracy: The American Experience of Media and Mass Persuasion* (Cambridge, UK: Cambridge University Press, 1997), 25.

[164] George Creel, *Wilson and the Issues* (New York: Century, 1916), 135–136.

[165] George Creel, "Public Opinion in War Time," *Annals of the American Academy of Political and Social Science*, Vol. 78 (July 1918), 185.

specifically to gain emotional support for the war.[166] Creel's rejection of charismatic techniques, however, was authentic and manifested itself throughout the CPI's activities. Creel's anti-charismatic approach was particularly obvious in the Committee's management of oratorical propaganda. Declaring "human speech" to be "the greatest swaying force in the world," the CPI made public speaking the centerpiece of its propaganda efforts.[167] Creel's "Four-Minute Men Bureau" soon mobilized some 75,000 volunteer orators to deliver brief popular addresses in support of the war. Bertram G. Nelson, a professor of public speaking at the University of Chicago, served as the Bureau's Associate Director and personally trained many of the volunteers.[168] Speaking at first during the four-minute delay between film reels at movie theaters, Four-Minute Men soon appeared at churches, voluntary associations, labor unions, lumber camps, and even remote Indian reservations.[169] By war's end, they had delivered over seven million speeches to over 130 million people.[170]

On the surface, the Four-Minute Men seemed a manifestation of Beecher's and Croly's charismatic ideal: a nation of trained orators addressing their fellow Americans on matters of national importance. The volunteer speakers, however, sought to win over audiences by persuasive argument, not charismatic technique. Wilson himself warned the Four-Minute Men not to use "the spoken word" to "light the fires of passion and unreason."[171] The *Four Minute Men News*, an official CPI organ written for the speakers, urged its readers to avoid emotional display in their public addresses. "We Four Minute Men must never forget our mission," the *News* argued, "not to arouse hatred, not to

166 George Creel, *Complete Report of the Chairman of the Committee on Public Information* (Washington, DC: Government Printing Office, 1920), 2–7.

167 "The War Work of the Four-Minute Men: With an Introductory Letter by President Wilson," *The Touchstone*, Vol. 3, No. 6 (September 1918), 507; Alfred E. Cornebise, *War as Advertised: The Four Minute Men and America's Crusade, 1917–1918* (Philadelphia: American Philosophical Society, 1984), 2.

168 Cornebise, *War as Advertised*, 15–16; Lisa Mastrangelo, "World War I, Public Intellectuals, and the Four Minute Men: Convergent Ideals of Public Speaking and Civic Participation," *Rhetoric & Public Affairs*, Vol. 12, No. 4 (Winter 2009), 607, 610.

169 Cornebise, *War as Advertised*, ix, 13–14; Stephen Vaughn, *Holding Fast the Inner Lines: Democracy, Nationalism, and the Committee on Public Information* (Chapel Hill, NC: University of North Carolina Press, 1980), 116–117.

170 George Creel, *How We Advertised America* (New York: Harper & Brothers, 1920), 85.

171 Woodrow Wilson to Four-Minute Men, November 9, 1917, in Four Minute Men Bulletin No. 20, "Carrying the Message" (Washington, DC: Committee on Public Information, November 26, 1917), 3.

inflame passion, but to show facts, to inspire deeper convictions."[172] The organization permitted some deviation from this model; certain speakers recounted stories of German atrocities, while one Four-Minute Man exhorted his audience to imitate the man carrying the message to Garcia.[173] The CPI, however, insisted that speakers normalize their messages as much as possible. Each *News* issue carried extracts of poorly delivered or overly emotional speeches, instructed the Four-Minute Men to forgo shouting or frequent gestures, and reminded them to obey the directives of the national office.[174] "The ax fell heavily," Creel boasted, when a speaker failed to follow these guidelines.[175] Ultimately, the Four-Minute Men were not a charismatic enterprise. When they stirred their listeners' emotions, they did so by rousing Americans to support a cause, not by convincing their listeners to follow the speakers themselves.

In spite of Wilson's persistent rejection of charismatic techniques, the end of the war marked the high point of the president's charismatic reception – though his most appreciative followers lived outside the United States. Wilson's wartime "Fourteen Points" address had thrilled people worldwide with its promises of national self-determination for colonial peoples and a League of Nations to enforce peace. When Wilson traveled to Europe in January 1919 to negotiate the treaty that would end the war, enthusiastic crowds in France, England, and Italy hailed him as an apostle of liberty.[176] Meanwhile, appeals from leaders of colonial peoples in Africa and Asia poured into Wilson's

[172] *Four Minute Men News*, Edition A (Washington, DC: Committee on Public Information, c. 1917), 2; James R. Mock and Cedric Larson, *Words that Won the War: The Story of the Committee on Public Information, 1917–1919* (Princeton: Princeton University Press, 1939), 122–124.

[173] M. C. Flaherty, "Like Message from Garcia," *Four Minute Men News*, Edition B (Washington, DC: Committee on Public Information, c. 1918), 11; Mock and Larson, *Words that Won the War*, 123; Thomas A. Hollihan, "Propagandizing in the Interest of War: A Rhetorical Study of the Committee on Public Information," *Southern Speech Communication Journal*, Vol. 49 (Spring 1984), 246; Jeanne Graham, "The Four Minute Men: Volunteers for Propaganda," *Southern Speech Journal*, Vol. 32 (Fall 1966), 54–55.

[174] *Four Minute Men News*, Edition D (Washington, DC: Committee on Public Information, c. 1918), 17; Glen N. Murray, "Do's and Don'ts," *Four Minute Men News*, Edition E (Washington, DC: Committee on Public Information, c. 1918), 28.

[175] Creel, *How We Advertised America*, 89.

[176] Erez Manela, *The Wilsonian Moment: Self-Determination and the International Origins of Anticolonial Nationalism* (New York: Oxford University Press, 2007), 19.

Paris headquarters.[177] Wilson "was transfigured in the eyes of men," H. G. Wells wrote later; "he became a Messiah. Millions believed him as the bringer of untold blessings; thousands would gladly have died for him."[178]

Though the resulting Treaty of Versailles was a decidedly equivocal document – Wilson got his League of Nations, but at the expense of many of his other demands – the president returned home convinced the treaty was a triumph. Buoyed by his reception overseas, Wilson was finally prepared to follow Croly's suggestion of a charismatic speaking campaign in favor of his platform. The treaty still had to be ratified by a hostile Senate, and for once, Wilson refused to negotiate directly with his Congressional opponents. Instead, he resolved to undertake a national speaking tour in favor of the treaty and the League. Just as Roosevelt had staked the future of progressivism on his charismatic abilities in 1912, Wilson was prepared to put his progressive vision for the world to the ultimate charismatic test. The *Anniston Star* cast Wilson's task as that of a Carlylean hero. "His personality is the most pronounced in world affairs today," wrote the *Star*. "On him rests, in no fanciful sense, the burden of the world's freedom. It can be said without exaggeration that the fullest success of the League of Nations depends on the life of President Wilson … [He] is the hope and confidence of not only our own people, but of all the ends of the earth."[179] Americans would soon learn whether that hope was justified.

* * *

Hiram Johnson, now a U.S. senator, invited two friends over for dinner one night in July 1919: William E. Borah, leader of the anti-treaty faction in the Senate, and editor James T. Williams. At dinner, Borah and Williams surprised Johnson with a proposition: the Californian, they argued, should undertake his own national speaking tour against the treaty and the League of Nations, matching Wilson speech for speech. Johnson, Williams reiterated in a July 26 letter, was the best choice for such a campaign. "The Man in the White House is more afraid of you in this particular fight than of any other member of the Senate," Williams explained. "I know this from men in his confidence, and my knowledge is

177 *Ibid.*, 5.

178 H. G. Wells, *The Shape of Things to Come* (New York: Macmillan, 1933), 82; *Ibid.*, 3.

179 "Personality in the Making of History, and President Wilson," *Anniston Star*, October 6, 1919, 4.

reenforced [*sic*] by reasons obvious to all. He never has stood up in a two fisted fight, and you are at all times a two-fisted fighter."[180]

A few weeks earlier, Johnson had ventured outside Washington to speak against the League in three New England cities. The results were startling: in Providence, Rhode Island, he had "stirred his audience of more than 2,000 persons to a wild pitch of enthusiasm," according to the local paper.[181] Evidently the old Bull Mooser had not lost his charismatic touch. Soon thereafter, speaking invitations began pouring in from around the country.[182] By August 1, Johnson had decided to take up Borah and Williams on their suggestion. "I would like," he wrote to his sons, "to talk to our people about this League ... I feel I ought to undergo any effort, physical or mental, to do my duty in this peculiar crisis."[183] Johnson's superior grasp of charismatic organization had made him a contrarian within the 1912 Roosevelt campaign; now he would play a similar role in the national debate with Wilson over the League.

After three weeks of oratorical competition with Wilson in the Western states, Johnson was delighted with the results of his tour. "It's been the toughest itinerary I ever tackled with the longest and most difficult jumps," he wrote his sons afterward. "But it's been wonderful ... I sensed the dramatic possibilities, and 'tho of course I had to face failure as well as success, I went to it." Old Bull Moosers had organized speaking engagements and filled the halls with eager listeners. "Chicago's meeting paralyzed everybody," Johnson declared. "No such demonstration had been seen there since Roosevelt's time." Johnson's audiences had been more impressive than Wilson's, too. "I actually outdrew him" in several cities, he wrote, while "whenever we could make comparisons of demonstrations and applause, we exceeded him many times over." In one city the audience, "perfunctorily courteous to the president, were a hundred fold more demonstrative at my meeting with them."[184] The senator's descriptions were largely accurate. Johnson "drives his thought into the minds of his audience with sledgehammer blows of utterance," the *New York Times*

180 James T. Williams, Jr., to Hiram W. Johnson, July 26, 1919, in Robert E. Burke, ed., *The Diary Letters of Hiram Johnson, 1917–1945*, Vol. 3 (New York: Garland, 1983).

181 *Providence Daily Journal*, July 8, 1919, quoted in Weatherson and Bochin, *Hiram Johnson*, 92.

182 Weatherson and Bochin, *Hiram Johnson*, 93.

183 Hiram W. Johnson to Hiram W. Johnson, Jr., and Archibald M. Johnson, August 1, 1919, in Burke, ed., *The Diary Letters of Hiram Johnson*, Vol. 3.

184 Hiram W. Johnson to Hiram W. Johnson, Jr., and Archibald M. Johnson, September 22, 1919, in Burke, ed., *The Diary Letters of Hiram Johnson*, Vol. 3.

reported; "he moves, rouses, and controls men who listen to him."[185] Newspapers on both sides of the League fight agreed that Johnson drew more supporters and more enthusiasm to his speeches than Wilson did.[186] "In oratory, Wilson is exacting," the *San Francisco Examiner* wrote in a typical analysis, "but a 'rabble rouser' he is not, or an inspirational orator. He does not get his hearers to their feet shouting hysterically. Hiram Johnson has it all over him in that quality ... Hiram, going at full steam could rouse a crowd to making ten times as much noise as the president evoked last night."[187]

For Wilson, it was William Cabell Bruce and the Jefferson Society all over again. While the charismatic Johnson was packing halls and energizing audiences, Wilson suffered from familiar difficulties. The president's tour could certainly boast some successes. "He is arousing a tide of emotion for the League which nothing can resist," the *New York Evening Post* insisted. "He is uttering the aspiration of the mass of the plain people of the land, and their voice will respond to him, like deep answering unto deep."[188] Too often, however, Wilson still appeared cold and aloof. The humor column "Potash and Perlmutter" produced a memorable description of Wilson's difficulty connecting with his audiences. Noting Wilson's desire to appeal personally to voters, one character remarks, "It begins to look like personal appealing wasn't Mr. Wilson's biggest asset exactly ... There is some critics of Mr. Wilson which when they see a moving picture of Mr. Wilson making a speech behind a pitcher of ice water, they pretend not to recognize which is the pitcher of ice water and which is the president, y'understand."[189]

As the tour progressed, with Joseph Tumulty urging a more combative stance and Johnson dogging the president's footsteps, Wilson began to embrace the charismatic techniques he had always rejected. The transformation began in Tacoma, Washington, and continued throughout Wilson's stops in Johnson's home state of California; with each successive

[185] "Senator Johnson's Exploit," *New York Times*, September 29, 1919, 9; Richard Coke Lower, *A Bloc of One: The Political Career of Hiram W. Johnson* (Stanford, CA: Stanford University Press, 1993), 136.

[186] Weatherson and Bochin, *Hiram Johnson*, 105–107.

[187] San Francisco Examiner, quoted in Robert T. Small, "Johnson's Stronghold Gives Huge Ovation to President Wilson," *Atlanta Constitution*, September 19, 1919, 17, quoted in J. Michael Hogan, *Woodrow Wilson's Western Tour: Rhetoric, Public Opinion, and the League of Nations* (College Station, TX: Texas A&M University Press, 2006), 118.

[188] *New York Evening Post*, September 5, 1919, 8.

[189] Montague Glass, "Potash and Perlmutter Talk over the President's Speaking Tour," *Idaho Statesman*, September 28, 1919, 5.

FIGURE 5.2 Woodrow Wilson had philosophical objections to charismatic oratory, but during the League fight in 1919 he began to use it anyway, beginning with this speech in Tacoma, Washington.
Source: Photo of Woodrow Wilson, Tacoma, WA, September 13, 1919, courtesy of the Department of Rare Books and Special Collections, Princeton University Library, Papers of Woodrow Wilson Project, Records Box 443, Folder 63.

speech, audiences responded more enthusiastically to the president's performance.[190] By the time the presidential train reached Pueblo, Colorado, on September 25, Wilson was finally ready to do what Croly and others had been urging all along: to become a democratic St. Francis, to speak as a charismatic leader rather than a Philip Dru–style administrator. Delivering one of the longest speeches of the tour, Wilson produced a charismatic effect unlike any he had ever created. Afterward, Tumulty described the scene. "A great wave of emotion," he wrote, "such as I have never witnessed at a public meeting, swept through the whole amphitheatre ... I saw men sneak the handkerchiefs out of their pockets and wipe the tears from their eyes." Tumulty's concluding words unwittingly reflected those of the St. Louis reporters who had witnessed Patrick Gilmore's magnetic performances over three decades earlier. "The President," he wrote, "was like a great organist playing upon the

[190] Hogan, *Woodrow Wilson's Western Tour*, 99–101, 108–109.

heart emotions of the thousands of people who were held spell-bound by what he said."[191]

Tragically, Wilson's first foray into charismatic oratory was also his last. That night, the physically fragile Wilson suffered a massive stroke from which he never fully recovered. While Wilson lay incapacitated in the White House, his supporters lost the Treaty fight in Congress, and the progressive movement itself disintegrated. Acutely conscious that a war which had cost 50,000 American lives had achieved little in terms of lasting international peace, Americans turned against the progressive leaders and policies that had brought them into the conflict. The president, bedridden and barely able to speak, could do nothing to win back his erstwhile supporters.[192]

Despite Wilson's equivocal relationship with charisma, the fall of progressivism led to a national backlash against magnetic techniques. Progressives had so dominated the discourse of charisma during the 1910s that charismatic movements had become popularly identified with progressivism, and many Americans had soured on the combination. Republican Warren Harding, running a conservative campaign for president in 1920, campaigned openly against the emotional politics of the previous decade. "America's present need is not heroics, but healing," he declared in a memorable speech; "not nostrums but normalcy; not revolution, but restoration; not agitation, but adjustment; not surgery, but serenity; not the dramatic, but the dispassionate … I pray for sober thinking in behalf of the future of America."[193] Voters elected Harding in the biggest landslide in a hundred years. Progressive charisma was no more.

* * *

Just as Roosevelt's 1912 loss had convinced Oscar King Davis that "the right of the people to rule is bunk," the failure of Wilson's Western tour and the electoral defeat of 1920 demoralized some of the charismatic

191 Tumulty, *Woodrow Wilson as I Know Him*, 449. J. Michael Hogan has questioned whether the audience response was really as enthusiastic as Tumulty indicates; see Hogan, *Woodrow Wilson's Western Tour*, 152–153.

192 David M. Kennedy, *Over Here: The First World War and American Society* (New York: Oxford University Press, 1980), 290; John A. Thompson, *Reformers and War: American Progressive Publicists and the First World War* (Cambridge, UK: Cambridge University Press, 1987), 258–259.

193 Warren G. Harding, "Back to Normal," speech delivered in Boston, May 14, 1920, in Frederick E. Schortemeier, *Rededicating America: Life and Recent Speeches of Warren G. Harding* (Indianapolis, IN: Bobbs-Merrill, 1920), 223, 228.

relationship's most ardent progressive backers. William Bayard Hale, who in 1911 had hailed Wilson as the "prophet and captain" of a "political revolution," condemned what he considered the president's emotional oratory in *The Story of a Style* (1920). Wilson, Hale wrote, "does not employ words because of any definite meaning they carry. He asks them only to possess a vague emotional content ... Therefore his fondness for large phrases dimly understanded [*sic*] of the people, but carrying with them mystic suggestions of profound wisdom." Such empty verbosity, Hale argued, was a form of falsehood that "emancipates [listeners] from the repressive thralldom of reality." Though Hale criticized Wilson for prevarication, his real problem with charismatic leadership was its overreliance on followers' instincts. It was a mistake, Hale felt, to trust ordinary people's ability to distinguish between truth and falsehood. Citing Gustave Le Bon's description of the crowd as a dangerous, mindless beast, he castigated the people in terms that recalled those Davis had used in 1914. "It is the way of the crowd," Hale concluded, "to bare its head at the pompous passing of a phrase, equally and with as sincere a thrill of reverence, whether the vehicle be occupied or empty."[194]

Herbert Croly was less eager than Hale to condemn the American people, but by 1920 he too had come to believe that their emotions could not be trusted. In an essay on "Religion in Life," Croly offered perhaps the progressives' most revealing assessment of charisma's failure to regenerate American society. "At present," he wrote, "our worst handicap in trying to conduct our lives in the light of truth is our inability to furnish to the conductor the truth about ourselves." The American people, Croly now believed, were not ready for a democratic St. Francis; indeed, they were more likely to support a dishonest demagogue, or to be manipulated into a poisonous militarism, than to identify and follow a truly enlightened leader. "We cannot prevent ourselves from going astray," he lamented, "not only because we cannot trust our spiritual Baedekers, but because our feelings and our preconceptions give us false information about our condition, our needs, our progress or retrogression and our capabilities." Croly still hoped that people could learn to interpret their emotions properly, but doing so would require an intense regimen of "systematic self-observation."[195] During the last ten years of his life,

[194] William Bayard Hale, *The Story of a Style* (New York: B. W. Huebsch, 1920), 247–249.

[195] Herbert Croly, "Religion in Life," unpublished paper, Houghton Library, Harvard University, MS Am 1291, 36–37.

Croly largely withdrew from politics and devoted himself to such a regimen under the tutelage of an austere Eastern mystic, George Ivanovich Gurdjieff.[196] In his own way, Croly, too, had surrendered to the notion that the people could not be trusted to change society in healthy or desirable ways.

In truth, this latent distrust of popular emotions had always been the key flaw in the progressive approach to charisma. Leaders such as Beecher, Bryan, Sunday, Debs, and even Hiram Johnson had recognized a democratic element in the charismatic relationship. These leaders offered an attractive vision of self-transformation, but they respected the right of ordinary Americans to make a free choice between competing platforms. They did not lecture their audiences like schoolmasters in an effort to change them; rather, in Beecher's Biblical paraphrase, they sought "to catch men" – to adapt themselves to their audiences in the hope of provoking voluntary conversions. "If you speak to the multitude and they do not respond," Bryan declared in a 1907 speech, "do not despise them, but rather examine what you have said." This openness to followers' desires and emotions won leaders enthusiastic converts and lent their movements strength and power. "Mankind," Bryan concluded, "deserves to be trusted."[197]

Distrustful of individualism, afraid of the agency possessed by ordinary Americans, the progressives never appreciated this democratic aspect of charisma. As Croly wrote in 1920, they rejected the view that "leaders must yield to the particular passions, grievances, animosities and interests which happen to prevail at any one time."[198] Like Wilson, they sought to change society by changing their followers – thereby inverting the charismatic structure. Wilson's "faith in the people," explained his brother-in-law Stockton Axson, "has never been a faith in the supreme wisdom of the people, but rather in the capacity of the people to be led right by those whom they elect and constitute their leaders."[199] "Much was futile," William Allen White wrote in 1926, "in that earlier vision which sought to give men freedom while they still

[196] Levy, *Herbert Croly of The New Republic*, 295–297.

[197] William Jennings Bryan, "Faith," speech delivered 1907, in Bryan, *Speeches of William Jennings Bryan*, Vol. 2 (New York: Funk & Wagnalls, 1909), 332.

[198] Herbert Croly, *The Breach in Civilization*, unpublished mss. (1920), 139, box 215 (microfilm: reel 135), Papers of Felix Frankfurter, Library of Congress.

[199] Stockton Axson, *"Brother Woodrow": A Memoir of Woodrow Wilson*, ed. Arthur S. Link (Princeton: Princeton University Press, 1993), 231.

carried servile hearts."[200] The progressives' unwillingness to grant their followers agency in the charismatic relationship weakened both the effect of their charismatic performances and the attachment of their followers. Yet at the same time, the ambitious progressives expected these weakened follower armies to achieve the impossible: to win the presidency or the League of Nations against the organized opposition of traditional parties and political machines. The failure of such efforts was virtually foreordained.

The fall of progressive charisma had broad consequences for the charismatic phenomenon as a whole. In the aftermath of World War I and Harding's 1920 victory, charismatic movements lost the cultural primacy they had held in the 1910s. Throughout the 1920s and 1930s, defenders of the charismatic relationship fought a rearguard action against a changing culture. Facing a series of threats to their existence, charismatic movements had to adapt in order to survive.

[200] William Allen White, "Introduction," in Fremont Older, *My Own Story* (New York: Macmillan, 1926), xiii; Mowry, *The California Progressives*, 301–302.

6

End of an Age

From Magnetism to Mass Communication, 1920–1940

One evening in the early 1930s, psychologist and public opinion researcher Hadley Cantril traveled to a meeting hall in Boston to observe a revival meeting. Though Cantril did not identify either the evangelist or the place, the occasion was likely a Billy Sunday campaign at the famous Tremont Temple.[1] Sunday's performances had worn thin with the years, and he no longer drew enough listeners to fill a massive tabernacle; nevertheless, there were still twice as many audience members as seats in the main hall. Accordingly, the organizers had set up overflow seating in the Temple's open basement, complete with a loudspeaker to broadcast the proceedings. The service would take place simultaneously for two essentially similar groups of listeners: a live audience upstairs and a radio audience downstairs. Sensing the opportunity for an experiment, Cantril made his way to the stairwell; from there, he could observe both audiences at once.

Ten minutes before Sunday's arrival at the podium, it was clear to Cantril that the two groups were in for very different experiences. A choir began singing hymns in the main hall; soon, Cantril wrote, the

[1] Cantril and Allport do not reveal which one of them was "the social psychologist" present at the meeting, but Cantril was a Harvard graduate student in the early 1930s and was a specialist in empirical research. They also do not name "the evangelist" who delivered the meeting, but some elements of the event, such as the organized handshaking and the phrase "hit the trail," were unique to Sunday's organization. Tremont Temple was Sunday's primary Boston revival location in the early 1930s and is structured similarly to Cantril and Allport's description, although the downstairs hall is smaller than the main auditorium. Hadley Cantril and Gordon W. Allport, *The Psychology of Radio* (New York: Harper & Brothers, 1935), 5; William G. McLoughlin, Jr., *Billy Sunday Was His Real Name* (Chicago: University of Chicago Press, 1955), 287–288.

upstairs listeners joined in. The downstairs crowd, however, remained "silent and impassive while it listens, in spite of the encouragement issued into the microphone by the song-leader." When Sunday appeared on stage, the upstairs audience produced "a tumult of applause, clearly heard by those in the radio audience but not provoking them to any visible or audible response. Why should they applaud when the evangelist can neither see nor hear them?" As he often did when beginning a revival meeting, Sunday began to make jokes. "There is loud laughter in the main group, but only a few chuckles below. Those who chuckle subside quickly, some glancing rather shamefacedly around." After Sunday said something especially meaningful, "[t]here is prolonged applause above," Cantril reported, "but only a few timid handclaps below."

Now came the climax of the meeting, as Sunday prepared to take up his collection and invite his audience to "hit the trail." "All those who are glad that I am in town," the evangelist prodded, "raise your hands." Upstairs, nearly 1,500 people complied with Sunday's request, Cantril noted, compared with only two listeners downstairs. Sunday's aides began passing the hat, but the financial offerings of the two audiences differed widely. "The collection basins upstairs," according to Cantril, "overflow with silver well silenced by bank notes; downstairs they rattle loosely with copper and nickel." Finally, Sunday issued his familiar call for converts to "hit the trail." Upstairs, a throng of people rushed forward, but Cantril was more interested in the response of the radio audience. "There is an awkward silence," he observed, "then a fumbling for coats and hats. The group below begins to disintegrate. Most of its members file out into the street, as stolid as when they arrived . . . None, so far as can be determined, joins the forward-moving crowds into the aisles, to seek salvation." The difference was striking. "With his major congregation," Cantril concluded, "the evangelist's efforts have been eminently successful, but with his radio congregation they have utterly failed."[2]

Sunday's Boston revival encapsulated the challenges charismatic movements faced in the two decades after World War I. As the responsive upstairs crowd demonstrated, Sunday and other charismatic speakers remained effective before a live audience, but their ability to reach that audience was eroding. Competition from new forms of entertainment such as motion pictures had diminished the number of Americans still interested in attending a Sunday revival; the 2,000 to 3,000 people who listened in Tremont Temple contrasted sharply with the 20,000 who, fifteen years earlier,

[2] Cantril and Allport, *The Psychology of Radio*, 5–6.

had filled Sunday's New York City tabernacle twice each day.[3] Meanwhile, the downstairs debacle showed that Sunday's oratorical style was unsuited to the radio medium, which dramatically changed the American soundscape and came to dominate public speaking opportunities during the interwar years.[4] It was certainly possible for charismatic speakers to reach radio audiences; as Cantril and his coauthor Gordon W. Allport recognized, Sunday could have adapted his presentation to the downstairs crowd had he chosen to do so. "A radio spellbinder," they wrote, "would have spoken quite differently. He would have used less bombast and more artistry, less brute force and more cunning. He would have directed his attention to the invisible audience and would have made each listener feel welcome as a member of the circle."[5] For charismatic leadership to survive in an age of mass communication, it would have to meet the demands of the new medium.

New communication technologies were not the only threat to charisma's persistence in American culture. In the aftermath of the war and of the progressives' coercive propaganda, American thinkers began to question charisma's compatibility with democracy. Henry Watterson died in 1921, but new voices rose up to renew his assault on charismatic leadership as a dangerous and demagogic phenomenon. Gradually, these anti-charismatic thinkers came to predominate in American society. At the same time, however, a new crop of political, religious, and activist leaders during the interwar years found ways to merge charismatic techniques successfully with new technologies and to adapt the charismatic relationship for modern use. By World War II, what remained of personal magnetism in American culture would have been unrecognizable to James Rush and Henry Ward Beecher; nevertheless, charisma had left a lasting mark on American society.

* * *

On September 19, 1919, during his Western tour in support of the League of Nations, Woodrow Wilson experienced the future of public address and rejected it outright. To carry Wilson's voice to a crowd of 50,000 without requiring the ill president to stand outside, San Diego civic leaders set up a loudspeaker system with an indoor microphone. Erroneously termed the "megabox" by Wilson's physician Cary Grayson, this

[3] McLoughlin, *Billy Sunday Was His Real Name*, xxiii, 63.

[4] Emily Thompson, *The Soundscape of Modernity: Architectural Acoustics and the Culture of Listening in America, 1900–1933* (Cambridge, MA: MIT Press, 2002), 233–240.

[5] Cantril and Allport, *The Psychology of Radio*, 7.

apparatus was actually the Magnavox sound system invented by Peter L. Jensen and Edwin Pridham.[6] Wilson was not the first charismatic politician to use the Magnavox; Wilson's old enemy Hiram Johnson had earned that distinction when he utilized the system during a December 1915 gubernatorial address. Johnson's speech had gone well, but the arrival of the war had forestalled further experimentation. Wilson's speaking needs now presented Jensen and Pridham with a new opportunity to demonstrate their system on a massive scale.[7] Standing "on a big glassed-in platform," Wilson delivered his speech "in an ordinary speaking voice," reported Philip Kinsley in the *Chicago Tribune*. "Over his head hung two black funnel-shaped horns. As he talked ... the horns picked it up and tossed it out over the sea of faces and they smiled, or grew thoughtful following every turn of his argument with as much ease as if he were talking in a small banquet room."[8] Despite the success of Wilson's speech, Grayson wrote in his diary, "The President did not relish this experience. He said afterwards that it was the most difficult speech he had ever tried to deliver in his life. He could not be free and natural because it was necessary that he remain at one spot talking so that his voice carried directly into the megaphones in front of him."[9]

Notwithstanding Wilson's dislike of electronic amplification, his demonstration of the technology helped to make it ubiquitous. By 1920, both political parties used loudspeakers at their national conventions and campaign events to increase the range of speakers' voices.[10] More significantly, engineers soon coupled recording devices with existing wireless technology to create a new communication medium: the radio. On November 2, 1920, station KDKA in Pittsburgh broadcast the first radio program: fittingly, given the civic implications of the new technology, a news feature on the results of the presidential election.[11] Radio's

6 Cary T. Grayson, *Woodrow Wilson: An Intimate Memoir* (New York: Holt, Rinehart, 1960), 7.

7 W. David Lewis, "Peter L. Jensen and the Amplification of Sound," in Carroll W. Pursell, Jr., ed., *Technology in America: A History of Individuals and Ideas*, 2nd ed. (orig. pub. 1979; Cambridge, MA: MIT Press, 1990), 203–206.

8 Philip Kinsley, "San Diego Opens 100,000 Arms to Embrace Wilson," *Chicago Tribune*, September 20, 1919, 5.

9 Cary T. Grayson, "From the Diary of Dr. Grayson," September 19, 1919, in Arthur S. Link, ed., *The Papers of Woodrow Wilson*, Vol. 63 (Princeton: Princeton University Press, 1990), 369–370.

10 Lewis, "Peter L. Jensen and the Amplification of Sound," 206.

11 J. Fred MacDonald, *Don't Touch That Dial! Radio Programming in American Life, 1920–1960* (Chicago: Nelson-Hall, 1991), 2.

subsequent growth was explosive. Within the next two years, over 500 new stations had acquired federal licenses; multicity networks and advertising had appeared by early 1923.[12] Insatiable consumers purchased radio sets just as quickly as the burgeoning industry could provide programming. In January 1921 Americans owned 50,000 radios; by December that number had shot up to a million.[13] By 1930, nearly half of American families owned a radio; by 1940, over 80 percent had one.[14]

The motion picture industry underwent a similar transformation. By 1928, over 20,000 movie theaters nationwide were selling sixty-five million tickets per week – over 50 percent more than they had sold just six years earlier.[15] By 1930, with the advent of talking pictures, the number of tickets sold had skyrocketed to ninety million per week.[16] In *Middletown*, their pioneering 1929 study of the "typical" American town of Muncie, Indiana, sociologists Robert and Helen Lynd found that the 36,000 residents bought over 100,000 movie tickets every month.[17] To accommodate such large audiences, the film industry built lavish "movie palaces" seating thousands of people for every show.[18] Though the film industry suffered during the Great Depression, the setback was only temporary. Six years after *Middletown*'s publication, the Lynds were surprised to find that a "resplendent" new 1,800-seat movie theater had sprung up in Muncie and was selling 14,000 tickets a week.[19] At a time when Billy Sunday's nightly audiences had declined to around a tenth of that number, the shift in popular tastes was palpable.

[12] *Ibid.*, 16, 18; Bruce Lenthall, *Radio's America: The Great Depression and the Rise of Modern Mass Culture* (Chicago: University of Chicago Press, 2007), 11; Susan J. Douglas, *Inventing American Broadcasting, 1899–1922* (Baltimore, MD: Johns Hopkins University Press, 1987), xv; Susan J. Douglas, *Listening in: Radio and the American Imagination* (New York: Random House, 1999), 61.

[13] MacDonald, *Don't Touch That Dial!*, 19.

[14] Lenthall, *Radio's America*, 12.

[15] Richard Koszarski, *An Evening's Entertainment: The Age of the Silent Feature Picture, 1915–1928* (New York: Scribner, 1990), 25–26; David Nasaw, *Going Out: The Rise and Fall of Public Amusements* (New York: Basic Books, 1993), 224, 241.

[16] Garth Jowett, *Film: The Democratic Art* (Boston: Little, Brown, 1976), 192.

[17] Robert S. Lynd and Helen Merrell Lynd, *Middletown: A Study in Modern American Culture* (New York: Harcourt Brace, 1929), 263–264.

[18] Jowett, *Film*, 59–61;

[19] Robert S. Lynd and Helen Merrell Lynd, *Middletown in Transition: A Study in Cultural Conflicts* (New York: Harcourt Brace, 1937), 260; Donald Crafton, *The Talkies: American Cinema's Transition to Sound, 1926–1931* (New York: Scribner, 1997), 188–191, 262.

It is hard to overstate the magnitude of this revolution in communication and entertainment. In 1919, Woodrow Wilson became just the second person to address a mass audience through electronic means; by the time Wilson died five years later, the world of platform oratory he inhabited had simply disappeared. The decline of the circuit Chautauquas demonstrated the suddenness and finality of the change. During the 1910s, dozens of leading speakers had spent months lecturing on the circuits; they had imparted charismatic oratory as well as entertainment to appreciative audiences across the country. "The progressive movement that now is sweeping the country," journalist French Strother had written during the 1912 campaign, "owes its strength very largely to the chautauqua ... Millions absorb from [Chautauqua assemblies] their political faith and are by them directed to their course of political action."[20] Theodore Roosevelt had called Chautauqua "the most American thing in America"; William Jennings Bryan had caused controversy by continuing to travel the circuit even while serving as secretary of state.[21] After World War I, however, competition from radio broadcasts and movie theaters ruined the circuits financially. "The final and most direct blow to the Chautauqua," manager Charles F. Horner remembered, "came from the radio and talking movies ... They really cut into our crowds."[22] In September 1932, as distraught employees looked on, the last remaining circuit struck its tent and shuttered its operations.[23]

To avoid meeting the same fate as the Chautauquas, public speakers had to adapt their speaking styles to fit the tastes of radio listeners. Like Wilson and Sunday, many charismatic orators found the transition jarring. Midwestern evangelist Bill Stidger considered radio preaching "a thrilling adventure" when he first tried it in the early 1920s, but he noted that successful radio performance required the ability to imagine a radio audience the speaker could not actually see. "As you sit there in the radio room talking," he explained, "you send your imagination hurtling out ... into the hearts and souls of your fellow men sitting in their homes by their own firesides ... waiting, listening, for your message; and the thing takes

[20] French Strother, "The Great American Forum," *The World's Work*, September 1912, 553.

[21] *Ibid.*, 564; "Chautauqua Stars," *Everybody's Magazine*, Vol. 33 (September 1915), 328.

[22] Charles F. Horner, *Strike the Tents: The Story of the Chautauqua* (Philadelphia: Dorrance, 1954), 189.

[23] Charlotte M. Canning, *The Most American Thing in America: Circuit Chautauqua as Performance* (Iowa City: University of Iowa Press, 2005), 220.

hold of your soul."[24] Just as Wilson had, magnetic speakers used to roaming the platform found it difficult to stand still in front of the microphone. Wisconsin senator Robert La Follette and New York governor Al Smith, who had served as political "spellbinders" in their youth, had to be physically restrained during broadcast speeches lest they unintentionally move out of radio range.[25] Meanwhile, Gilbert Austin's system of gestures, which many magnetic speakers had painstakingly mastered, was obviously useless before a radio audience.

The biggest change brought about by radio, however, was in elocutionary style. As charismatic figures quickly learned, success "on the air" required a completely new type of public speaking: a flat, conversational approach that tended to appeal more to radio listeners than did emotional oratory. In part, as Cantril discovered at the Billy Sunday revival, the physical separation between speaker and audience explained the shift in audience tastes. Huddled around radio sets with their families, audience members did not react to charismatic oratory as they did in the emotionally charged mass atmosphere of the lecture hall; without the close connection between leader and follower, charismatic speaking techniques seemed overemotional and ridiculous over the radio. "Detached from the excitement of the mob," explained Orrin Dunlap in 1936, "the voter sits comfortably at home and eavesdrops on the appeals. He is swayed by cold facts and voice personality. He may be honestly persuaded but seldom swept off his feet."[26]

In part, too, the change reflected a broader shift in American emotional culture during the interwar years. In the late nineteenth century, Americans unsettled by industrial capitalism had sought intense emotional experiences, and they had felt comfortable expressing the resulting emotions publicly. Drawing on nineteenth-century Romanticism's frank celebration of strong emotions, most Americans had seen nothing shameful in experiencing laughter, tears, or awe. After World War I,

[24] William L. Stidger, *That God's House May Be Filled: A Book of Modern Church Methods and Workable Plans* (New York: George H. Doran, 1924), 145; Jack Hyland, *Evangelism's First Modern Media Star: The Life of Reverend Bill Stidger* (New York: Cooper Square Press, 2002), 157–158.

[25] Edward Ranson, *The Role of Radio in the American Presidential Election of 1924: How a New Communications Technology Shapes the Political Process* (Lewiston, NY: Edwin Mellen, 2010), 108; Douglas B. Craig, *Fireside Politics: Radio and Political Culture in the United States, 1920–1940* (Baltimore, MD: Johns Hopkins University Press, 2000), 168–170.

[26] Orrin E. Dunlap, Jr., *Talking on the Radio: A Practical Guide for Writing and Broadcasting a Speech* (New York: Greenberg, 1936), 30.

however, the growth of consumerism helped ease sexual and cultural taboos and led Americans to replace these strictures by more closely regulating their emotions. The resulting cultural embrace of "American cool" emphasized an even temperament and a laid-back approach toward emotional experience.[27] In an era favoring both conservative reaction and emotional self-regulation, conversational speaking was the oratorical equivalent of a return to normalcy.

Whatever the reasons for the change, observers agreed that "Brevity and Appeal to Reason Make Radio Talks Magnetic," as the *New York Times* put it in 1928.[28] Radio "has slain the political orator," Samuel Blythe insisted in 1929. "He is out. The day of the spellbinder is over."[29] In radio broadcasting, Dunlap agreed, "[T]here is no place ... for electromagnetic mud-slinging, high-sounding phraseology, hot air, meaningless platitudes and the bunkum of soap-box oratory."[30] In such an environment, extemporaneous speaking made little impression on audiences. The radio "is a godsend to the public speaker who reads his speeches," Al Smith wrote in 1930. "The listeners ... feel he is making a great oration when, as a matter of fact, he is reading the entire thing from a piece of paper. He needs no personal appeal or magnetism."[31]

Given the new medium's stylistic demands, it was no surprise that Calvin Coolidge was the first politician to become a radio star.[32] Nasal-voiced, taciturn, and prone to reading his speeches in a bored monotone, the thirtieth president nevertheless appealed to radio listeners with his measured, matter-of-fact delivery.[33] Coolidge's radio following surprised even his supporters. "He had never been known as an orator,"

[27] Peter N. Stearns, *American Cool: Constructing a Twentieth-Century Emotional Style* (New York: New York University Press, 1994), 1–6, 199; Brenton J. Malin, *Feeling Mediated: A History of Media Technology and Emotion in America* (New York: New York University Press, 2014), 110–111, 139.

[28] "Brevity and Appeal to Reason Make Radio Talks Magnetic," *New York Times*, March 25, 1928, 156; Malin, *Feeling Mediated*, 143.

[29] Samuel Blythe, "Political Publicity," *Saturday Evening Post*, Vol. 201 (February 2, 1929), 9; Craig, *Fireside Politics*, 168.

[30] Dunlap, *Talking On the Radio*, 211; Craig, *Fireside Politics*, 172.

[31] Alfred E. Smith, "Spellbinding," *Saturday Evening Post*, Vol. 202, No. 47 (May 24, 1930), 144.

[32] Barnet Baskerville, *The People's Voice: The Orator in American Society* (Lexington, KY: University Press of Kentucky, 1979), 157.

[33] *Ibid.*, 159–160; MacDonald, *Don't Touch That Dial!*, 7–8; Arthur F. Fleser, *A Rhetorical Study of the Speaking of Calvin Coolidge* (Lewiston, NY: Edwin Mellen, 1990), 58–59, 73, 83; Erik Barnouw, *A Tower in Babel: A History of Broadcasting in the United States*, Vol. 1 – to 1933 (New York: Oxford University Press, 1966), 146–147.

Indiana senator James E. Watson remembered, "did not possess any of the graces of oratory, spoke part of the time through his nose with a very clear nasal twang, manifested no enthusiasm in the enunciation of his sentences, and usually talked along in quite a humdrum fashion from beginning to end."[34] Coolidge "drawled in the twang of Vermont, with no grace of delivery or art of oratory," wrote his secretary C. Bascom Slemp, but his speech still "captured and held the minds of men." The radio, Slemp continued, "seemed to have been invented for him. His voice is perfectly adapted to its use in an enunciation clear and distinct. The invisible audience without the dramatic experience of the speaker must listen, if at all, to the thought of the speaker. In this rôle the President shines."[35]

There was nothing accidental about the Coolidge style. As a youth, Coolidge had been attracted to the oratorical tradition in much the same way as had his progressive predecessors. "So long as wickedness and misery, injustice, and wretchedness prevail on the earth," Coolidge had declared in 1890 at the age of seventeen, "so long as the Millennium is still distant and Utopia a dream, the voice of the orator will still be needed to warn, to denounce, to terrify, and to overwhelm."[36] By the 1920s, however, Coolidge had changed his views on oratory. Recognizing his own elocutionary strengths and the changes radio brought to the art of public speaking, the president chose to embrace the new, more restrained style of successful radio performance. "I can't make an engaging, rousing, or oratorical speech to a crowd," Coolidge confided humbly to Watson, "and so all I can do is to stand up and talk to them in a matter-of-fact way about the issues of the campaign; but I have a good radio voice, and now I can get my messages across to them without acquainting them with my lack of oratorical ability."[37]

The 1924 presidential campaign featured a battle of the airwaves between the old charismatic style and the new Coolidge approach. Coolidge followed the advice of advertising executive Bruce Barton, whose firm would soon feature the first radio advertising department. "The time may easily come," Barton had written in 1922 – "and soon – when the president of the United States in the White House can sit at his own desk and . . . be heard by every

[34] James E. Watson, *As I Knew Them* (Indianapolis, IN: Bobbs-Merrill, 1936), 236.

[35] C. Bascom Slemp, *The Mind of the President, as Revealed by Himself in His Own Words* (Garden City, NY: Doubleday, Page, 1926), 7, 10.

[36] Calvin Coolidge, "Jam Tempus Agi Res: Oratory in History," Dartmouth College, Hanover, NH, quoted in Fleser, *A Rhetorical Study of the Speaking of Calvin Coolidge*, 22.

[37] Quoted in Watson, *As I Knew Them*, 239; Craig, *Fireside Politics*, 142.

household in the nation where there is a radio set."[38] At Barton's suggestion, Coolidge eschewed the charismatic speaking tour in favor of a series of White House radio addresses delivered in his trademark monotone; listeners responded enthusiastically.[39] Meanwhile, aging progressive Robert La Follette, waging a third-party campaign, fared much worse. The radio, La Follette found, stripped him of every charismatic advantage he had traditionally enjoyed. In addition to finding it difficult to remain in one place during a speech, the senator had trouble keeping his addresses short enough to fit the allotted time. To prevent himself from wandering off extemporaneously, La Follette resorted to reading his speeches off a printed text – exactly what Coolidge was doing, only the president's voice sounded better over the radio.[40] Coolidge's radio advantage contributed to his decisive victory in November. By 1927, "Silent Cal" was speaking to radio audiences of thirty million at a time.[41] Coolidge's voice had "reached more hearers than that of any other speaker in history," W. P. Sandford noted in the same year. "Say what you will of his style," Sandford pointed out, "it is simple, direct and restrained. Moreover, its effect must be reckoned with. At the moment this paragraph is being typed, forty-three radio stations carry his voice to no one knows how many millions. More than any other speaker, he is moulding the popular concept of public address."[42]

Coolidge's conversational style soon became a sought-after commodity even beyond the confines of the radio. Female rhetoricians had been preaching the value of conversational rhetoric for a century, but it was not until the 1920s that most Americans began looking to everyday discourse as a model for public address.[43] (Ironically, many 1920s radio

[38] David Greenberg, *Republic of Spin: An Inside History of the American Presidency* (New York: W. W. Norton, 2016), 192; Bruce Barton, "This Magic Called Radio," *American Magazine*, June, 1922, 72.

[39] Craig, *Fireside Politics*, 144; Ranson, *The Role of Radio in the American Presidential Election of 1924*, 87, 140, 148; Timothy D. Taylor, *The Sounds of Capitalism: Advertising, Music, and the Conquest of Culture* (Chicago: University of Chicago Press, 2012), 44.

[40] Ranson, *The Role of Radio in the American Presidential Election of 1924*, 107–108.

[41] Fleser, *A Rhetorical Study of the Speaking of Calvin Coolidge*, 85.

[42] W. P. Sandford, review of Calvin Coolidge, *Foundations of the Republic: Speeches and Addresses* (New York: Scribner, 1926), *Quarterly Journal of Speech Education*, Vol. 13, No. 2 (April 1927), 197, 199; Baskerville, *The People's Voice*, 160.

[43] Jane Donawerth, *Conversational Rhetoric: The Rise and Fall of a Women's Tradition, 1600–1900* (Carbondale, IL: Southern Illinois University Press, 2012), 16; Kathleen Hall Jamieson, *Eloquence in an Electronic Age: The Transformation of Political Speechmaking* (New York: Oxford University Press, 1988), 53–56.

experts argued that female voices were innately emotional and therefore unsuited to the conversational radio style.)[44] Dale Carnegie, a farmer's son, a failed actor, and like his hero Elbert Hubbard a sometime soap salesman, built a successful career in the 1920s and 1930s by teaching businessmen how to improve their public speaking skills.[45] Carnegie had grown up around charismatic oratory; his mother was a revival preacher, his father was a Populist and a Bryanite, and Dale himself was inspired by both the eloquence of traveling Chautauqua lecturers and the New Thought ideals of Hubbard and Orison Swett Marden.[46] At the Missouri State Normal School in Warrensburg, Carnegie trained in the Delsarte system of oratory and became an outstanding public speaker.[47]

Nevertheless, the adult Carnegie flatly rejected the techniques that had made Beecher, Bryan, and others so popular. "Old-fashioned 'elocution' " and "the ornate 'oratory' of Webster and Ingersoll," he wrote in 1926, were an "abomination in the sight of God and man ... The verbal fireworks that were once the vogue would no longer be tolerated by an audience in this year of grace." Instead, inspired by his Delsarte training – "The great essential is a solid foundation of conversational delivery," his college textbook had declared – he substituted the more straightforward style pioneered by Coolidge.[48] "An entirely new school of speaking has sprung up since the Civil War," Carnegie continued. "It is as modern as the *Saturday Evening Post*, direct as a telegram, businesslike as an automobile advertisement ... A modern audience ... wants the speaker to talk just as directly as he would in a chat, and in the same general manner that he would employ in speaking to one of them in conversation."[49]

The Coolidge–Carnegie model of conversational speech pervaded American public discourse by the end of the decade. Even college speech departments reflected the change. During the 1910s and 1920s, public speaking teachers rejected elocution and charismatic stylings in favor of

44 Malin, *Feeling Mediated*, 146–147.

45 Giles Kemp and Edward Claflin, *Dale Carnegie: The Man Who Influenced Millions* (New York: St. Martin's Press, 1989), 53, 91.

46 Steven Watts, *Self-Help Messiah: Dale Carnegie and Success in Modern America* (New York: Other Press, 2013), 26–29, 42–43, 140–142.

47 *Ibid.*, 50–52.

48 *Ibid.*, 51; F. Townsend Southwick, *Elocution and Action* (New York: Edgar S. Werner, 1890), 6.

49 Dale Carnegie, *Public Speaking: A Practical Course for Business Men* (New York: Pocket Books, 1926), 197–198; Kenneth Cmiel, *Democratic Eloquence: The Fight over Popular Speech in Nineteenth-Century America* (Berkeley, CA: University of California Press, 1990), 259.

the new conversational ethos – though the shift was often incomplete, allowing some of Rush's magnetic recommendations to coexist with the new ideas.[50] "Professors of public speaking," noted speech instructor Edward Z. Rowell in 1930, "appear to be unanimous in urging that the proper mode for speakers in our day is the conversational as against the elocutionary or the formally oratorical style." Rowell followed this observation by incongruously attributing the earliest conversational oratory to Barber's student Wendell Phillips.[51] Malvern Rosenberg, a young education student at Northwestern University in the late 1920s, recorded in her class notes a lecture on "Attributes of a Beautiful Voice" by Northwestern professor of oratory Winifred Ward. Ward, who had studied public speaking with Billy Sunday's teacher Robert McLean Cumnock, first outlined a series of speaking techniques drawn straight from the work of James Rush – including an expanded pitch range ("ups and downs of a wide range") and the orotund voice ("relaxed throat").[52] Having described the magnetic style approvingly, however, Ward rejected the elocutionary techniques with which it was associated. "This is the day of the natural conversational manner," read Rosenberg's notes; "elocution out."[53]

Though Coolidge's conversational style endeared him to national audiences, the president resisted Bruce Barton's advice that he address his constituents regularly by radio outside of the campaign context. Just as Woodrow Wilson had rejected Croly's calls for national speaking tours, Coolidge believed that sort of regular contact with voters was unnecessary and counterproductive. Herbert Hoover, Coolidge's presidential successor, was similarly wary of building a national following through the radio.[54] For now, American presidents were unwilling to participate in something that, despite its lack of magnetic performance practice, looked suspiciously like a charismatic movement. The reluctance of Coolidge and Hoover to embrace fully the "radio presidency" reflected, in part, the deep

50 Malin, *Feeling Mediated*, 114; Herman Cohen, *The History of Speech Communication: The Emergence of a Discipline, 1914–1945* (Washington, DC: National Communication Association, 1994), 12.

51 Edward Z. Rowell, "Public Speaking in a New Era," orig. pub. *Quarterly Journal of Speech*, Vol. 16, No. 1 (February 1930), 62.

52 M. S. Moss, "Guide to the Winifred Ward (1884–1975) Papers" (Northwestern University, 1974), accessed March 29, 2014, http://findingaids.library.northwestern.edu/catalog/inu-ead-nua-archon-1144.

53 Malvern Ross [Malvern Rosenberg Starkstein], "Notes on Winifred Ward," n.d. (c. late 1920s), unpublished mss., private collection.

54 Craig, *Fireside Politics*, 145, 150–151.

unpopularity of charismatic leaders and movements during the 1920s. In the decade after the war, the anti-charismatic sentiment first displayed by frustrated progressives grew more pervasive and influential. By the time Coolidge triumphed in the 1924 election, American charisma found itself under attack in a way not seen since the days of Henry Ward Beecher.

* * *

Much had happened to Frederic C. Howe since that 1901 evening when a Tom L. Johnson speech had invested his life with meaning and purpose. Howe had served ten years as Mayor Johnson's lieutenant in Cleveland, won a term in the Ohio State Senate, hobnobbed with the left-wing intellectuals of Greenwich Village, written nearly a dozen books, and served from 1914 to 1919 as the immigration commissioner at Ellis Island.[55] Despite this record of activity and achievement, Howe found himself, in the aftermath of Woodrow Wilson's failure in the treaty fight, disillusioned once again. Howe had venerated Wilson during his graduate years at Johns Hopkins, had voted for him in 1912, and had worked for him as immigration commissioner since 1914.[56] Nevertheless, Howe felt Wilson had betrayed his own ideals at Versailles and then, what was worse, had returned home pretending that the compromise treaty was an idealistic triumph. "The people did not believe what he said," Howe wrote. "They heckled him in his meetings. They forced him to see himself. It was then that his strength gave way, his health broke. He lost his vision of himself ... That was the tragedy of the Peace Messiah."[57]

Amid the bitterness of his disappointment, Howe "began to face myself." This cycle of followership and disillusionment, he realized, had characterized every stage of his life. "Authority had always been necessary to me," he wrote. "In my boyhood it had been the neighbors; what 'they' would say ... At Johns Hopkins, my professors. I had always had a leader and a herd. I had abandoned one authority for another – in that, as I look back over my life, there had been original movement of my mind. But I had been a lieutenant, not a leader."[58] Desperate to find meaning in his life, Howe stared his own lifelong charismatic followership full in the face. The effect was shattering. "I had lost the illusions I had spent a lifetime in hoarding ... Drafts on my mind came back indorsed: 'No funds.'"[59]

[55] Kenneth E. Miller, *From Progressive to New Dealer: Frederic C. Howe and American Liberalism* (University Park, PA: Pennsylvania State University Press, 2010), 1–2, 434.

[56] *Ibid.*, 163; Frederic C. Howe, *The Confessions of a Reformer* (New York: Scribner, 1925), 7.

[57] Howe, *The Confessions of a Reformer*, 316. [58] *Ibid.*, 320–321. [59] *Ibid.*, 325.

Howe emerged from his self-reflection a changed man. He rejected charismatic movements, retreated from politics, and withdrew to a Nantucket farm. Though his "conscience still troubles me often," he wrote in 1925, he had found a modicum of peace. "Unobligated to movements or to reforms, I find a kind of verity that I did not know before. In a deeper way I now find the same content in living as I choose and being myself."[60] Happiness, he had found, could no longer coincide with charismatic followership.

Howe was far from the only progressive to turn against charisma in the aftermath of wartime disappointment; indeed, his was among the mildest of progressive reactions. Walter Lippmann, Herbert Croly's protégé at *The New Republic*, experienced a more violent break with charismatic ideas. Lippmann had spent the 1910s as a dedicated supporter of the charismatic relationship and of the progressive leaders who sought to harness its power. In a 1916 essay, he had praised Theodore Roosevelt for his charismatic abilities. "He is forever tantalizing us with the hope that we have in him a leader equal to our needs," Lippmann had written. "That is the political meaning of his rich and abounding personality. That is why he survives every defeat."[61] Later, he had supported U.S. intervention in Europe, worked for President Wilson's reelection, and served in the wartime government as head of an Army propaganda bureau.[62] Like Croly and Howe, however, Lippmann was horrified by the equivocal, imperialist Treaty of Versailles; for Lippmann, the failed treaty retroactively discredited the whole American war effort as a meaningless sacrifice.[63] Demoralized by the fate of the progressive enterprise in which he had participated, Lippmann began to condemn not just the Wilson administration but the democratic process itself – and, by extension, the charismatic relationship.

The problem, Lippmann explained – in a familiar refrain of disillusioned progressives – lay with the people. Lippmann began his book *Public Opinion* (1922) with Plato's allegory of the cave – quoting a passage in which the Greek philosopher described ordinary citizens as "strange prisoners," trapped in an underground cavern, who could not

[60] *Ibid.*, 340, 343.

[61] Walter Lippmann, "Integrated America," *The New Republic*, February 19, 1916, in *The New Republic Book: Selections from the First Hundred Issues* (New York: Republic Pub. Co., 1916), 138.

[62] Ronald Steel, *Walter Lippmann and the American Century* (orig. pub. Little, Brown, 1980; New Brunswick, NJ: Transaction Pub., 1999), 94, 107, 117, 142.

[63] *Ibid.*, 158–161.

"see anything but the shadows" directly in front of them.[64] It was impossible, Lippmann continued, for people to participate directly in their own governance, because they could never possess enough information to make informed policy judgments. All people really knew of the world were the false and incomplete impressions inside their minds – mere shadows in the cave of knowledge. Worse, popular emotions interfered with effective reasoning. "On many subjects of great public importance," Lippmann wrote, "the threads of memory and emotion are in a snarl . . . In the uncriticised parts of the mind there is a vast amount of association by mere clang, contact, and succession."[65] Lacking information and rationality, the people were susceptible to charismatic demagogues who used their ignorance as a weapon against intelligent opinion. "The practice of appealing to the public on all sorts of intricate matters," Lippmann charged, "means almost always a desire to escape criticism from those who know by enlisting a large majority which has had no chance to know. The verdict is made to depend on who has the loudest or the most entrancing voice."[66] The unreasoning public could always be swayed by a George Creel or a Four-Minute Man. Creel and his lecturers had eschewed charismatic techniques, but Lippmann no longer saw a distinction between propaganda and charisma. Four-Minute Men and charismatic progressives, he believed, had jointly persuaded Americans to support a pointless and destructive war; their success demonstrated that ordinary people were susceptible to both emotional manipulation and faulty logic.

The solution to this problem, Lippmann concluded, was to take most decisions out of the hands of the people entirely – "not to burden every citizen with expert opinions on all questions, but to push that burden away from him towards the responsible administrator."[67] It was an "intolerable and unworkable fiction that each of us must acquire a competent opinion about all public affairs"; the public should intervene only occasionally, to ensure the government did its job.[68] In *The Phantom Public* (1925), Lippmann stated his position more baldly. "The public must be put in its place," he declared, in part "so that each of us may live free of the trampling and the roar of a bewildered herd . . . I set no great store on what can be done by public opinion and the action of masses."[69]

[64] Plato, *Republic*, quoted in Walter Lippmann, *Public Opinion* (New York: Harcourt, Brace, 1922), viii.

[65] Lippmann, *Public Opinion*, 406. [66] *Ibid.*, 401. [67] *Ibid.*, 399. [68] *Ibid.*, 31.

[69] Walter Lippmann, *The Phantom Public* (New York: Harcourt, Brace, 1925), 155, 199.

So long as the people remained the "bewildered" playthings of demagogues, Lippmann insisted, the charismatic relationship was a negative influence on American society and should be avoided or suppressed.[70]

Lippmann's views on public opinion drew a rejoinder from *Baltimore Sun* editorialist Henry Louis Mencken. In his iconoclastic opposition to charismatic leaders, Mencken had established himself as a worthy successor to Henry Watterson. "All that is necessary to raise a piece of imbecility into what the mob regards as a piece of profundity," Mencken wrote in 1925, "is to lift it off the floor and put it on a platform."[71] Much of Mencken's journalistic career consisted of artful skewers of such platform personalities. "In his dealings with men in the mass," Mencken wrote in 1919, Theodore Roosevelt "was a charlatan of the very highest skill – and there was in him, it goes without saying, the persuasive charm of the charlatan."[72] Roosevelt's fellow Bull Moosers were "mere disordered enthusiasts – believing in anything and everything, pathetic victims of the credulity complex, habitual followers of jitney messiahs, incurable hopers and snufflers."[73] Woodrow Wilson, meanwhile, was "the self-bamboozled Presbyterian . . . the perfect model of the Christian cad."[74] In an approving review of William Bayard Hale's *The Story of a Style*, Mencken excoriated Wilson's charismatic speech as extravagant "buncombe." "When Wilson got upon his legs in those days," Mencken commented, "he seems to have gone into a sort of trance, with all the peculiar illusions and delusions that belong to a frenzied pedagogue." To Mencken, Wilson was a charlatan who had seduced Americans with vacuous emotionalism. "He knew how to make them glow, and weep," he declared. "He wasted no time upon the heads of his dupes, but aimed directly at their ears, diaphragms and hearts . . . It is difficult to believe that even idiots ever succumbed to . . . so vast and obvious a nonsensicality."[75]

Mencken's problem with Lippmann, put simply, was the latter's continuing belief in the perfectibility of the people. "What he says, in brief,"

[70] See also Steel, *Walter Lippmann and the American Century*, 180–183, 212–213; J. Michael Sproule, *Propaganda and Democracy: The American Experience of Media and Mass Persuasion* (Cambridge, UK: Cambridge University Press, 1997), 94.

[71] H. L. Mencken and George Jean Nathan, "Clinical Notes," *The American Mercury*, Vol. 5, No. 17 (May 1925), 95.

[72] H. L. Mencken, "Roosevelt: An Autopsy," in Mencken, *Prejudices: Second Series* (New York: Knopf, 1920), 125.

[73] *Ibid.*, 122. [74] *Ibid.*, 102.

[75] H. L. Mencken, "The Style of Woodrow," in Mencken, *H. L. Mencken's Smart Set Criticism*, ed. William H. Nolte (Ithaca, NY: Cornell University Press, 1968), 119–121.

Mencken wrote, "is that we must keep on hoping that the mob will one day grow intelligent, despite the colossal improbability of it." Mencken, appealing to "Gustave Le Bon's half-forgotten pioneer treatise, *The Crowd*," disagreed with Lippmann's approach. "The fact is, of course, that it is absolutely hopeless to think of filling the great masses of men with even the most elemental sense." Since people could not be perfected, demagogues would always be able to control them. A leader with a "feeling of kinship for ignorant and degraded men," who professed himself "willing to submit with alacrity to the mob's mandates," and who was "enormously skillful at appealing to the savage prejudices that lie in the depths of [the mob's] consciousness ... the great body of ignoble hopes and poltroonish fears out of which flow all its customary rages and enthusiasms" – such a figure could make people "do or believe almost everything."[76] This popular susceptibility to demagogues, Mencken believed, struck at the heart of democracy's claim to good government.

Mencken perceived a solution to this crisis, however, in the wartime propaganda machine that had disillusioned Lippmann. Mencken, too, now viewed Creel and his coterie as emotional manipulators rather than as the rational persuaders they had claimed to be, and he incongruously linked them with the charismatic techniques they had avoided. Through the Four-Minute Men program and other Creel Committee efforts, "men who are normally too sniffish to engage in any such enterprise" had executed "potent raids upon the boob emotions," had engaged in the basest demagoguery, out of a sense of patriotism. "They performed their duties very skilfully [*sic*] and effectively," Mencken wrote approvingly. Momentarily abandoning his opposition to charismatic oratory, the columnist proposed that such "members of the *intelligentsia*" use similar emotional techniques to manipulate the people constantly and cynically toward support of enlightened policies. Democracy could thrive, Mencken concluded, only if intelligent leaders "devoted themselves to the arts of the demagogue" in order to "debauch the booboisie into accepting ideas of a relatively high soundness."[77] Where Lippmann sought to limit the scope of popular government, Mencken, in his cynicism about charisma, had adopted Le Bon's views and had written free choice out of popular rule altogether. Lippmann, for his part, charged

[76] H. L. Mencken, "Vox Populi," in Mencken, *H. L. Mencken's Smart Set Criticism*, 112–123, 127–129.

[77] *Ibid.*, 128–129; italics in original.

that Mencken's "childlike faith in the omnipotence of words" made the columnist no better than those he criticized. "His science," Lippmann charged, "is of the same stuff at bottom as Mr. Bryan's or Billy Sunday's."[78]

Such antidemocratic approaches to the leader–follower relationship were ubiquitous in the 1920s.[79] Scholars, psychologists, reformers, writers, and businessmen united in reviving the old Le Bonian shibboleths about charismatic movements: emotionally driven crowds were dangerous and must either be rationalized through education or cynically manipulated. "Our society is becoming a veritable babel of gibbering crowds," warned Everett Dean Martin in 1920. "The councils of democracy are conducted on about the psychological level of commercial advertising ... I know of nothing which to-day so menaces not only the values of civilization, but also ... the achievement of personality and true knowledge of self, as the growing habit of behaving as crowds."[80] "Familiarity with the ruling public has bred contempt," agreed sociologist Harold D. Lasswell in 1927. Summarizing the views of the "despondent democrat," Lasswell wrote that "the public has not reigned with benignity and restraint. The good life is not in the mighty rushing wind of public sentiment. It is no organic secretion of the horde, but the tedious achievement of the few."[81] Theologian Reinhold Niebuhr, writing in 1932, condemned "the brutal character of the behavior of all human collectives." "In every human group," he continued, "there is less reason to guide and to check impulse, less capacity for self-transcendence, less ability to comprehend the needs of others and therefore more unrestrained egoism than the individuals, who compose the group, reveal in their personal relationships."[82] The reverse of this argument also held currency. Before the rise of Adolf Hitler rendered the idea moot, American filmmakers and auto manufacturers promoted the idea of a presidential dictator who would solve the country's problems in

[78] Walter Lippmann, "The New Machiavelli," *The New Republic*, May 31, 1922, 13–14; Greenberg, *Republic of Spin*, 148.

[79] Daria Frezza, *The Leader and the Crowd: Democracy in American Public Discourse, 1880–1941*, tr. Martha King (Athens, GA: University of Georgia Press, 2007), 145–148.

[80] Everett Dean Martin, *The Behavior of Crowds: A Psychological Study* (New York: Harper & Brothers, 1920), 6–7.

[81] Harold D. Lasswell, *Propaganda Technique in the World War* (New York: Peter Smith, 1927), 4.

[82] Reinhold Niebuhr, *Moral Man and Immoral Society: A Study in Ethics and Politics* (New York: Scribner, 1932), xi–xii, xx; Wilfred M. McClay, *The Masterless: Self & Society in Modern America* (Chapel Hill, NC: University of North Carolina Press, 1994), 178–179.

undemocratic fashion – a charismatic figure to be sure, but one who deprived his submissive followers of agency.[83]

Perhaps the strongest efforts toward the cynical exploitation of the masses came from the growing advertising industry. The success of the Creel Committee's propaganda efforts touched off an advertising revolution during the 1920s; financial outlays for advertisements quadrupled between 1914 and 1929.[84] The new advertisers saw less value in the charismatic relationship than had their prewar predecessors, though. During the Progressive Era, Elbert Hubbard had offered a vision of society in which advertising served as a bridge between charisma and conservative business interests. In Hubbard's ideal, advertisers promoted charismatic hero narratives that inspired ordinary Americans to work hand in hand with their employers in service of the "established order." After the war, however, the advertising industry broke decisively with charismatic techniques and with the democratic attitudes of earlier charismatic thinkers. Their goal was no longer to improve society by bringing out the best tendencies in Americans; instead, they embraced a more sinister and calculating brand of manipulation in order, as Hubbard would have said, to "sell the goods."[85]

In adopting this mechanistic view of social influence, advertisers drew not only on wartime propaganda but on ideas gaining currency in the psychological field. In the 1910s and 1920s, the behaviorist approach promoted by Johns Hopkins professor John B. Watson became increasingly popular among American psychologists. Rejecting the introspective investigations of religious and emotional experience pioneered by William James, Watson boldly declared that human behavior was a purely mechanical set of "responses" conditioned by external "stimuli." By studying the relationship between stimulus and response, Watson reasoned, psychologists could develop "*laws and principles whereby*

[83] Benjamin L. Alpers, *Dictators, Democracy, & American Public Culture: Envisioning the Totalitarian Enemy, 1920s-1950s* (Chapel Hill, NC: University of North Carolina Press, 2003), 15–16, 30–35, 77.

[84] Scott M. Cutlip, *The Unseen Power: Public Relations, A History* (Hillsdale, NJ: Lawrence Erlbaum, 1994), 105, 107; Lynn Dumenil, *The Modern Temper: American Culture and Society in the 1920s* (New York: Hill and Wang, 1995), 88–89; Roland Marchand, *Advertising the American Dream: Making Way for Modernity, 1920–1940* (Berkeley, CA: University of California Press, 1985), 5–7.

[85] T. J. Jackson Lears, "From Salvation to Self-Realization: Advertising and the Therapeutic Roots of the Consumer Culture, 1880–1930," Richard Wightman Fox and T. J. Jackson Lears, ed., *The Culture of Consumption: Critical Essays in American History, 1880–1980* (New York: Pantheon, 1983), 19–20.

man's actions can be controlled by organized society."[86] Although Watson's desire for social control via emotional manipulation echoed Le Bon's work, the behaviorist denounced religious revivalism and other crowd phenomena as creating uncontrollable and counterproductive emotional responses.[87] Like Warren Harding, Watson preferred the moderate emotions of "normalcy" to the exaggerated emotionalism of charismatic movements; his goal was not to change society but to exploit it for profit. "If psychology would follow the plan I suggest," he insisted, "the educator, the physician, the jurist and the business man could utilize our data in a practical way, as soon as we are able, experimentally, to obtain them."[88] Forced from his position at Johns Hopkins in 1920 following an affair with a graduate student, Watson took his behaviorist approach to the J. Walter Thompson advertising agency and helped to design ad campaigns for a number of consumer brands and to promote products over the radio.[89] "The consumer is to … the advertising agencies," he told a group of executives in 1922, "what the green frog is to the physiologist."[90]

Bruce Barton, the advertising pioneer who had advised Coolidge to give regular radio speeches, exemplified the industry's changed view of the leader–follower relationship. Barton, like Lippmann, was steeped in the charismatic tradition; his father was a preacher and a biographer of Lincoln, and Barton himself had achieved prominence through two fawning magazine profiles of Billy Sunday.[91] "Emotions affect votes much more than logic," he had written while advising Coolidge in 1923.[92] Like Hubbard before him, Barton penned a biography of Jesus Christ in which he portrayed the Son of God as a charismatic figure. "He had the voice and manner of the leader," Barton wrote in *The Man Nobody Knows*

[86] John B. Watson, *Psychology from the Standpoint of a Behaviorist* (Philadelphia: Lippincott, 1919), 2, 9–10; italics in original.

[87] Kerry W. Buckley, *Mechanical Man: John Broadus Watson and the Beginnings of Behaviorism* (New York: Guilford Press, 1989), 120.

[88] John B. Watson, "Psychology as the Behaviorist Views It," *Psychological Review*, Vol. 20, No. 2 (March 1, 1913), 168.

[89] David Cohen, *J. B. Watson: The Founder of Behaviourism* (London: Routledge and Kegan Paul, 1979), 182–183.

[90] John B. Watson, "The Ideal Executive," speech delivered to Macy's graduating class of young executives, April 20, 1922, John Broadus Watson Papers, Library of Congress, quoted in Buckley, *Mechanical Man*, 137.

[91] Lears, "From Salvation to Self-Realization," 30–31; Bruce Barton, "In the Wake of Billy Sunday," *Home Herald*, Vol. 20, No. 22 (June 2, 1909), 3–5; Bruce Barton, "Billy Sunday, Baseball Evangelist," *Collier's*, Vol. 51, No. 19 (July 26, 1913), 7–8, 30.

[92] Quoted in Greenberg, *Republic of Spin*, 156.

(1925) – "the personal magnetism which begets loyalty and commands respect."[93] While Hubbard's Jesus had filled an authentic need for a charismatic Messiah, however, Barton presented Christ prosaically as the "founder of modern business." "He picked up twelve men from the bottom ranks of business," Barton crowed, "and forged them into an organization that conquered the world."[94] In Barton's vision, Jesus became a Dale Carnegie poster boy, winning friends and influencing people throughout the Middle East. "No other public character ever had a more interesting list of friends," Barton wrote.[95] "The secret of Jesus' success was an affection for folks which so shone in his eyes and rang in his tones, that even the commonest man in a crowd felt instinctively that here was a friend."[96] The divine miracles Jesus performed were "front page stories" designed to advertise his creed.[97] His exhortations to serve others were the forerunners of automotive companies' claims to provide customers with the best service.[98] "Every one of the 'principles of modern salesmanship' on which business men so much pride themselves," Barton concluded, "are brilliantly exemplified in Jesus' talk and work ... He proved his right to be the silent partner in every modern business; to sit at the head of every directors' table."[99] Barton's Jesus possessed charismatic abilities, but they were purely self-serving; Jesus' motivation was not to improve society, but to grow his organization and sell his product.

In his book *Propaganda* (1928), Edward L. Bernays came close to establishing a unified field theory of the relationship between advertising, charisma, and the public. A nephew of Sigmund Freud, Bernays had worked for the Creel Committee as a young man and established himself in the 1920s as one of America's leading public relations professionals.[100] Creel's propagandistic ideal, Bernays argued, should be applied to all aspects of public life – not just business, but the arts, education, social activism, and even government. Bernays made explicit the antidemocratic nature of his argument. "No serious sociologist any longer believes that the voice of the people expresses any divine or specially wise and lofty idea," he declared. "The voice of the people expresses the mind of the people, and that mind is made up for it by the group leaders in whom it believes and by those persons who understand the manipulation of public

[93] Bruce Barton, *The Man Nobody Knows: A Discovery of the Real Jesus* (orig. pub. Indianapolis, IN: Bobbs-Merrill, 1925; Chicago: Ivan R. Dee, 2000), 13.

[94] *Ibid.*, 4–5. [95] *Ibid.*, 35. [96] *Ibid.*, 49. [97] *Ibid.*, 61. [98] *Ibid.*, 77.

[99] *Ibid.*, 50, 88. [100] Cutlip, *The Unseen Power*, 160–161, 164–165.

opinion ... Fortunately, the sincere and gifted politician is able, by the instrument of propaganda, to mold and form the will of the people."[101] "Times had changed," Bernays argued, since the halcyon days when "the masses promised to become king." Today, "the minority has discovered a powerful help in influencing majorities. It has been found possible so to mold the mind of the masses that they will throw their newly gained strength in the desired direction."[102] Tellingly, charismatic speaking and organization played a very small part in Bernays' worldview. "The emotions of oratory have ben warn down through long years of overuse," he declared. "The haphazard staging of emotional events without regard to their value as part of the whole campaign, is a waste of effort, just as it would be a waste of effort for the manufacturer of hockey skates to advertise a picture of a church surrounded by spring foliage."[103] When the goal was to manipulate the masses emotionally for private profit, Bernays agreed with Watson: charismatic appeals were merely an inefficient and wasteful technique.

The social consequences of this line of thinking were inevitable. In 1928, at the height of the postwar stock market bubble, Americans listening to the weekly "Halsey-Stuart Radio Hour" enjoyed the resonant tones of a man identified only as the "Old Counselor." In a calm, confident voice perfectly suited to the radio audience, the Old Counselor dispensed seemingly innocuous investment advice. Often, he would promote stocks belonging to a dubious holding company controlled by utilities magnate Samuel Insull – a company in which Halsey, Stuart, & Co. just happened to have invested millions themselves. The Insull holdings collapsed during the Great Depression, wiping out the savings of thousands who had followed the Old Counselor's advice. During the ensuing congressional hearings, Halsey, Stuart, & Co. president Harold L. Stuart caused a minor scandal when he admitted that the trusted Old Counselor was not an economics expert at all; he was none other than Bertram G. Nelson, the speech professor who had trained the Four-Minute Men in the arts of persuasion during the war. For a salary of fifty dollars an episode, the congressmen learned, Nelson had put the same skills to use hawking Insull stocks – repeating in a "mellow voice" lines written for him by the investment bankers themselves.[104]

101 Edward L. Bernays, *Propaganda* (New York: Liveright, 1928), 92. 102 *Ibid.*, 19.

103 *Ibid.*, 100–101.

104 U.S. Senate, Committee on Banking and Currency, *Stock Exchange Practices Hearing*, Part 5 (Insull), February 15, 16, and 17, 1933 (Washington, DC: Government Printing

The spectacle of a former Four-Minute Men organizer defrauding the public for fifty dollars a week exemplified the dominance of sometimes anti-charismatic, always anti-populist attitudes in 1920s America. Most cultural commentators viewed charismatic appeals either as dangerous and counterproductive or as permissible only when promoting consumerism or the commentator's own particular idea of good government. In such an atmosphere, charismatic leaders who believed, as Bryan did, that "mankind deserves to be trusted" had to fight the prevailing cultural winds. Some charismatic figures succumbed to withering attacks or were caricatured as dangerous demagogues. Yet others managed to evolve successfully, crafting new and innovative charismatic approaches more in keeping with their era's cultural standards. Overall, the struggles of charismatic leaders to thrive in a culture increasingly hostile to charisma yielded decidedly mixed results.

* * *

When William Jennings Bryan delivered his "Cross of Gold" speech at the 1896 Democratic National Convention, he did not know that one member of his audience would wage a fierce battle against him three decades later. From his seat at the convention, Clarence Darrow watched as Bryan, displaying "his idealism and zeal and force," swept the audience before him.[105] "Men and women cheered and laughed and cried," Darrow recalled in his autobiography. "Here was a political Messiah who was to lift the burdens that the oppressed had borne so long."[106] Yet Darrow already had a political messiah, sitting near him in the Chicago crowd: Illinois governor John Peter Altgeld. The young defense attorney had been a devoted follower of Altgeld since reading the governor's book of legal philosophy as a young man; when Darrow moved to Chicago, he became part of Altgeld's political machine.[107] Darrow's charismatic devotion to Altgeld knew no bounds. "I used to go to the governor's quarter," he wrote, "and sit and look at him in silence, just to be with him."[108]

Office, 1933), 1610–1611, 1625; "Advised on Investments," *Charleston Daily Mail*, February 28, 1933, 8; " 'Old Counselor,' " orig. pub. *New York World Telegram*; *Pittsburgh Press*, February 24, 1933, 12; Michael Perino, *The Hellhound of Wall Street: How Ferdinand Pecora's Investigation of the Great Crash Forever Changed American Finance* (New York: Penguin, 2010), 123–124; Kenneth G. Hance, H. O. Hendrickson, and Edwin W. Schoenberger, "The Later National Period, 1860–1930," in William Norwood Brigance, ed., *A History and Criticism of American Public Address*, Vol. 1 (New York: McGraw-Hill, 1943), 119.

[105] Clarence Darrow, *The Story of My Life* (New York: Scribner, 1932), 277.

[106] *Ibid.*, 91. [107] *Ibid.*, 41, 89–90. [108] *Ibid.*, 103.

In addition to being a radical and a charismatic leader, Altgeld was something of an oratorical expert. His views on public speaking, however, were closer to Woodrow Wilson's than to Bryan's. In *Oratory: Its Requirements and Its Rewards* (1901), Altgeld advised budding orators to avoid handshakes and "needless gesture[s]" and to project instead "the earnestness that comes from a burning soul . . . The feet of the orator must walk in the sun and every fiber in his body must speak to the audience, not in rant, or quaver, but in the simple fervor of the patriot."[109] Conversely, "[t]he mere fact that a speaker can work himself into a glow of excitement," Altgeld wrote, "does not by any means prove that he is eloquent. Generally this is simply rant and wearies the audience."[110] Given Altgeld's oratorical theories, it is not surprising that the governor found Bryan's dramatic, emotional performance distasteful. "It takes more than speeches to win real victories," Altgeld told Darrow the next day. "Applause lasts but a little while . . . I have been thinking over Bryan's speech. What did he say, anyhow?"[111]

Thirty years later, Darrow found himself staring at Bryan across the aisle of a courtroom. After World War I, Bryan had established himself as a leader of the burgeoning Christian fundamentalist movement in the United States. He began using his charismatic speaking skills to attack evolutionary biologists and to promote laws banning the teaching of evolution in public schools.[112] Darrow, a committed agnostic, found Bryan's attacks on science and scientists intolerable. "Thinking of the years through which he had busied himself tormenting intelligent professors . . . and seeking to arouse the ignoramuses and bigots to drive them out of their positions," Darrow became truly angry at Bryan. "It is a terrible transgression to intimidate and awe teachers with fear of want."[113] When Bryan agreed to help prosecute high school science teacher John T. Scopes for teaching evolution in violation of Tennessee

109 John P. Altgeld, *Oratory: Its Requirements and Its Rewards* (Chicago: Charles H. Kerr, 1901), 12–14, 42.

110 *Ibid.*, 25. 111 Darrow, *The Story of My Life*, 92.

112 John A. Farrell, *Clarence Darrow: Attorney for the Damned* (New York: Doubleday, 2011), 361–362; Andrew E. Kersten, *Clarence Darrow: American Iconoclast* (New York: Hill and Wang, 2011), 205–206; Michael Kazin, *A Godly Hero: The Life of William Jennings Bryan* (New York: Knopf, 2006), 273–277; Lawrence W. Levine, *Defender of the Faith: William Jennings Bryan: The Last Decade, 1915–1925* (New York: Oxford University Press, 1965), 266–272; Edward J. Larson, *Summer for the Gods: The Scopes Trial and America's Continuing Debate over Science and Religion* (New York: Basic Books, 1997), 41–43.

113 Darrow, *The Story of My Life*, 267.

law, Darrow eagerly volunteered to represent Scopes.[114] The fight was on.

The battle Darrow and Bryan waged in July 1925 at the Rhea County Courthouse in Dayton, Tennessee, was a complex one. The trial's many players pursued multiple objectives simultaneously: each sought to win the case, to change or defend the state law, and to shape public attitudes toward evolution.[115] Hidden at times in the ideological conflicts, however, was the war Darrow waged on Bryan's charismatic oratory itself. In his long career, Darrow had delivered emotional speeches before juries, toured on the Chautauqua circuit, defended Eugene Debs and Big Bill Haywood in court, followed Governor Altgeld in a charismatic fashion, and voted for Bryan three times.[116] But by 1925, Darrow had come to agree with Altgeld that Bryan's speechifying was distasteful, that the "Great Commoner" from Nebraska sought merely to trick audiences with his melodious voice. Writing in 1932, Darrow mocked his own youthful tendency "to cover up such ideas as I had in a cloud of sounding metrical phrases" – a characteristic of James Rush's magnetic style. "In later years," Darrow continued, "nothing has disturbed my taste along that line more than being called an 'orator,' and I strive to use simpler words and shorter sentences, to make my statements plain and direct."[117] Like many of his fellow Americans, Darrow had become a crusader against charismatic oratory and the charismatic relationship. In his battle with Bryan at Dayton, he not only attacked the ideas of the "Boy Orator of the Platte," but sought to destroy Bryan as a charismatic figure.

In a pair of speeches before the trial, Bryan laid out the stakes of the battle to come. More was at issue in the Scopes case, he declared, than merely legal or theological concerns; the future of democracy itself was at stake. "Who made the courts?" he asked rhetorically. "The people. Who made the Constitution? The people. The people can change the Constitution and if necessary they can change the decisions of the

[114] Levine, *Defender of the Faith*, 329–330; Larson, *Summer for the Gods*, 99–101.

[115] Michael Lienesch, *In the Beginning: Fundamentalism, the Scopes Trial, and the Making of the Antievolution Movement* (Chapel Hill, NC: University of North Carolina Press, 2007), 141, 155–156.

[116] Richard J. Jensen, *Clarence Darrow: The Creation of an American Myth* (New York: Greenwood Press, 1992), 42; Martin Maloney, "Clarence Darrow," in Marie Kathryn Hochmuth, ed., *A History and Criticism of American Public Address*, Vol. 3 (New York: Longmans, Green, 1955), 300; Larson, *Summer for the Gods*, 71.

[117] Darrow, *The Story of My Life*, 42.

courts."[118] *New York Times* reporter Ike Shuman was mesmerized by Bryan. "His voice ... vibrated with feeling," Shuman wrote; "his whole being was synchronized into a graceful machine for driving home his word." Looking around, Shuman saw that the entire audience was transfixed by the speech. "The people of Dayton," he reported, "look upon Mr. Bryan as their champion against the hosts of evil."[119] Bryan believed his charismatic power would sway the jury just as it had moved the crowd in Dayton. Darrow knew better, though. By nature and training, the defense attorney was a debater rather than an orator – skilled in the give-and-take of cross-examination rather than declamation. Bryan, who had not practiced law since 1896, lacked this debating background.[120] Dayton's people were Bryan's people, but the Rhea County Courthouse was Darrow's domain – and the defense counsel was prepared to make the most of his advantage.

In the courtroom, Darrow consistently found ways to frustrate Bryan's efforts at charismatic oratory. At the climax of the trial, Darrow called Bryan himself to the stand and interrogated him about the Bible and Bryan's views on Biblical truth. Dodging and weaving, attacking and counterattacking, Darrow deftly jabbed Bryan over and over while interrupting the aging "Boy Orator" whenever he tried to deliver a speech from the witness stand. Finally, Darrow trapped Bryan in an error: the former presidential candidate admitted he did not believe the six days of Biblical creation were necessarily twenty-four-hour periods. The crowd gasped: the fundamentalist leader had been caught interpreting the Bible, a lapse that, to some, called his entire commitment to Biblical literalism into question.[121] The exchange was devastating for Bryan. "Two old men," Paul Y. Anderson wrote in the *St. Louis Labor*, "one eloquent, magnetic and passionate, the other cold, impassive, and philosophical," had met in intellectual combat; afterward, "Bryan was broken, if ever a man was broken ... To see this wonderful man ... this man whose silver voice and majestic mien had stirred millions, to see him humbled and humiliated before the vast crowd which had come to adore him, was sheer tragedy, nothing less."[122] After the court adjourned, Darrow found himself thronged by supporters. "The great gathering began to surge toward me," he wrote. "They seemed to have changed sides in a single

118 "Bryan Threatens National Campaign to Bar Evolution," *New York Times*, July 9, 1925, 1.

119 "Bryan in Dayton, Calls Scopes Trial Duel to the Death," *New York Times*, July 8, 1925, 1; John T. Scopes and James Presley, *Center of the Storm: Memoirs of John T. Scopes* (New York: Holt, Rinehart and Winston, 1967), 95.

120 Jamieson, *Eloquence in an Electronic Age*, 35–36. 121 *Ibid.*, 36–41.

122 *St. Louis Labor*, July 21, 1925, quoted in L. Sprague de Camp, *The Great Monkey Trial* (Garden City, NY: Doubleday, 1968), 413.

afternoon."[123] Bryan's followers had deserted him. "He was left alone on that green, spacious lawn," Scopes recalled, "a forgotten, forlorn man."[124]

Bryan felt the loss keenly, but he still hoped to win back the people through a charismatic closing statement to the jury. "He has worked for two months on the speech which he is to make in the Scopes trial," Shuman wrote. "It will undoubtedly be his greatest oratorical effort since his famous 'Cross of Gold' speech."[125] Bryan never had a chance to deliver his peroration, however. At the conclusion of the trial, the defense declined to make a closing argument – a legal maneuver that prevented Bryan from speaking as well. "We knew that Mr. Bryan was there to make a closing speech about 'The Prince of Peace,' " Darrow explained later, "and that the closing address he meant should thrill the world was doubtless prepared for the press in manifold copies ... By not making a closing argument on our side we could cut him out." Darrow had not merely defeated his opponent on the witness stand; he had "cut out" Bryan's charismatic oratory by depriving the great leader of his audience. Bryan could not even induce the journalists present at the trial to print copies of his undelivered address.[126] The Great Commoner never had a chance to recover; a week after the trial ended, Bryan died in his sleep.[127]

In the battle over evolution, both camps found much to celebrate in the outcome of the Scopes trial.[128] The charismatic conflict, however, was more one-sided. H. L. Mencken, in Dayton covering the trial, portrayed the Scopes affair as a catastrophic defeat for Bryan's approach to charisma. In a lacerating editorial, he declared the greatest charismatic leader of the age "a charlatan, a mountebank, a zany without shame or dignity." Bryan "was the most sedulous fly-catcher in American history," but he sought to catch not the common housefly but the charismatic follower. "For forty years he tracked it with coo and bellow, up and down the rustic backways of the Republic," Mencken wrote. "He was born with a roaring voice, and it had the trick of inflaming half-wits. His whole career was devoted to raising those half-wits against their betters, that he himself might shine." The power and nobility Bryan had shown in 1896 had long

123 Darrow, *The Story of My Life*, 267.

124 Scopes and Presley, *Center of the Storm*, 183.

125 "Bryan Threatens National Campaign to Bar Evolution," *New York Times*, July 9, 1925, 1.

126 Darrow, *The Story of My Life*, 259–260, 269.

127 Larson, *Summer for the Gods*, 199.

128 Lienesch, *In the Beginning*, 169–170; Larson, *Summer for the Gods*, 192; Ronald L. Numbers, *Darwinism Comes to America* (Cambridge, MA: Harvard University Press, 1998), 85.

since faded, leaving only a bitter shell of a man. "He came into life a hero, a Galahad, in bright and shining armor," Mencken concluded. "He was passing out a poor mountebank."[129] In private, Mencken allowed himself to gloat. "Well," he remarked, "we killed the son-of-a-bitch!"[130]

Mencken's gleeful obituary for charismatic leadership was premature, however. While the Scopes Trial demonstrated the obstacles facing traditional charismatic figures such as Bryan who practiced the Rush style of personal magnetism, younger magnetic leaders were busily refashioning charismatic techniques to circumvent these obstacles. As Coolidge and Hoover demonstrated, mainstream politicians in the 1920s were cautious about using charismatic appeals as a political strategy. Activists for extremist, downtrodden, and minority groups, on the other hand, gladly appropriated magnetic techniques to rally their supporters. Some of these figures – proto-fascist reactionaries such as Silver Shirts founder and Elbert Hubbard devotee William Dudley Pelley, Ku Klux Klan Grand Dragon D. C. Stephenson, and right-wing evangelical minister Gerald L. K. Smith – were easy to marginalize as extremists.[131] Other leaders, though, were a force to be reckoned with. In particular, the years after World War I were something of a charismatic renaissance among women and minority populations. Deflecting anti-charismatic attacks both from outside opponents and from within their own ideological camps, these leaders used innovative magnetic approaches to develop their movements, with varying degrees of success.

Marcus Mosiah Garvey was both a typical and an outstanding case. Born on August 17, 1887, in Jamaica to a struggling stonemason father and spice trader mother, the Afro-Jamaican Garvey showed little interest in political leadership as a young man.[132] In 1914, however, Garvey read Booker T. Washington's autobiography *Up from Slavery*; soon after, he

[129] H. L. Mencken, "In Memoriam: W. J. B.," in Mencken, *Prejudices: Fifth Series* (New York: Knopf, 1926), 64–72.

[130] Quoted in William Manchester, *Disturber of the Peace: The Life of H. L. Mencken* (New York: Harper & Brothers, 1950), 185.

[131] Scott Beekman, *William Dudley Pelley: A Life in Right-Wing Extremism and the Occult* (Syracuse, NY: Syracuse University Press, 2005), 1, 6–7; M. William Lutholtz, *Grand Dragon: D. C. Stephenson and the Ku Klux Klan in Indiana* (West Lafayette, IN: Purdue University Press, 1991), 9, 11–12; Leonard J. Moore, *Citizen Klansmen: The Ku Klux Klan in Indiana, 1921–1928* (Chapel Hill, NC: University of North Carolina Press, 1991), 46; Glen Jeansonne, *Gerald L. K. Smith: Minister of Hate* (New Haven, CT: Yale University Press, 1988), 39–40.

[132] Judith Stein, *The World of Marcus Garvey: Race and Class in Modern Society* (Baton Rouge, LA: Louisiana State University Press, 1986), 24–25.

wrote, "My doom . . . of being a race leader dawned upon me . . . I asked, 'Where is the black man's Government?' 'Where is his King and his kingdom?' . . . I could not find them, and then I declared, 'I will help to make them.' "[133] Two years later, Garvey and his wife moved to Harlem, where Garvey came under the influence of fellow West Indian immigrant Hubert H. Harrison. Harrison was an early advocate of pan-Africanism – an ideology arguing that peoples of African descent worldwide should separate from local white-dominated societies and unite, in Africa or elsewhere, in defense of their racial prerogatives.[134] For many African Americans, pan-Africanism was an attractive alternative to Washington's "Atlanta Compromise" or the educational "uplift" strategy advocated by Washington's opponents; Harrison's ideas offered racial pride and an immediate, muscular response to the demoralizing effects of Jim Crow.

Garvey was already thinking along similar lines. During the war years, he served a sort of charismatic apprenticeship. The young leader, who may have studied elocution in Jamaica, further honed his speaking skills as a Harlem soapbox orator and drew inspiration from Billy Sunday's tabernacle meetings.[135] On June 12, 1917, Harrison arranged for Garvey to lecture at a mass meeting in Harlem. "The man spoke," author James Weldon Johnson wrote later, "and his magnetic personality, torrential eloquence, and intuitive knowledge of crowd psychology were all brought into play."[136] Over the next five years, Garvey's powerful oratory won him and his pan-African organization, the Universal Negro Improvement Association (UNIA), a national following.

[133] Marcus Garvey, "The Negro's Greatest Enemy," orig. pub. *Current History*, September 1923, in Amy Jacques Garvey, ed., *The Philosophy & Opinions of Marcus Garvey: Or, Africa for the Africans*, Vol. 2 (New York: Universal Publishing House, 1923), 126; E. David Cronon, *Black Moses: The Story of Marcus Garvey and the Universal Negro Improvement Association* (Madison, WI: University of Wisconsin Press, 1955), 16.

[134] Jeffrey B. Perry, *Hubert Harrison: The Voice of Harlem Radicalism, 1883–1918* (New York: Columbia University Press, 2009), 299–300.

[135] Tony Martin, *Race First: The Ideological and Organizational Struggles of Marcus Garvey and the Universal Negro Improvement Association* (Westport, CT: Greenwood Press, 1976), 9, 111; Colin Grant, *Negro with a Hat: The Rise and Fall of Marcus Garvey* (New York: Oxford University Press, 2008), 80; Kevin K. Gaines, *Uplifting the Race: Black Leadership, Politics, and Culture in the Twentieth Century* (Chapel Hill, NC: University of North Carolina Press, 1996), 239; Graham Knox, "Political Change in Jamaica (1866–1906) and the Local Reaction to the Policies of the Crown Colony Government," in F. M. Andic and T. G. Mathews, ed., *The Caribbean in Transition: Papers on Social, Political, and Economic Development* (Rio Piedras, PR: Institute of Caribbean Studies, 1965), 161.

[136] James Weldon Johnson, *Black Manhattan* (New York: Knopf, 1930), 253.

During the interwar years, many ambitious charismatic leaders arose in the African American community; the early pan-Africanist "Chief" Alfred Sam, the self-proclaimed deity Father Divine, and the religious leader "Sweet Daddy" Grace were some of the most notable.[137] Garvey outshone them all. While Washington had appealed chiefly to a white audience, and ministers such as Alexander Crummell and Henry McNeal Turner to the black middle class, Garvey tailored his appeals to the millions of poor African Americans across the United States – something no African American leader before him had done on such a massive scale. Accordingly, his UNIA boasted nearly three million American members by 1923 and four million by 1930, making it the largest secular mass movement in African American history, before or since.[138] The movement's apparatus included nearly a thousand organized chapters in the United States, a weekly newspaper with an international circulation of 75,000, and even a small fleet of ships to dramatize Garvey's back-to-Africa platform.[139] During parades and funeral processions, UNIA members marched down the streets of Harlem in full military dress.[140] At the center was Garvey himself; his use of religious rhetoric, his sense of pageantry, and above all his magnetic oratory bound followers to his cause.[141] "When he spoke," Virginia Collins remembered eighty years later in a remarkable interview, "It was as if you were speaking yourself.

[137] William E. Bittle and Gilbert Geis, *The Longest Way Home: Chief Alfred C. Sam's Back-to-Africa Movement* (Detroit, MI: Wayne State University Press, 1964), 8–13; Jill Watts, *God, Harlem, U.S.A.: The Father Divine Story* (Berkeley, CA: University of California Press, 1992), ix–x; Kenneth E. Burnham, *God Comes to America: Father Divine and the Peace Mission Movement* (Boston: Lambeth Press, 1979), 1–2; Marie W. Dallam, *Daddy Grace: A Celebrity Preacher and His House of Prayer* (New York: New York University Press, 2007), 89, 104.

[138] Martin, *Race First*, 13–14.

[139] Mary G. Rolinson, *Grassroots Garveyism: The Universal Negro Improvement Association in the Rural South, 1920–1927* (Chapel Hill, NC: University of North Carolina Press, 2007), 17, 103, 107; Claudrena N. Harold, *The Rise and Fall of the Garvey Movement in the Urban South, 1918–1942* (New York: Routledge, 2007), 32–35.

[140] Martin Summers, *Manliness and Its Discontents: The Black Middle Class and the Transformation of Masculinity, 1900–1930* (Chapel Hill, NC: University of North Carolina Press, 2004), 17.

[141] Randall K. Burkett, *Garveyism as a Religious Movement: The Institutionalization of a Black Civil Religion* (Metuchen, NJ: Scarecrow Press and American Theological Library Association, 1978), 7–9, 17; Theodore G. Vincent, *Black Power and the Garvey Movement* (Berkeley, CA: Ramparts Press, 1971), 153–154; Lawrence W. Levine, "Marcus Garvey and the Politics of Revitalization," in Levine, *The Unpredictable Past: Explorations in American Cultural History* (New York: Oxford University Press, 1993), 121–122; Adam Ewing, *The Age of Garvey: How a Jamaican Activist Created a Mass Movement and Changed Global Black Politics* (Princeton: Princeton University Press, 2014), 144.

FIGURE 6.1 Marcus Garvey (shown at a 1920 UNIA meeting) was a magnetic orator; hearing him speak, remembered one of his followers, was "something like fire, like lightning."
Source: Convention Address by Hon. Marcus Garvey Delivering Constitution for Negro Rights, courtesy of the Library of Congress, Prints and Photographs Division, LC-USZ62-109628.

It was not like somebody speaking to you, but like he was you, or you was he, and it just was a connected link and it was something like fire, like lightning, like something that went through everybody at the same time."[142]

By the early 1920s, Garvey was arguably the most successful charismatic leader in America – but his success was short-lived. In part, Garvey created his own bad luck; poor financial management of the UNIA, a bizarre endorsement of the Ku Klux Klan, and the death of a rival under questionable circumstances helped to doom his enterprise. Other African American leaders, however, helped hasten Garvey's demise by attacking him on anti-charismatic grounds. African American intellectual W. E. B. Du Bois, for instance, unleashed a fusillade of attacks on Garvey from the editorial page of *The Crisis*. "Garvey is an extraordinary leader of men," Du Bois admitted in 1920. "Thousands of people believe in him. He is able to stir them with singular eloquence and the general run of his thought is of a high plane. He has become to thousands of people a sort of religion."[143] Du Bois, however, had little respect for this sort of leadership. "Garvey is ... a stubborn, domineering leader of the mass," he charged; "his methods are bombastic, wasteful, illogical and ineffective and almost illegal."[144] In 1923, Du Bois made this argument more explicit. Garvey, he wrote, "screams his propaganda" nightly from his Harlem lecture hall. "With all the arts of the demagogue, Garvey appealed to crowds of people with persuasive eloquence ... It was the sort of appeal that easily throws ignorant and inexperienced people into orgies of response and generosity." The only African Americans who followed Garvey were "the ignorant, drawn by eloquence and sound."[145] Garvey, Du Bois concluded in 1924, "is, without doubt, the most dangerous enemy of the Negro race in America and in the world. He is either a lunatic or a traitor ... [who] should be locked up or sent home."[146]

In his attacks on Garvey's charismatic leadership and his call to imprison or deport the Jamaican-born leader, Du Bois spoke for the black middle-class establishment. Garvey was "a blustering West Indian

[142] Interview with Virginia Collins in *Marcus Garvey: Look for Me in the Whirlwind*, dir. Stanley Nelson (Arlington, VA: PBS Home Video, 2001); Erica R. Edwards, *Charisma and the Fictions of Black Leadership* (Minneapolis, MN: University of Minnesota Press, 2012), 31.

[143] W. E. B. Du Bois, "Marcus Garvey," *The Crisis*, Vol. 21, No. 2 (December 1920), 60.

[144] W. E. B. Du Bois, "Marcus Garvey," *The Crisis*, Vol. 21, No. 3 (January 1921), 115.

[145] W. E. B. Du Bois, "Back to Africa," *The Century Magazine*, February 1923, 546, 548.

[146] W. E. B. Du Bois, "A Lunatic or a Traitor," *The Crisis*, Vol. 28, No. 1 (May 1924), 8–9.

demagogue," wrote Chandler Owen and A. Philip Randolph in *The Messenger*, "who preys upon the ignorant, unsuspecting poor West Indian working men and women who believe Garvey is some sort of Moses."[147] The U.S. government had come to the same conclusion. In a 1922 civil case involving Garvey, Judge Jacob Panken – himself a charismatic follower of Eugene Debs – assailed not only Garvey's financial shenanigans but his charismatic ambitions. "There is a form of paranoia," Panken declared, "which manifests itself in believing oneself to be a great man."[148] In early 1923, U.S. attorney general Harry Daugherty arrested Garvey for mail fraud; eight African American businessmen signed a letter urging Daugherty to prosecute Garvey to the fullest extent of the law. On June 18, a jury convicted Garvey and sentenced him to five years in jail.[149] After exhausting his appeals, Garvey bid his followers goodbye. "Look for me in the whirlwind or the storm," he said, "look for me all around you, for ... I shall rise with God's grace and blessing to lead the millions up the heights of triumph."[150] In 1927, the government deported Garvey to Jamaica; he never set foot in the United States again.[151] Despite the abrupt end to Garvey's American tenure, however, the pan-African leader exerted a lasting influence on the American scene. The massive UNIA continued to grow after Garvey's departure and remained powerful well into the 1930s. Meanwhile, the transnational impact of Garvey's publications was even greater. In the early 1920s, Anglo-Irish writer Joyce Cary, then in West Africa, was surprised to hear local villagers describe Garvey as "a black king ... coming, with a great iron ship full of black soldiers, to drive all the whites out of Africa."[152] Postcolonial African politicians such as Kwame Nkrumah and Jomo Kenyatta considered Garvey a key philosophical forerunner, and by the 1970s many Jamaicans viewed Garvey as that nation's version of George Washington.[153]

147 Chandler Owen and A. Philip Randolph, editorial in *The Messenger*, Vol. 4 (July 1922), 437, quoted in Leon Fink, *Progressive Intellectuals and the Dilemmas of Democratic Containment* (Cambridge, MA: Harvard University Press, 1997), 192.

148 Quoted in W. E. B. Du Bois, "The Black Star Line," *The Crisis*, Vol. 24, No. 5 (September 1922), 214.

149 Grant, *Negro with a Hat*, 363, 371–372.

150 Marcus Garvey, "First Message to the Negroes of the World from Atlanta Prison," speech delivered February 10, 1925, in Amy Jacques Garvey, ed., *The Philosophy & Opinions of Marcus Garvey*, Vol. 2, 239.

151 Grant, *Negro with a Hat*, 411.

152 Joyce Cary, *The Case for African Freedom* (London: Secker & Warburg, 1944), 20; Ewing, *The Age of Garvey*, 76.

153 Vincent, *Black Power and the Garvey Movement*, 244–246.

No female charismatic figure of the 1920s possessed Garvey's national reach, but Aimee Semple McPherson came close. Born in Canada on October 9, 1890, the young McPherson learned elocution at a local Methodist church and won prizes in oratorical contests sponsored by Frances Willard's Women's Christian Temperance Union.[154] Deep religious belief came later. Three days after hearing Pentecostal evangelist Robert Semple speak in tongues, the seventeen-year-old McPherson underwent a powerful conversion.[155] "Immediately the most wonderful change took place in my soul," she wrote later. "Darkness passed away and light entered. The sky was filled with brightness ... So conscious was I of the pardoning blood of Jesus that I seemed to feel it flowing over me."[156] Things moved quickly after that. By 1915, McPherson had been married twice – first to Semple, who died while on an evangelical mission, then to businessman Harold McPherson – and had decided to become a traveling revivalist. At first touring the nation by car, Aimee Semple McPherson eventually founded a new Pentecostal denomination, the International Church of the Foursquare Gospel, based at the Angelus Temple in Los Angeles. When she was not conducting national revivals, she preached at the Temple every night and three times on Sundays, always to standing-room-only crowds of over 5,000 people.[157] An advocate of women's involvement in the ministry, McPherson also mentored a generation of "girl evangelists" who spread her message across the country.[158]

McPherson's captivating and extravagant performances were legendary even in a Hollywood saturated with various forms of entertainment. "Sister Aimee," as she called herself, combined the show-stopping religious practices of Maria Woodworth-Etter – faith healing and speaking in tongues – with theatrical practices borrowed from the movies and the stage. She pioneered

[154] William G. McLoughlin Jr., "Aimee Semple McPherson: 'Your Sister in the King's Glad Service,'" *Journal of Popular Culture*, Vol. 1, No. 3 (Winter 1967), 196; Aimee Semple McPherson, *This Is That: Personal Experiences, Sermons and Writings* (Los Angeles, CA: Bridal Call Publishing House, 1919), 27.

[155] McPherson, *This Is That*, 38–39, 42–43; Matthew Avery Sutton, *Aimee Semple McPherson and the Resurrection of Christian America* (Cambridge, MA: Harvard University Press, 2007), 10; Edith L. Blumhofer, *Aimee Semple McPherson: Everybody's Sister* (Grand Rapids, MI: Eerdmans, 1993), 62–63.

[156] McPherson, *This Is That*, 42.

[157] Sutton, *Aimee Semple McPherson and the Resurrection of Christian America*, 12–15, 20–23; Blumhofer, *Aimee Semple McPherson*, 5–6.

[158] Thomas A. Robinson and Lanette D. Ruff, *Out of the Mouths of Babes: Girl Evangelists in the Flapper Era* (New York: Oxford University Press, 2012), 152–153.

FIGURE 6.2 Aimee Semple McPherson (shown in Boston in 1931) developed a multifaceted charismatic technique that included faith healing, speaking in tongues, and theatrical and radio performances.
Source: Photo of Aimee Semple McPherson, Boston Gardens, Boston, MA, October 1931, courtesy of the International Church of the Foursquare Gospel, Heritage Department.

the "illustrated sermon," a Vaudeville-style performance complete with professional lighting, props, sets, costumes, makeup, an angelic choir, and a full cast of actors. The endlessly creative McPherson wrote and designed all of the illustrated sermons herself.[159] Then there was the minister's own dazzling charismatic performance in the pulpit. "This complete control over the mood of her audience she exercises from the instant she arrives upon the platform," journalist Sarah Comstock wrote in 1927. "Mrs. McPherson's magnetism is of that inexplicable sort which occurs but rarely in a puzzled world ... The glance of her companionable eye,

159 Wendy A. Danforth Wilson, "The Theatricality of Revivalism as Exemplified in the Artistry of Billy Sunday and Aimee Semple McPherson" (M.A. thesis, University of Oregon, 1974), 75–82.

the flash of her comprehending smile possess the electrical quality to an all-conquering degree."[160]

McPherson did not neglect traditional charismatic techniques, either. She designed audience seating in Angelus Temple in a semicircular shape to maximize her connection with listeners; she preceded each sermon with an hour of preparatory music. The Foursquare denomination produced a weekly newspaper, the *Bridal Call*, to spread McPherson's message to the faithful across the country. McPherson's church even owned its own radio station so that her sermons could be broadcast throughout the region. True to charismatic form, the evangelist often turned this impressive machinery toward concrete policy aims, women's equality, and even political campaigns; one illustrated sermon depicted Socialist California gubernatorial candidate Upton Sinclair, whose platform the evangelist disliked, being deported to the USSR by Uncle Sam.[161]

Just as Garvey's magnetism raised enemies in his path, McPherson's charismatic leadership eventually got her into trouble. On May 18, 1926, McPherson disappeared while vacationing at California's Venice Beach. She resurfaced five weeks later, weak, exhausted, and on foot, in Agua Prieta, Mexico. The minister claimed she had been kidnapped and held for ransom before finally escaping from her captors; others suspected she had simply run off with a lover. Rival radio evangelist Robert "Fighting Bob" Shuler was the most vocal skeptic. Shuler had railed for years against McPherson's "almost unbelievable ... hypnotic powers" that "[play] on every chord of emotionalism that there is left in human nature."[162] Recalling criticisms of Henry Ward Beecher in the 1870s, Shuler's attacks on McPherson emphasized the sexual transgressions supposedly inherent in charisma. "She fondles, kisses and embraces literally hundreds of women," Shuler complained; the woman evangelist's "strange power" over her followers was "very closely related to the sex appeal."[163]

160 Sarah Comstock, "Aimee Semple McPherson: Prima Donna of Revivalism," *Harper's Monthly Magazine*, December 1927, 17–18; Grant Wacker, *Heaven Below: Early Pentecostals and American Culture* (Cambridge, MA: Harvard University Press, 2001), 115.

161 Sutton, *Aimee Semple McPherson and the Resurrection of Christian America*, 2–3, 79.

162 *Ibid.*, 36; Robert P. "Bob," Shuler, *McPhersonism* (Los Angeles, CA: Robert P. Shuler, 1924), 4.

163 Shuler, *McPhersonism*, 4; Robert P. "Bob" Shuler, "In the Name of Jesus, the Christ," *Bob Shuler's Magazine*, Vol. 3 (December 1924), 502, quoted in Sutton, *Aimee Semple McPherson and the Resurrection of Christian America*, 60; Robert P. Shuler III, *Fighting Bob Shuler of Los Angeles: God's Man for the Issues of His Time* (Indianapolis, IN: Dog Ear Publishing, 2011), 159.

The kidnapping incident led other local ministers to endorse Shuler's position. Eight of them signed a petition calling for Los Angeles County District Attorney Asa Keyes to investigate not the alleged kidnappers, but Sister Aimee herself, for criminal acts related to the incident.[164] Incredibly, Keyes obliged; he convened a grand jury and eventually charged McPherson with criminal conspiracy. Soon, McPherson was on trial, while eager journalists published sensational tales about her sexuality and attacked her charismatic persona.

H. L. Mencken had little sympathy for most charismatic leaders, but while covering the McPherson libel trial he concluded that Sister Aimee was being railroaded by the civic leaders of Los Angeles. Writing in December 1926, Mencken observed that the evangelist faced "two sets of enemies, both powerful." One group consisted of Shuler and "the other town clergy," who "resented her raids upon their customers." McPherson's other opponents were "the town Babbitts," drab businessmen and city fathers of the type depicted in a Sinclair Lewis novel of that name. These civic leaders feared that McPherson's charismatic antics were bad for the city's reputation – that "her growing celebrity," as Mencken put it, "was making Los Angeles ridiculous."[165] Mencken's editorial represented a useful typology of the forces arrayed against charismatic leaders in the 1920s. As the cases of Garvey and McPherson demonstrated, postwar charismatic figures had to walk a difficult gauntlet of jealous charismatic rivals and critics of charismatic leadership – a united opposition possessing great societal power.

Nevertheless, the wily McPherson managed to save her charismatic enterprise. McPherson succeeded in getting the charges dropped through an unknown means – possibly by blackmailing publisher William Randolph Hearst into bribing the district attorney.[166] For Sister Aimee, the costs of the trial were high: many members of her church left in the aftermath of her arrest, related legal cases dragged her back into court again and again, and she experienced a nervous breakdown. By 1933, she was forced to appear on Broadway to finance her struggling denomination.[167] McPherson and her movement eventually made a full recovery, however, and the Foursquare church remains active to this day. Still, the

[164] Sutton, *Aimee Semple McPherson and the Resurrection of Christian America*, 120.

[165] H. L. Mencken, "Sister Aimee," *Baltimore Evening Sun*, December 13, 1926, 21.

[166] Sutton, *Aimee Semple McPherson and the Resurrection of Christian America*, 108, 118, 139.

[167] Blumhofer, *Aimee Semple McPherson*, 300, 307, 336; McLoughlin, "Aimee Semple McPherson," 213.

evangelist was in no mood to repeat the experience. When McPherson's charismatic associate pastor Rheba Crawford Splivalo – the inspiration for Salvation Army Sergeant Sarah Brown in the Frank Loesser musical *Guys and Dolls* – began her own crusade against city corruption in 1936, McPherson summarily terminated Splivalo's contract.[168]

As the experiences of Garvey and McPherson demonstrated, the charismatic relationship remained a viable strategy in the 1920s, particularly for leaders and causes relegated to the margins of society. By appealing to populations previously ignored by charismatic leaders, by borrowing film and radio techniques to achieve new communication styles, these figures managed to parry anti-charismatic opponents and develop large and successful followings. As Bryan's defeat in Dayton showed, however, the traditional techniques of personal magnetism no longer carried the significance they once did. The way forward for charismatic movements lay in adapting to the requirements of radio and film technology and to the elocutionary preferences of modern audiences. In the 1930s, an American leader would finally merge charismatic ideas with mass media and the new conversational idiom to create a successful leadership style for the modern age.

* * *

March 12, 1933, was only Franklin Delano Roosevelt's ninth day as president, and already he faced a national crisis. It was the low point of the Great Depression; nearly a quarter of adult Americans were out of work, with no relief in sight. A rash of bank failures had led Roosevelt to close banks nationwide; reopening them, he feared, might cause a panic that would collapse the nation's financial system. To rally American confidence and prevent financial disaster, Roosevelt would have to act quickly and decisively. It was time, he determined, to address the nation by radio.

Ignoring the rhetorical recommendations of the Treasury Department, speechwriter Samuel Rosenman remembered, Roosevelt wrote the text of the speech himself. "He dictated it in simple, ordinary language," Rosenman wrote later – "he looked for words that he would use in an informal conversation with one or two of his friends. He found the kind of language that everyone could understand."[169] At 10:00 that evening, as

[168] Judy Pearson, "Rheba Crawford's Public Ministry" (M.A. thesis, California State University, Long Beach, 1995), 90, 95, 98.

[169] Samuel I. Rosenman, *Working with Roosevelt* (New York: Harper & Brothers, 1952), 92–93.

Roosevelt sat at a desk behind a bank of microphones, an audience of sixty million people – twice as many as Coolidge had ever reached – listened anxiously for the president's words. A radio announcer introduced the speaker without fanfare: "Ladies and gentlemen, the president of the United States." Perhaps moved by the connection he felt with his radio listeners, Roosevelt uttered two words not written on the page in front of him: "My friends."[170] Then, in a calm, cheerful, fatherly voice, he began to read from his prepared text. "I want to talk for a few minutes with the people of the United States about banking," he said. "I want to tell you what has been done in the last few days, and why it was done, and what the next steps are going to be ... And I know that when you understand what we in Washington have been about I shall continue to have your cooperation as fully as I have had your sympathy and your help during the past week.[171]

That the president would attempt a radio appeal to the masses at this moment of crisis was in some ways surprising. At first glance, Roosevelt's background made it seem unlikely that he would be able to communicate well with ordinary American voters. For the fourteen years following his birth on January 30, 1882, Roosevelt inhabited the rarefied world of the upper class. Servants, private tutors, riding and sailing lessons, yearly European tours, summers on the island of Campobello, frequent family trips to the White House – such features of Roosevelt's childhood separated him firmly from the middle-class charismatic figures of earlier decades.[172] Roosevelt's life changed, however, when he attended Groton School and came under the spell of its rector, Endicott Peabody. A deeply spiritual man, Peabody sought to inspire two traits in his charges: a belief in civic responsibility and a commitment to hard work.[173] At the same time, Peabody provided Roosevelt and his fellow students with the model of a charismatic, if reserved, leadership figure. "The master [of the school] is the key to the situation," Peabody explained. "The man must have the qualities of the teacher, one who not only knows but can inspire his pupils. It is not methods, which are over-emphasized today, that count, but men

[170] Address of President Roosevelt by Radio, March 12, 1933, Box 23, Section 1820 (Speeches), Franklin D. Roosevelt Papers as President, President's Personal File, Franklin D. Roosevelt Library, Hyde Park, New York.

[171] Franklin D. Roosevelt, "The Banking Crisis," in Russell D. Buhite and David W. Levy, *FDR's Fireside Chats* (Norman, OK: University of Oklahoma Press, 1992), 12–13.

[172] Jean Edward Smith, *FDR* (New York: Random House, 2007), 22–25; Frank Freidel, *Franklin D. Roosevelt: A Rendezvous with Destiny* (Boston: Little, Brown, 1990), 6–8.

[173] Freidel, *Franklin D. Roosevelt*, 10; Smith, *FDR*, 28.

who create interest through their vivacious and enthusiastic personality."[174] "As long as I live," Roosevelt declared later, "the influence of ... Peabody means and will mean more to me than that of any other people next to my mother and father."[175] The pupil took more than just the rector's message of diligence and civic engagement to heart; Roosevelt's March 1933 radio address clearly reflected the influence of Peabody's warm, fatherly brand of charismatic leadership.

For Roosevelt, the two decades after Groton consisted of a relatively easy climb to political prominence. After earning degrees from Harvard and Columbia, he won a seat in the New York State Senate, served as assistant secretary of the Navy during World War I, and ran for vice president on the losing 1920 Democratic ticket. Then, tragedy struck. In the summer of 1921, Roosevelt contracted a mysterious condition now thought to have been Guillain–Barré syndrome; though he recovered, he lost the use of his legs. Displaying the work ethic he had learned from Peabody, Roosevelt labored tirelessly to reclaim his political position. With the help of devoted aide Louis McHenry Howe, he returned triumphantly to the national spotlight in 1924 by delivering the nominating speech for Al Smith's presidential campaign; four years later, he succeeded Smith as governor of New York. In 1932, with the nation in the throes of the Great Depression, Roosevelt concluded his remarkable comeback by winning the presidency.[176]

Despite Roosevelt's vigorous campaign ethic – he traveled with steel leg braces and a portable podium so he could deliver speeches across the country while standing upright – his inability to walk and his determination to hide his paralysis ensured that he would never again perform as effectively on the platform as he had in 1920.[177] Gripping the podium in an effort to remain on his feet, Roosevelt could not stride across the stage or gesture to his listeners in the traditional magnetic style; he could not walk a rope line shaking hands; he could not even emerge from behind the lectern without alerting audience members to his disability. For Roosevelt, more than for almost any other politician, radio seemed a godsend: a new

[174] Quoted in Frank D. Ashburn, *Peabody of Groton: A Portrait* (New York: Coward McCann, 1944), 74.

[175] Quoted in "Roosevelt Relives His Boyhood Days," *New York Times*, June 3, 1934, 5; Smith, *FDR*, 28.

[176] Smith, *FDR*, 211, 227–228, 287.

[177] Halford R. Ryan, *Franklin D. Roosevelt's Rhetorical Presidency* (New York: Greenwood Press, 1988), 14.

medium perfectly designed to maximize the candidate's appealing personality while masking his physical condition.[178]

Besides, Roosevelt had an excellent radio presence. "Franklin Roosevelt," noted a *New York Times* reporter as early as 1924, "has [a radio personality] because of his knack for making things sound personal and informal ... The radio audiences like to feel that the speaker has dropped into its parlor for an informal chat."[179] As New York governor, Roosevelt delivered radio speeches several times a month, often to apply pressure on recalcitrant state legislators.[180] Roosevelt purposely crafted a distinctly conversational idiom; he relied on small words and colloquial expressions to make his audience feel at home.[181] Rather than thinking of his audiences as "the masses," Labor Secretary Frances Perkins recalled, Roosevelt "thought of them individually. He thought of them in family groups ... When he talked on the radio, he saw them gathered in the little parlor, listening with their neighbors." Roosevelt spoke to these listeners "as though he were actually sitting on the front porch or in the parlor with them," Perkins concluded. "His voice and his facial expression as he spoke were those of an intimate friend."[182] Indeed, the metaphor of the "Good Neighbor," usually linked with Roosevelt's foreign policy, was an accurate description of how he conceived of the radio audience; deploying religious and military rhetoric, he molded his hearers into a unified community, transcending local and class interests.[183]

From Groton to his physical tragedy to the governorship and the presidential campaign, everything in Roosevelt's life had seemingly prepared him for that moment before the microphones in March 1933. But when the president delivered the first of what broadcasting manager Harry C. Butcher soon named "fireside chats" – conversational speeches designed specifically for a radio audience – he had no way of

[178] Craig, *Fireside Politics*, 157.

[179] *New York Times*, July 29, 1924, 4, quoted in G. Joseph Wolfe, "Some Reactions to the Advent of Campaigning by Radio," *Journal of Broadcasting*, Vol. 13, No. 3 (Summer 1969), 309.

[180] Craig, *Fireside Politics*, 154; Russell D. Buhite and David W. Levy, "Introduction," in Buhite and Levy, eds., *FDR's Fireside Chats*, xiv; Lenthall, *Radio's America*, 88.

[181] Earnest Brandenberg and Waldo W. Braden, "Franklin Delano Roosevelt," in Hochmuth, ed., *A History and Criticism of American Public Address*, 509, 515.

[182] Frances Perkins, *The Roosevelt I Knew* (New York: Viking Press, 1946), 71–72.

[183] Mary E. Stuckey, *The Good Neighbor: Franklin D. Roosevelt and the Rhetoric of American Power* (East Lansing, MI: Michigan State University Press, 2013), 2, 33, 54.

knowing what would happen next.[184] Would his sixty million listeners respond by investing Roosevelt with their confidence, as he hoped? Or would they panic and bring down the banking system, as he feared? As soon as Roosevelt's speech ended, "the White House switchboard was deluged with telephone calls from all sections," reported the Associated Press, "each caller praising Mr. Roosevelt's outline of the problem."[185] Then the letters began to appear at the White House, and Roosevelt had his answer.

In some ways, the letters closely resembled earlier charismatic follower testimonials. For one thing, they were effusive and deeply emotional. "When your radio talk began," wrote New York Supreme Court Justice Frank J. Cregg, "everyone seemed to become hypnotized, because there wasn't a word spoken by anyone until you had finished and then as if one voice were speaking all spoke in unison 'We are saved.' "[186] At the end of the banking chat, Bertha M. Lindquist told the president, her father had "tears in his eyes."[187] "I heard you on the radio," Josie D'Natale agreed, "and I started to cry."[188] Many missives featured religious allusions identical to those used by charismatic followers. "Yours was ... a message from heaven," declared Samuel B. Altman, "answering the silent prayers of millions of people."[189] "Our little home seemed a church," agreed Louise Hill, "our radio the pulpit, and you the preacher."[190] Roosevelt's correspondents linked him with other sacred or sacralized historical figures. "As God had sent Moses to deliver his chosen people out of the land of bondage," wrote Thomas Kennedy, "so also I think he sent you to

184 Waldo W. Braden and Earnest Brandenburg, "Roosevelt's Fireside Chats," *Speech Monographs*, Vol. 22, No. 5 (November 1955), 290, 292.

185 "Messages to White House Reflect Confidence," unknown newspaper clipping, in E. H. Mengel to Franklin D. Roosevelt, March 13, 1933, Folder Me-My, Box 10, President's Personal File 220B, Public Reaction Letters, Roosevelt Papers.

186 Frank J. Cregg to Franklin D. Roosevelt, March 14, 1933, Folder I-J, Box 9, President's Personal File 200B, Public Reaction Letters, Roosevelt Papers; Lawrence W. Levine and Cornelia R. Levine, *The People and the President: America's Conversation with FDR* (Boston: Beacon Press, 2002), 37.

187 Bertha M. Lindquist to Franklin D. Roosevelt, March 12, 1933, in Levine and Levine, *The People and the President*, 41.

188 Josie D'Natale to Franklin D. Roosevelt, March 13, 1933, Folder N-O, Box 10, President's Personal File 200B, Public Reaction Letters, Roosevelt Papers; Levine and Levine, *The People and the President*, 56.

189 Samuel B. Altman to Franklin D. Roosevelt, March 13, 1933, Folder A, Box 8, President's Personal File 200B, Public Reaction Letters, Roosevelt Papers.

190 Louise Hill to Franklin D. Roosevelt, March 13, 1933, Folder H, Box 9, President's Personal File 200B, Public Reaction Letters, Roosevelt Papers; Levine and Levine, *The People and the President*, 37.

free us from the hands of a lot of robbers like Wall St."[191] God "sent Moses to deliver the oppressed," agreed Mrs. J. R. Adams. "Then he sent Jesus Christ . . . Then you."[192] Others compared Roosevelt to King David, Julius Caesar, Jesus Christ (again), George Washington, Abraham Lincoln, and William Jennings Bryan.[193] A number of writers, too, referenced the fatherly persona Roosevelt had inherited from Peabody. "I liken it to a Christian father calling his family together and taking them in to his full and loving confidence," explained W. T. Rowland.[194] "It seemed as if a father were talking to me," remarked a "dear young girl" to Florence N. Betts, "and I felt like throwing my arms about his neck, he cheered me up so."[195] "We look upon you," wrote Lewis Gardner Muller, "as the Indians did – 'as the Great White Father in Washington.' "[196]

In other respects, however, the letters to Roosevelt described a type of follower experience more intensely personal than anything produced by turn-of-the-century charismatic movements. For many Americans, as Louis Howe put it, the president's fireside chat created "an actual, intimate bond between themselves and the man in the mansion on Pennsylvania Avenue."[197] Where Bryan spoke to Americans from a convention hall or the rear platform of his train, Roosevelt seemed to come right into their living rooms. "At ten o'clock P. M.," wrote Thomas A. Keller, "I opened the doors of my Radio and admitted you to my home."[198] "We invited some friends in 'to meet the President,' " reported

[191] Thomas Kennedy to Franklin D. Roosevelt, n.d., Folder K, Box 10, President's Personal File 200B, Public Reaction Letters, Roosevelt Papers.

[192] Mrs. J. R. Adams to Franklin D. Roosevelt, n.d., Folder A, Box 8, President's Personal File 200B, Public Reaction Letters, Roosevelt Papers; Levine and Levine, *The People and the President*, 45.

[193] Fred Brown to Franklin D. Roosevelt, March 13, 1933, Folder B, Box 9; Thomas Q. Lempertz to Franklin D. Roosevelt, March 15, 1933, Folder L, Box 10; Mary A. Curley to Franklin D. Roosevelt, March 13, 1933, Folder C, Box 9; May Foster to Franklin D. Roosevelt, March 13, 1933, Folder E-F, Box 9; Ruth Lieberman to Franklin D. Roosevelt, March 14, 1933, Folder L, Box 10; and John W. Mitchell to Franklin D. Roosevelt, May 10, 1933, Folder M, Box 12, President's Personal File 200B, Public Reaction Letters, Roosevelt Papers.

[194] W. T. Rowland to Franklin D. Roosevelt, March 14, 1933, Folder R, Box 10, President's Personal File 200B, Public Reaction Letters, Roosevelt Papers.

[195] Florence N. Betts to Franklin D. Roosevelt, March 28, 1933, Folder B, Box 8, President's Personal File 200B, Public Reaction Letters, Roosevelt Papers.

[196] Lewis Gardner Muller to Franklin D. Roosevelt, March 14, 1933, Folder Me-My, Box 10, President's Personal File 200B, Public Reaction Letters, Roosevelt Papers.

[197] Howe, "The President's Mail Bag!" 120.

[198] Thomas A. Keller to Franklin D. Roosevelt, March 17, 1933, Folder K, Box 10, President's Personal File 200B, Public Reaction Letters, Roosevelt Papers.

FIGURE 6.3 In "Champions!" (1934), Burris Jenkins, Jr., captured the new radio-based leader–follower relationship pioneered by Franklin Roosevelt – an emotional connection that did not require physical proximity to the leader.
Source: Burris Jenkins, Jr., "Champions!" editorial cartoon, *New York Evening Journal*, January 30, 1934, 21, courtesy of the Library of Congress, Serial and Government Publications Division.

F. W. Myers, "not forgetting to place an easy chair by the fireplace for the guest of honor, and when your voice came, so clear and vibrant and confident, we had but to close our eyes to see you sitting there with us, talking things over in friendly fashion."[199] "I can see you seated in the big armchair in my living room," Simon Miller concurred, "pipe in mouth and talking on the crisis that confronts us all."[200] Roosevelt's impromptu salutation, too, served to emphasize his accessibility: "Your address of 'My Friends,' to us" left Edna Kempton Merritt "with a feeling of your

[199] F. W. Meyers to Franklin D. Roosevelt, n.d., Folder Me-My, Box 10, President's Personal File 200B, Public Reaction Letters, Roosevelt Papers.

[200] Simon Miller to Franklin D. Roosevelt, March 13, 1933, Folder Me-My, Box 10, President's Personal File 200B, Public Reaction Letters, Roosevelt Papers.

very nearness to every American ... I am now a convert to all that you plan to do."[201] A 1934 *New York Evening Journal* cartoon by Burris Jenkins, Jr., captured the nature of the relationship between president and radio audience. In the image, a middle-class American family sits around the dinner table, enraptured, as the family patriarch raises a toast to the disembodied visage of Roosevelt.[202]

The letters were overwhelmingly positive toward the president's fiscal policies, as was national sentiment generally. Mollified by Roosevelt's cheerful confidence, Americans exercised restraint and allowed the banks to reopen without a panic. Roosevelt continued to deliver fireside chats every few months, and they remained wildly popular over the course of his presidency; by 1941, more than three-quarters of the American people were listening each time Roosevelt made a radio appearance.[203] Writer Saul Bellow remembered walking down a street during one such chat and being able to "follow without missing a single word" by listening to the radios of the cars parked up and down the drive.[204] Roosevelt's eager listeners continued to deluge the White House with mail, too. Even before the first fireside chat, 450,000 letters arrived during the new administration's first week – over twice as many as Bryan had received during the entire 1896 campaign, and at a rate over ten times that of Roosevelt's predecessor Herbert Hoover.[205] The two staffers in the White House mail room, whose job was to forward issue-based correspondence to various executive branch departments, were quickly overwhelmed with letters that specifically referenced the president's speeches and begged for a personal response.[206]

201 Edna Kempton Merritt to Franklin D. Roosevelt, March 13, 1933, Folder Me-My, Box 10, President's Personal File 200B, Public Reaction Letters, Roosevelt Papers.

202 Burris Jenkins, Jr., "Champions!" editorial cartoon, *New York Evening Journal*, January 30, 1934, 21.

203 Kenneth D. Yeilding and Paul H. Carlson, comp., *Ah That Voice: The Fireside Chats of Franklin Delano Roosevelt* (Odessa, TX: The John Ben Shepperd, Jr., Library of the Presidents, The Presidential Museum, 1974), xii; Craig, *Fireside Politics*, 156.

204 Saul Bellow, *It All Adds Up: From the Dim Past to the Uncertain Future: A Nonfiction Collection* (New York: Viking Press, 1994), 28; Jason Loviglio, *Radio's Intimate Public: Network Broadcasting and Mass-Mediated Democracy* (Minneapolis, MN: University of Minnesota Press, 2005), xiii.

205 Leila A. Sussmann, *Dear FDR: A Study of Political Letter-Writing* (Totowa, NJ: Bedminster Press, 1963), 9; Ira R. T. Smith and Joe Alex Morris, *"Dear Mr. President ...": The Story of Fifty Years in the White House Mail Room* (New York: Julian Messner, 1949), 150.

206 Gabrielle Forbush interview by Jerry Deyo, October 26, 1966, Box 1, Oral History Interviews, Franklin D. Roosevelt Library.

This massive increase in correspondence seemed to be a hallmark of radio-based leader–follower communication. Bill Stidger had noticed the same phenomenon in the early 1920s; after his first radio sermon, letters had streamed into his office "at the rate of twenty-five a day for two weeks."[207] In the past, charismatic followers who heard magnetic leaders speak in person had written letters primarily to fix a magnetic encounter in their own minds. Absent the opportunity for a handshake or personal meeting with the radio leader, however, letters grew far more important as followers sought to craft what one scholar has called an "epistolary public sphere" – a direct connection through the mail to replace the one they could not forge in person.[208] "After hearing you discuss the banking situation Sunday night," reported L. A. Wisenbaker to Roosevelt, "I felt like shaking your hand"; he wrote the president a letter instead.[209] Frank Benenati felt the new practice mirrored the old. "Your speech of March 12," he wrote, "was like a hand-shake with all the people."[210]

With more letters coming in every day, Louis Howe made the remarkable decision that each author should receive an individualized response.[211] The resulting mail policy was both very personal and strangely impersonal. "A staff room of some twenty-five or thirty attractive, intelligent girls," wrote Howe's secretary Lela Stiles, penned detailed responses to each letter in the style – and under the name – of Roosevelt himself.[212] Gabrielle Forbush, who supervised the response writers during the mid-1930s, instructed her team to mimic Roosevelt's affectations, his warmth, and his masculinity, always keeping in mind that "he is a man and you are a woman."[213] Americans who wrote to the president thus received personalized responses purportedly from their hero – who had, in most cases, read neither letters nor replies.

[207] Stidger, *That God's House May Be Filled*, 146.

[208] Gerard A. Hauser, *Vernacular Voices: The Rhetoric of Publics and Public Spheres* (Columbia, SC: University of South Carolina Press, 1999), 240–242, 264–265.

[209] L. A. Wisenbaker to Franklin D. Roosevelt, March 16, 1933, Folder W, Box 11, President's Personal File 200B, Public Reaction Letters, Roosevelt Papers.

[210] Frank Benenati to Franklin D. Roosevelt, March 4, 1933, Folder B, Box 8, President's Personal File 200B, Public Reaction Letters, Roosevelt Papers.

[211] Louis McHenry Howe, "The President's Mail Bag!" *The American Magazine*, June 1934, 22.

[212] Lela Stiles, *The Man behind Roosevelt: The Story of Louis McHenry Howe* (Cleveland, OH: World Pub. Co., 1954), 241–242.

[213] Gabrielle Forbush interview by Leila A. Sussmann, December 4, 1954, quoted in Sussmann, *Dear FDR*, 52–53.

This added layer of artificiality, however, did not seem to bother Roosevelt's followers. Forbush kept a file of letters from Americans who had received ghostwritten responses from the New York governor during the 1932 presidential campaign; if this selection of correspondence is to be believed, Americans were overjoyed at the personal replies. Many declared happily that they would frame the letters from Roosevelt or pass them down to their grandchildren and great-grandchildren. Roosevelt's letter "gave me new hopes and visions that will linger in memory of you throughout my life," wrote Forney B. Ray. "You are small enough to know us – great and strong enough to protect us." A group of workers in Hallsville, Missouri, identified these personalized responses as themselves a new development in the leader–follower relationship: "They had never heard of it being done before," reported Mrs. F. L. Faucett – "and you do things that have not been done before . . . – that's why we love you and work for you so cheerfully." Several writers recognized that Roosevelt may not have been able to write the letters himself, but they did not seem to care. "I have not been sure whether you really are the super-man who is capable of being so decent to so many people at once, or whether some thoroughly capable person on your staff has been doing a splendid job of kidding me along," wrote H. R. Hadfield, who had received several letters from the candidate. "Which ever way it is, . . . I am persuaded that any man who can either keep so much detail in his mind or so organize his staff as to at[t]ain such efficiency deserves my support, all of it, all of the time, and you have it."[214]

Did Roosevelt's fireside chats and staff-generated responses generate a charismatic relationship with his radio audience? Certainly, they differed in many ways from the old techniques of Beecher, Bryan, and others. The president's speech did contain some elements of Rush's magnetic style; public speaking professor Glenn Merry, in a 1922 study, captured in graphic form an instance of expanded pitch range in one of Roosevelt's early recorded addresses.[215] Roosevelt's vocal cords, reported one listener, were "more sensitive, more susceptible to the influence of the man's emotions than the strings of a violin to the master touch of the bow."[216] During his fireside chats, however, Roosevelt largely suppressed these magnetic characteristics in favor of the new conversational ethos.

[214] Ms. 67–9, Gabrielle Forbush Papers, Franklin D. Roosevelt Library.

[215] Glenn N. Merry, "Voice Inflection in Speech," *Psychological Monographs*, Vol. 31, No. 1 (1922), 226.

[216] Quoted in Dunlap, *Talking on the Radio*, 38.

Roosevelt's radio addresses bore no trace of the orotund voice or the melody of speech that were so central to Rush's recommendations. Absent any visible gestures or elocutionary techniques, Roosevelt's speaking style was not a magnetic one. Despite this clear shift in method, however, the old terminology appeared several times in the letters, indicating that for many listeners the effect was the same. "I cannot refrain from telling you," wrote Sarah Chisling in a typical letter, "how I feel your magnetic personality enter my room while you talk over the radio."[217]

Some commentators, too, argued that the distance radio created between speaker and hearers weakened the emotional bond between the two, at least compared with in-person charismatic meetings. "The radio listener," *The Nation* had noted in 1924, "is lonely; there is no mob presence to sweep him out of his Yankee cynicism. He is an onlooker, not a participant, and is more likely to turn off his instrument with a smile than to thrust his fist into the solitary air and cry 'Hurray for Cal.'"[218] Radio "has destroyed the old fresh contact between the speaker and his audience," the *New York Times* concurred in 1936, "deprived him of the inspiration which comes from the sight of attentive and even fascinated listeners, and robbed him of the direct fire of flashing eyes and expressive features."[219] In a 1934 essay, novelist John Dos Passos outlined a more substantial complaint. Roosevelt's fireside chats, he acknowledged, comforted listeners beaten down by the "northeast gale" of the Depression. "No wonder they all go to bed happy. But what about it when they wake up and find the wagecut, the bank foreclosing just the same, prices going up on groceries at the chain stores, and the coal dealers bill ... and that it's still raining?"[220]

Notwithstanding such concerns, however, and despite all the differences between Roosevelt's efforts and those of charismatic leaders, Americans responded to the president with the same intense emotion they had reserved for Beecher, Bryan, and other magnetic personalities. On the other hand, Roosevelt's radio-adapted, conversational speaking style; his composite, artificial letter-writing persona; and his avoidance of

[217] Sarah Chisling to Franklin D. Roosevelt, March 16, 1933, Folder C, Box 9, President's Personal File 200B, Public Reaction Letters, Roosevelt Papers.

[218] "Radio Convention Year," *The Nation*, July 9, 1924, 34, quoted in Wolfe, "Some Reactions to the Advent of Campaigning by Radio," 310.

[219] "Political Speaking and the Radio," *New York Times*, October 4, 1936, E8; Ranson, *The Role of Radio in the American Presidential Election of 1924*, 110.

[220] John Dos Passos, "The Radio Voice," *Common Sense*, Vol. 3, No. 2 (February 1934), 17; Craig, *Fireside Politics*, 186.

nearly all traditional charismatic techniques testified that his connection with followers represented something new and different from a charismatic movement. Instead, Roosevelt had drawn on charismatic precedents to develop an entirely new type of leader–follower relationship – one with a broader reach, with more physical distance but more emotional closeness, featuring new stagecraft but familiar emotional responses. Roosevelt "is made personal rather than a figure on a pedestal whose actions are akin to those of the gods and as incomprehensible," opined the *Knickerbocker Press* after the president's second fireside chat. "This progressive concept of the relationship between the people and the administration may well be one of the greatest single advances resulting from the present upheaval."[221]

Americans who wrote to Roosevelt after the first fireside chat seemed to recognize that they had experienced a remarkable shift in American culture – a momentous change in the leader–follower relationship as significant as that represented by William Jennings Bryan's "Cross of Gold" speech nearly forty years earlier. "It is the first time in my memory," declared Morgan Royce, "that a god from Olympus has taken 'human' form and called upon the citizenry, or even feigned to care about us."[222] "In the past," explained C. G. Adams, "the government of our country,as embodied in President, Cabinet, and Congress, has seemed so far away, so distant from the people; and your talk was like the intimate confidence of a father to his family."[223] "Some how, last night, we were made too [*sic*] feel that we are a part of the government and that we have some responsibility," wrote minister Newton C. Fetter. "There was an intimacy and a summons about those fifteen minutes that had a tremendously wholesome effect on us all."[224] Mildred I. Goldstein's letter perfectly captured the consequences of the change. "Until last night," she wrote, "to me, the President of the United States was merely a legend. A picture to look at. A newspaper item. But you are real. I know your voice; what you are trying to do."[225]

221 *Knickerbocker Press*, May 9, 1933, in William F. McDonald to Marvin H. McIntyre, May 9, 1933, Folder M, Box 12, President's Personal File 200B, Public Reaction Letters, Roosevelt Papers.

222 Morgan Royce to Franklin D. Roosevelt, March 15, 1933, Folder R, Box 10, President's Personal File 200B, Public Reaction Letters, Roosevelt Papers.

223 C. G. Adams to Franklin D. Roosevelt, March 15, 1933, Folder A, Box 8, President's Personal File 200B, Public Reaction Letters, Roosevelt Papers.

224 Newton C. Fetter to Franklin D. Roosevelt, March 15, 1933, Folder E-F, Box 9, President's Personal File 200B, Public Reaction Letters, Roosevelt Papers.

225 Mildred I. Goldstein to Franklin D. Roosevelt, March 13, 1933, Folder G, Box 9, President's Personal File 200B, Public Reaction Letters, Roosevelt Papers.

In crafting a communication style that preserved and even augmented the emotional content of the charismatic relationship while allowing for the use of mass media and a physical separation between leader and led, the president had built what would become the dominant model of leader–follower relations in the years to come. In merging the charismatic connection with modern social organization, Roosevelt had ensured a lasting legacy for charisma.

* * *

Taken together, the events of the interwar years heralded the end of charismatic movements as a significant phenomenon in American life. The changes in speech education ensured that few Americans born after 1900 received training in the speaking style pioneered by James Rush. Indeed, no magnetic orators achieved prominence in the United States after 1940; just twenty years later, Fredric March's portrayal of a lightly fictionalized William Jennings Bryan in the film *Inherit the Wind* lampooned the Great Commoner's now-antiquated style of delivery.[226] The charismatic ideal of using emotional public speaking to change society aged just as poorly. Never again would American attitudes be as positive toward emotionally charged oratory as they were between the Civil War and World War I. Nor did charismatic national speaking tours seem necessary in an age of electronic mass media. Instead, Americans embraced the new type of leader–follower connection pioneered by Franklin Roosevelt: a social movement helmed by a leader who used mass communication and a conversational idiom to move and inspire audiences and who received written professions of followership in return.

The charismatic phenomenon did have a bizarre epilogue of sorts, in the person of Huey Pierce Long, Jr. Born on August 30, 1893, in rural Winnfield, Louisiana, Long dropped out of high school after two years on the debate team and gained the rest of his public speaking experience in the same way Hubbard and Dale Carnegie had – as a traveling salesman.[227] After a brief legal career, Long immediately inserted himself into state politics; in 1928, at the age of thirty-four, he won the governorship by defeating an oligarchy that had controlled the state for a

[226] *Inherit the Wind*, dir. Stanley Kramer (Beverly Hills, CA: United Artists, 1960).

[227] Robert S. Iltis, "Reconsidering the Demagoguery of Huey Long," in Thomas W. Benson, ed., *American Rhetoric in the New Deal Era, 1932–1945* (East Lansing, MI: Michigan State University Press, 2006), 377.

half century.[228] Over the next seven years, Long established a near-dictatorial machine in Louisiana. Nicknaming himself "the Kingfish," he bribed, destroyed, and even kidnapped political opponents; he cut off federal aid to jurisdictions that opposed him; at one point, he held the governorship and a U.S. Senate seat simultaneously.[229] Long was unscrupulous, power-mad, corrupt, and an alcoholic; despite a complete lack of elocutionary training, he also fancied himself a powerful charismatic leader.[230] Unlike virtually any other interwar figure, he made himself equally effective in person and on the radio by adapting his folksy, rambling style to both media.[231] Following charismatic precedents, Long's apparatus included a weekly newspaper and a national network of "Share Our Wealth" clubs dedicated to the Kingfish's pet wealth-taxation scheme.[232] Even his campaign slogan, "Every Man a King," was paraphrased from a William Jennings Bryan epigram.[233]

For a brief period in early 1935, it looked as though Long might singlehandedly revive the charismatic tradition by blending his eccentric persona with the once-ubiquitous charismatic organizing techniques Roosevelt and others had abandoned. Stumping the country on an anti-Roosevelt speaking tour, Long gathered tens of thousands of listeners at each stop; he received over 100,000 letters after each radio broadcast.[234] He began to attract the support of other idiosyncratic reformers, including the radio priest Father Charles Coughlin of Royal Oak, Michigan, whose public speaking style resembled Adolf Hitler's in some respects; the old-age pension advocate Dr. Francis Townsend from Long Beach, California; and the fiery right-wing evangelist Gerald L. K. Smith, who ran Long's Share Our Wealth clubs.[235] Flush with allies and supporters, Long began openly discussing a third-party presidential run against Roosevelt and

[228] Richard D. White, Jr., *Kingfish: The Reign of Huey P. Long* (New York: Random House, 2006), 8–10, 15.

[229] *Ibid.*, 110, 141.

[230] T. Harry Williams, *Huey Long* (New York: Knopf, 1969), 4–5; Iltis, "Reconsidering the Demagoguery of Huey Long," 406.

[231] White, *Kingfish*, 18; Alan Brinkley, *Voices of Protest: Huey Long, Father Coughlin, and the Great Depression* (New York: Knopf, 1982), 62.

[232] Brinkley, *Voices of Protest*, 70–71; White, *Kingfish*, 97, 197.

[233] Brinkley, *Voices of Protest*, 20. [234] *Ibid.*, 169; White, *Kingfish*, 240–242.

[235] Donald Warren, *Radio Priest: Charles Coughlin, The Father of Hate Radio* (New York: The Free Press, 1996), 24, 71, 76; Ronald H. Carpenter, *Father Charles E. Coughlin: Surrogate Spokesman for the Disaffected* (Westport, CT: Greenwood Press, 1998), 6–10; Michael Kazin, *The Populist Persuasion: An American History* (New York: Basic Books, 1995), 114, 124; Edwin Amenta, *When Movements Matter: The*

the Republicans in the 1936 election.[236] The Democratic National Committee conducted an opinion poll to determine how Long would fare as a third-party candidate. The results showed the Louisiana senator drawing as much as 11 percent of the vote nationwide – enough to throw a close election into the House of Representatives and make the Kingfish a kingmaker.[237] "Huey Long," bank president W. E. Warren wrote ominously to Roosevelt, "is the man we thought you were when we voted for you."[238]

Alarmed, Roosevelt sent administration official General Hugh Johnson out to attack Long and Coughlin for their charismatic oratory. Comparing Coughlin and Long to Pied Pipers hypnotizing their followers, Johnson told a group of reporters that the two leaders' "dangerous demagogy" put the entire nation at risk. "They have emotions rather than beliefs," Johnson explained. "In fact Huey is the Hitler of one of our sovereign States – not in the forcible seizure of absolute and arbitrary powers alone but in the ... undoubted personal magnetism that cause[s] people to put their emotions before their reason and go stampeding off to nothing like a frightened flock of sheep." "This country," the general concluded, "was never under a greater menace."[239]

The stage seemed set for a symbolic final battle between Long's more traditional charismatic style and Roosevelt's post-charismatic approach – but that opportunity passed when an assassin's bullet felled Huey Long on September 8, 1935. Undaunted, the remaining Long and Coughlin forces forged ahead with a national third-party campaign. Now under Coughlin's direction, they regrouped around a pugnacious congressman, William Lemke, who had grown up amid the Populist and Bryan movements.[240] It soon became clear, however, that the challengers' charismatic organization was no match for Roosevelt's

Townsend Plan & the Rise of Social Security (Princeton, NJ: Princeton University Press, 2006), 4; Jeansonne, *Gerald L. K. Smith*, 39, 53; Craig, *Fireside Politics*, 160.

236 White, *Kingfish*, 242. 237 Brinkley, *Voices of Protest*, 284–285.

238 W. E. Warren to Franklin Roosevelt, February 14, 1935, Official File 1403, Franklin Delano Roosevelt Library, quoted in *Ibid.*, 198.

239 Hugh S. Johnson, "Text of General Johnson's Denouncement of Father Coughlin and Huey Long," *New York Times*, March 5, 1935, 10.

240 On the debate over Lemke's charismatic abilities, see Edward C. Blackorby, *Prairie Rebel: The Public Life of William Lemke* (Lincoln, NE: University of Nebraska Press, 1963), 117–118, 199; David H. Bennett, *Demagogues in the Depression: American Radicals and the Union Party, 1932–1936* (New Brunswick, NJ: Rutgers University Press, 1969), 232.

modern social movement or his massive following; the Kingfish's outsize personality had made his movement appear more powerful than it was. Roosevelt romped to a double-digit victory in November, while the hapless Lemke won less than 2 percent of the vote. With that, the age of charisma was over.

Conclusion

"It was a whole bunch of people made into one crawling beast," declares Jody Tiflin's grandfather in John Steinbeck's 1936 short story "The Leader of the People." Sitting on the steps of the Tiflins' front porch, Grandfather is struggling to explain why it was important, in his youth, to help push back the Western frontier. "It was westering and westering," he tells Jody. "Every man wanted something for himself, but the big beast that was all of them wanted only westering." Though Grandfather led wagon trains full of these pioneer settlers, he is circumspect about his importance to the project. "I was the leader, but if I hadn't been there, someone else would have been the head," he remembers. "The thing had to have a head." As the pioneers moved west, their shared endeavor took on an almost religious significance. "The westering was as big as God," he recalls, "and the slow steps that made the movement piled up and piled up until the continent was crossed." But the time of such movements is over now, and Jody cannot "lead the people some day" as Grandfather did. "There's no place to go," Grandfather smiles ruefully. "There's the ocean to stop you. There's a line of old men along the shore hating the ocean because it stopped them." Besides, "Westering has died out of the people. Westering isn't a hunger any more ... It is finished." Moved and saddened, Jody can offer Grandfather nothing but lemonade in consolation.[1]

Steinbeck's lament for the collective undertaking "as big as God" is perhaps only nominally about the desire to go west. Grandfather was,

[1] John Steinbeck, "The Leader of the People," *Argosy*, August 1936, 106.

after all, a "leader of the people" – a charismatic figure under whose stewardship an assortment of followers united into a "crawling beast" of humanity and pursued a great collective goal. The West was symbolic for Steinbeck; in his novels, it often represented the unfulfilled longing and the frustrated hopes he saw embedded in American culture.[2] In the story of Jody and his grandfather, Steinbeck's "westering" was merely another word for the charismatic phenomenon Americans had always struggled to name – a phenomenon that, Steinbeck felt, was now irrevocably lost.

"Westering has died out of the people." In its emotional content, Steinbeck's mournful epitaph for charisma mirrors the general tendency of commentators since World War I to imagine the late nineteenth and early twentieth centuries in general, and the career of Woodrow Wilson in particular, as an apotheosis, a declension narrative, or a missed chance for national salvation. The titles of these books speak for themselves: *The End of American Innocence*, *When the Cheering Stopped*, *Breaking the Heart of the World*.[3] "Another act of the tragedy had come to an end," Frederick Lewis Allen wrote of Wilson's collapse in *Only Yesterday*. "He had given all he had to the cause, and it had not been enough."[4] Historical fiction has told much the same story. John Dos Passos closed his novel *1919* with the image of a broken and cynical Wilson mutely placing a bouquet of bloodstained poppies on the Tomb of the Unknown Soldier.[5] "The era of Ragtime," E. L. Doctorow concluded in his book on the period, "had run out, with the heavy breath of the machine, as if history were no more than a tune on a player piano."[6]

The United States did in fact lose much during World War I and its aftermath; the lives of over 50,000 Americans during the conflict certainly rank at the top of the list. Many of these narratives stress the failure of progressive policy initiatives, the weakening of the welfare state, the

[2] Louis Owens, "The Culpable Joads: Desentimentalizing *The Grapes of Wrath*," in John Ditsky, ed., *Critical Essays on Steinbeck's The Grapes of Wrath* (Boston: G. K. Hall, 1989), 112; Richard Astro, "John Steinbeck," in J. Golden Taylor and Thomas J. Lyon, eds., *A Literary History of the American West* (Fort Worth, TX: Texas Christian University Press, 1987), 431, 441;

[3] Henry F. May, *The End of American Innocence: A Study of the First Years of Our Own Time, 1912–1917* (New York: Knopf, 1959); Gene Smith, *When the Cheering Stopped: The Last Years of Woodrow Wilson* (New York: William Morrow, 1964); John Milton Cooper, Jr., *Breaking the Heart of the World: Woodrow Wilson and the Fight for the League of Nations* (New York: Cambridge University Press, 2001).

[4] Frederick Lewis Allen, *Only Yesterday: An Informal History of the Nineteen-Twenties* (New York: Harper & Brothers, 1931), 34.

[5] John Dos Passos, *1919* (orig. pub. 1932; Boston: Houghton Mifflin, 2000), 74, 380.

[6] E. L. Doctorow, *Ragtime* (orig. pub. 1974; New York: Plume, 1996), 270.

economic ruination of the Great Depression, or Wilson's inability to "make the world safe for democracy." Leaving aside their policy content, however, these laments reflect a pervasive sense of loss that suggests at least some of their nostalgia is emotional rather than political. During the decades surrounding 1900, charismatic movements provided Americans with an intense emotional fulfillment that often appears absent from modern society. Ordinary citizens found lasting meaning and purpose through commitment to religious, social, and political causes; emotive charismatic leaders promoted visions of a new society in ways that thrilled and inspired Americans. "Never was oratory more orotund, propaganda more reckless, denunciation more bitter, reform more strident," declared Howard Mumford Jones in *The Age of Energy*. "A people thus verbally unrestrained must have been filled with exuberance and wrath."[7]

Some elements of this age of charisma are surely gone for good. The magnetic speaking style developed by James Rush and Jonathan Barber has all but vanished from modern society; a few poor-quality recordings of aging orators are the only evidence of its prior ubiquity, and the testimonials of long-dead listeners are the only proof of its once-great power to move audiences. Today, leaders who appear overly persuasive or emotional, and followers who respond to them, invariably awaken anti-charismatic criticism recalling the attacks of Watterson and Mencken. Where Gustave Le Bon once raised the specters of Napoleon and Boulanger to argue that charismatic leaders were unscrupulous and demagogic, the twentieth century created new charismatic bogeymen in the form of genocidal dictators such as Benito Mussolini, Adolf Hitler, and Joseph Stalin.[8] Modern Americans rarely compare their leaders with Moses, Jesus, or other messianic figures.[9] The progressive distrust of individual agency and the charismatic glorification of mass movements have given way to a culture celebrating Emersonian individualism and independence. When contemporary Americans witness a performance by a musical ensemble, they no longer see, as Patrick Gilmore's audiences did in 1885, "the parts of one grand organ" bending inexorably to their

[7] Howard Mumford Jones, *The Age of Energy: Varieties of American Experience, 1865–1915* (New York: Viking, 1971), xii.

[8] Benjamin L. Alpers, *Dictators, Democracy, and American Public Culture: Envisioning the Totalitarian Enemy, 1920s–1950s* (Chapel Hill, NC: University of North Carolina Press, 2003), 77–78.

[9] Gregory P. Downs, *Declarations of Dependence: The Long Reconstruction of Popular Politics in the South, 1861–1908* (Chapel Hill, NC: University of North Carolina Press, 2011), 218.

leader's will. Instead, they recognize the players as a collection of individuals whose harmonious blending is a credit to their own separate talents. By contrast, the once-powerful conductor seems almost superfluous; groups such as the Orpheus Chamber Orchestra have done away with the baton-wielding leader altogether.[10]

Unlike an orchestra leader, however, charisma's lasting influence on American culture cannot be easily dismissed. In *Meet John Doe* (1941), filmmaker Frank Capra investigated the charismatic relationship in the age of radio and found, to his surprise, that audiences did not share his ambivalence about charismatic movements. In the film, a newspaper looking for cheap publicity transforms drifter John Willoughby into a charismatic leader. In exchange for money, Willoughby agrees to impersonate a fictitious "John Doe" and read an inspiring speech, written by one of the paper's columnists, over the radio. The speech gains Willoughby a national army of charismatic followers who idolize the Doe character and establish "John Doe clubs" dedicated to his "love-thy-neighbor" philosophy. Soon, however, Willoughby realizes he is being used to pave the way for a presidential run by the paper's shadowy publisher D. B. Norton. When Willoughby tries to expose the publisher's plan, Norton instead reveals Willoughby as a fake, and the John Doe clubs turn on their onetime idol. Despondent, Willoughby decides to draw attention to the conspiracy by jumping to his death.

Does John Doe jump, thereby affirming the moral bankruptcy of charismatic movements? Capra could not decide. He shot four different endings for the film and screened them for audiences; in each case, viewers left the theater disappointed. "For seven-eighths of the film," Capra wrote later, "we had made The Great American Motion Picture; but in the last eighth, it fizzled into The Great American Letdown."[11] In the end, Capra's viewers seized control of the film's message and rewrote it as a defense of the charismatic relationship. Just before *Doe*'s nationwide release, Capra received a letter from a man, signing himself "John Doe," who had attended some of the early screenings. "I have seen your film with many different endings," he wrote, "all bad, I thought … The only thing that can keep John Doe from jumping to his death is the John Does themselves … if they ask him." Capra adopted the suggestion and released the film with a new ending showing the false Doe saved by the real ones; in the final film, the

[10] Jamie James, "Bringing Haydn to Hanoi," *New York Times*, November 17, 1998, E1.

[11] Frank Capra, *The Name above the Title: An Autobiography* (New York: Macmillan, 1971), 304; *Meet John Doe*, dir. Frank Capra (Warner Bros., 1941).

followers insist on keeping their charismatic idol even though they know he is a fraud.[12]

As Capra's fan mail indicates, the audience's reinterpretation of *Meet John Doe* did not end with the film's conclusion. The film itself, wrote M. Gluck to the director, created the very effect the fictional Doe inspired in his audiences. "By the time you had the band play the Star Spangled Banner," Gluck wrote, "You *had* a John Doe Club right there in the theater."[13] Other writers demanded that Capra himself take up the role of a real-life Doe. "The responsibility falls on your shoulder," Charles H. Martin wrote; "to you will come the plea to carry through that which you have started."[14] "I'm just one of the millions of John Does," insisted George B. Nordman, "who are sick of wars ... and the eventual taxes that are piled on us; of the cheap petty politics with their intrigue and selfishness ... There are millions of more John Does who believe the same thing, but who are waiting for someone to bring it to their attention." Declaring *Meet John Doe* "one of the most powerful sermons since the one on the mount," Nordman begged Capra to make a second *Doe* film in which the director himself would come out from behind the curtain and instruct "those in the audience to get together on the John Doe principle."[15] Real-life charismatic movements may have been anachronistic by 1941, but popular interest in the charismatic relationship was clearly alive and well.

Indeed, while charismatic speakers on national tours are no longer ubiquitous, the leader–follower model developed by Franklin Roosevelt – in which Americans experience an intimate emotional connection with a leader via mass communication technologies – has continued to thrive in the decades since *Meet John Doe*. Beginning in the 1940s, Billy Graham coupled in-person revivals with a dizzying array of newspaper columns, radio broadcasts, films, and televised sermons to become the most successful evangelist in American history. Despite Graham's extensive use of mass media, his followers displayed similar attachments to their

12 Capra, *The Name above the Title*, 305.

13 M. Gluck to Frank Capra, March 13, 1941, Frank Capra Collection, Wesleyan University Cinema Archives, Middletown, CT, quoted in Eric Smoodin, " 'This Business of America': Fan Mail, Film Reception, and Meet John Doe," *Screen*, Vol. 37, No. 2 (Summer 1996), 123; italics in original.

14 Charles H. Martin to Frank Capra, May 13, 1941, Frank Capra Collection, quoted in Smoodin, " 'This Business of America,' " 123.

15 George B. Nordman to Frank Capra, undated letter, Frank Capra collection, quoted in Smoodin, " 'This Business of America,' " 123–124.

leader as had Billy Sunday's trail-hitters decades earlier.[16] Since the 1960s, evangelical ministers such as Jerry Falwell, Pat Robertson, and Graham's friend Robert Schuller have developed national television followings. Oprah Winfrey, whose media empire dwarfs that of any televangelist, has so mesmerized her millions of viewers that she has been likened to a religious leader promoting a theology of consumerism. Winfrey also dabbled in turn-of-the-century charismatic techniques when she stumped the country for Barack Obama's 2008 presidential campaign.[17] In the political realm, activists such as Martin Luther King, Jr., and presidents such as Obama, John F. Kennedy, and Ronald Reagan have used televised speeches to motivate and inspire followers. Even Jimmy Carter, not a particularly notable orator, tried to save his floundering presidency in 1979 with a televised address, "A Crisis of Confidence." Although the speech failed to improve Carter's electoral prospects, it still inspired letters comparing the president to Moses and a *New York Times* article comparing him to William Jennings Bryan.[18]

Perhaps the ultimate proof of charisma's continuing relevance in modern American culture is the popularity of charisma itself – the modern lexical term, not the historical phenomenon. As charismatic movements were disappearing in the 1930s, sociologists such as Robert Michels, Talcott Parsons, H. H. Gerth, and C. Wright Mills were introducing Max Weber's new word into American scholarship.[19] After Gerth and Mills published the first partial English translation of Weber's *Economy and Society* in 1946, charisma began to attract wider cultural circulation in the United States.[20] Explaining the term to a skeptical *Fortune* editor in 1949, sociologist Daniel Bell described it as the "magnetic presence" exuded by individuals such as Huey Long.[21] By the 1960s, the word was ubiquitous in popular descriptions of every kind of leader, from presidents

[16] Grant Wacker, *America's Pastor: Billy Graham and the Shaping of a Nation* (Cambridge, MA: Belknap Press of Harvard University Press, 2014), 13–15, 258.

[17] Kathryn E. Lofton, *Oprah: The Gospel of an Icon* (Berkeley, CA: University of California Press, 2011), 2, 218.

[18] Kevin Mattson, *"What the Heck Are You Up To, Mr. President?": Jimmy Carter, America's "Malaise," and the Speech That Should Have Changed the Country* (New York: Bloomsbury, 2009), 159–161, 163, 172; Francis X. Clines, "About Chautauqua: The Circuit Is Gone but Not the Oratory," *New York Times*, August 2, 1979, B4.

[19] Joshua Derman, *Max Weber in Politics and Social Thought: From Charisma to Canonization* (Cambridge, UK: Cambridge University Press, 2012), 198–206.

[20] Max Weber, *From Max Weber: Essays in Sociology*, ed. and tr. H. H. Gerth and C. Wright Mills (New York: Oxford University Press, 1946).

[21] Daniel Bell, "The Day *Fortune* Lost Charisma," in *Writing for Fortune: Nineteen Authors Remember Life on the Staff of a Remarkable Magazine* (New York: Time, 1980), 163.

to ministers to football coaches.[22] Its meaning was roughly the same as that of personal magnetism decades earlier, though the new term lacked the elocutionary connotations of the old. "Charisma is something you have which gives you what Hollywood used to call 'oomph,' " concurred *Los Angeles Times* columnist Hal Humphrey in the same year, "and especially on TV."[23] Pollster George Gallup, who as a youth had supported Bryan, helped to popularize the term by creating a "charisma poll" of the 1968 presidential candidates. "In its current use," Gallup wrote, charisma "means the ability of a person to lead and to inspire people."[24] Though commentators found the word well suited to modern society, they were largely ignorant of the connections Weber had drawn between charisma and the social movements of earlier years. "Franklin D. Roosevelt got elected four times," sniffed columnist and erstwhile Debs follower Harry Golden in 1969, "and he never heard of 'charisma' let alone knew what it meant."[25]

Today, charisma is virtually a national obsession in the United States. Just as the books of Orison Swett Marden and Webster Edgerly once promised to unlock the secrets of personal magnetism, contemporary self-help literature is filled with advice on how to introduce charismatic elements into one's personality. Relying on the Biblical meaning of the term, a new generation of Pentecostal believers branded themselves "charismatic" in the 1960s and helped to reintroduce the concept of charisma to American Christianity. After political scientist James MacGregor Burns, inspired by Weber's ideas, called in 1978 for a renaissance in "transforming leadership," business leaders in boardrooms across the United States adopted Burns' recommendations and joined the charismatic revolution.[26] In the past few decades, scholars have resumed the study of charismatic oratory; several have rediscovered the value of expanded pitch range and other James Rush–style techniques in the speech of modern charismatic figures.[27] Motivational speakers,

[22] Derman, *Max Weber in Politics and Social Thought*, 213–214.

[23] Hal Humphrey, "Charisma – You're Dead without It," *Los Angeles Times*, April 30, 1968, C14.

[24] George Gallup, "Nixon Tops Opponents on Charisma Scale," *Hartford Courant*, September 25, 1968, 32; David Greenberg, *Republic of Spin: An Inside History of the American Presidency* (New York: W. W. Norton, 2016), 260.

[25] Harry Golden, " 'Charisma' and Options," *Chicago Defender*, April 14, 1969, 13.

[26] James MacGregor Burns, *Leadership* (New York: Harper & Row, 1978), 4.

[27] Max Atkinson, *Our Masters' Voices: The Language and Body Language of Politics* (New York: Methuen, 1984), 60, 108–109; Boas Shamir, Robert J. House, and Michael B. Arthur, "The Motivational Effects of Charismatic Leadership: A Self-Concept Based

leadership training courses, religious sermons, and political commentators all affirm the importance of charisma as a central feature of contemporary life. Notwithstanding the wistfulness of cultural commentators for turn-of-the-century charismatic movements, it seems at times as if personal magnetism never left at all.

The modern fascination with charisma, of course, has no direct connection with the historical movements Beecher, Bryan, and their fellow magnetic personalities once led, nor does it indicate any meaningful resurgence of either the old elocutionary speaking style or the sacralized relationships that accompanied it. Contemporary charismatic discourse, however, reflects the pervasive influence of perhaps charisma's most important element. The historical phenomenon of charisma was not merely a speaking style or an organizational structure; it also represented a new and significant approach to the relationship between leaders and followers. Charismatic movements taught leaders that they must appeal to followers' emotions as well as to their reason, that leadership required giving something of themselves to the people they hoped to represent; it showed followers that their emotional experience could provide them with agency within both social movements and society at large. Americans have learned these lessons well. Gone are the days when a politician could run for national office without making a single speech or encountering a single voter, when a minister could read a sermon monotonously off a printed text without ever making eye contact with the congregation. Today, Americans require that their spiritual mentors inspire and connect with them and that their politicians shake hands, kiss babies, and demonstrate an interest in the lives of ordinary people. Leaders in all realms of society must demonstrate their fitness for leadership not by creating emotional distance from followers, but by forging emotional connections with them. This newfound emotional availability among leaders reflects a substantial shift in cultural expectations of leadership and represents a democratic element in American culture that Americans take for granted – an element that represents charisma's most substantial legacy in American society.

"Not until human nature is other than it is," Henry Ward Beecher declared in 1886, "will the function of the living voice – the greatest force

Theory," *Organization Science*, Vol. 4, No. 4 (November 1993), 582–584; Rosario Signorello and Didier Demolin, "The Physiological Use of the Charismatic Voice in Political Speech," Proceedings of Interspeech 2013, Lyon, FR, August 25–29, 2013, 989.

on earth among men – cease."[28] Beecher's confident prediction of the timelessness of charismatic oratory was only half wrong. In the end, there were two ages of charisma: one, a historically bounded phenomenon; the other, a social philosophy that has earned a lasting place in American culture. Americans who look back nostalgically at the intense emotions of a hundred years ago neglect the enduring influence of charismatic ideas on modern life. As a magnetic speaking style, a performance practice, and an organizational structure, the age of charisma is over. But as a commitment to the emotional connection between leaders and followers – and as a testament to the power of emotional experience to shape American culture – the age of charisma is with us still.

[28] Henry Ward Beecher, "Oratory" (Philadelphia: National School of Oratory, 1886), 46.

Bibliography

MANUSCRIPT AND ARCHIVAL SOURCES

Numerous collections of charismatic follower testimonials exist in American archives, usually in the public or private papers of charismatic leaders. Though all of these collections have been "selected" in some fashion by correspondence secretaries or by the leaders themselves, enough variety remains among the letters to provide a reasonably accurate picture of the follower experience. For this project, I located particularly rich veins of follower correspondence in the Papers of William and Helen Sunday at Grace College and Theological Seminary, Winona Lake, Indiana; the William Jennings Bryan Papers at the Library of Congress (particularly for the 1896 campaign); the (Eugene) Debs Collection at Indiana State University, Terre Haute, Indiana; and the Franklin D. Roosevelt Papers as President (President's Personal File) at the Franklin D. Roosevelt Library, Hyde Park, New York. Other useful manuscript collections containing follower correspondence include the Theodore Roosevelt Papers at the Library of Congress (for the 1912 election); the Woodrow Wilson Papers at the Library of Congress; and the Jane Addams Papers/Swarthmore College Peace Collection at Swarthmore College, Swarthmore, Pennsylvania. A helpful collection of noncharismatic follower testimonials can be found in the Benjamin Harrison Papers at the Library of Congress (particularly for the 1888 election).

Several additional archival collections contain follower testimonials elicited through either surveys or oral histories. The two most valuable of these collections are J. Robert Constantine, ed., *Debs Remembered: A Collection of Reminiscences* (Terre Haute, IN: Indiana State University [unpublished], 1981) on reel 5 of the Papers of Eugene V. Debs microfilm edition; and the Charlotte Evangelistic Campaigns Research Project, Collection 295 at the Archives of the Billy Graham Center, Wheaton College, Wheaton, Illinois, a sociological survey of Billy Sunday followers conducted by Ivan J. Fahs. Other useful collections include Robert Shuster's interviews with Andrew Wyzenbeek and Kathryn Marie Hess Feldi, Collections 43 and 487 at the Archives of the Billy Graham Center.

Many valuable collections of follower testimonials have been published and are available in book or article form. Ruth Le Prade, ed., *Debs and the Poets* (Pasadena, CA: Upton Sinclair, 1920), is a collection of testimonials about Eugene V. Debs collected from supportive poets and writers. Jeannette Smith-Irvin, *Footsoldiers of the Universal Negro Improvement Association: Their Own Words* (Trenton, NJ: Africa World Press, 1989), contains six oral histories of followers of Marcus Garvey. "Personal Gains from the Sunday Campaign: A Sheaf of Testimonies," *The Congregationalist*, February 22, 1917: 256–257, contains several testimonials from converts and followers of Billy Sunday. Selected letters to Franklin Roosevelt from the Roosevelt Papers as President (President's Personal File) can be found in several published works; the three most useful for the study of charisma are Leila A. Sussmann, *Dear FDR: A Study of Political Letter-Writing* (Totowa, NJ: Bedminster Press, 1963); Robert S. McElvaine, ed., *Down & Out in the Great Depression: Letters from the Forgotten Man* (Chapel Hill, NC: University of North Carolina Press, 1983); and Lawrence W. Levine and Cornelia R. Levine, *The People and the President: America's Conversation with FDR* (Boston: Beacon Press, 2002). Louis R. Harlan, ed., *The Booker T. Washington Papers*, 12 vols. (Urbana, IL: University of Illinois Press, 1972–1988), contains several letters from followers of Washington.

Finally, numerous additional collections contain manuscript writings and correspondence essential for understanding the mindset of various charismatic leaders and other commentators on charisma. The Rush Family Papers, Library Company of Philadelphia, include manuscript drafts and correspondence showing the development of James Rush's ideas on public speaking and his connections with the Barber brothers and other influential forebears of the charismatic speaking style. Herbert Croly's important unpublished manuscripts "Religion in Life" (undated) and *The Breach in Civilization* (1920) can be found respectively in the Houghton Library, Harvard University (MS Am 1291), and in the Papers of Felix Frankfurter at the Library of Congress. The Elbert Hubbard Papers at the Harry Ransom Center, University of Texas at Austin, contain correspondence relevant to Hubbard's views on charisma and his dealings with the Rockefeller and Carnegie families. The Henry Watterson Papers at the University of Louisville contain a number of Watterson's *Louisville Courier-Journal* editorials on charisma and magnetism. For Presidents Theodore Roosevelt and Woodrow Wilson, several published collections reproduce useful archival correspondence. For Roosevelt, these include *The Letters of Theodore Roosevelt*, 8 vols., ed. Elting E. Morison (Cambridge, MA: Harvard University Press, 1951–1954); Joseph Bucklin Bishop, *Theodore Roosevelt and His Time, Shown in His Own Letters*, 2 vols. (New York: Scribner, 1920); and *Letters from Theodore Roosevelt to Anna Roosevelt Cowles, 1879–1918* (New York: Scribner, 1924). For Wilson, they include *The Papers of Woodrow Wilson*, 69 vols., ed. Arthur S. Link (Princeton: Princeton University Press, 1966–1994); and *The Public Papers of Woodrow Wilson*, 6 vols., ed. Ray Stannard Baker and William E. Dodd (New York: Harper & Brothers, 1925–1926). Malvern Rosenberg Starkstein's collegiate "Notes on Winifred Ward," in the possession of Karen Raskin-Young (mother of the author), contain an invaluable record of Northwestern University professor Winifred Ward's discussion of elocution teaching in the 1930s. Other useful collections include the W. E. B. Du Bois Papers at the University of Massachusetts Amherst; the Carry Amelia Nation Papers at the Kansas Historical Society, Topeka, Kansas; the Keith/Albee Collection at the University of Iowa Library; the Prints and Photographs Division at the Library of Congress; the *United States Census of Population*; and the *Congressional Record.*

NEWSPAPERS

Aberdeen Daily American
Anniston Star
Atchison Daily Globe
Baltimore Evening Sun
Bisbee Daily Review
Bismarck Daily Tribune
Boston Daily Advertiser
Boston Investigator
Charleston Daily Mail
Charlotte Daily Observer
Chicago Daily Inter Ocean
Chicago Defender
Chicago Sunday Times
Chicago Tribune
Cleveland Daily Herald
Cleveland Plain Dealer
Colorado Springs Gazette
Columbus Enquirer-Sun
Dallas Morning News
Denver Evening Post
Denver Rocky Mountain News
Duluth News-Tribune
Evening Independent
Galveston Daily News
Grand Forks Daily Herald
Grand Rapids Evening Press
Hamilton Daily Republican-News
Harrisburg Patriot
Hartford Courant
Idaho Daily Statesman
Idaho Falls Times
Industrial Worker
Kansas City Star
Kansas City Times
Langston City Herald
Lexington Morning Herald
Little Rock Gazette
Los Angeles Times

Louisville Courier-Journal
Maysville Daily Public Ledger
Milwaukee Daily Journal
New Hampshire Sentinel
New Haven Evening Register
New Orleans Daily Picayune
New York Evangelist
New York Evening Journal
New York Evening Post
New York Globe
New York Herald
New York Sun
New York Times
New York Tribune
Omaha Sunday World-Herald
Philadelphia Inquirer
Phoenix Republican-Herald
Pittsburg Dispatch
Pittsburgh Press
Portland Morning Oregonian
Salem Register
Springfield Republican
The State
St. Louis Globe-Democrat
St. Louis Republican
Trenton Evening Times
Tucson Daily Citizen
Washington Post
Yenowine's Illustrated News

PERIODICALS

The American Magazine
The American Mercury
American Review of Reviews
The Arena
Atlantic Monthly
The Bookman
The Century Magazine
Collier's Weekly
Common Sense
The Commoner
The Congregationalist
The Crisis
Current Literature
The Etude

Everybody's Magazine
Everyman
The Forum
Four Minute Men News
The Fra
Frank Leslie's Illustrated Newspaper
Harper's Monthly
Harper's Weekly
Home Herald
The Independent
John Swinton's Paper
London Review of Books
The Miners' Magazine
Munsey's Magazine
The New Republic
Northwestern University Alumni News
The Outlook
The Philistine: A Periodical of Protest
The Princetonian
The Saturday Evening Post
Scribner's Monthly
The Socialist Woman
The Touchstone
The World To-Day
The World's Work

PRIMARY SOURCES

Abbott, Lyman. *Henry Ward Beecher*. Boston: Houghton, Mifflin, 1903.
Silhouettes of My Contemporaries. Garden City, NY: Doubleday, Page, 1922.
Addams, Jane. *Democracy and Social Ethics*. New York: Macmillan, 1902.
Twenty Years at Hull-House, with Autobiographical Notes. New York: Macmillan, 1910.
Austin, Gilbert. *Chironomia: Or a Treatise on Rhetorical Delivery*. London: T. Cadell and W. Davies, 1806.
Axson, Stockton. *"Brother Woodrow": A Memoir of Woodrow Wilson*. Arthur S. Link, ed. Princeton: Princeton University Press, 1993.
Badger, Joseph E., Jr. *Major Magnet, The Man of Nerve; or, the Muck-a-Mucks of Animas*. Beadle's New York Dime Library. New York: Beadle & Adams, 1889.
Baker, Ray Stannard. *Woodrow Wilson: Life and Letters*. 8 vols. Garden City, NY: Doubleday, Page, 1927–1939.
Balch, William Ralston. *Life and Public Services of James G. Blaine, with the Facts in the Career of John A. Logan*. Philadelphia: Thayer, Merriam, 1884.
Barber, Jonathan. *A Grammar of Elocution*. New Haven, CT: A. H. Maltby, 1830.

A Practical Treatise on Gesture. Cambridge, MA: Hilliard and Brown, 1831.

Barrows, John Henry. *Henry Ward Beecher: The Shakespeare of the Pulpit*. New York: Funk & Wagnalls, 1893.

Barton, Bruce. *The Man Nobody Knows: A Discovery of the Real Jesus*. Orig. pub. Indianapolis, IN: Bobbs-Merrill, 1925. Chicago: Ivan R. Dee, 2000.

Beecher, Henry Ward. "Oratory." Philadelphia: National School of Oratory, 1886.

Yale Lectures on Preaching. 3 vols. New York: J. B. Ford, 1872–1874.

Beecher, William C. and Samuel Scoville. *A Biography of Rev. Henry Ward Beecher*. New York: Charles L. Webster, 1888.

Beer, Thomas. *Hanna*. New York: Knopf, 1929.

Bell, Daniel. "The Day *Fortune* Lost Charisma." *Writing for Fortune: Nineteen Authors Remember Life on the Staff of a Remarkable Magazine*. New York: Time, 1980.

Bellow, Saul. *It All Adds Up: From the Dim Past to the Uncertain Future: A Nonfiction Collection*. New York: Viking Press, 1994.

Bentson, Henry Arthur. "A Psychological Study of a 'Billy' Sunday Revival." Ph. D. diss., Columbia University, 1916.

Bernays, Edward L. *Propaganda*. New York: Liveright, 1928.

Betts, Frederick W. *Billy Sunday: The Man and Method*. Boston: Murray, 1916.

The Billy Sunday Story, Irvin S. Yeaworth, Jr., dir. Orig. pub. Chester Springs, PA: Sacred Cinema/Westchester Films, ca. 1960. Garland, TX: Beacon Video Ministries, 1989.

Bishop, Joseph Bucklin. *Theodore Roosevelt and His Time, Shown in His Own Letters*. 2 vols. New York: Scribner, 1920.

Blaine, James G. "James A. Garfield Memorial Address." February 27, 1882. Washington, DC: Government Printing Office, 1882.

Political Discussions, Legislative, Diplomatic, and Popular, 1856–1886. Norwich, CT: Henry Bill, 1887.

Boyd, James P. *Life and Public Services of James G. Blaine, the Illustrious American Orator, Diplomat and Statesman*. Philadelphia: Publishers' Union, 1893.

Braniff, E. A. "How I Ran Out on Carrie Nation." *The Commonweal*, March 19, 1948: 558–560.

Bruce, William Cabell. *Recollections* and *The Inn of Existence*. Orig. pub. 1936. Rev. ed. Baltimore, MD: Gateway Press, 1998.

Bryan, William Jennings. *The First Battle: A Story of the Campaign of 1896*. Chicago: W. B. Conkey, 1896.

"Introduction." *The World's Famous Orations*, Vol. I, ed. William Jennings Bryan (New York: Funk and Wagnalls, 1906): x–xxx.

Speeches of William Jennings Bryan. 2 vols. New York: Funk & Wagnalls, 1909.

and Mary Baird Bryan. *The Memoirs of William Jennings Bryan*. Chicago: John C. Winston, 1925.

Buhite, Russell D. and David W. Levy, eds. *FDR's Fireside Chats*. Norman, OK: University of Oklahoma Press, 1992.

Burke, Robert E., ed. *The Diary Letters of Hiram Johnson, 1917–1945*. 7 vols. New York: Garland, 1983.
Cantril, Hadley and Gordon W. Allport. *The Psychology of Radio*. New York: Harper & Brothers, 1935.
Capra, Frank. *The Name above the Title: An Autobiography*. New York: Macmillan, 1971.
Carlyle, Thomas. *On Heroes, Hero-Worship, and the Heroic in History*. London: James Fraser, 1841.
Carnegie, Andrew. "The Negro in America." Speech delivered October 16, 1907. Inverness: Committee of Twelve, 1907.
Carnegie, Dale. *Public Speaking: A Practical Course for Business Men*. New York: Pocket Books, 1926.
Cary, Joyce. *The Case for African Freedom*. London: Secker & Warburg, 1944.
Commission on Industrial Relations. *Industrial Relations: Final Report and Testimony*. Vol. VII. Washington, DC: Government Printing Office, 1916.
"*Confessions of a Magnetizer*." Boston: Gleason's Publishing Hall, 1845.
Constantine, J. Robert, ed. *Debs Remembered: A Collection of Reminiscences*. Terre Haute, IN: Indiana State University (unpublished), 1981. Reel 5, Papers of Eugene V. Debs microfilm edition.
Conwell, Russell Herman. *Acres of Diamonds*. New York: Harper & Brothers, 1915.
Cooper, Thomas V. *Biographies of James G. Blaine, the Republican Candidate for President, and John A. Logan, the Republican Candidate for Vice President*. Chicago: Baird & Dillon, 1884.
Craig, Hardin. "Woodrow Wilson as an Orator." *Quarterly Journal of Speech*, Vol. 38 (April 1952): 145–148.
Crawford, Theron Clark. *James G. Blaine: A Study of His Life and Career*. Cleveland, OH: Edgewood Pub. Co., 1893.
Creel, George. *Complete Report of the Chairman of the Committee on Public Information*. Washington, DC: Government Printing Office, 1920.
How We Advertised America. New York: Harper & Brothers, 1920.
"Public Opinion in War Time." *Annals of the American Academy of Political and Social Science*, Vol. 78 (July 1918): 185–194.
Rebel at Large: Recollections of Fifty Crowded Years. New York: G. P. Putnam's Sons, 1947.
Wilson and the Issues. New York: Century, 1916.
Croly, Herbert David. "In Memoriam: David Goodman Croly – Estimates of the Man, His Character, and His Life's Work." *Real Estate Record and Builder's Guide*, May 18, 1889: 7.
The Promise of American Life. New York: Macmillan, 1909.
"Why I Wrote My Latest Book: My Aim in 'The Promise of American Life.'" *The World's Work*, Vol. 20 (June 1910): 13086.
Cumnock, Robert McLean. *Choice Readings for Public and Private Entertainments*. Rev. ed. Chicago: McClurg, 1898.
Daniels, George H. "'A Message to Garcia': How It Came to Be Written and Why a Million Copies of It Are Being Printed." Speech in New York, May, 22, 1899.

Darrow, Clarence. *The Story of My Life*. New York: Scribner, 1932.

Davis, Oscar King. *Released for Publication: Some Inside Political History of Theodore Roosevelt and His Times, 1898–1918*. Boston: Houghton Mifflin, 1925.

Debs, Eugene V. *Industrial Unionism*. Speech delivered December 10, 1905. New York: New York Labor News Co., 1906.

Labor and Freedom: The Voice and Pen of Eugene V. Debs. St. Louis: Phil Wagner, 1916.

Dell, Floyd. *Women as World Builders: Studies in Modern Feminism*. Chicago: Forbes, 1913.

Depew, Chauncey M. "Editorial Foreword." *The Library of Oratory: Ancient and Modern*, Vol. I, ed. Chauncey M. Depew (Akron, OH: The New Werner Co., 1902): i–iv.

The Disposal of the Subsidies Granted Certain Railroad Companies. Miscellaneous Documents, Report No. 176. House of Representatives, 44th Congress, First Session, 1876.

Doctorow, E. L. *Ragtime*. Orig. pub. 1974. New York: Plume, 1996.

Dos Passos, John. *1919*. Orig. pub. 1932. Boston: Houghton Mifflin, 2000.

"The Radio Voice." *Common Sense*, Vol. 3, No. 2 (February 1934): 17.

Du Bois, W. E. Burghardt. *The Souls of Black Folk: Essays and Sketches*. Chicago: A. C. McClurg, 1903.

Dunlap, Orrin E., Jr. *Talking On the Radio: A Practical Guide for Writing and Broadcasting a Speech*. New York: Greenberg, 1936.

Ellis, William T. *"Billy" Sunday: The Man and His Message*. Philadelphia: John C. Winston, 1914.

Emerson, Ralph Waldo. *The Journals and Miscellaneous Notebooks of Ralph Waldo Emerson, 1838–1842*. A. W. Plumstead and Harrison Hayward, eds. Cambridge, MA: Harvard University Press, 1969.

"Self-Reliance." Ralph Waldo Emerson, *Essays, First Series* (New York: Crowell, 1841): 32–68.

Finney, Charles Grandison. *Lectures on Revivals of Religion*. New York: Leavitt, Lord, & Co., 1835.

The Memoirs of Charles G. Finney: The Complete Restored Text. Garth M. Rosell and Richard A. G. Dupuis, eds. Grand Rapids, MI: Zondervan, 1989.

Sermons on Important Subjects. New York: John S. Taylor, 1834.

Flynn, Elizabeth Gurley. *The Rebel Girl: An Autobiography, My First Life (1906–1926)*. New York: International Publishers, 1973.

Fogarty, Robert S. *Desire & Duty at Oneida: Tirzah Miller's Intimate Memoir*. Bloomington, IN: Indiana University Press, 2000.

Foner, Philip S. and Robert James Branham, eds. *Lift Every Voice: African American Oratory, 1787–1900*. Tuscaloosa, AL: University of Alabama Press, 1998.

Foster, William Z. *From Bryan to Stalin*. New York: International Publishers, 1937.

Four Minute Men Bulletin No. 20, "Carrying the Message." Washington, DC: Committee on Public Information, November 26, 1917.

Frankenberg, Theodore Thomas. *Billy Sunday, His Tabernacles and Sawdust Trails: A Biographical Sketch of the Famous Baseball Evangelist.* Columbus, OH: F. J. Heer, 1917.

Fuessle, Milton. "Elbert Hubbard: Master of Advertising and Retailing." *The Advertising World*, Vol. 20, No. 3 (August–September 1915): 139–144.

Garland, Hamlin. *Roadside Meetings.* New York: Macmillan, 1930.

Garvey, Amy Jacques. *Garvey and Garveyism.* Kingston, Jamaica: United Printers, 1963.

ed. *The Philosophy & Opinions of Marcus Garvey: Or, Africa for the Africans.* 2 vols. New York: Universal Publishing House, 1923.

Gordon, Anna A. *The Beautiful Life of Frances E. Willard: A Memorial Volume.* Chicago: Woman's Temperance Publishing Association, 1898.

Grant, Robert. *Unleavened Bread.* New York: Scribner, 1900.

Grayson, Cary T. *Woodrow Wilson: An Intimate Memoir.* New York: Holt, Rinehart, 1960.

Hackett, Francis. *The Invisible Censor.* New York: B. W. Huebsch, 1921.

Hale, William Bayard. *The Story of a Style.* New York: B. W. Huebsch, 1920.

Hamill, S. S. *The Science of Elocution.* New York: Nelson & Phillips, 1872.

Harding, Warren G. "Back to Normal," speech delivered in Boston, May 14, 1920. Frederick E. Schortemeier, *Rededicating America: Life and Recent Speeches of Warren G. Harding* (Indianapolis, IN: Bobbs-Merrill, 1920): 223–229.

Harlan, Louis R., ed. *The Booker T. Washington Papers.* 12 vols. Urbana, IL: University of Illinois Press, 1972–1988.

Haywood, William D. "The Agitator." *The Miners' Magazine*, Vol. 3 (February 1902): 6.

Hill, Adams Sherman. *The Principles of Rhetoric and Their Application.* New York: Harper and Brothers, 1893.

House, Edward Mandell. *Philip Dru: Administrator.* New York: B. W. Huebsch, 1912.

Howe, Frederic C. *Confessions of a Reformer.* Kent, OH: Kent State University Press, 1925.

Howland, Harold. *Theodore Roosevelt and His Times: A Chronicle of the Progressive Movement.* New Haven, CT: Yale University Press, 1921.

Hubbard, Elbert. *A Message to Garcia: Being a Preachment.* East Aurora, NY: The Roycrofters, 1899.

In the Spotlight: Personal Experiences of Elbert Hubbard on the American Stage. Comp. John T. Hoyle. East Aurora, NY: The Roycrofters, 1917.

"Introduction." Henry Dickson, *Dickson's How to Speak in Public*, 3rd ed. (Chicago: Dickson School of Oratory, 1911): 5.

Little Journeys to the Homes of Eminent Orators. New York: G. P. Putnam/Knickerbocker Press, 1907.

Little Journeys to the Homes of Great Business Men: Andrew Carnegie. East Aurora, NY: The Roycrofters, 1909.

The Man of Sorrows: Being a Little Journey to the Home of Jesus of Nazareth. East Aurora, NY: The Roycrofters, 1908.

Hubbard, Elbert, II, ed. *In Memoriam: Elbert and Alice Hubbard.* East Aurora, NY: The Roycrofters, 1915.

Inherit the Wind. Stanley Kramer, dir. Beverly Hills, CA: United Artists, 1960.

James, Henry. "The Speech of American Women." *Henry James on Culture: Collected Essays on Politics and the American Social Scene*, ed. Pierre A. Walker (Lincoln, NE: University of Nebraska Press, 1999): 58–81.

James, William. "The Moral Equivalent of War." Leaflet no. 27. New York: American Association for International Conciliation, 1910.

Review of Gustave Le Bon, *The Crowd: A Study of the Popular Mind* (New York: Macmillan, 1896). *Psychological Review*, Vol. 4 (May 1897): 313–316.

The Varieties of Religious Experience: A Study in Human Nature. New York: Longmans, Green, 1902.

Johnson, James Weldon. *Black Manhattan*. New York: Knopf, 1930.

Johnson, Tom L. *My Story*. Elizabeth J. Hauser, ed. New York: B. W. Huebsch, 1911.

Johnson, Willis Fletcher. *Life of James G. Blaine, "The Plumed Knight."* Philadelphia: Atlantic Pub. Co., 1893.

Kerney, James. *The Political Education of Woodrow Wilson*. New York: Century, 1926.

Knox, Thomas W. *The Lives of James G. Blaine and John A. Logan, Republican Presidential Candidates of 1884*. Hartford, CT: Hartford Pub. Co., 1884.

Lansing, Robert. *War Memoirs of Robert Lansing*. Indianapolis, IN: Bobbs-Merrill, 1935.

Lasswell, Harold D. *Propaganda Technique in the World War*. New York: Peter Smith, 1927.

Le Bon, Gustave. *The Crowd: A Study of the Popular Mind*. Tr. of *La psychologie des foules*. New York: Macmillan, 1896.

Le Prade, Ruth, ed. *Debs and the Poets*. Pasadena, CA: Upton Sinclair, 1920.

Levine, Lawrence W. and Cornelia R. Levine. *The People and the President: America's Conversation with FDR*. Boston: Beacon Press, 2002.

Link, Arthur S., ed. *The Papers of Woodrow Wilson*. 69 vols. Princeton: Princeton University Press, 1966–1994.

Lippmann, Walter. *Drift and Mastery: An Attempt to Diagnose the Current Unrest*. New York: Kennerley, 1914.

"Integrated America." *The New Republic Book: Selections from the First Hundred Issues* (New York: Republic Pub. Co., 1916): 124–138.

The Phantom Public. New York: Harcourt, Brace, 1925.

Public Opinion. New York: Harcourt, Brace, 1922.

Lodge, Henry Cabot and Theodore Roosevelt. *Hero Tales from American History*. New York: Century, 1895.

Lynd, Robert S. and Helen Merrell Lynd. *Middletown: A Study in Modern American Culture*. New York: Harcourt Brace, 1929.

Middletown in Transition: A Study in Cultural Conflicts. New York: Harcourt Brace, 1937.

MacDonald, J. Ramsay. *Syndicalism: A Critical Examination*. London: Constable & Co., 1912.

Marcus Garvey: Look for Me in the Whirlwind. Stanley Nelson, dir. Arlington, VA: PBS Home Video, 2001.

Marden, Orison Swett. *Little Visits with Great Americans*. New York: The Success Company, 1903.

The Power of Personality. New York: T. Y. Crowell, 1906.

Marshall, Charles F. *The True History of the Brooklyn Scandal*. Philadelphia: National Publishing Company, 1874.

Martin, Everett Dean. *The Behavior of Crowds: A Psychological Study*. New York: Harper & Brothers, 1920.

McClure, Samuel Sidney. *My Autobiography*. New York: Frederick A. Stokes, 1914.

McCombs, William F. *Making Woodrow Wilson President*. Louis Jay Lang, ed. New York: Fairview, 1921.

McElvaine, Robert S., ed. *Down & Out in the Great Depression: Letters from the Forgotten Man*. Chapel Hill, NC: University of North Carolina Press, 1983.

McPherson, Aimee Semple. *This Is That: Personal Experiences, Sermons and Writings*. Los Angeles, CA: Bridal Call Publishing House, 1919.

Meet John Doe. Frank Capra, dir. Hollywood, CA: Warner Bros., 1941.

Maine State Legislature. *Memorial Addresses on the Life and Character of James Gillespie Blaine of Augusta*. Augusta, ME: Burleigh & Flynt, 1893.

Mencken, H. L. *H. L. Mencken's Smart Set Criticism*. William H. Nolte, ed. Ithaca, NY: Cornell University Press, 1968.

Prejudices. 6 vols. New York: Knopf, 1919–1927.

Merriam, Charles Edward. *Four American Party Leaders*. New York: Macmillan, 1926.

Merry, Glenn N. "Voice Inflection in Speech." *Psychological Monographs*, Vol. 31, No. 1 (1922): 205–229.

Mr. Blaine's Record: The Investigation of 1876 and the Mulligan Letters. Boston: Committee of One Hundred, 1884.

Mulzac, Hugh. *A Star to Steer By*. As told to Louis Burnham and Norval Welch. New York: International Publishers, 1963.

Niebuhr, Reinhold. *Moral Man and Immoral Society: A Study in Ethics and Politics*. New York: Scribner, 1932.

Nomad [Felicite Clarke]. *Varied Verse on Billy Sunday*. Tarrytown, NY: Roe Printing Co., 1924.

O'Hare, Kate Richards. "How I Became a Socialist Agitator." *The Socialist Woman*, Vol. 2 (October 1908): 4–5.

Oliver, Leon. *The Great Sensation*. Chicago: Beverly, 1873.

Outterson, Leslie A. *This I Believe – Thank You, Billy Sunday, for the Goodness and Mercy Which I Know*. Hicksville, NY: Exposition Press, 1977.

Paine, Albert Bigelow. *Th. Nast: His Period and His Pictures*. New York: Macmillan, 1904.

Parton, James. *Famous Americans of Recent Times*. Boston: Houghton, Mifflin, 1890.

Patterson, A. W. *Personal Recollections of Woodrow Wilson*. Richmond, VA: Whittet & Shepperson, 1929.

Payne, George Henry. *The Birth of the New Party, or Progressive Democracy*. Napierville, IL: H. E. Rennels, 1912.

Perkins, Frances. *The Roosevelt I Knew*. New York: Viking Press, 1946.

"Personal Gains from the Sunday Campaign: A Sheaf of Testimonies." *The Congregationalist*, February 22, 1917: 256–257.

Pinchot, Amos. *History of the Progressive Party 1912–1916*. Helene Maxwell Hooker, ed. Washington Square, NY: New York University Press, 1958.

Pond, James Burton. *Eccentricities of Genius: Memories of Famous Men and Women of the Platform and Stage*. New York: G. W. Dillingham, 1900.

Rauschenbusch, Walter. *Christianity and the Social Crisis*. New York: Macmillan, 1907.

Reisner, Christian F. *Roosevelt's Religion*. New York: Abingdon Press, 1922.

Richberg, Donald. *Tents of the Mighty*. New York: Willett, Clark & Colby, 1930.

Ridpath, John Clark and Selden Connor. *Life and Work of James G. Blaine*. Chicago: Dominion, 1893.

Rodeheaver, Homer. *Twenty Years with Billy Sunday*. Winona Lake, IN: Rodeheaver Hall-Mack, 1936.

Roosevelt, Theodore. *An Autobiography*. New York: Scribner, 1913.

Letters from Theodore Roosevelt to Anna Roosevelt Cowles, 1879–1918. New York: Scribner, 1924.

The Letters of Theodore Roosevelt. Elting E. Morison, ed. 8 vols. Cambridge, MA: Harvard University Press, 1951–1954.

"The Strenuous Life." Theodore Roosevelt, *The Strenuous Life: Essays and Addresses* (New York: Century, 1900): 1–24.

The Works of Theodore Roosevelt, memorial ed. Hermann Hagedorn, ed. 24 vols. New York: Scribner, 1923–1926.

Rosenman, Samuel I. *Working with Roosevelt*. New York: Harper & Brothers, 1952.

Ross, Edward Alsworth. *Seventy Years of It: An Autobiography*. New York: D. Appleton-Century, 1936.

Rush, James. *The Collected Works of James Rush*. Melvin H. Bernstein, ed. 4 vols. Weston, MA: M&S Press, 1974.

The Philosophy of the Human Voice. Philadelphia: J. Maxwell, 1827.

Russell, Charles Edward. *Blaine of Maine: His Life and Times*. New York: Cosmopolitan, 1931.

Sandburg, Carl. *The Letters of Carl Sandburg*. Herbert Mitgang, ed. New York: Harcourt, Brace and World, 1968.

Sandford, W. P. Review of Calvin Coolidge, *Foundations of the Republic: Speeches and Addresses* (New York: Scribner, 1926). *Quarterly Journal of Speech Education*, Vol. 13, No. 2 (April 1927): 197–199.

Sankey, Ira D. *My Life and the Story of the Gospel Hymns*. Philadelphia: The Sunday School Times Co., 1906.

Scopes, John T. and James Presley. *Center of the Storm: Memoirs of John T. Scopes*. New York: Holt, Rinehart and Winston, 1967.

Sedgwick, Ellery. *The Happy Profession*. Boston: Little, Brown, 1946.

Shaftesbury, Edmund [(Albert) Webster Edgerly]. *Sex Magnetism*. Meridien, CT: Ralston University Press, 1924.

The Two Sexes. Washington, DC: The Ralston Club, 1898.

Shaw, Anna Howard and Elizabeth Jordan. *The Story of a Pioneer*. New York: Harper & Brothers, 1915.

Shay, Felix. *Elbert Hubbard of East Aurora*. New York: William H. Wise, 1926.

Shuler, Robert P. "Bob." *McPhersonism: A Study of Healing Cults and Modern Day "Tongues" Movements*. Los Angeles, CA: Robert P. Shuler, 1924.

Sinclair, Upton. *The Brass Check: A Study of American Journalism*. Pasadena, CA: Upton Sinclair, 1920.

Slemp, C. Bascom. *The Mind of the President, as Revealed by Himself in His Own Words*. Garden City, NY: Doubleday, Page, 1926.

Smiles, Samuel. *Self-Help, with Illustrations of Character and Conduct*. London: John Murray, 1859.

Smith, Arthur D. Howden. *Mr. House of Texas*. New York: Funk and Wagnalls, 1940.

Smith-Irvin, Jeannette. *Footsoldiers of the Universal Negro Improvement Association: Their Own Words*. Trenton, NJ: Africa World Press, 1989.

Sohm, Rudolf. *Outlines of Church History*. Tr. May Sinclair. Orig. pub. 1895. London: Macmillan, 1931.

Southwick, F. Townsend. *Elocution and Action*. New York: Edgar S. Werner, 1890.

Stanton, Elizabeth Cady, Susan B. Anthony, and Matilda Joslyn Gage. *History of Woman Suffrage*. Vol. II, 1861–1876. Rochester, NY: Susan B. Anthony, 1881.

Steinbeck, John. "The Leader of the People." *Argosy*, August 1936: 99–106.

Stidger, William L. *That God's House May Be Filled: A Book of Modern Church Methods and Workable Plans*. New York: George H. Doran, 1924.

Stiles, Lela. *The Man behind Roosevelt: The Story of Louis McHenry Howe*. Cleveland, OH: World Pub. Co., 1954.

Stowe, Harriet Beecher. *Men of Our Times; Or, Leading Patriots of the Day*. Hartford, CT: Hartford Publishing Co., 1868.

Straus, Oscar S. *Under Four Administrations: From Cleveland to Taft*. Boston: Houghton Mifflin, 1922.

Sunday, Billy. *The Sawdust Trail: Billy Sunday in His Own Words*. Orig. pub. *Ladies' Home Journal*, September, October, November, December 1932, February, April 1933. Iowa City: University of Iowa Press, 2005.

Tarbell, Ida M. *A Short Life of Napoleon Bonaparte*. Orig. pub. *McClure's Magazine*, 1894. New York: S. S. McClure, 1895.

The Life of Abraham Lincoln. 2 vols. Orig. pub. *McClure's Magazine*, 1895. New York: S. S. McClure, 1895.

Tewksbury, J. H., ed. *Henry Ward Beecher as His Friends Saw Him*. New York: Pilgrim Press, 1904.

Theodore Tilton vs. Henry Ward Beecher, Action for Crim. Con. Tried in the City Court of Brooklyn. New York: McDivitt, Campbell, 1875.

Trachtenberg, Alexander. *Heritage of Gene Debs*. New York: International Publishers, 1928.

Tumulty, Joseph P. *Woodrow Wilson as I Know Him*. Garden City, NY: Doubleday, Page, 1921.

Twain, Mark [Samuel Clemens]. *Autobiography of Mark Twain: The Complete and Authoritative Edition.* Vol. 1. Harriet Elinor Smith, ed. Berkeley, CA: University of California Press, 2010.

U.S. Senate, Committee on Banking and Currency. *Stock Exchange Practices Hearing*, Part 5 (Insull), February 15, 16, and 17, 1933. Washington, DC: Government Printing Office, 1933.

Van Zile, Edward S. "A Magnetic Man." *Pittsburg Dispatch*, August 4, 1889: 9–10.

Washburn, Charles G. *Theodore Roosevelt: The Logic of His Career.* Boston: Houghton Mifflin, 1916.

Washington, Booker T. *Up from Slavery: An Autobiography.* New York: A. L. Burt, 1900.

Watson, James E. *As I Knew Them.* Indianapolis, IN: Bobbs-Merrill, 1936.

Watson, John B. "Psychology as the Behaviorist Views It," *Psychological Review*, Vol. 20, No. 2 (March 1, 1913): 158–177.

Psychology from the Standpoint of a Behaviorist. Philadelphia: Lippincott, 1919.

Weber, Max. *Economy and Society: An Outline of Interpretive Sociology.* 2 vols. Guenther Roth and Claus Wittich, ed. Tr. Ephraim Fischoff et al. Orig. pub. New York: Bedminster Press, 1968. Berkeley, CA: University of California Press, 1978.

From Max Weber: Essays in Sociology. H. H. Gerth and C. Wright Mills, ed. and tr. New York: Oxford University Press, 1946.

The Protestant Ethic and the Spirit of Capitalism. Tr. Talcott Parsons. Orig. pub. New York: Charles Scribner's Sons, 1930. Los Angeles, CA: Roxbury Publishing Co., 1996.

Wells, H. G. *The Shape of Things to Come.* New York: Macmillan, 1933.

Wescott, John W. *Woodrow Wilson's Eloquence.* Camden, NJ: I. F. Huntzinger, 1922.

White, Alma. *The Story of My Life.* Zarephath, NJ: Pillar of Fire, 1919.

White, William Allen. *The Autobiography of William Allen White.* New York: Macmillan, 1946.

"Introduction." Fremont Older, *My Own Story* (New York: Macmillan, 1926): v–xii.

Selected Letters of William Allen White. Walter Johnson, ed. New York: Henry Holt, 1947.

Whitlock, Brand. *Forty Years of It.* New York: D. Appleton, 1914.

Whitman, Walt. *Memoranda During the War.* Camden, NJ: Walt Whitman, 1875.

Willard, Frances E. *Glimpses of Fifty Years: The Autobiography of an American Woman.* Chicago: H. J. Smith, 1889.

Woman in the Pulpit. Boston: D. Lothrop, 1888.

Willson, Meredith. *The Music Man.* Morton DaCosta, dir. Burbank, CA: Warner Bros., 1962.

Wilson, Woodrow. *The Public Papers of Woodrow Wilson.* Ray Stannard Baker and William E. Dodd, eds. 6 vols. New York: Harper & Brothers, 1925–1926.

Wister, Owen. *Roosevelt: The Story of a Friendship.* New York: Macmillan, 1930.

Wood, Frederick S. *Roosevelt as We Knew Him*. Philadelphia: John C. Winston, 1927.

Yeilding, Kenneth D. and Paul H. Carlson, comp. *Ah That Voice: The Fireside Chats of Franklin Delano Roosevelt*. Odessa, TX: The John Ben Shepperd, Jr., Library of the Presidents, The Presidential Museum, 1974.

SECONDARY SOURCES

Adler, William M. *The Man who Never Died: The Life, Times, and Legacy of Joe Hill, American Labor Icon*. New York: Bloomsbury, 2011.

Albanese, Catherine L. *A Republic of Mind and Spirit: A Cultural History of American Metaphysical Religion*. New Haven, CT: Yale University Press, 2007.

Allen, Frederick Lewis. *Only Yesterday: An Informal History of the Nineteen-Twenties*. New York: Harper & Brothers, 1931.

Allen, Judith A. *The Feminism of Charlotte Perkins Gilman: Sexualities, Histories, Progressivism*. Chicago: University of Chicago Press, 2009.

Alpers, Benjamin L. *Dictators, Democracy, and American Public Culture: Envisioning the Totalitarian Enemy, 1920s-1950s*. Chapel Hill, NC: University of North Carolina Press, 2003.

Amenta, Edwin. *When Movements Matter: The Townsend Plan & the Rise of Social Security*. Princeton, NJ: Princeton University Press, 2006.

Applegate, Debby. *The Most Famous Man in America: The Biography of Henry Ward Beecher*. New York: Doubleday, 2006.

Ashburn, Frank D. *Peabody of Groton: A Portrait*. New York: Coward McCann, 1944.

Astro, Richard. "John Steinbeck." *A Literary History of the American West*, ed. J. Golden Taylor and Thomas J. Lyon (Fort Worth, TX: Texas Christian University Press, 1987): 424–446.

Atkinson, Max. *Our Masters' Voices: The Language and Body Language of Politics*. New York: Methuen, 1984.

Axelrod, Alan. *Selling the Great War: The Making of American Propaganda*. New York: Palgrave Macmillan, 2009.

Baker, Paula. "The Domestication of Politics: Women and American Political Society, 1780–1920." *American Historical Review*, Vol. 89, No. 3 (June 1984): 620–647.

Barnouw, Erik. *A Tower in Babel: A History of Broadcasting in the United States. Vol. 1 – to 1933*. New York: Oxford University Press, 1966.

Barrows, Susanna. *Distorting Mirrors: Visions of the Crowd in Late Nineteenth-Century France*. New Haven, CT: Yale University Press, 1981.

Baskerville, Barnet. *The People's Voice: The Orator in American Society*. Lexington, KY: University Press of Kentucky, 1979.

Basler, Roy P. *The Lincoln Legend: A Study in Changing Conceptions*. Boston: Houghton Mifflin, 1935.

Beard, Mary. "The Public Voice of Women." *London Review of Books*, Vol. 36, No. 6 (March 20, 2014): 11–14.

Beekman, Scott. *William Dudley Pelley: A Life in Right-Wing Extremism and the Occult*. Syracuse, NY: Syracuse University Press, 2005.

Behl, William Auburn. "The Speaking and Speeches of Theodore Roosevelt." Ph.D. diss., Northwestern University, 1942.

"Theodore Roosevelt's Principles of Speech Preparation and Delivery." *Speech Monographs*, Vol. 12, No. 1 (1945): 112–122.

Beisner, Robert L. "'Commune' in East Aurora." *American Heritage*, Vol. 22, No. 2 (February 1971): 72–75, 106–109.

Bennett, David H. *Demagogues in the Depression: American Radicals and the Union Party, 1932–1936*. New Brunswick, NJ: Rutgers University Press, 1969.

Bensel, Richard Franklin. *Passion and Preferences: William Jennings Bryan and the 1896 Democratic National Convention*. New York: Cambridge University Press, 2008.

Benson, Thomas W., ed., *American Rhetoric in the New Deal Era, 1932–1945*. East Lansing, MI: Michigan State University Press, 2006.

Bierley, Paul E. *John Philip Sousa, American Phenomenon*. Westerville, OH: Integrity Press, 1973.

Bittle, William E. and Gilbert Geis. *The Longest Way Home: Chief Alfred C. Sam's Back-to- Africa Movement*. Detroit, MI: Wayne State University Press, 1964.

Blackorby, Edward C. *Prairie Rebel: The Public Life of William Lemke*. Lincoln, NE: University of Nebraska Press, 1963.

Blight, David W. *Race and Reunion: The Civil War in American Memory*. Cambridge, MA: Belknap Press of Harvard University Press, 2001.

Blocker, Jack S., Jr. *"Give to the Winds Thy Fears": The Women's Temperance Crusade, 1873–1874*. Westport, CT: Greenwood Press, 1985.

Blumhofer, Edith L. *Aimee Semple McPherson: Everybody's Sister*. Grand Rapids, MI: Eerdmans, 1993.

Bode, Carl. *The American Lyceum: Town Meeting of the Mind*. Carbondale, IL: Southern Illinois University Press, 1956.

Bordin, Ruth. *Frances Willard: A Biography*. Chapel Hill, NC: University of North Carolina Press, 1986.

Boris, Eileen. *Art and Labor: Ruskin, Morris, and the Craftsman Ideal in America*. Philadelphia: Temple University Press, 1986.

Bowman, Matthew. *The Urban Pulpit: New York City and the Fate of Liberal Evangelicalism*. New York: Oxford University Press, 2014.

Boyer, Paul. *Urban Masses and Moral Order in America, 1820–1920*. Cambridge, MA and London: Harvard University Press, 1978.

Braden, Waldo W. and Earnest Brandenburg. "Roosevelt's Fireside Chats." *Speech Monographs*, Vol. 22, No. 5 (November 1955): 290–302.

Brands, H. W. "Politics as Performance Art: The Body English of Theodore Roosevelt." *The Presidency and Rhetorical Leadership*, ed. Leroy G. Dorsey (College Station, TX: Texas A&M University Press, 2002): 115–128.

Brawley, Benjamin. *The Negro in Literature and Art in the United States*. New York: Duffield, 1921.

Brigance, William Norwood, ed. *A History and Criticism of American Public Address*. Vols. 1–2. New York: McGraw-Hill, 1943.

"In the Workshop of Great Speakers." *American Speech*, Vol. 1 (August 1, 1926): 589–595.

Brinkley, Alan. *Voices of Protest: Huey Long, Father Coughlin, and the Great Depression*. New York: Knopf, 1982.

Broderick, Francis L. *Progressivism at Risk: Electing a President in 1912*. New York: Greenwood Press, 1989.

Brodsky, Alyn. *Benjamin Rush: Patriot and Physician*. New York: St. Martin's Press, 2004.

Brown, Victoria Bissell. *The Education of Jane Addams*. Philadelphia: University of Pennsylvania Press, 2004.

Buchanan, Lindal. *Regendering Delivery: The Fifth Canon and Antebellum Women Rhetors*. Carbondale, IL: Southern Illinois University Press, 2005.

Buckley, Kerry W. *Mechanical Man: John Broadus Watson and the Beginnings of Behaviorism*. New York: Guilford Press, 1989.

Burkett, Randall K. *Garveyism as a Religious Movement: The Institutionalization of a Black Civil Religion*. Metuchen, NJ: Scarecrow Press and American Theological Library Association, 1978.

Burnham, Kenneth E. *God Comes to America: Father Divine and the Peace Mission Movement*. Boston: Lambeth Press, 1979.

Burns, David. *The Life and Death of the Radical Historical Jesus*. New York: Oxford University Press, 2013.

Burns, James MacGregor. *Leadership*. New York: Harper & Row, 1978.

Calhoun, Charles W. *Benjamin Harrison*. New York: Henry Holt, 2005.

Minority Victory: Gilded Age Politics and the Front Porch Campaign of 1888. Lawrence, KS: University Press of Kansas, 2008.

Camic, Charles, Philip S. Gorski, and David M. Trubek, eds. *Max Weber's Economy and Society: A Critical Companion*. Stanford, CA: Stanford University Press, 2005.

Campbell, Karlyn Kohrs. *Man Cannot Speak For Her*. 2 vols. New York: Praeger, 1989.

Canning, Charlotte M. *The Most American Thing in America: Circuit Chautauqua as Performance*. Iowa City: University of Iowa Press, 2005.

Carlson, Peter. *Roughneck: The Life and Times of Big Bill Haywood*. New York: W. W. Norton, 1983.

Carpenter, Ronald H. *Father Charles E. Coughlin: Surrogate Spokesman for the Disaffected*. Westport, CT: Greenwood Press, 1998.

Carwardine, Richard J. *Evangelicals and Politics in Antebellum America*. New Haven, CT: Yale University Press, 1993.

Champney, Freeman. *Art & Glory: The Story of Elbert Hubbard*. New York: Crown Pub., 1968.

Chandler, Alfred D., Jr. *The Visible Hand: The Managerial Revolution in American Business*. Cambridge, MA: Belknap Press, 1977.

Chesebrough, David B. *Charles G. Finney: Revivalistic Rhetoric*. Westport, CT: Greenwood Press, 2002.

Clark, Clifford E., Jr. *Henry Ward Beecher: Spokesman for a Middle-Class America*. Urbana, IL: University of Illinois Press, 1978.

Clark, Gregory and S. Michael Halloran, eds. *Oratorical Culture in Nineteenth-Century America: Transformations in the Theory and Practice of Rhetoric*. Carbondale, IL: Southern Illinois University Press, 1993.

Cmiel, Kenneth. *Democratic Eloquence: The Fight over Popular Speech in Nineteenth-Century America*. New York: William Morrow, 1990.

Coffman, Edward M. *The War to End All Wars: The American Military Experience in World War I*. New York: Oxford University Press, 1968.

Cohen, David. *J. B. Watson: The Founder of Behaviourism*. London: Routledge and Kegan Paul, 1979.

Cohen, Herman. *The History of Speech Communication: The Emergence of a Discipline, 1914–1945*. Washington, DC: National Communication Association, 1994.

Coletta, Paolo E. *William Jennings Bryan*. 3 vols. Lincoln, NE: University of Nebraska Press, 1964–1969.

Conway, Jill. "Women Reformers and American Culture, 1870–1930." *Social History*, Vol. 5, No. 2 (Winter 1971–1972): 164–177.

Cooper, John Milton, Jr. *Breaking the Heart of the World: Woodrow Wilson and the Fight for the League of Nations*. New York: Cambridge University Press, 2001.

The Warrior and the Priest: Woodrow Wilson and Theodore Roosevelt. Cambridge, MA: Belknap Press of Harvard University Press, 1983.

Woodrow Wilson: A Biography. New York: Knopf, 2009.

Cornebise, Alfred E. *War as Advertised: The Four Minute Men and America's Crusade, 1917–1918*. Philadelphia: American Philosophical Society, 1984.

Corrigan, John. *Business of the Heart: Religion and Emotion in the Nineteenth Century*. Berkeley, CA: University of California Press, 2002.

Cott, Nancy F. *The Grounding of Modern Feminism*. New Haven, CT: Yale University Press, 1989.

Crafton, Donald. *The Talkies: American Cinema's Transition to Sound, 1926–1931*. New York: Scribner, 1997.

Craig, Douglas B. *Fireside Politics: Radio and Political Culture in the United States, 1920–1940*. Baltimore: Johns Hopkins University Press, 2000.

Cronon, E. David. *Black Moses: The Story of Marcus Garvey and the Universal Negro Improvement Association*. Madison, WI: University of Wisconsin Press, 1955.

Crunden, Robert M. *Ministers of Reform: The Progressives' Achievement in American Civilization, 1889–1920*. New York: Basic Books, 1982.

Cutlip, Scott M. *The Unseen Power: Public Relations, a History*. Hillsdale, NJ: Lawrence Erlbaum, 1994.

Dallam, Marie W. *Daddy Grace: A Celebrity Preacher and His House of Prayer*. New York: New York University Press, 2007.

Dalton, Kathleen. *Theodore Roosevelt: A Strenuous Life*. New York: Knopf, 2002.

"Why America Loved Theodore Roosevelt: Or Charisma is in the Eyes of the Beholders." *Psychohistory Review*, Vol. 8 (Winter 1979): 16–26.

Darnton, Robert. *Mesmerism and the End of the Enlightenment in France*. Cambridge, MA: Harvard University Press, 1968.

de Camp, L. Sprague. *The Great Monkey Trial*. Garden City, NY: Doubleday, 1968.

De Caux, Len. *The Living Spirit of the Wobblies*. New York: International Publishers, 1978.

Derman, Joshua. *Max Weber in Politics and Social Thought: From Charisma to Canonization*. Cambridge, UK: Cambridge University Press, 2012.

Donald, David. "Getting Right with Lincoln." David Donald, *Lincoln Reconsidered: Essays on the Civil War Era* (New York: Knopf, 1956): 3–14.

Donawerth, Jane. *Conversational Rhetoric: The Rise and Fall of a Women's Tradition, 1600–1900*. Carbondale, IL: Southern Illinois University Press, 2012.

Dorsett, Lyle W. *A Passion for Souls: The Life of D. L. Moody*. Chicago: Moody Press, 1997.

Billy Sunday and the Redemption of Urban America. Grand Rapids, MI: Eerdmans, 1991.

Douglas, Susan J. *Inventing American Broadcasting, 1899–1922*. Baltimore, MD: Johns Hopkins University Press, 1987.

Listening In: Radio and the American Imagination. New York: Random House, 1999.

Downs, Gregory P. *Declarations of Dependence: The Long Reconstruction of Popular Politics in the South, 1861–1908*. Chapel Hill, NC: University of North Carolina Press, 2011.

Dubofsky, Melvyn. *"Big Bill" Haywood*. New York: St. Martin's Press, 1987.

Dumenil, Lynn. *The Modern Temper: American Culture and Society in the 1920s*. New York: Hill and Wang, 1995.

Eastman, Carolyn. *A Nation of Speechifiers: Making an American Public after the Revolution*. Chicago: University of Chicago Press, 2009.

Edwards, Erica R. *Charisma and the Fictions of Black Leadership*. Minneapolis, MN: University of Minnesota Press, 2012.

Edwards, Rebecca. "Mary E. Lease and the Populists: A Reconsideration." *Kansas History: A Journal of the Central Plains*, Vol. 35 (Spring 2012): 26–41.

Evensen, Bruce J. *God's Man for the Gilded Age: D. L. Moody and the Rise of Modern Mass Evangelism*. New York: Oxford University Press, 2003.

Ewing, Adam. *The Age of Garvey: How a Jamaican Activist Created a Mass Movement and Changed Global Black Politics*. Princeton: Princeton University Press, 2014.

Farrell, John A. *Clarence Darrow: Attorney for the Damned*. New York: Doubleday, 2011.

Fink, Leon. *Progressive Intellectuals and the Dilemmas of Democratic Containment*. Cambridge, MA: Harvard University Press, 1997.

Fleser, Arthur F. *A Rhetorical Study of the Speaking of Calvin Coolidge*. Lewiston, NY: Edwin Mellen, 1990.

Forcey, Charles. *The Crossroads of Liberalism: Croly, Weyl, Lippmann, and the Progressive Era, 1900–1925*. New York: Oxford University Press, 1961.

Fox, Richard Wightman. *Jesus in America: Personal Savior, Cultural Hero, National Obsession*. New York: HarperCollins, 2004.

Trials of Intimacy: Love and Loss in the Beecher-Tilton Scandal. Chicago: University of Chicago Press, 1999.

Franzen, Trisha. *Anna Howard Shaw: The Work of Woman Suffrage*. Urbana, IL: University of Illinois Press, 2014.

Freidel, Frank. *Franklin D. Roosevelt: A Rendezvous with Destiny*. Boston: Little, Brown, 1990.

Frezza, Daria. *The Leader and the Crowd: Democracy in American Public Discourse, 1880–1941*. Tr. Martha King. Athens, GA: University of Georgia Press, 2007.

Friedenberg, Robert V. *Theodore Roosevelt and the Rhetoric of Militant Decency*. New York: Greenwood Press, 1990.

Frisken, Amanda. *Victoria Woodhull's Sexual Revolution: Political Theater and the Popular Press in Nineteenth-Century America*. Philadelphia: University of Pennsylvania Press, 2004.

Fuller, Robert C. *Mesmerism and the American Cure of Souls*. Philadelphia: University of Pennsylvania Press, 1982.

Fulop, Timothy E. " 'The Future Golden Day of the Race': Millennialism and Black Americans in the Nadir, 1877–1901." *Harvard Theological Review*, Vol. 84, No. 1 (January 1991): 75–99.

Gable, John Allen. *The Bull Moose Years: Theodore Roosevelt and the Progressive Party*. Port Washington, NY: Kennikat Press, 1978.

Gaines, Kevin K. *Uplifting the Race: Black Leadership, Politics, and Culture in the Twentieth Century*. Chapel Hill, NC: University of North Carolina Press, 1996.

Gallman, J. Matthew. *America's Joan of Arc: The Life of Anna Elizabeth Dickinson*. New York: Oxford University Press, 2006.

Gardner, Joseph L. *Departing Glory: Theodore Roosevelt as Ex-President*. New York: Scribner, 1973.

Gauld, Alan. *A History of Hypnotism*. Cambridge, UK: Cambridge University Press, 1992.

Gold, David and Catherine L. Hobbs, eds. *Rhetoric, History, and Women's Oratorical Education: American Women Learn to Speak*. New York: Routledge, 2013.

Goodale, Greg. "The Presidential Sound: From Orotund to Instructional Speech, 1892–1912." *Quarterly Journal of Speech*, Vol. 96, No. 2 (May 2010): 164–184.

Goodwyn, Lawrence. *Democratic Promise: The Populist Moment in America*. New York: Oxford University Press, 1976.

Gores, Stan. "The Attempted Assassination of Teddy Roosevelt." *The Wisconsin Magazine of History*, Vol. 53, No. 4 (Summer 1970): 269–277.

Gorn, Elliott J. *Mother Jones: The Most Dangerous Woman in America*. New York: Hill and Wang, 2001.

Gottschalk, Jane. "The Rhetorical Strategy of Booker T. Washington." *Phylon*, Vol. 27, No. 4 (4th Quarter 1966): 388–395.

Gould, Lewis L. *Four Hats in the Ring: The 1912 Election and the Birth of Modern American Politics*. Lawrence, KS: University Press of Kansas, 2008.

Grace, Fran. *Carry A. Nation: Retelling the Life*. Bloomington, IN: Indiana University Press, 2001.

Graham, Jeanne. "The Four Minute Men: Volunteers for Propaganda." *Southern Speech Journal*, Vol. 32 (Fall 1966): 49–57.

Grant, Colin. *Negro with a Hat: The Rise and Fall of Marcus Garvey*. New York: Oxford University Press, 2008.

Greenberg, David. *Republic of Spin: An Inside History of the American Presidency*. New York: W. W. Norton, 2016.

Greene, Theodore P. *America's Heroes: The Changing Models of Success in American Magazines*. New York: Oxford University Press, 1970.

Griffith, R. Marie. " 'Joy Unspeakable and Full of Glory': The Vocabulary of Pious Emotion in the Narratives of American Pentecostal Women, 1910–1945." *An Emotional History of the United States*, ed. Peter N. Stearns and Jan Lewis (New York: New York University Press, 1998): 218–241.

Grover, David H. "Elocution at Harvard: The Saga of Jonathan Barber." *Quarterly Journal of Speech*, Vol. 51, No. 1 (February 1965): 62–67.

Gutman, Herbert G. "Protestantism and the American Labor Movement: The Christian Spirit in the Gilded Age." *American Historical Review*, Vol. 72, No. 1 (October 1966): 74–101.

Hall, David D. "Review Essay: What is the Place of 'Experience' in Religious History?" *Religion and American Culture: A Journal of Interpretation*, Vol. 13, No. 2 (Summer 2003): 241–250.

Halloran, Fiona Deans. *Thomas Nast: The Father of Modern Political Cartoons*. Chapel Hill, NC: University of North Carolina Press, 2012.

Halttunen, Karen. *Confidence Men and Painted Women: A Study of Middle-Class Culture in America, 1830–1870*. New Haven: Yale University Press, 1982.

Hambrick-Stowe, Charles E. *Charles G. Finney and the Spirit of American Evangelicalism*. Grand Rapids, MI: Eerdmans, 1996.

Hamilton, Charles F. *As Bees in Honey Drown: Elbert Hubbard and the Roycrofters*. South Brunswick, UK: A. S. Barnes, 1973.

Hammer, Rusty. *P. S. Gilmore: The Authorized Biography of America's First Superstar*. Gainesville, FL: Rusty Hammer, 2006.

Hardman, Keith J. *Charles Grandison Finney, 1792–1875: Revivalist and Reformer*. Syracuse, NY: Syracuse University Press, 1987.

Harlan, Louis R. *Booker T. Washington: The Making of a Black Leader, 1856–1901*. New York: Oxford University Press, 1972.

Booker T. Washington: The Wizard of Tuskegee, 1901–1915. New York: Oxford University Press, 1983.

Harlow, Alvin F. *The Road of the Century: The Story of the New York Central*. New York: Creative Age Press, 1947.

Harold, Claudrena N. *The Rise and Fall of the Garvey Movement in the Urban South, 1918–1942*. New York: Routledge, 2007.

Harpine, William D. *From the Front Porch to the Front Page: McKinley and Bryan in the 1896 Presidential Campaign*. College Station, TX: Texas A&M University Press, 2005.

Harris, Neil. *Cultural Excursions: Marketing Appetites and Cultural Tastes in Modern America*. Chicago: University of Chicago Press, 1990.

Hauser, Gerard A. *Vernacular Voices: The Rhetoric of Publics and Public Spheres*. Columbia, SC: University of South Carolina Press, 1999.

Heckscher, August. *Woodrow Wilson*. New York: Scribner, 1991.

Helferich, Gerard. *Theodore Roosevelt and the Assassin: Madness, Vengeance, and the Campaign of 1912*. Guilford, CT: Lyons Press, 2013.

Hilgendorf, Maynard Donavon. "Billy Sunday: 'I Am Glad I Came to Detroit,' A Study of Rhetorical Strategies in the 1916 Campaign." Ph.D. diss., University of Michigan, 1985.

Hochmuth, Marie Kathryn, ed. *A History and Criticism of American Public Address*. Vol. 3. New York: Longmans, Green, 1955.

Hodgson, Godfrey. *Woodrow Wilson's Right Hand: The Life of Colonel Edward M. House*. New Haven, CT: Yale University Press, 2006.

Hofstadter, Richard. *The Age of Reform: From Bryan to F. D. R.* New York: Knopf, 1955.

The American Political Tradition and the Men Who Made It. Orig. pub. New York: Knopf, 1948. New York: Vintage Books, 1989.

Hogan, J. Michael. *Woodrow Wilson's Western Tour: Rhetoric, Public Opinion, and the League of Nations*. College Station, TX: Texas A&M University Press, 2006.

ed. *Rhetoric and Reform in the Progressive Era*. East Lansing, MI: Michigan State University Press, 2003.

Hollihan, Thomas A. "Propagandizing in the Interest of War: A Rhetorical Study of the Committee on Public Information." *Southern Speech Communication Journal*, Vol. 49 (Spring 1984): 241–257.

Horner, Charles F. *Strike the Tents: The Story of the Chautauqua*. Philadelphia: Dorrance, 1954.

Horowitz, Joseph. *Wagner Nights: An American History*. Berkeley, CA: University of California Press, 1994.

Howe, Daniel Walker. *Making the American Self: Jonathan Edwards to Abraham Lincoln*. Cambridge, MA: Harvard University Press, 1997.

Hungerford, Edward. *Men and Iron: The History of the New York Central*. New York: Thomas Y. Crowell, 1938.

Hyland, Jack. *Evangelism's First Modern Media Star: The Life of Reverend Bill Stidger*. New York: Cooper Square Press, 2002.

Jackson, David H., Jr. *Booker T. Washington and the Struggle against White Supremacy: The Southern Educational Tours, 1908–1912*. New York: Palgrave Macmillan, 2008.

Jacoby, Susan. *The Great Agnostic: Robert Ingersoll and American Freethought*. New Haven: Yale University Press, 2013.

Jamieson, Kathleen Hall. *Eloquence in an Electronic Age: The Transformation of Political Speechmaking*. New York: Oxford University Press, 1988.

Jeansonne, Glen. *Gerald L. K. Smith: Minister of Hate*. New Haven, CT: Yale University Press, 1988.

Jensen, Richard J. *Clarence Darrow: The Creation of an American Myth*. New York: Greenwood Press, 1992.

Jividen, Jason R. *Claiming Lincoln: Progressivism, Equality, and the Battle for Lincoln's Legacy in Presidential Rhetoric*. DeKalb, IL: Northern Illinois University Press, 2011.

Johnson, Nan. *Gender and Rhetorical Space in American Life, 1866–1910*. Carbondale, IL: Southern Illinois University Press, 2002.

Joiner, Thekla Ellen. *Sin in the City: Chicago and Revivalism, 1880–1920*. Columbia, MO: University of Missouri Press, 2007.

Jones, Howard Mumford. *The Age of Energy: Varieties of American Experience, 1865–1915*. New York: Viking, 1971.

Jones, Stanley Llewellyn. *The Presidential Election of 1896*. Madison, WI: University of Wisconsin Press, 1964.

Jowett, Garth. *Film: The Democratic Art*. Boston: Little, Brown, 1976.

Kasson, John F. *Houdini, Tarzan, and the Perfect Man: The White Male Body and the Challenge of Modernity in America*. New York: Hill and Wang, 2001.

Kazin, Michael. *A Godly Hero: The Life of William Jennings Bryan*. New York: Knopf, 2006.

The Populist Persuasion: An American History. New York: Basic Books, 1995.

Keller, Morton. *The Art and Politics of Thomas Nast*. New York: Oxford University Press, 1968.

Kelley, Robin D. G. *Race Rebels: Culture, Politics, and the Black Working Class*. New York: The Free Press, 1994.

Kemp, Giles and Edward Claflin. *Dale Carnegie: The Man Who Influenced Millions*. New York: St. Martin's Press, 1989.

Kennedy, David M. *Over Here: The First World War and American Society*. New York: Oxford University Press, 1980.

Kersten, Andrew E. *Clarence Darrow: American Iconoclast*. New York: Hill and Wang, 2011.

Kidd, Thomas S. *George Whitefield: America's Spiritual Founding Father*. New Haven: Yale University Press, 2014.

Kloppenberg, James T. *Uncertain Victory: Social Democracy and Progressivism in European and American Thought, 1870–1920*. New York: Oxford University Press, 1986.

Knight, Louise W. *Citizen: Jane Addams and the Struggle for Democracy*. Chicago: University of Chicago Press, 2005.

Knox, Graham. "Political Change in Jamaica (1866–1906) and the Local Reaction to the Policies of the Crown Colony Government." *The Caribbean in Transition: Papers on Social, Political, and Economic Development*, ed. F. M. Andic and T. G. Mathews (Rio Piedras, PR: Institute of Caribbean Studies, 1965): 141–162.

Kostlevy, William. *Holy Jumpers: Evangelicals and Radicals in Progressive Era America*. New York: Oxford University Press, 2010.

Koszarski, Richard. *An Evening's Entertainment: The Age of the Silent Feature Picture, 1915–1928*. New York: Scribner, 1990.

Kraig, Robert Alexander. *Woodrow Wilson and the Lost World of the Oratorical Statesman*. College Station, TX: Texas A&M University Press, 2004.

Kramer, Jacob. *The New Freedom and the Radicals: Woodrow Wilson, Progressive Views of Radicalism, and the Origins of Repressive Tolerance*. Philadelphia: Temple University Press, 2015.

Ladefoged, Peter and Ian Maddieson. *The Sounds of the World's Languages*. Malden, MA: Blackwell Publishing, 1996.

Larson, Edward J. *Summer for the Gods: The Scopes Trial and America's Continuing Debate over Science and Religion*. New York: Basic Books, 1997.

Leach, William. *Land of Desire: Merchants, Power, and the Rise of a New American Culture*. New York: Pantheon, 1993.

Lears, T. J. Jackson. "From Salvation to Self-Realization: Advertising and the Therapeutic Roots of the Consumer Culture, 1880–1930." *The Culture of Consumption: Critical Essays in American History, 1880–1930*, ed. Richard Wightman Fox and T. J. Jackson Lears (New York: Pantheon, 1983): 3–38.

No Place of Grace: Antimodernism and the Transformation of American Culture, 1880–1920. New York: Pantheon, 1981.

"Sherwood Anderson: Looking for the White Spot." *The Power of Culture: Critical Essays in American History*, ed. Richard Wightman Fox and T. J. Jackson Lears (Chicago: University of Chicago Press, 1993), 13–37.

Lenthall, Bruce. *Radio's America: The Great Depression and the Rise of Modern Mass Culture*. Chicago: University of Chicago Press, 2007.

Leone, Massimo. *Religious Conversion and Identity: The Semiotic Analysis of Texts*. London: Routledge, 2004.

Levander, Caroline Field. *Voices of the Nation: Women and Public Speech in Nineteenth-Century American Literature and Culture*. Cambridge, UK: Cambridge University Press, 1998.

Levine, Lawrence W. *Defender of the Faith: William Jennings Bryan: The Last Decade, 1915–1925*. New York: Oxford University Press, 1965.

The Unpredictable Past: Explorations in American Cultural History. New York: Oxford University Press, 1993.

Levy, David W. *Herbert Croly of* The New Republic*: The Life and Thought of an American Progressive*. Princeton: Princeton University Press, 1985.

Lewis, David Levering. *W. E. B. Du Bois, 1868–1919: Biography of a Race*. New York: Henry Holt, 1993.

Lewis, W. David. "Peter L. Jensen and the Amplification of Sound." *Technology in America: A History of Individuals and Ideas*, 2nd ed., ed. Carroll W. Pursell, Jr. (orig. pub. 1979; Cambridge, MA: MIT Press, 1990): 190–210.

Lienesch, Michael. *In the Beginning: Fundamentalism, the Scopes Trial, and the Making of the Antievolution Movement*. Chapel Hill, NC: University of North Carolina Press, 2007.

Link, Arthur S. *Wilson: Campaigns for Progressivism and Peace, 1916–1917*. Princeton: Princeton University Press, 1965.

Linkugel, Wil A. and Martha Solomon. *Anna Howard Shaw: Suffrage Orator and Reformer*. New York: Greenwood Press, 1991.

Litwack, Leon F. *Trouble in Mind: Black Southerners in the Age of Jim Crow*. New York: Knopf, 1998.

Lofton, Kathryn E. *Oprah: The Gospel of an Icon*. Berkeley, CA: University of California Press, 2011.

"The Preacher Paradigm: Promotional Biographies and the Modern-Made Evangelist." *Religion and American Culture: A Journal of Interpretation*, Vol. 16, No. 1 (Winter 2006): 95–123.

Logan, Rayford W. *The Negro in American Life and Thought: The Nadir, 1877–1901*. New York: Dial Press, 1954.

Loviglio, Jason. *Radio's Intimate Public: Network Broadcasting and Mass-Mediated Democracy*. Minneapolis, MN: University of Minnesota Press, 2005.

Lower, Richard Coke. *A Bloc of One: The Political Career of Hiram W. Johnson*. Stanford, CA: Stanford University Press, 1993.

Lunsford, Andrea A., ed. *Reclaiming Rhetorica: Women in the Rhetorical Tradition*. Pittsburgh, PA: University of Pittsburgh Press, 1995.

Lutholtz, M. William. *Grand Dragon: D. C. Stephenson and the Ku Klux Klan in Indiana*. West Lafayette, IN: Purdue University Press, 1991.

MacDonald, J. Fred. *Don't Touch That Dial! Radio Programming in American Life, 1920–1960*. Chicago: Nelson-Hall, 1991.

Malin, Brenton J. *Feeling Mediated: A History of Media Technology and Emotion in America*. New York: New York University Press, 2014.

Manchester, William. *Disturber of the Peace: The Life of H. L. Mencken*. New York: Harper & Brothers, 1950.

Manela, Erez. *The Wilsonian Moment: Self-Determination and the International Origins of Anticolonial Nationalism*. New York: Oxford University Press, 2007.

Marchand, Roland. *Advertising the American Dream: Making Way for Modernity, 1920–1940*. Berkeley, CA: University of California Press, 1985.

Martin, Robert F. *Hero of the Heartland: Billy Sunday and the Transformation of American Society, 1862–1935*. Bloomington, IN: Indiana University Press, 2002.

Martin, Tony. *Race First: The Ideological and Organizational Struggles of Marcus Garvey and the Universal Negro Improvement Association*. Westport, CT: Greenwood Press, 1976.

Mastrangelo, Lisa. "World War I, Public Intellectuals, and the Four Minute Men: Convergent Ideals of Public Speaking and Civic Participation." *Rhetoric & Public Affairs*, Vol. 12, No. 4 (Winter 2009): 607–633.

Mattern, Grace. "The Biography of Robert McLean Cumnock." M.A. thesis, Northwestern University, 1929.

Mattson, Kevin. *Creating a Democratic Public: The Struggle for Urban Participatory Democracy During the Progressive Era*. University Park, PA: Pennsylvania State University Press, 1998.

"What the Heck Are You Up To, Mr. President?": Jimmy Carter, America's "Malaise," and the Speech That Should Have Changed the Country. New York: Bloomsbury, 2009.

May, Henry F. *The End of American Innocence: A Study of the First Years of Our Own Time, 1912–1917*. New York: Knopf, 1959.

McClay, Wilfred M. *The Masterless: Self & Society in Modern America*. Chapel Hill, NC: University of North Carolina Press, 1994.

McCormick, Mike. *Terre Haute: Queen City of the Wabash*. Charleston, SC: Arcadia Publishing, 2005.

McGerr, Michael E. *A Fierce Discontent: The Rise and Fall of the Progressive Movement in America, 1870–1920*. Orig. pub. The Free Press, 2003. New York: Oxford University Press, 2005.

The Decline of Popular Politics: The American North, 1865–1928. New York: Oxford University Press, 1986.

"Political Style and Women's Power, 1830–1930." *Journal of American History*, Vol. 77, No. 3 (December 1990): 864–885.

McKanan, Dan. *Prophetic Encounters: Religion and the American Radical Tradition*. Boston: Beacon Press, 2011.

McLoughlin, William G., Jr. "Aimee Semple McPherson: 'Your Sister in the King's Glad Service.' " *Journal of Popular Culture*, Vol. 1, No. 3 (Winter 1967): 193–217.

"Billy Sunday and the Working Girl of 1915." *Journal of Presbyterian History*, Vol. 54 (Fall 1976): 376–384.

Billy Sunday Was His Real Name. Chicago: University of Chicago Press, 1955.

The Meaning of Henry Ward Beecher: An Essay on the Shifting Values of Mid-Victorian America, 1840–1870. New York: Knopf, 1970.

Modern Revivalism: Charles Grandison Finney to Billy Graham. New York: Ronald Press, 1959.

"Professional Evangelism: The Social Significance of Religious Revivals since 1865." 2 vols. Ph.D. diss., Harvard University, 1953.

Revivals, Awakenings, and Reform: An Essay on Religion and Social Change in America, 1607–1977. Chicago: University of Chicago Press, 1978.

McMullen, Josh. *Under the Big Top: Big Tent Revivalism and American Culture, 1885–1925*. New York: Oxford University Press, 2015.

Melder, Keith. "Bryan the Campaigner." *Contributions from the Museum of History and Technology*, Paper 46. Washington, DC: Smithsonian, 1965.

Milkis, Sidney M. *Theodore Roosevelt, the Progressive Party, and the Transformation of American Democracy*. Lawrence, KS: University Press of Kansas, 2009.

Miller, Kenneth E. *From Progressive to New Dealer: Frederic C. Howe and American Liberalism*. University Park, PA: Pennsylvania State University Press, 2010.

Mock, James R. and Cedric Larson. *Words that Won the War: The Story of the Committee on Public Information, 1917–1919*. Princeton: Princeton University Press, 1939.

Moore, Leonard J. *Citizen Klansmen: The Ku Klux Klan in Indiana, 1921–1928*. Chapel Hill, NC: University of North Carolina Press, 1991.

Moore, R. Laurence. *Selling God: American Religion in the Marketplace of Culture*. New York: Oxford University Press, 1994.

Morgan, David. "Protestant Visual Culture and the Challenges of Urban America during the Progressive Era." *Faith in the Market: Religion and the Rise of Urban Commercial Culture*, ed. John M. Giggie and Diane Winston (New Brunswick, NJ: Rutgers University Press, 2002): 37–56.

Morgan, H. Wayne. *Eugene V. Debs: Socialist for President*. Syracuse, NY: Syracuse University Press, 1962.

Morris, Edmund. *The Rise of Theodore Roosevelt*. New York: Coward, McCann and Geoghegan, 1979.

Moses, Wilson Jeremiah. *Black Messiahs and Uncle Toms: Social and Literary Manipulations of a Religious Myth*. University Park, PA: Pennsylvania State University Press, 1982.

Moss, M. S. "Guide to the Winifred Ward (1884–1975) Papers." Northwestern University, 1974. Accessed March 29, 2014. http://findingaids.library.northwestern.edu/catalog/inu-ead-nua-archon-1144.

Mowry, George E. *The California Progressives*. Berkeley, CA: University of California Press, 1951.

Theodore Roosevelt and the Progressive Movement. New York: Hill and Wang, 1946.

Muzzey, David Saville. *James G. Blaine: A Political Idol of Other Days*. New York: Dodd, Mead, 1935.

Nadis, Fred. *Wonder Shows: Performing Science, Magic, and Religion in America*. New Brunswick, NJ: Rutgers University Press, 2005.

Nasaw, David. *Going Out: The Rise and Fall of Public Amusements*. New York: Basic Books, 1993.

Nelson, H. Viscount "Berky." *The Rise and Fall of Modern Black Leadership: Chronicle of a Twentieth Century Tragedy*. Lanham, MD: University Press of America, 2003.

Neu, Charles E. *Colonel House: A Biography of Woodrow Wilson's Silent Partner*. New York: Oxford University Press, 2015.

Norrell, Robert J. *Up from History: The Life of Booker T. Washington*. Cambridge, MA: Belknap Press of Harvard University Press, 2009.

Numbers, Ronald L. *Darwinism Comes to America*. Cambridge, MA: Harvard University Press, 1998.

Nye, Robert A. *The Origins of Crowd Psychology: Gustave Le Bon and the Crisis of Mass Democracy in the Third Republic*. London: Sage Publications, 1975.

O'Toole, Patricia. *When Trumpets Call: Theodore Roosevelt After the White House*. New York: Simon & Schuster, 2005.

Osborn, George C. "Woodrow Wilson as a Speaker." *Southern Speech Journal*, Vol. 22, No. 2 (1956): 61–72.

Owens, Louis. "The Culpable Joads: Desentimentalizing the Grapes of Wrath." *Critical Essays on Steinbeck's The Grapes of Wrath*, ed. John Ditsky (Boston: G. K. Hall, 1989): 108–116.

Pearson, Judy. "Rheba Crawford's Public Ministry." M.A. thesis, California State University, Long Beach, 1995.

Peretti, Burton W. *The Leading Man: Hollywood and the Presidential Image*. New Brunswick, NJ: Rutgers University Press, 2012.

Perino, Michael. *The Hellhound of Wall Street: How Ferdinand Pecora's Investigation of the Great Crash Forever Changed American Finance*. New York: Penguin, 2010.

Perry, Jeffrey B. *Hubert Harrison: The Voice of Harlem Radicalism, 1883–1918*. New York: Columbia University Press, 2009.

Pitzer, Donald Elden. "The Ohio Campaigns of Billy Sunday with Special Emphasis upon the 1913 Columbus Revival." M.A. thesis, Ohio State University, 1962.

Pope-Levison, Priscilla. *Building the Old Time Religion: Women Evangelists in the Progressive Era*. New York: New York University Press, 2013.

Postel, Charles. *The Populist Vision*. New York: Oxford University Press, 2007.

Potts, John. *A History of Charisma*. Houndmills, UK: Palgrave Macmillan, 2009.

Putnam, Carleton. *Theodore Roosevelt: The Formative Years, 1858–1886*. New York: Scribner, 1958.

Putney, Clifford. *Muscular Christianity: Manhood and Sports in Protestant America, 1880–1920*. Cambridge, MA: Harvard University Press, 2001.

Rambo, Lewis R. *Understanding Religious Conversion*. New Haven, CT: Yale University Press, 1993.

Ranson, Edward. *The Role of Radio in the American Presidential Election of 1924: How a New Communications Technology Shapes the Political Process*. Lewiston, NY: Edwin Mellen, 2010.

Ray, Angela G. *The Lyceum and Public Culture in the Nineteenth-Century United States*. East Lansing, MI: Michigan State University Press, 2005.

Reynolds, John F. "The Hustling Candidate and the Advent of the Direct Primary: A California Case Study." *Journal of the Gilded Age and Progressive Era*, Vol. 12, No. 1 (January 2013): 31–64.

Rieser, Andrew C. *The Chautauqua Moment: Protestants, Progressives, and the Culture of Modern Liberalism*. New York: Columbia University Press, 2003.

Robinson, Thomas A. and Lanette D. Ruff. *Out of the Mouths of Babes: Girl Evangelists in the Flapper Era*. New York: Oxford University Press, 2012.

Rolde, Neil. *Continental Liar from the State of Maine: James G. Blaine*. Gardiner, ME: Tilbury House, 2006.

Rolinson, Mary G. *Grassroots Garveyism: The Universal Negro Improvement Association in the Rural South, 1920–1927*. Chapel Hill, NC: University of North Carolina Press, 2007.

Ross, Thomas Richard. *Jonathan Prentiss Dolliver: A Study in Political Integrity and Independence*. Iowa City, IA: State Historical Society of Iowa, 1958.

Ryan, Halford R. *Franklin D. Roosevelt's Rhetorical Presidency*. New York: Greenwood Press, 1988.

Henry Ward Beecher: Peripatetic Preacher. New York: Greenwood Press, 1990.

Salvatore, Nick. *Eugene V. Debs: Citizen and Socialist*. 2nd ed. Urbana, IL: University of Illinois Press, 2007.

Schonberg, Harold C. *The Great Conductors*. New York: Simon and Schuster, 1967.

Schultz, James R. *The Romance of Small-Town Chautauquas*. Columbia, MO: University of Missouri Press, 2002.

Schuster, David G. *Neurasthenic Nation: America's Search for Health, Happiness, and Comfort, 1869–1920*. New Brunswick, NJ: Rutgers University Press, 2011.

Seymour, Harold and Dorothy Seymour Mills. *Baseball: The Golden Age*. New York: Oxford University Press, 1989.

Shamir, Boas, Robert J. House, and Michael B. Arthur. "The Motivational Effects of Charismatic Leadership: A Self-Concept Based Theory." *Organization Science*, Vol. 4, No. 4 (November 1993): 577–594.

Sharf, Robert H. "Experience."*Critical Terms for Religious Studies*, ed. Mark C. Taylor (Chicago: University of Chicago Press, 1998): 94–116.

Shuler, Robert P., III. *Fighting Bob Shuler of Los Angeles: God's Man for the Issues of His Time*. Indianapolis, IN: Dog Ear Publishing, 2011.

Sicherman, Barbara. *Well-Read Lives: How Books Inspired a Generation of American Women*. Charlotte, NC: University of North Carolina Press, 2010.

Sievers, Harry J. *Benjamin Harrison, Hoosier Statesman: From the Civil War to the White House, 1865–1888*. New York: University Publishers, 1959.

Signorello, Rosario and Didier Demolin. "The Physiological Use of the Charismatic Voice in Political Speech." Proceedings of Interspeech 2013, Lyon, FR, August 25–29, 2013, 987–991.

Six, Janet L. "Hidden History of Ralston Heights: The Story of New Jersey's Failed 'Garden of Eden.' " *Archaeology*, Vol. 57, No. 3 (May/June 2004): 30–35.

"Material Symbol: The Role of the Garden in the Transmission of Meaning." M.A. thesis, University of Pennsylvania, 2003.

Sizer, Sandra S. *Gospel Hymns and Social Religion: The Rhetoric of Nineteenth-Century Revivalism*. Philadelphia: Temple University Press, 1978.

Sklansky, Jeffrey. *The Soul's Economy: Market Society and Selfhood in American Thought, 1820–1920*. Chapel Hill, NC: University of North Carolina Press, 2002.

Skocpol, Theda. "The Tocqueville Problem: Civic Engagement in American Democracy." *Social Science History*, Vol. 21, No. 4 (Winter 1997): 455–479.

Slout, William Lawrence. *Theatre in a Tent: The Development of a Provincial Entertainment*. Bowling Green, OH: Bowling Green University Popular Press, 1972.

Smith, Gene. *When the Cheering Stopped: The Last Years of Woodrow Wilson*. New York: William Morrow, 1964.

Smith, Ira R. T. and Joe Alex Morris. *"Dear Mr. President . . .": The Story of Fifty Years in the White House Mail Room*. New York: Julian Messner, 1949.

Smith, Jean Edward. *FDR*. New York: Random House, 2007.

Smoodin, Eric. " 'This Business of America': Fan Mail, Film Reception, and Meet John Doe." *Screen*, Vol. 37, No. 2 (Summer 1996): 111–128.

Spencer, Samuel R., Jr. *Booker T. Washington and the Negro's Place in American Life*. New York: Little, Brown, 1955.

Springen, Donald K. *William Jennings Bryan: Orator of Small-Town America*. New York: Greenwood Press, 1991.

Sproule, J. Michael. *Propaganda and Democracy: The American Experience of Media and Mass Persuasion*. Cambridge, UK: Cambridge University Press, 1997.

Stanger, Howard R. "From Factory to Family: The Creation of a Corporate Culture in the Larkin Company of Buffalo, New York." *Business History Review*, Vol. 74, No. 3 (Autumn 2000): 407–433.

Stanley, Susie Cunningham. *Feminist Pillar of Fire: The Life of Alma White*. Cleveland, OH: Pilgrim Press, 1993.

Stearns, Peter N. *American Cool: Constructing a Twentieth-Century Emotional Style*. New York: New York University Press, 1994.

and Carol Z. Stearns. "Emotionology: Clarifying the History of Emotions and Emotional Standards." *American Historical Review*, Vol. 90, No. 4 (October 1985): 813–836.

Steel, Ronald. *Walter Lippmann and the American Century*. Orig. pub. Little, Brown, 1980. New Brunswick, NJ: Transaction Pub., 1999.

Stein, Judith. *The World of Marcus Garvey: Race and Class in Modern Society*. Baton Rouge, LA: Louisiana State University Press, 1986.

Stettner, Edward A. *Shaping Modern Liberalism: Herbert Croly and Progressive Thought*. Lawrence, KS: University Press of Kansas, 1993.

Stid, Daniel. "Rhetorical Leadership and 'Common Counsel' in the Presidency of Woodrow Wilson." *Speaking to the People: The Rhetorical Presidency in Historical Perspective*, ed. Richard J. Ellis (Amherst, MA: University of Massachusetts Press, 1998): 162–181.

Stout, Harry S. *The Divine Dramatist: George Whitefield and the Rise of Modern Evangelicalism*. Grand Rapids, MI: Eerdmans, 1991.

Stuckey, Mary E. *The Good Neighbor: Franklin D. Roosevelt and the Rhetoric of American Power*. East Lansing, MI: Michigan State University Press, 2013.

Summers, Martin. *Manliness and Its Discontents: The Black Middle Class and the Transformation of Masculinity, 1900–1930*. Chapel Hill, NC: University of North Carolina Press, 2004.

Sumner, Nancy Ann McCowan. "Orison Swett Marden: The American Samuel Smiles." Ph.D. diss., Brown University, 1981.

Susman, Warren I. *Culture as History*. New York: Pantheon, 1984.

Sussmann, Leila A. *Dear FDR: A Study of Political Letter-Writing*. Totowa, NJ: Bedminster Press, 1963.

Sutton, Matthew Avery. *Aimee Semple McPherson and the Resurrection of Christian America*. Cambridge, MA: Harvard University Press, 2007.

American Apocalypse: A History of Modern Evangelicalism. Cambridge, MA: Belknap Press of Harvard University Press, 2014.

Tapia, John E. *Circuit Chautauqua: From Rural Education to Popular Entertainment*. Jefferson, NC: McFarland & Co., 1997.

Taves, Ann. *Fits, Trances, & Visions: Experiencing Religion and Explaining Experience from Wesley to James*. Princeton: Princeton University Press, 1999.

Taylor, Timothy D. *The Sounds of Capitalism: Advertising, Music, and the Conquest of Culture*. Chicago: University of Chicago Press, 2012.

Thompson, Emily. *The Soundscape of Modernity: Architectural Acoustics and the Culture of Listening in America, 1900–1933*. Cambridge, MA: MIT Press, 2002.

Thompson, John A. *Reformers and War: American Progressive Publicists and the First World War*. Cambridge, UK: Cambridge University Press, 1987.

Thornbrough, Emma L. "Booker T. Washington as Seen by His White Contemporaries." *Journal of Negro History*, Vol. 53, No. 2 (April 1968): 161–182.

Tipson, Baird. "How Can the Religious Experience of the Past Be Recovered? The Examples of Puritanism and Pietism." *Journal of the American Academy of Religion*, Vol. 43, No. 4 (December 1975): 695–707.

Tulis, Jeffrey K. *The Rhetorical Presidency*. Princeton: Princeton University Press, 1987.

Turner, Henry A. "Woodrow Wilson and Public Opinion." *Public Opinion Quarterly*, Vol. 21, No. 4 (Winter 1957–1958): 505–520.

Tutorow. Norman E. *James Gillespie Blaine and the Presidency: A Documentary Study and Source Book*. New York: Peter Lang, 1989.

Valentine, Leslie R. "Evangelist Billy Sunday's Clean-Up Campaign in Omaha: Local Reaction to His 50-Day Revival, 1915." *Nebraska History*, Vol. 64 (1983): 209–227.

Vaughn, Stephen. *Holding Fast the Inner Lines: Democracy, Nationalism, and the Committee on Public Information*. Chapel Hill, NC: University of North Carolina Press, 1980.

Venet, Wendy Hamand. *A Strong-Minded Woman: The Life of Mary A. Livermore*. Amherst, MA: University of Massachusetts Press, 2005.

Vincent, Theodore G. *Black Power and the Garvey Movement*. Berkeley, CA: Ramparts Press, 1971.

Wacker, Grant. *America's Pastor: Billy Graham and the Shaping of a Nation*. Cambridge, MA: Belknap Press of Harvard University Press, 2014.

Heaven Below: Early Pentecostals and American Culture. Cambridge, MA: Harvard University Press, 2001.

Wallace, Karl L., ed. *History of Speech Education in America: Background Studies*. New York: Appleton-Century-Crofts, 1954.

Waller, Altina L. *Reverend Beecher and Mrs. Tilton: Sex and Class in Victorian America*. Amherst, MA: University of Massachusetts Press, 1982.

Warner, Wayne E. *The Woman Evangelist: The Life and Times of Charismatic Evangelist Maria B. Woodworth-Etter*. Metuchen, NJ: Scarecrow Press, 1986.

Warren, Donald. *Radio Priest: Charles Coughlin, The Father of Hate Radio*. New York: The Free Press, 1996.

Watson, Martha S. and Thomas R. Burkholder, eds. *The Rhetoric of Nineteenth-Century Reform*. East Lansing, MI: Michigan State University Press, 2008.

Watts, Jill. *God, Harlem, U.S.A.: The Father Divine Story*. Berkeley, CA: University of California Press, 1992.

Watts, Sarah. *Rough Rider in the White House: Theodore Roosevelt and the Politics of Desire*. Chicago: University of Chicago Press, 2003.

Watts, Steven. *Self-Help Messiah: Dale Carnegie and Success in Modern America*. New York: Other Press, 2013.

Weatherson, Michael A. and Hal W. Bochin. *Hiram Johnson: Political Revivalist*. Lanham, MD: University Press of America, 1995.

Wecter, Dixon. *The Hero in America: A Chronicle of Hero-Worship*. Orig. pub. New York: Scribner, 1941. Ann Arbor, MI: University of Michigan Press, 1963.

Welke, Barbara Young. *Recasting American Liberty: Gender, Race, Law, and the Railroad Revolution, 1865–1920*. Cambridge, UK: Cambridge University Press, 2001.

Wheeler, Edward L. *Uplifting the Race: The Black Minister in the New South, 1865–1902*. Lanham, MD: University Press of America, 1986.

White, Barbara A. *The Beecher Sisters*. New Haven: Yale University Press, 2003.

White, Bruce A. *Elbert Hubbard's* The Philistine: *A Periodical of Protest (1895–1915)*. Lanham, MD: University Press of America, 1989.

White, Richard D., Jr. *Kingfish: The Reign of Huey P. Long*. New York: Random House, 2006.

Wiebe, Robert H. *The Search for Order, 1877–1920*. New York: Hill and Wang, 1967.

Willard, Carla. "Timing Impossible Subjects: The Marketing Style of Booker T. Washington." *American Quarterly*, Vol. 53, No. 4 (December 2001): 624–669.

Williams, T. Harry. *Huey Long*. New York: Knopf, 1969.

Williams, Wade. "Religion, Science, and Rhetoric in Revolutionary America: The Case of Dr. Benjamin Rush." *Rhetoric Society Quarterly*, Vol. 30, No. 3 (Summer 2000): 55–72.

Wilson, Christopher P. " 'Unleavened Bread': The Representation of Robert Grant." *American Literary Realism, 1870–1910*, Vol. 22, No. 3 (Spring 1990): 17–35.

Wilson, Kirt H. "The Politics of Place and Presidential Rhetoric in the United States, 1875–1901." *Civil Rights Rhetoric and the American Presidency*, ed. James Arnt Aune and Enrique D. Rigsby (College Station, TX: Texas A&M University Press, 2005): 16–40.

Wilson, Wendy A. Danforth. "The Theatricality of Revivalism as Exemplified in the Artistry of Billy Sunday and Aimee Semple McPherson." M.A. thesis, University of Oregon, 1974.

Winters, Donald E., Jr. *The Soul of the Wobblies: The I. W. W., Religion, and American Culture in the Progressive Era, 1905–1917*. Westport, CT: Greenwood Press, 1985.

Wolfe, G. Joseph. "Some Reactions to the Advent of Campaigning by Radio." *Journal of Broadcasting*, Vol. 13, No. 3 (Summer 1969): 305–314.

Wolmar, Christian. *The Great Railroad Revolution: The History of Trains in America*. New York: PublicAffairs, 2012.

Woodward, C. Vann. *Tom Watson: Agrarian Rebel*. Orig. pub. New York: Macmillan, 1938. New York: Oxford University Press, 1963.

Index